MW01255178

Soviet Strategic Aviation

in the Cold War

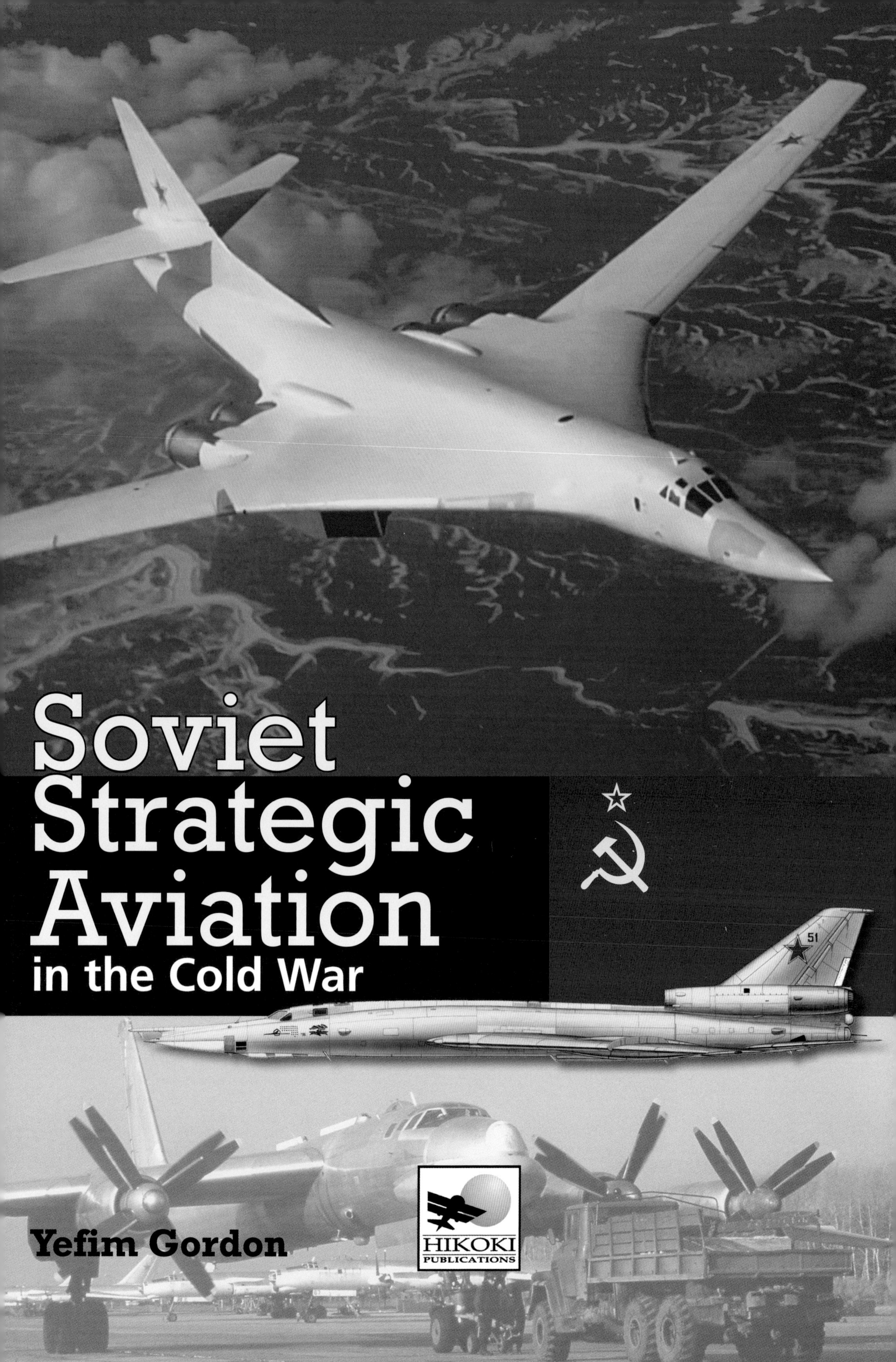
Soviet
Strategic
Aviation
in the Cold War
51
Yefim Gordon
HIKOKI
PUBLICATIONS

First published in 2009 by
Hikoki Publications Ltd
1a Ringway Trading Est
Shadowmoss Rd
Manchester
M22 5LH
England

Reprinted 2013

Email: enquiries@crecy.co.uk
www.crecy.co.uk

Original translation by Dmitriy Komissarov
Layout by Polygon Press Ltd., Moscow

Colour profiles: © Andrey Yurgenson,
Sergey Ignat'yev, Viktor Mil'yachenko,
Aleksandr Gavrilov
Line drawings: © the late Vladimir Klimov,
Andrey Yurgenson, Avico-Press

ISBN 9 781902 109084

Printed in China

Contents

Acknowledgements 6

Introduction 7

1 Into the Nuclear Age 9

2 The Strategic Breakthrough 31

3 Operations in the Arctic 75

4 The Long-Range Aviation's Involvement in Nuclear Testing 83

5 Soviet Air-Launched Missile Systems 93

6 Beyond the Sound Barrier 133

7 The Long-Range Aviation in Times of Cutbacks 185

8 In Support of 'Friendly Nations' 201

9 The Long-Range Aviation in the Afghan War 205

10 The Aircraft of the Long-Range Aviation 215

11 In Times of Change: The Demise of the Soviet Union 255

Index 270

Acknowledgements

The author wishes to thank Vladimir Rigmant and Sergey Burdin who kindly supplied materials used in the making of this book.

The book is illustrated by photos by Yefim Gordon, the late Sergey Skrynnikov, Vasiliy P. Kunyayev, Yuriy Skuratov.

The book includes information and photos from the following sources: Novosti Press Agency, ITAR-TASS, United States Air Force, United States Navy, Royal Air Force, Royal Swedish Air Force, Royal Norwegian Air Force, the archives of the Tupolev PLC and the Myasishchev Experimental Machinery Plant, the archive of the Russian Aviation Research Trust (RART), as well as the personal archives of Yefim Gordon, Sergey Burdin, Vladimir Rigmant, Sergey and Dmitriy Komissarov, and from the following web sources: www.globalsecurity.org, www.aviaforum.ru, www.forum.keypublishing.co.uk.

A Tu-95K-22 (foreground) and a Tu-95U on the hardstand at Ryazan

Introduction

In August 1941, just over a month after the outbreak of the Great Patriotic War – that is, the German invasion of the Soviet Union – the existing Air Corps of what was then called the Workers' and Peasants' Red Army Air Force (VVS RKKA – *Voyenno-vozdooshnyye seely Raboche-krest'yanskoy Krasnoy Armii*) were disbanded and replaced by six Independent Air Divisions of the High Command. Pursuant to Directive No. 1392 issued by the State Defence Committee on 5th March 1942 a long-range bomber arm of the Red Army Air Force – the Long-Range Aviation (then known as the ADD – *Aviahtsiya dahl'nevo deystviya*) – was established, reporting directly to the Headquarters of the Supreme High Command. In April 1944 the ADD was reorganised – or rather demoted, becoming the 18th Air Army (VA – *vozdooshnaya armiya*).

Considering that the Long-Range Aviation was one of the key factors behind the Soviet victory in the Great Patriotic War and the defeat of Nazi Germany, its importance as a military-political instrument increased dramatically in the post-war period. The development of the US nuclear weapons programme, the destruction of Hiroshima and Nagasaki by American atomic bombs and the establishment of the Strategic Air Command (SAC) within the USAAF compelled the Soviet government to take appropriate countermeasures. Thus, after only two years of existence the 18th VA was reorganised again (see below).

In the immediate post-war years the DA had virtually no state-of-the-art aircraft left – only a handful of four-engined long-range bombers remained. The Il'yushin IL-4 twin-engined medium bombers had reached the end of their service lives; the Tupolev Tu-2 twin-engined tactical bombers were totally unsuitable for strategic missions (the same was true for the IL-4) and only a small number of Tu-2s survived the war anyway. To be sure, the national aircraft industry – to be precise, the aircraft design bureaux headed by Andrey N. Tupolev and Vladimir M. Myasishchev – had embarked on the design of modern four-engined strategic bombers having a tricycle landing gear, an adequate offensive warload and potent defensive armament, but this work was going to take a while and the government could not wait. The USA – now regarded as a potential adversary – clearly would not wait either.

In this situation the Soviet government – first and foremost the Soviet leader Iosif V. Stalin – took the decision to reverse-engineer the Boeing B-29 Superfortress bomber. This was made possible by the circumstance that four USAAF B-29s damaged in action over Japan had force-landed in the Soviet Far East in August-November 1944 and had been interned by the Russians. (In May 1941 the Soviet Union had signed a Pact of Neutrality with Japan and observed this pact strictly. The reason is obvious – the Soviet Union could not afford to wage war on two fronts, and should Japan undertake an offensive in the East, this could mean total disaster, at least in 1942-43. in April 1945, when it was clear that Germany had lost the war, the Soviet Union denounced this Pact and supported the Allies on the Far Eastern theatre of operations.)

Within a very short time the Tupolev OKB and other Soviet aircraft industry enterprises accomplished the monstrous task of copying the Superfortress and adapting it to the metric system of measurements and Soviet manufacturing standards. The Soviet version of the B-29 entered production as the Tupolev Tu-4, improving the offensive capability of the Soviet Air Force no end.

On 9th April 1946 the Soviet Council of Ministers and the Communist Party Central Committee issued directive No. 721-283 according to which the 18th VA was reorganised into a separate branch of the Air Force, becoming the reborn Long-Range Aviation – now rendered as the DA (*Dahl'nyaya aviahtsiya*, equivalent to the US Strategic Air Command). In its new iteration the Long-Range Aviation comprised three Air Armies:

- the 1st VA headquartered at Smolensk (in western Russia) and commanded by Col.-Gen. G. S. Shchotchikov (he was succeeded as Commander by Lt.-Gen. Ye. M. Nikolayenko as early as June 1946);
- the 2nd VA headquartered at Vinnitsa (in central Ukraine) and commanded by Col.-Gen. V. N. Aladinskiy;
- the 3rd VA headquartered at Khabarovsk (in the Far East) and commanded by Col.-Gen. V. N. Zhdanov.

As the Air Armies were established, the units with the highest level of combat readiness were picked for inclusion – including some units which had not been part of the ADD during the war (for example, certain tactical aviation regiments). Each Air Army included two Corps, which in turn consisted of two Air Divisions comprising four Air Regiments each. This, for example, pursuant to the General Headquarters Chief of Staff's directive No. ORG/5/248913 dated 26th August 1946 the 1st VA consisted of the 1st GvBAK (*Gvardeyskiy bombardirovochnyy aviakorpus* – Guards Bomber Corps) and the 3rd GvBAK, which comprised the 11th GvBAD (*Gvardeyskaya*

During the Great Patriotic War the Soviet Long-Range Aviation (ADD) operated large numbers of Mitchells, like this B-25C.

*bombardi***rov***ochnaya* **a***viadi***vee***ziya* – Guards Bomber Division), 22nd GvBAD, 57th GvBAD and 45th TBAD (*tya***zhol***aya bombardi***rov***ochnaya* **a***viadi***vee***ziya* – Heavy Bomber Division). In turn, these four divisions comprised:

• the 18th GvTAP (*Gvar***dey***skiy* **trahnsportnyy** **a***via***polk** – Guards Airlift Regiment);

• the 37th, 121st, 157th, 208th, 171st, 240th, 170th and 108th GvBAP (*Gvar***dey***skiy bombardi***rov***ochnyy* *avia***polk** – Guards Bomber Regiment) flying IL-4 bombers;

• the 200th GvBAP, 210th GvBAP, 111th BAP and 330th BAP flying North American B-25C/D/J Mitchell bombers;

• the 52nd GvBAP, 203rd GvBAP, 362nd BAP and 890th BAP operating Petlyakov Pe-8, Boeing B-17F/G Flying Fortress and Consolidated B-24A/D Liberator bombers.

The Army's Military Council included 1st VA Commander Lt.-Gen. Yevgeniy M. Nikolayenko (holder of the Hero of the Soviet Union title), Maj.-Gen. Mikhail M. Moskalyov and Chief of Staff Lt.-Gen. Konstantin I. Tel'nov. Air Chief Marshal Aleksandr Ye. Golovanov was appointed Commander of the Long-Range Aviation.

At that time the IL-4 made up the backbone of the DA, 336 of these aircraft remaining on strength. The DA also operated 26 surviving Pe-8 heavy bombers and a large number of B-25s supplied under the Lend-Lease Act (252 aircraft remained active). The B-17s and B-24s recovered by the Soviet forces after making forced landings in Eastern Europe due to enemy action were few and were used chiefly as trainers, easing the transition to the Tu-4.

The Yermolayev Yer-2 (here an AM-37 powered example) was one of the ADD's main types at the end of the war.

The Petlyakov Pe-8 was the ADD's sole indigenous heavy bomber at the end of the war. This one is powered by Charomskiy M-40 diesels.

Opposite page: A full frontal of a production Tu-4 bomber. Note the instrument landing system aerial under the nose.

1 Into the Nuclear Age

Now that the Second World War was over, the Soviet Union began recovering from the ravages of war and switching to a peacetime economy. Yet it was a bit too early to think of complete disarmament; on the contrary, the nuclear bombardment of Hiroshima and Nagasaki in August 1945 showed the world that weapons of untold power had been created in the USA. The one-time ally in the fight against Nazism was now rapidly turning into the Soviet Union's potential adversary No. 1. In order to maintain the balance of military and political power the Soviet Union urgently needed to create weapons matching those in the American arsenal.

Development work on Soviet atomic bombs was already in progress under the leadership of Academician Igor' V. Kurchatov, head of the Nuclear Physics Institute. Yet the bombs were worthless without a proper means of delivery. Strategic bombers with intercontinental range were viewed as the optimum delivery vehicle. Yet the Soviet Air Force lacked such aircraft, the Long-Range Aviation still being equipped with obsolete bombers of 1930s/early 1940s vintage (the IL-4, Pe-8 and Yermolayev Yer-2) which lacked the required performance. A completely new aircraft was required – one that would be able to carry powerful nuclear munitions characterised by large dimensions and weight over long distances.

As mentioned earlier, in order to speed up the development and service entry of a delivery vehicle for the Soviet nuclear weapons, the Soviet government took the decision to use the Boeing B-29 as a pattern. After all, it was the B-29 that had dropped the atomic bombs on Hiroshima and Nagasaki. Repeated attempts to procure the Superfortress officially had been undertaken by the Soviet authorities during the war but the US government had refused to supply the bomber. Thus, a windfall of four B-29s that force-landed in the Soviet Far East in late 1944 (three of them could be returned to airworthy condition) was most welcome. The bombers were ferried to Moscow and OKB-156 (***op****ytno-kon****strook****torskoye byu****ro*** –

experimental design bureau) under Chief Designer Andrey N. Tupolev was tasked with copying the Superfortress.

A hectic period began at the Tupolev OKB – the work schedule set out in the Council of Ministers and Communist Party Central Committee directive regarding the B-29 was rather tight. It took about a year to take the American bomber apart, study it to the tiniest detail and adapt it to the capabilities of the Soviet aircraft industry. In particular, the available structural materials differed somewhat from the American ones, and so did the sheet metal thicknesses used by the Soviet industry.

The 'Soviet Stratofortress' was originally designated B-4 but the designation was soon

A brand-new Tu-4 awaiting delivery at Kazan'-Borisoglebskoye.

Tu-4 operations at a grass airstrip – probably a forward operating location.

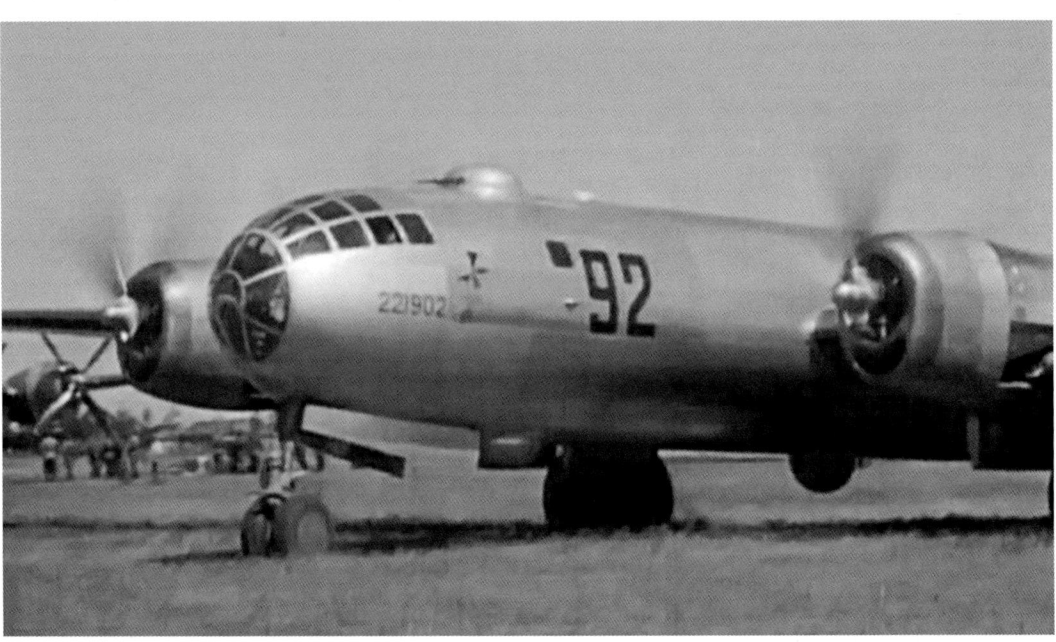

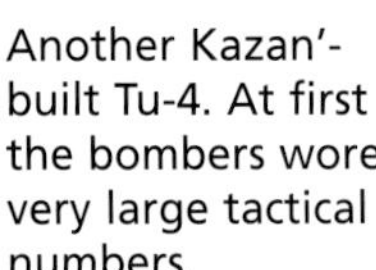
Another Kazan'-built Tu-4. At first the bombers wore very large tactical numbers.

changed to Tu-4 (in keeping with the Soviet system under which the initial letters of the OKB founder's last name were used as a 'brand'). For security reasons it was referred to in paperwork as *samolyot* R (aircraft R) or *izdeliye* R (product R). The first Soviet-built example was completed at the Kazan' aircraft factory, a major production plant in the capital of the Tatar Autonomous Soviet Socialist Republic, in the spring of 1947. Thus it could be regarded as the first pre-production example. (As distinct from the western world, the Soviet aircraft design bureaux had no production plants of their own, only limited prototype manufacturing facilities; the production plants were separate enterprises under the Ministry of Aircraft Industry umbrella.)

The B-4 (Tu-4) made its maiden flight from Kazan'-Borisoglebskoye airfield on 19th May 1947 with aircraft captain Nikolay S. Rybko and co-pilot Aleksandr P. Vasil'chenko at the controls. Large-scale production began shortly afterwards, and a total of 847 was manufactured at three factories (No. 22 in Kazan', No. 23 in Moscow and No. 18 in Kuibyshev) until 1952.

The Tu-4 long-range bomber was not a 100% carbon copy of the B-29, having a different powerplant (indigenous ASh-73TK engines) and heavier defensive armament. For one thing, rather than copy the Wright R-3350-23A radial, the Soviet designers chose to use the indigenous Shvetsov ASh-73TK engine – a turbosupercharged version of the M-72 and likewise an 18-cylinder radial (though based on licensed Wright technology). For another, there was no point in copying the Browning machine-guns, and the first three Kazan'-built examples featured 12.7-mm (.50 calibre) Berezin UBK machine-guns – two each in the dorsal and ventral barbettes and three in the tail barbette. From the fourth aircraft onwards the machine-guns were replaced with 20-mm (.78 calibre) Berezin B-20E cannons (two in each barbette). Later, as the bomber was progressively upgraded in the course of production, these gave way to 23-mm (.90 calibre) NR-23 cannons developed by A. E. Nudel'man and A. A. Rikhter.

The Tu-4 achieved initial operational capability (IOC) with the Soviet Air Force service in 1947. Mass introduction of the type began in 1951; during the first ten-year period after the war it saw service with 20 heavy bomber regiments. The aircraft was intended for delivering massive bomb strikes with conventional bombs against strategic targets located deep in the enemy's rear area, both singly and in groups, day and night, in any weather.

As noted earlier, the advent of nuclear weapons brought about a need to bolster the Soviet Air Force's bomber component and made the Soviet government admit it had made a mistake by 'demoting' the ADD to an Air Army during the war. Now this mistake

The captain of a Tu-4 as seen from the navigator's workstation.

The crew of an 840th TBAP Tu-4 receives a briefing prior to a mission.

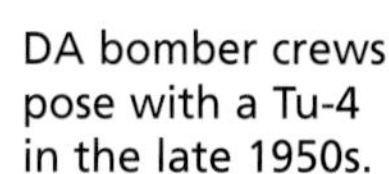

DA bomber crews pose with a Tu-4 in the late 1950s.

Early production Tu-4s at a snow-bound airbase.

was put right when the DA was (re)established in April 1946. The 'new' Long-Range Aviation consisted of three Air Armies that were initially designated as the 1st, 2nd and 3rd VA. Pursuant to the General Headquarters Chief of Staff's directive No. ORG/1/120030 dated 10th January 1949, however, these formations were renumbered as the 50th, 43rd and 65th Air Armies respectively, effective from 15th February that year. Another eight years later the 65th VA was reorganised to become the 5th VA headquartered in Blagoveshchensk, also in the Far East.

The large-scale introduction of the Tu-4 coincided with the addition of nuclear munitions to the Long-Range Aviation's inventory. Wartime bomber pilots, many of whom became commanders of DA regiments and divisions, were the first to master the operational use of the Tu-4. Well-known airmen who had earned the Hero of the Soviet Union (HSU) title in combat – Aleksandr I. Molodchiy, Vasiliy V. Reshetnikov, A. V. Ivanov, Serafim K. Biryukov, Vladimir M. Bezbokov and Pavel A. Taran – spearheaded the aircrew conversion effort.

The DA (and the Soviet defence industry) also successfully took on the issue of weapons upgrading. The ballistic parameters of free-fall bombs were greatly enhanced, their blast effect was increased, new types of high-explosive, marker and other bombs were developed and tested. The Air Force's tactics and strategy

The flight line of a heavy bomber regiment equipped with early Tu-4s having no under-nose ILS aerials.

Another view of the same hard-stand. All of the unit's Tu-4s are Kazan'-built.

changed to reflect both the experience gained in the past war and the availability of new weapons and other systems. In particular, a wingtip-to-wingtip in-flight refuelling (IFR) system was developed at the Flight Research Institute (LII – ***Lyot**no-is**sled**ovatel'skiy insti**toot***), finding its first practical application on the Tu-4 and extending the bomber's range. In order to enhance the protection of bombers flying in close formation against enemy interceptors the DA went so far as to establish its own escort fighter units. This turned out to be a bad idea, as the contemporary Soviet fighters then in service with the Air Force lacked the necessary range to fulfil the escort mission effectively.

On 18th August 1947 a group of three Tu-4s made the type's public debut at the traditional Aviation Day air event at Moscow-Tushino airfield, seat of the Central Air Club. The parade formation was led by Air Chief Marshal Aleksandr Ye. Golovanov, with test pilots Nikolay S. Rybko and Mark L. Gallai as his wingmen. After that the Tu-4 was given the NATO reporting name *Bull*.

Before that, concurrently with the decision to copy the Superfortress, the 890th Bryanskiy BAP forming part of the 45th Gomel'skaya BAD of the 50th VA was redeployed from a base in Belorussia to Kazan'. (The honorary appellations *Bryanskiy* and *Gomel'skaya* were given for liberating the cities of Bryansk

The same Tu-4s seen from the rear; note the open entry hatch of the centre pressure cabin.

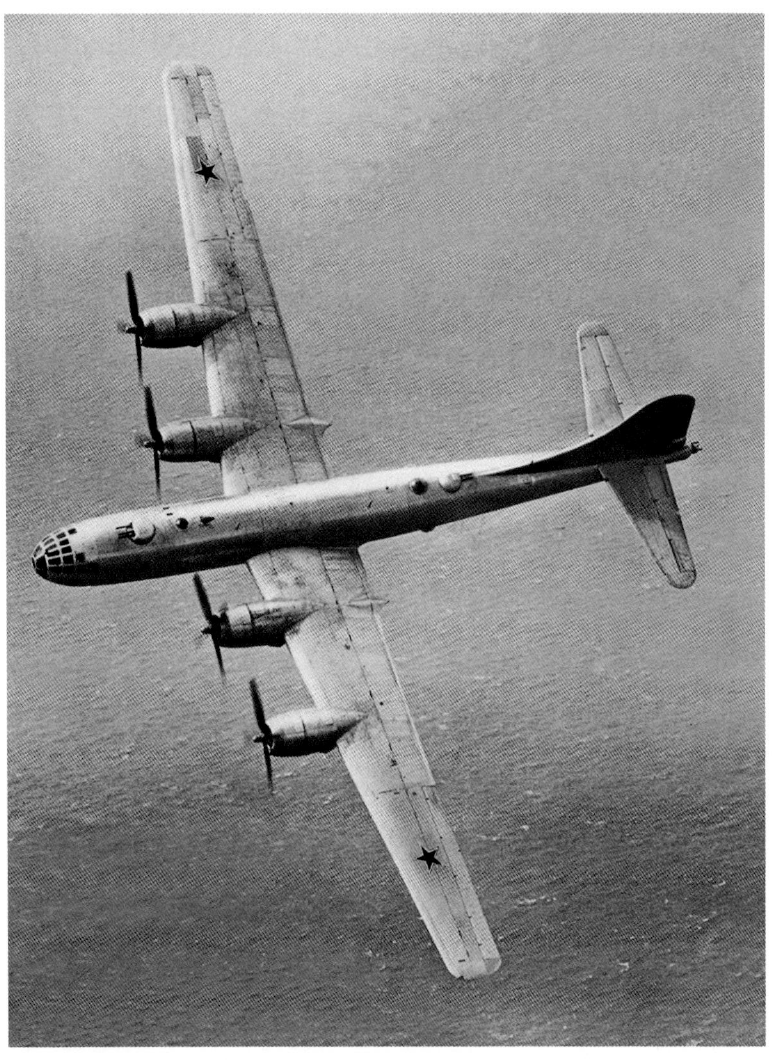

A Tu-4 on an overwater mission.

A trio of Tu-4s on a mission.

(Russia) and Gomel' (Belorussia) in the Great Patriotic War.) The regiment's pilots had accumulated considerable experience of operating the Pe-8, B-17, B-24 and B-25. At the new location the unit was redesignated the 890th Bryanskiy OUTAP (*ot**del'**nyy oo**cheb**no-treni**rov**ochnyy **a**via**polk*** – Independent Instructional & Training Air Regiment), reporting directly to the Long-Range Aviation HQ, and Col. Vladimir V. Abramov was appointed regiment CO. Thus was born an operational conversion unit easing the DA aircrews' transition to the new Tu-4 strategic bomber.

When the remaining units of the 45th BAD had undertaken their training, in late 1948 it was the turn of the 13th *Dnepropetrovsko-Budapeshtskaya* GvBAD of the 43rd VA to start the transition to the Tu-4. This division comprised the 185th, 202nd and 226th Bomber Regiments, all equipped with IL-4s. (The honorary appellation was given for liberating the cities of Dnepropetrovsk (the Ukraine) and Budapest in the Great Patriotic War. The division was also decorated with the Suvorov Order, one of the highest Soviet military awards.)

In November 1948 the division's technical personnel were dispatched to the Kazan' aircraft factory to familiarise themselves with the bomber's design. Between January and April 1949 the flight crews took conversion training both at the factory and in the 890th OUTAP; the 185th and 226th TBAPs (*tya**zhol**yy bombardi**rov**ochnyy **a**via**polk*** – Heavy Bomber Regiment) were the first to do so, followed by the 202nd BAP in April 1949. The B-25 was used as a transitional trainer by virtue of its tricycle landing gear. Meanwhile, the navigators/bomb-aimers took conversion training courses in operational units under the guidance of tutors and instructors from the training centre; flight training took place at the training centre in Ivanovo, central Russia.

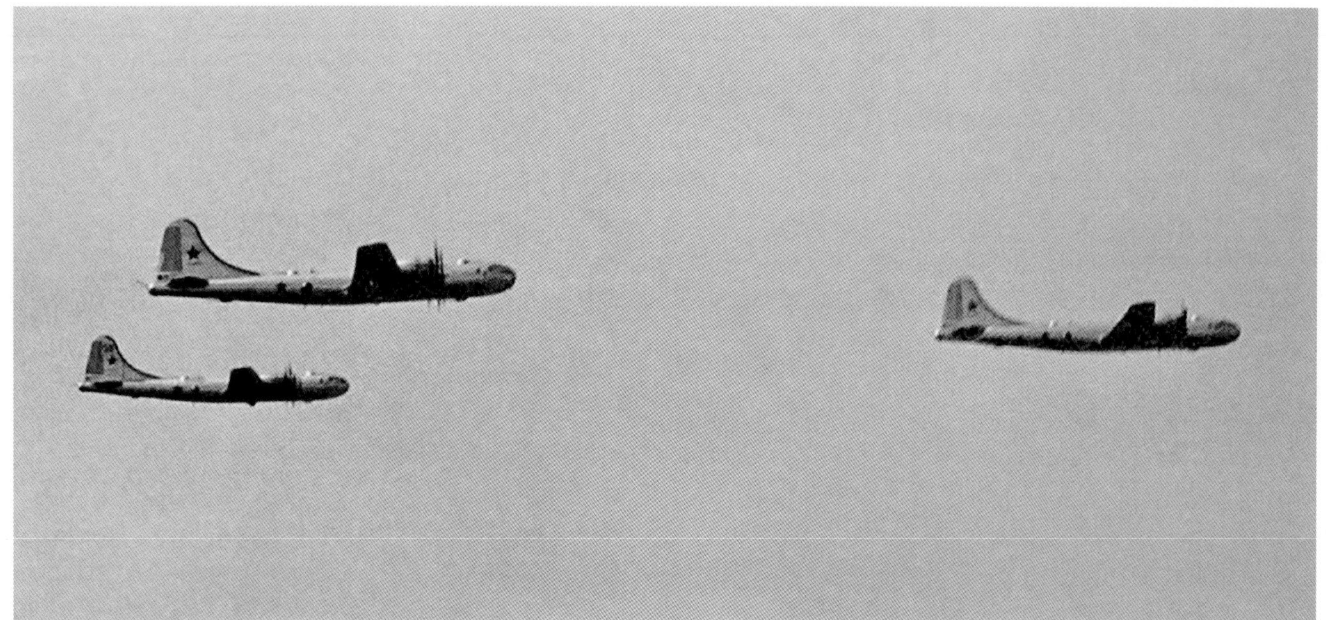

Tu-4s in a V formation similar to the USAF's 'Hometown' defensive formation.

The first six Tu-4s delivered to the 185th GvTBAP arrived at Poltava (the Ukraine), the regiment's home base, in July 1949; by the middle of the month the crews assigned to the bombers had started flying them. The Tu-4 had a flight crew of 12 and a ground crew of ten. The flight crew comprised the captain, co-pilot, chief navigator, navigator/bomb-aimer, navigator/radar operator, flight engineer, flight technician, radio operator, chief gunner (defensive fire commander), two beam gunners (so called because their gunsights – not the actual guns – were located at the lateral sighting blisters) and tail gunner.

In early September 1949 the crews captained by the regiment's command staff – the regiment CO and the squadron commanders – started practicing flights along designated routes involving weapons training; soon the other crews followed suit. All in all, 72 aircraft captains and 67 complete crews received their type ratings on the Tu-4 in the 13th GvBAD; the average flight time logged in the process of conversion training was 14 hours. However, the mastery of Tu-4 combat techniques in the division continued all the way to 1952.

In November 1949 Lt.-Gen. Yevgeniy M. Nikolayenko was appointed Commander of the Long-Range Aviation. He stayed in office for less than a year, being succeeded by Air Marshal Sergey I. Rudenko in August 1950.

In the late 1940s and early 1950s the technical staff of the Long-Range Aviation regiments shouldered a large workload, getting to grips with totally new hardware within very tight time limits. The technicians had to deal with remote control systems and electronic equipment the likes of which had not been seen in the USSR. Many DA generals and officers, including I. V. Markov, V. G. Balashov, N. D. Grebennikov, Yu. G. Mamsurov, I. K. Sklyarenko, P. I. Vostrikov, N. U. Timoshok, N. Ye. Yefimov, A. V. Omel'chenko, V. M. Semyonov and G. T. Fomin, did a lot to facilitate and expedite this process.

Two Tu-4s make a low pass.

'41 Black', a Kazan'-built Tu-4, at a grass airfield.

A Tu-4 passes overhead, apparently on landing approach.

The Long-Range Aviation command gave much attention to the aerial gunnery service which was responsible for training the flight crews in anti-fighter defence techniques. This was also a time when bomber crews trained intensively in low-level and ultra-low-level flying as a means of penetrating enemy air defences. This was a highly complex job, and the absence of special equipment enhancing flight safety (radio altimeters and ground proximity warning systems) on the Tu-4 did not make it any easier.

One of the top-priority tasks facing the DA was the enhancement of poor-weather flying capability in daytime and at night. The importance of this aspect was so high that on 15th January 1950 the Council of Ministers issued a special directive dealing with the outfitting of airfields with blind landing systems. A system of aircrew qualification ratings was introduced (Pilot 3rd Class, Pilot 2nd Class, Pilot 1st Class, Merited Military Pilot; the same system applied to navigators). In accordance with this system, airmen with higher qualification ratings received various bonuses (including financial ones) and were eligible for state awards for mastering the technique of flying in instrument meteorological conditions (IMC). The document introducing this system also introduced qualification badges to be worn on the airmen's uniforms. The incentive worked: by the end of 1950 no less than 74% of the DA's pilots had received qualification ratings.

Between 1952 and 1955 the 13th GvBAD perfected the crews' flying skills in daytime and night maximum-range flights in IMC during operations by flights, squadrons and entire regiments. The crews became proficient in the bombardment of targets obscured by clouds or darkness, as well as of moving maritime targets, using the *Kobal't* (Cobalt) bomb-aiming radar and the OPB-4 optical bomb sight (*op**tich**eskiy pri**tsel** bombardi**rov**ochnyy*). Additionally, the crews were trained to make evasive manoeuvres when the bomber was caught by air defence searchlights. In 1950-51 each Tu-4 crew logged an average 80-100 flight hours per annum; in 1952-54 this figure rose to 120-140 hours.

Apart from combat training, the units operating the Tu-4 fulfilled other tasks of national importance. For example, in 1950 the 185th and 226th TBAPs took part in military parades in Moscow – events of major psycho-

A Tu-4 retracts its undercarriage after take-off.

Parades were part of the job. Here, a Tu-4 escorted by four Lavochkin La-11s performs at a military parade.

logical importance that imbued the Soviet people with confidence and demonstrated the Soviet Union's military might to the outside world ('hear ye, fear ye').

Between February and October 1954 Tu-4s were used for air sampling to determine radiation levels in the wake of nuclear tests. In March-June 1954 a detachment of 226th TBAP Tu-4s commanded by Lt.-Col. Kirsanov was temporarily deployed in China on a special assignment. Missions flown by Tu-4s included reconnaissance flights of more than 12 hours' duration along the northern borders of Turkey, Iran and Afghanistan in order to prompt the air defence radars located there into 'painting' the aircraft and revealing themselves. Many airmen of the 13th GvBAD received combat awards for successfully mastering the new hardware and for fulfilling various special assignments.

In 1951 the operational Tu-4 gained nuclear capability. This was preceded by highly complex tests which warrant a more detailed description.

A Tu-4 with fighter escort passes over Moscow's History Museum during a parade in Red Square. Another Tu-4 brings up the rear.

Soviet officers in winter uniforms pose with a late-production Kuibyshev-built Tu-4.

A version of the Tu-4 designated Tu-4A (***ah**tomnyy* – in this context, nuclear-capable) was developed as a delivery vehicle for the first Soviet free-fall nuclear bombs. It differed from the basic Tu-4 in having an electrically heated, thermostabilised bomb bay equipped with an electronic control system. The suspension system for the bulky nuclear munition had to be designed anew and special shielding installed in the pressure cabins to protect the crew from radiation in flight.

The badge awarded to graduates of one of the Soviet Air Force flying schools (class of 1954).

Ballistic tests of the first Soviet nuclear bomb, the RDS-1 (also known as *izdeliye* 501), began in the first half of 1948; it was developed by the KB-11 design bureau. Initially dummy bombs were dropped by a Tu-4 at the proving ground near the town of Noginsk in the eastern suburbs of Moscow which was run by the 4th Directorate of the Soviet Air Force State Research Institute named after Valeriy P. Chkalov (GK NII VVS – *Gosoo**dar**stvennyy Krasnozna**myon**nyy na**ooch**no-is**sle**dovatel'-*

Air Force personnel receive a briefing in front of a Moscow-built Tu-4 coded '35 Red'.

*skiy insti**toot** Vo**yen**no-voz**doosh**nykh seel*). The bomber was flown by LII test pilots Aleksey P. Yakimov and Stepan F. Mashkovskiy. These test drops and other research conducted by KB-11 jointly with the Central Aero-Hydrodynamic Institute named after Nikolay Ye. Zhukovskiy (TsAGI – *Tsen**trahl'**nyy **a**ero- i **ghid**rodina**mich**eskiy insti**toot***) showed that the bomb was not stable enough as it travelled on its ballistic trajectory. The manufacturer had to optimise the design by streamlining the bomb, shifting the CG and altering the inertia forces.

Further ballistic tests were then performed at the 71st Test Range at Totskoye in the Orenburg Region. No fewer than 30 test drops from a Tu-4 were required before KB-11 had achieved the required accuracy and made the

Top and centre right: The hardstands of the 840th TBAP.

Above: Group operations of red-coded Tu-4s during an exercise.

Centre left: A large-calibre bomb is hoisted into the bomb bay of a Tu-4. Note the special trench over which the aircraft is parked to facilitate the loading procedure.

Above left: The captain of an operational Tu-4.

Left: A nuclear bomb seen seconds after falling away from a Tu-4.

Above: Tu-4s taking part in a military exercise.

Right: The nose of a Tu-4A.

Far right: An RDS-3 atomic bomb is towed on a dolly to the flight line of a unit equipped with Tu-4As.

Far right, below: The RDS-3 in the bomb bay of a Tu-4A.

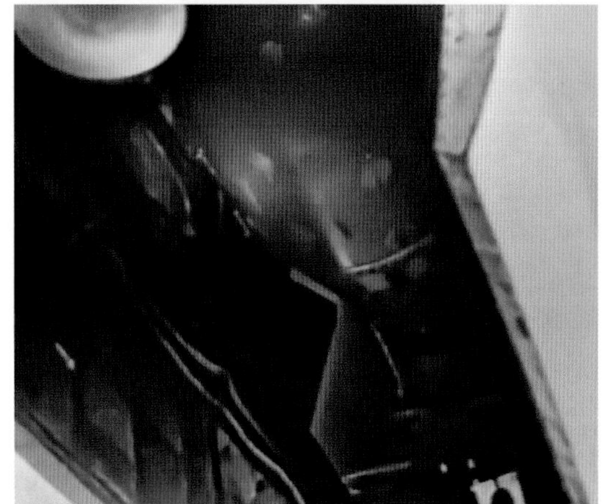

Above and right: A Tu-4A in flight.

Far right: Here the Tu-4A is accompanied by an IL-28 jet bomber, possibly monitoring radiation levels.

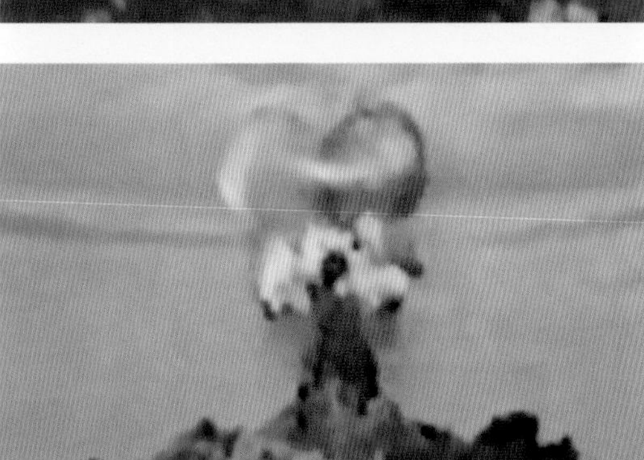

Left column:

The crew of Tu-4A '207 Black' receives the final briefing before a nuclear test.

The captain of '207 Black' in his seat.

Tu-4A '207 Black' cruises towards the test range.

'207 Black' pictured on take-off.

Right column:

An RDS-4 bomb (note the more elongated body) seconds after being released by the aircraft.

The first few seconds after the nuclear blast: a huge ball of flame rises above the spot...

...and the tell-tale mushroom cloud forms.

A late-production Kuibyshev-built Tu-4
43rd Air Army, November 1956; note post 1955 insignia placement

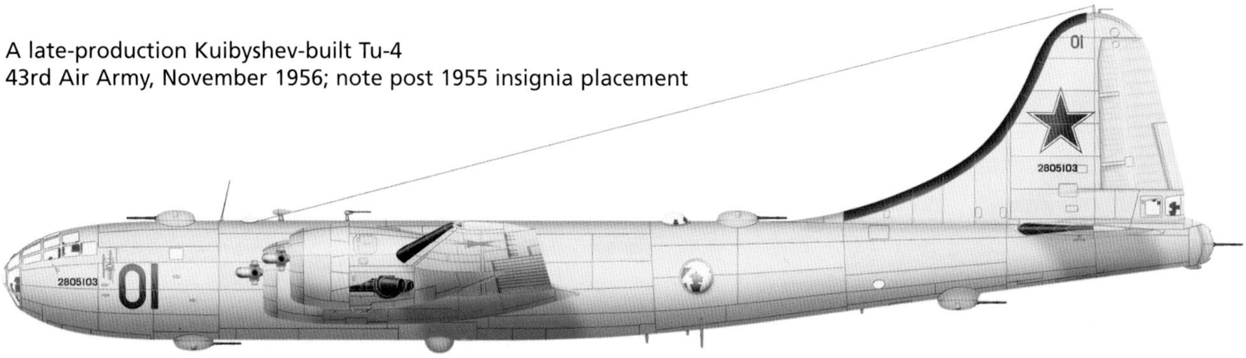

An early Kazan'-built Tu-4
(possibly operated by the 840th TBAP)

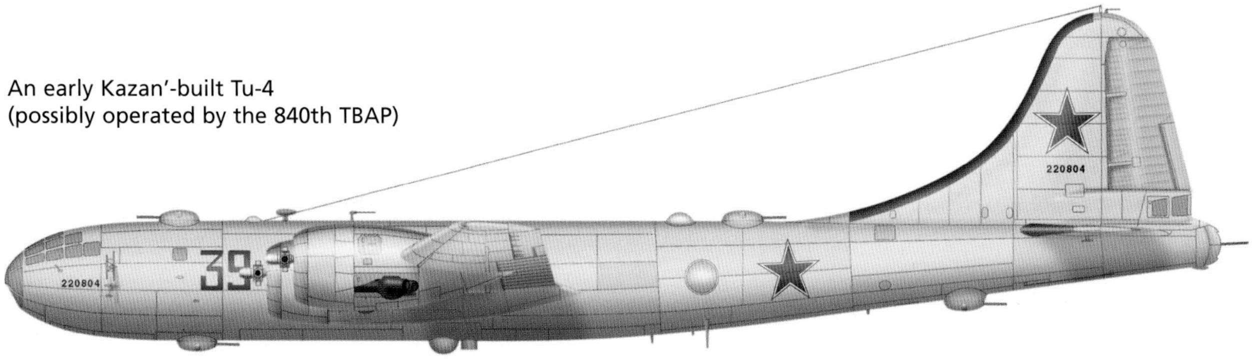

A late-production Kuibyshev-built Tu-4
Tushino flypast, Moscow, 1956 (?)

A late-production Kuibyshev-built Tu-4
in pre-1955 markings

necessary trajectory measurements to be used in developing the *izdeliye* 501's automatic control system.

Tests of the Tu-4A nuclear-capable bomber and its specialised equipment were duly completed in 1951. On 17th May 1951 the Air Force Commander-in-Chief signed an order appointing a State commission for holding ground tests and flight tests of two *Bulls* which had been converted by OKB-156 to Tu-4A standard. The commission was chaired by Maj.-Gen. G. O. Komarov, Director of the 71st Test Range; it included representatives from the Tupolev OKB and KB-11.

Upon completion of the tests the commission ruled that the Tu-4As were suitable for carrying and accurately delivering RDS-3 (*izdeliye* 501-M) nuclear bombs and that a series of measurements could be undertaken in the interests of both design bureaux. The commission did not focus on the carrier aircraft's flight safety when subjected to the factors of a nuclear explosion; this aspect would have to be dealt with separately.

Live tests of the RDS-3 nuclear bomb were scheduled for 18th October 1951. A highly experienced Tu-4 crew was entrusted with performing the first-ever live drop. It comprised crew captain Lt.-Col. Konstantin I. Urzhuntsev (HSU), co-pilot Lieutenant (Senior Grade) Ivan M. Koshkarov, navigator Capt. Vladimir S. Suvorov, bomb-aimer Capt. Boris D. Davydov, radar operator Lt. (SG) Nikolay D. Kiriushkin, radio operator Lieutenant (Junior Grade) Vladimir V. Yakovlev, flight engineer Maj. Vasiliy N. Trofimov, gunner Private Arkadiy F. Yevgodashin, technician Lt. Arkadiy F. Kuznetsov and test engineer for the nuclear bomb Lt. Al'vian N. Stebel'kov.

For the sake of reliability a second Tu-4 was to accompany Urzhuntsev's aircraft. The crew of this aircraft comprised crew captain Capt. Konstantin I. Usachov, co-pilot Lt. (SG) Vasiliy I. Kooreyev, navigator Capt. Aleksey A. Pastoonin, bomb-aimer Lt. (SG) Gheorgiy A. Sablin, radar operator Lt. (SG) Nikita I. Svechnikov, radio operator Sgt (SG) Vladimir B. Zolotaryov, flight engineer Lt. Pyotr P. Cherepanov, gunner Sgt (SG) Nikolay D. Borzdov, technician Lt. Filaret I. Zolotookhin and test engineer Lt. Leonid A. Blagov.

Extremely tough security measures were taken during the final preparations. The armed, checked and re-checked RDS-3 bomb was placed on a ground handling dolly, carefully draped in tarpaulins to disguise its outline and slowly towed to the parking ramp where the Tu-4A was waiting. The ramp itself was surrounded by a tall fence and had a separate checkpoint at the only entrance, which was the taxiway. The refuelled aircraft was parked over a special trench lined with concrete; this was necessary because the bomber's ground clearance was insufficient to accommodate the bomb on its ground handling dolly. By then the bomb bay doors had been opened and fitted with four mechanical hoists for the bomb. To enhance security the bomb bay area was curtained off by a canvas tent preventing unauthorised personnel from seeing the bomb. After the RDS-3 had been uncovered and slowly hoisted into the bomb bay, an electrical connector was locked into place on the bomb's rear section and the approved time delay and critical barometric altitude settings were downloaded to the detonation mechanism, using the aircraft's control panel.

Next, the crew began the pre-flight check. The captain and the navigator inspected the

An unusual aspect of a Tu-4; the picture was possibly taken through the upper sighting blister of a sister ship.

Tu-4s were updated in the course of their service; this one has a different (forked) ILS aerial under the nose.

A Tu-4A with the forward bomb bay open.

bomb bay, satisfying themselves that the bomb was properly secured and all electrical connectors were in place. Together with a representative of KB-11 they activated the bomb's electric locks, checking that the appropriate signal lights were on; the keys were then handed over to the crew captain in case the aircraft had to make an emergency landing away from its home base. After checking the bomb control panel readings to see that they matched the entries in the log the bomb bay doors were closed and sealed by a Ministry of State Security (MGB – *Mini**ster**stvo gosu**dar**stvennoy bezo**pahs**-nosti*, the forerunner of the KGB) officer. Finally the crew captain and the navigator signed their acceptance of the aircraft in the log book.

The 'sunburst' flag of the Soviet Air Force.

With the entire crew lined up in front of the bomber, Urzhuntsev reported his readiness to Major-General Komarov and the KB-11 representative. Receiving the go-ahead, the crew took their seats and the aircraft taxied out for take-off. At 7.00 am Moscow time on 18th October 1951 the Tu-4A lifted off the runway at Zhana-Semey airfield in Kazakhstan; the first-ever take-off with a nuclear bomb in the Soviet Union went without a hitch.

Minutes later the backup aircraft captained by Usachov took off. This *Bull* carried a dummy FAB-1500 HE bomb (*foo**gahs**naya **a**via**bom**ba*). In the event the nuclear-armed aircraft's targeting systems failed the backup aircraft would become the flight leader, proceeding to the target range as planned while transmitting a series of tone-modulated radio signals to the Tu-4A until the predesignated bomb release time. The signals and the moment when the backup aircraft dropped the dummy bomb would tell the crew of the Tu-4A when it was time to drop the real thing.

En route to the target the bombers were escorted and protected by constantly shifting pairs of Lavochkin La-11 fighters. The flight was controlled from the Main Command Centre where all the people in charge of the tests were assembled; these were Igor' V. Kurchatov (head of the Nuclear Physics Institute), Yu. B. Khariton, Ya. B. Zel'dovich, B. L. Vannikov, P. M. Zernov, M. I. Nedelin, V. A. Boliatko and, representing the Air Force, Gen. G. O. Komarov and engineer Maj. S. M. Kulikov.

The Tu-4A climbed to 10,000 m (32,800 ft) and proceeded to the target in strict accordance with the schedule; its progress was monitored on a map display at the Main Command Centre. The Centre maintained HF and VHF radio communication with the bomber, using special code tables; for good measure the most important commands to the crew were backed up by the target range's support service.

The weather was favourable, all systems functioned perfectly, and right on schedule the Tu-4A crew was authorised to make a practice pass over the target while transmitting special radio signals so that the final adjustments could be made to the test range instrumentation. Finally it was time for the live bombing run. The range command post reported 'all systems are go' and the permission to drop the bomb was given. The bomber began sending special signals over the HF and VHF channels: T minus 60 seconds... T minus 15 seconds...

The last signal came at 9.52:08 when radar operator Kiriushkin pushed the bomb release button. Lights started illuminating on the display showing the bomb's trajectory as the automatic control system was powered up, the multi-stage safety system was deactivated, the detonator was armed and the barometric altitude sensors switched on. This was the first evidence that the bomb was functioning normally. The next and final evidence was earth-shattering; the ground shook violently and a tremendous boom came from outside, confirming that the Soviet Union's first mid-air nuclear test had been successfully performed. The 42-kiloton RDS-3 had detonated at 380 m (1,250 ft) above ground level.

The Tu-4A landed safely at its home base. In his post-flight report Konstantin I. Urzhuntsev described how the effects of the explosion were felt inside the aircraft. He reported that no problems were experienced with flying the aircraft manually (as recommended by TsAGI and Chief Designer Andrey N. Tupolev) when the blast wave hit. No equipment failures occurred as a result of the blast. We'll let his bomb-aimer Boris D. Davydov tell the story:

'The weather that day was good enough for me to see the target in time, take aim and drop the bomb accurately. All systems, including the transmitters sending radio signals which activated the ground equipment, functioned without a hitch. When the bomb was gone and the doors were closed the crew prepared for the flash and the blast wave: we switched off the autopilot, drew the protective curtains and donned protective dark goggles, decompressed the cabins and put on our oxygen masks. We used a stopwatch to check the anticipated moment of detonation.

The first thing we knew was a tremendous flash. Then the first and quite powerful blast wave caught up with the aircraft, followed by a weaker second wave and a still weaker third wave. The flight instruments went crazy, the needles spinning round and round. Dust filled the cabin, even though the aircraft had been vacuumed clean before the flight. Then we watched as the dust and debris cloud grew; it quickly mounted right up to our own flight level and billowed out into a mushroom. There was every thinkable colour to that cloud. I am lost for words to describe what I felt after I had dropped the bomb; I perceived the whole world, everything I could see, in a different way. I guess that was because I had my mind focused on this important mission, which I could not fail, for many days before the drop and it just shut out everything else.

After landing we taxied to our special parking area and climbed out of the aircraft still wearing our parachutes and oxygen masks – we were still breathing pure oxygen from the bottles that came with the parachutes. The ground crew checked us and the aircraft for radioactive contamination; a washing-down station had been set up at the aircraft parking area, and after showering and changing into fresh clothes we were taken by car to the headquarters to file our reports.'

The State commission declared that the Tu-4A carrier aircraft equipped with a bomb bay heating system, modified bombing equipment and other associated mission equipment permitted safe and reliable carriage of the RDS-3 nuclear bomb and accurate delivery of same. By decree of the Presidium of the USSR

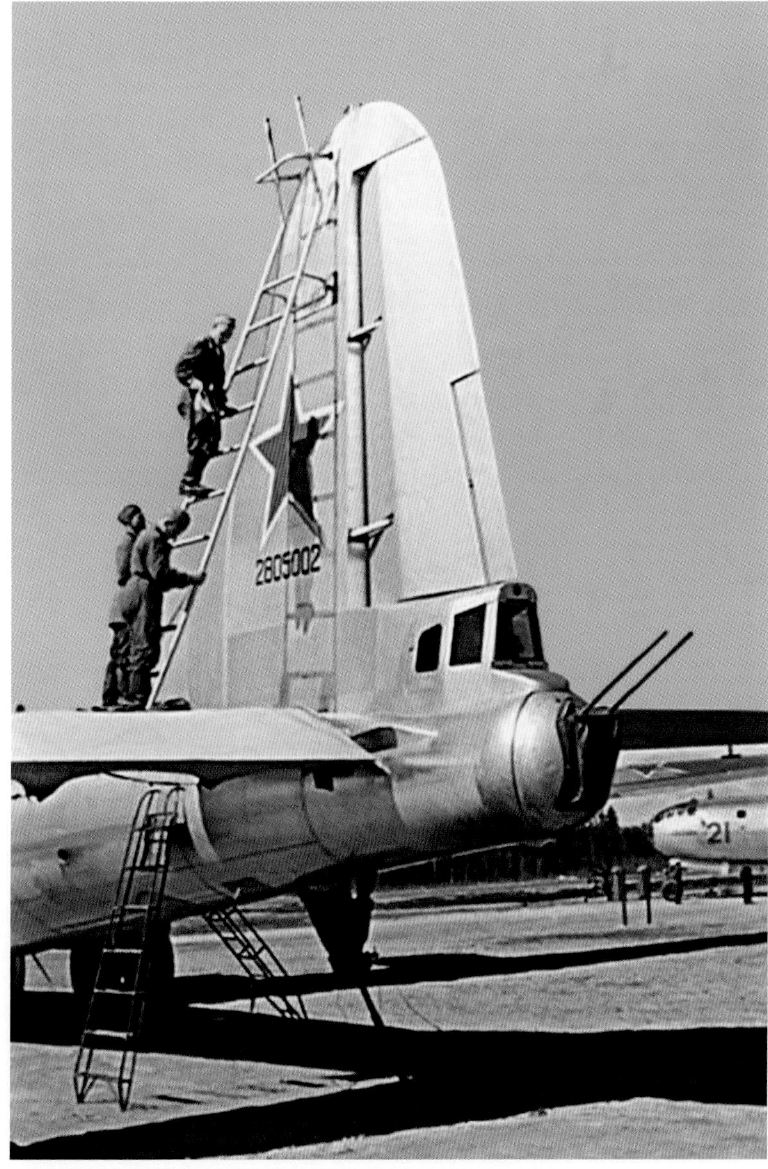

Technicians use a special ladder for maintenance of a Tu-4 coded '22 Blue'.

Another sortie is due to start soon for the crew of Tu-4 '28 Blue'.

Supreme Soviet dated 8th December 1951 Lt.-Col. Konstantin I. Urzhuntsev was awarded the Order of Lenin; Capt. Boris D. Davydov (promoted to Major after the test), Capt. Konstantin I. Usachov, Lt Al'vian N. Stebel'kov and Lt Leonid A. Blagov were awarded the Order of the Red Banner of Combat. All the other crew members of both aircraft involved in the first test also received Government decorations.

The successful first test prompted the decision to add nuclear weapons to the inventory of the Air Force and launch series production of the Tu-4A and the RDS-3 and RDS-4 bombs. As early as 7th November 1951 the HQ of the 45th TBAD and the division's three regiments (the 52nd, 203rd and 362nd TBAPs) urgently moved out from their home base – Balbasovo AB near the Belorussian town of Orsha – to other bases. The division's best crews were hand-picked for inclusion into the so-called 'atomic group', which became a separate military unit referred to as Unit 78724 and commanded by Col. Vasiliy A. Tryokhin from the 52nd TBAP. Next, construction units assigned to the MGB arrived at Balbasovo and set to work. The first thing they did was to put up a triple barbed wire fence around the base perimeter and erect watchtowers. Then they proceeded to construct nuclear bomb storage bunkers and special hardstands featuring trenches over which the bombers would be parked to facilitate the loading of the big bombs. Strict security measures were introduced in the garrison and enforced by MGB officers; this applied to all aspects of the unit's activities.

Once the reconstruction of the base was complete, Unit 78724 started taking delivery of Tu-4A bombers, as well as IAB-3000 and IAB-500 practice bombs (*imitatsi**on**naya* ***a****vi-a****bom****ba* – 'simulation bomb'). These bombs were filled with a flammable mixture to replicate reasonably accurately the flash of a nuclear explosion and the tell-tale mushroom cloud during exercises. Special training stands were set up and manuals for the use of nuclear bombs were issued. Instructions were developed for the flight and ground crews, rigidly prescribing the entire nuclear weapons utilisation procedure from the moment the order to deliver a nuclear strike came in and to the moment when the bomb release button was pushed.

The 'Excellent Air Force Serviceman' badge awarded for good results in combat training.

Thus was established the Soviet Union's first operational nuclear-capable bomber unit. Its mission was to destroy the enemy's key military targets and industrial centres.

In 1952 a production Tu-4A bomber and an RDS-3 from the first production batches passed checkout tests at the Totskoye range.

In mid-1953 four Tu-4As were deployed to Kazakhstan along with several other aircraft to undertake live nuclear bomb drops at the nuclear test range near Semipalatinsk. In addition to the actual drops, two such aircraft fitted with dose meters were used to measure radiation levels near the mushroom clouds and at long distances from the epicentre – right up to the Sino-Soviet border. On these missions the crews wore isolating gas masks to protect their lungs; tragically, on one occasion a defective gas mask cost one of the crewmen his life.

In September 1953 the Tu-4A took part in the tests of the new RDS-5 nuclear bomb; these served to check some of the bomb's design features, including the neutron initialisation system. As had been the case with the very first test, a pair of Tu-4As ('live' and back-up) was involved, with V. Ya. Kutyrchev and F. P. Golovashko as crew captains; the drops were performed at 9,000 m (29,530 ft).

Considering that the USA was still harbouring plans of a nuclear attack on the Soviet Union, in 1953 the Soviet government took the decision to establish several nuclear-capable bomber units within the Long-Range Aviation. The first of these was the 402nd TBAP.

In early 1954, pursuant to a directive issued by the DA Commander, a group of 78 persons was hand-picked from the flying and ground personnel of the 43rd VA. All of them were highly competent specialists with an excellent record of military discipline, unblemished moral character and no incriminating circumstances in their biographies. With a few exceptions, all of them had fought in the Great Patriotic War, and all had taken conversion training for the Tu-4. The group was dispatched to Balbasovo AB where Air Maj.-Gen. Nikolay I. Parygin was to set up the first regiment of nuclear bomb carriers. The personnel and aircraft of the resident Unit 78724, together with the newly arrived group, formed the core of this regiment. The task facing them was of truly national importance – for the first time in Soviet Air Force history it was necessary to prepare an air unit for nuclear warfare.

In September 1953 the newly formed 402nd TBAP was commissioned, with Lt.-Col. V. N. Shevchenko as Chief of Staff and Lt.-Col. Ye. N. Bashkatov as Deputy CO (Maintenance). Shortly afterwards, a second operational Tu-4A regiment – the 291st TBAP commanded

A slightly different version of the same badge.

Below and overleaf: Rare photos of the dispersal area at a base hosting a Tu-4 unit taken by a Soviet Yak-25R recce aircraft in the late 1950s. Note the varying types of pavement slabs.

by Col. N. M. Kalinin – was formed at Balbasovo; both units became part of the 160th TBAD commanded by Col. Vasiliy A. Tryokhin. This bomber division enjoyed a special status, reporting directly to Air Lt.-Gen. N. I. Sazhin, Assistant to the Air Force C-in-C.

Initially the mission preparation time was extremely long – it was nearly 24 hours before the aircraft could become airborne. This may have been due in part to the high security levels which hampered the work at times; in the division garrison alone there were nearly 50 MGB officers. Additionally, the first teams assembling and checking the atomic bombs were not Air Force personnel; they consisted largely of civilians employed by the Ministry of Medium Machinery (this odd-sounding name applied to the agency responsible for the Soviet nuclear programme).

On the other hand, the crews' training levels were always high. Many of the 160th TBAD's aircraft captains (V. F. Martynenko, K. K. Liasnikov, V. A. Kutyrchev and others) later tested nuclear bombs at the 71st Test Range in Totskoye.

In April-July 1954 seven Tu-4s captained by Zharkov, Korshunov, Kisilyov, Lootsik, Polyanin, Stroonov and Kholodov were again detailed for measuring radiation levels along the Soviet Union's western border and the Sino-Soviet border in the wake of nuclear tests at Semipalatinsk. For this mission the aircraft captains were awarded the Order of the Red Banner of Combat.

On 14th September 1954 the Soviet Union held the first all-arms exercise involving the use of nuclear weapons for the purpose of training the troops to operate in a nuclear environment. Within the scenario of this exercise, which took place at the 71st Test Range in Totskoye, the target replicated exactly the defensive positions of a US Army battalion. The exercise was commanded by Marshal Gheorgiy K. Zhookov, the Commander of the Soviet Army's Ground Forces.

An atomic bomb dropped by a Tu-4A (the crew included captain V. A. Kutyrchev, navigator V. Babets and radar operator Nikolay D. Kiriushkin) detonated at 0933 hours Moscow time at an altitude of 8,000 m (26,250 ft). The nuclear attack was followed by an assault by Mikoyan MiG-15 *Fagot* jet fighters from the 165th IAP (*istre**bit**el'nyy* ***a**via**polk*** – Fighter Regiment) and finally an assault by a mechanised infantry regiment.

Opposite page: Front view of a Myasishchev M-4-2 tanker.

In October 1954 a pair of 226th TBAP Tu-4As captained by L. P. Lootsik and M. L. Bondarenko again undertook air sampling after a nuclear test at Semipalatinsk, flying right through the pillar of the mushroom cloud. The same aircraft also measured radiation levels after the cloud dissipated and followed it as it was borne on the wind all the way to China.

Here we have to go back in time a little. The growing political confrontation between the Soviet Union and the USA eventually escalated into outright warfare when the Korean War broke out on 25th June 1950. This was the first time the Cold War opponents flexed their military muscles, and the situation could explode into an all-out war any minute. Luckily the opponents had the common sense not to use the 'aces' in their military 'decks of cards' – nuclear weapons; the Americans knew from intelligence reports that the Soviet Union, too, now possessed nuclear weapons and would answer in kind if a nuclear attack were launched.

On 26th November China entered the Korean War as well, supporting the Communist North. The Soviet Union, though officially maintaining neutrality, supported North Korea as well; the participation of Soviet pilots flying MiG-15s in the air war over Korea made it possible to assess the capabilities of various aircraft. It was then that the B-29's inadequacy as a nuclear bomb delivery vehicle became apparent; given properly organised interceptor operations, the B-29 would stand no chance of penetrating the Soviet air defences. The US Department of Defense was quick to draw the appropriate conclusions and gave orders to accelerate the development of the Boeing B-47 Stratojet – a much faster swept-wing bomber powered by six turbojet engines.

The Soviet side, too, learned much the same lessons from the Korean War. Accordingly, the DA's aircraft fleet was soon augmented by the Tupolev Tu-16 twin-turbojet medium bomber (NATO reporting name *Badger*) which could carry three types of nuclear bombs – the RDS-3, RDS-4 and RDS-5. As early as January 1955 the aircrews of the 13th TBAD started conversion training for the Tu-16 in keeping with the Soviet Minister of Defence's order No. 00230-54.

After Iosif V. Stalin's death on 5th March 1953, a wave of change swept the country and there were considerable changes in the political an military management. Thus, as early as June 1953 Air Chief Marshal Aleksandr A. Novikov was appointed the new Commander of the Long-Range Aviation.

2 The Strategic Breakthrough

The Soviet political and military leaders were well aware that introduction of the piston-engined Tu-4 was no more than a stopgap measure and would not ensure parity with the potential adversary. In the USA and Great Britain, development of long-range jet bombers capable of transonic flight at high altitude was going full steam ahead. Hence, as early as 1948-49 the Soviet aircraft design bureaux initiated design studies of jet bombers as well. The design work was a two-pronged effort. One specification called for the development of a jet bomber capable of hauling a 3,000-kg (6,610-lb) bomb load over a range of some 6,000 km (3,720 miles). To meet this requirement the Tupolev OKB brought out the famous Tu-16 (NATO reporting name *Badger*); powered by two Mikulin AM-3 turbojet engines, the bomber could attain a top speed of 960 km/h (596 mph) at 12,800 m (42,000 ft).The Tu-16 entered production in 1953, and re-equipment of bomber regiments flying the Tu-4 started in 1954.

The other direction of work was to create a strategic bomber having transcontinental range in excess of 12,000 km (7,450 miles). This work culminated in the creation of two very different aircraft – the four-turboprop Tu-95 *Bear* and the four-turbojet M-4 *Bison-A* developed by OKB-23 under Chief Designer Vladimir M. Myasishchev. The first prototype Tu-95 ('95/1') entered flight test in 1952, followed by its jet competitor a year later. Even though the range of both aircraft fell somewhat short of the design target, both bombers eventually entered production and achieved initial operational capability with the Soviet Air Force as early as 1954-55.

In fact, the M-4 powered by four of the same AM-3 turbojets as the Tu-16 was the first to enter service, despite the competitor's head start. Two new heavy bomber regiments, the 1096th and 1230th TBAPs, were specially established to operate the type at Engels-2 AB in the town of Engels, Saratov Region, southern Russia; the two units constituted the newly formed 201st TBAD. In 1956 the M-4 was thoroughly upgraded, receiving a longer and reshaped fuselage nose, a zero-dihedral horizontal tail and new, more powerful Dobrynin VD-7B turbofans; the resulting aircraft was designated 3M and codenamed *Bison-B*. In addition to the two units operating the M-4, which converted to the 3M in due course, from 1957 onwards the *Bison-B* equipped two new bomber regiments – the 40th and 79th TBAPs at Ookraïnka AB in the Far East constitut-

The first production M-4 in take-off configuration.

ing the newly formed 73rd TBAD. The *Bison-B* was built in two versions – the 3MS powered by Mikulin RD-3M-500 engines (hence the S for ***sta****ryye* ***dvig****ateli* – old engines) and the 3MN powered by VD-7Bs (hence the N for ***nov****yye* ***dvig****ateli* – new engines). The latter variety evolved into the 3MN *Bison-C* with its distinctive pointed nose tipped with an in-flight refuelling probe; the 3MD was conceived as a missile carrier but the missile armament was never fitted and the aircraft was used purely as a bomber.

In the mid-1950s the Myasishchev OKB began experimenting with IFR systems. A few M-4s were fitted with an IFR probe on top of the nose; the 3MS and 3MN had a similarly located probe fitted as standard. Later, many *Bison-A/Bs* were converted into single-point hose-and-drogue tankers which, depending on the original version, were designated M-4-2, 3MS-2 and 3MN-2

All in all, aircraft factory No. 23 in Moscow built 33 M-4s and 37 bombers of the 3M series between 1954 and 1960. The aircraft remained in service until the late 1980s, albeit many were converted to tankers fairly quickly, serving with the Long-Range Aviation in this capacity for nearly a quarter of a century. The *Bison*'s career as a strategic bomber proved to be relatively brief, and the examples that were

A late-production *Bison-A* begins the landing gear retraction sequence; note the position of the nose gear bogie.

not converted to tankers remained in storage for many years until they were finally broken up in 1989.

The Tu-95 had a happier fate, despite its initial troubles associated with the powerplant. In 1955 the Air Force took delivery of the first production Tu-95s powered by Kuznetsov NK-12 turboprops; the aircraft entered service with the newly formed 409th TBAP stationed at Uzin AB (pronounced *oo**zin***) near Kiev. A year later a second heavy bomber regiment – the 1006th TBAP – was established at Uzin, likewise operating the *Bear-A*. In 1957 the Tu-95 underwent an upgrade and officially entered the Soviet Air Force inventory as the Tu-95M *Bear-A*. That same year two further regiments operating the type – the 1023rd and 1226th TBAPs – were set up at Dolon' AB near Semipalatinsk in Kazakhstan.

Despite being turboprop-powered, the Tu-95 was capable of speeds in excess of 800 km/h (496 mph), matching the performance of its turbojet-powered competitors; the bomber's non-stop range was 12,100 km (7,518 miles). By the beginning of 1958 the Kuibyshev aircraft factory No. 18 had completed 50 *Bear-As*, including a number of nuclear-capable Tu-95As and Tu-95MAs; after that, production switched to the Tu-95K *Bear-B* missile carrier. The original bomber evolved into a whole family of specialised versions, including the Tu-95RTs *Bear-D* maritime reconnaissance/over-the-horizon targeting aircraft and the Tu-142 *Bear-F* anti-submarine warfare (ASW) aircraft, and became the basis for the Tu-114 *Cleat* long-haul airliner which, in turn, served as the basis for the Tu-126 *Moss* airborne early warning aircraft. We might as well say now that the final versions of the *Bear* family remained in production until the early 1990s; few strategic aircraft can boast a 40-year-plus production record.

This view illustrates well the M-4's high aspect ratio wings.

The Tu-16 family was even more prolific and varied. Although the *Badger* was in production for a much shorter period (1953-63), no fewer than 1,507 aircraft in more than 30 versions were manufactured by three plants (No. 22 in Kazan', No. 1 in Kuibyshev and No. 64 in Voronezh). These versions included the Tu-16A *Badger-A* nuclear-capable bomber, the Tu-16R *Badger-E/F/K/L* series of photo reconnaissance and electronic intelligence (ELINT) versions, the Tu-16K-10 *Badger-C* and Tu-16K-11-16 *Badger-G* naval missile strike aircraft, the Tu-16P *Badger-J* and Tu-16E *Badger-H* electronic countermeasures (ECM)

Routine maintenance of a 3M *Bison-B*; note the zero-dihedral tailplane.

This *Bison-A* has been converted to an M-4-2 refuelling tanker.

Another M-4-2 illustrates the type's colour scheme with white undersides and rudder.

variant, the Tu-16Z and Tu-16N *Badger-A* IFR tankers and so on. In addition to new-build versions, many variants of the Tu-16 emerged as mid-life upgrades. The Long-Range Aviation took delivery of Tu-16 *sans suffixe* and Tu-16A bombers, Tu-16R reconnaissance aircraft and Tu-16P and Tu-16E ECM aircraft. No fewer than 18 heavy bomber regiments converted to the Tupolev twinjet in the mid/late 1950s; the first units to do so were the 203rd GvTBAP commanded by Col. A. V. Ivanov, the 52nd GvTBAP commanded by Col. V. A. Tryokhin and the 402nd TBAP commanded by Col. N. I. Parygin. Later, in 1955, the units of the 13th TBAD also re-equipped with the *Badger*.

The main thrust of the Tu-16 family's development was directed at creating missile carrier versions which are dealt with in Chapters 4 and 8.

The advent of the Tu-16, Tu-95 and M-4/3M series took the Soviet Air Force's long-range bomber arm to a qualitatively new level, making it a component of the Soviet nuclear triad. From then on the Long-Range Aviation evolved by fielding progressively more sophisticated air-launched missile strike systems.

This chapter deals with the operational history of the *Bison*, *Bear* and *Badger* in the Long-Range Aviation (with the exception of the missile-carrying versions).

This view shows clearly one of the *Bison*'s weaknesses. The bicycle landing gear and large wingspan meant the outrigger struts were outside the paved taxiways.

The world became aware of Myasishchev's giant jet bomber on 1st May 1954 when the first prototype M-4 streaked over Moscow's Red Square during the traditional May Day parade, escorted by four MiG-17 *Fresco-A* fighters. Heated discussions about the Soviets' new wonder weapon broke out in the Western press. For a while the West had no idea who was responsible for the bomber, and one source misidentified the aircraft as the Il'yushin IL-38! (This real IL-38, in fact, was a shore-based ASW aircraft based on the IL-18 *Coot* four-turboprop airliner and codenamed *May*.)

Western experts rightly concluded that the aircraft unveiled on May Day 1954 was a high-altitude long-range bomber. The wing span was estimated as 48-52 m (157 ft 5¾ in to 170 ft 7¼ in), which was not too far from the truth. However, it was presumed that the turbojet engines buried in the wing roots were rated at about 6,800 kgp (14,990 lbst) each, that the aircraft had a maximum design speed of about Mach 0.95 and a take-off weight of some 113.5 tons (250,220 lb). The weight and thrust estimates turned out to be way off the mark. Little did the Western experts know that the Russians could create a turbojet delivering 8,750 kgp (19,290 lbst); nothing in the same league existed then on their side of the Iron Curtain.

The service pilots of the DA were wary of the M-4 at first. One of the reasons was the unfamiliar bicycle landing gear used for the first time on such a heavy aircraft. A lot of consternation was caused by the wings flexing up and down in flight – sometimes the wingtips travelled a dozen feet or more. On one occasion during the evaluation period at Engels-2 AB the aircraft unexpectedly dumped the entire bomb load instead of dropping just one bomb as planned; the force acting on the aircraft was so great that the elastic wings propelled the aircraft upwards like a springboard! All attempts to get to the core of the problem on the ground failed and the crew, being rather shaken, did not want to push their luck.

GK NII VVS Chief Navigator Col. A. N. Rekunov came to Engels to take the matter in hand. After analysing the incident he took the decision to fly a sortie. The first drop went normally but on the second try the scenario was repeated – the bomber's wings creaked threateningly under the sudden stress as the entire remaining load of heavy-calibre bombs tumbled earthwards. The defect was eventually traced to a seemingly minor error – the wires

The wing/fuselage junction and engine housings of the M-4.

The forward fuselage of the 'glass-nosed' M-4, showing the crew entry hatch.

in the bomb release control circuit had been cross-wired to the wrong connectors. This again proves the old adage: in aviation there are no trifling matters!

Pretty soon the M-4s (and later their 3M stablemates) started venturing out over international waters. The *Bisons* and other Soviet bombers frequently 'harassed' NATO naval task forces and skirted the maritime borders of NATO nations and Japan. Apart from the 'show of force', these sorties involved an extremely important photo reconnaissance mission, including night-time recce. To this end the M-4 featured a tilting camera mount with AFA-42 day cameras (***a****ero****fot****oappa****raht*** – aerial camera) or NAFA-MK night cameras (*noch**noy** **a**ero**fot**oappa**raht***), while a fairly large bay further aft housed flare bombs.

M-4-2 '62 Red' is refuelled at Engels-2 AB.

The bomber's main mission was the destruction of key military and industrial centres. Standard armament options included two special munitions (a euphemism for nuclear bombs), two 9,000-kg (19,840-lb) FAB-9000 high-explosive bombs or four 6,000-kg (13,230-lb) FAB-6000 bombs. Smaller bombs or torpedoes could also be carried in cassette- or on bridge-type racks. If one FAB-9000 was carried, the bomb bay also accommodated two long-range fuel tanks.

Meanwhile, the Boeing B-52 Stratofortress eight-turbojet heavy bomber entered flight test in 1952. The initial-production B-52A was broadly similar in performance to the M-4, except that the American bomber's service ceiling was nearly 5,000 m (16,400 ft) higher, which was considered an important advantage for air defence penetration purposes in the 1950s. The B-52's higher payload/weight ratio and take-off weight (204 tons/449,735 lb versus the M-4's 184 tons/405,640 lb) also gave it slightly longer range. The only area where the B-52 was inferior was the defensive armament, which initially consisted of only two 12.7-mm (.50 calibre) machine-guns.

Now we come to the big question: could the *Bison* penetrate the air defence system of the NATO nations? The numerous radar pickets, surface-to-air missile (SAM) sites and the supersonic interceptors stationed in Western Europe and North America virtually negated any chances of getting through, even in a first-strike scenario. The six cannons of the M-4 would hardly give it enough protection. The only hope the bomber's crew had lay in the SPS-2 active jammer (***stahn**tsiya po**mekh**ovykh sig**nah**lov* – lit. 'interference signals emitter'), the chaff dispensers and the armour plating protecting the crew.

The service introduction of both the M-4 and the 3M was by no means trouble-free. For instance, on the *Bison-A* there were two cases of the elevator skin ripping away in flight; fortunately on both occasions the crew managed to land the aircraft in one piece. This dangerous defect was cured by altering the elevator design and stiffening the elevator control rods.

Fatal and non-fatal accidents occurred both during tests and in service. For instance, on 21st March 1955 the main crew cabin of an M-4 (construction number 5300609) decompressed at 5,000 m (16,400 ft) during a test flight from Zhukovskiy. Test pilots L. P. Vinogradov and L. V. Soomtsov brought the bomber home and attempted a landing but were foiled by a sudden blizzard. After three unsuccessful attempts the aircraft made an off-field forced landing, touching down fast and breaking up; navigator/radar operator Leonov lost his life.

Maintenance platforms have been erected beside this M-4. The warning sign in front of the aircraft says electric power is on.

On another occasion a reservoir in the back-up hydraulic system failed just as an M-4 captained by the famous test pilot Mark L. Gallai was about to become airborne. The massive cast-iron reservoir burst like a bomb, the fragments severing the rudder control runs and the No. 3 engine's fuel line. As soon as the bomber became airborne it veered sharply to one side because of the inoperative rudder; Gallai had to wait until he had got up to about 50 m (165 ft) before he could counteract the turn by opposite bank. As he did, the No. 3 engine failed due to fuel starvation and the tail gunner reported there was a serious fuel leak.

With extreme caution the pilots turned the stricken bomber around for an emergency landing. Care had to be exercised in handling

A production 3MN-1 *Bison-B* bomber in flight.

the throttles because the exhaust plume changed its shape as the engines were throttled back and could ignite both the aircraft and the pall of kerosene mist stretching for hundreds of feet behind it – and then the chances of survival would be very slim indeed. As the aircraft touched down the flight engineer shut down the outer engines to reduce the fire hazard; the No. 2 engine was shut down on the hardstand, but a bit too early; with all hydraulic power gone, the huge bomber (which was still under momentum)

A 3MN is being serviced. The fairing has been removed from the dorsal barbette, exposing the breeches of the AM-23 cannons.

Another maintenance scene as a 3M is jacked up.

Head-on view of an IFR-capable 3M (it is impossible to tell the engine type from this angle).

ran off the edge of the hardstand and struck a discarded fuselage, suffering minor damage.

On 25th August 1955, M-4 c/n 5301417 became airborne with a slight right bank. The bank angle steadily grew, reaching 60-80° by the time the aircraft climbed to 25-40 m (80-130 ft; eyewitness accounts varied), whereupon the *Bison* side-slipped, crashed and burst into flames. The crew of seven captained by I. P. Pronin perished. Pilot error was cited as the cause, but the underlying reason was the M-4's poor roll stability at critical angles of attack reached when the nose gear bogie tilted automatically to increase the AoA before lift-off.

Almost a year later, on 26th June 1955, M-4 c/n 5300912 crashed in similar circumstances while taking off from Engels-2 AB. The cause of the crash was never determined because the M-4 had no 'black boxes' (flight

Two more aspects of the same bomber.

A Tu-16R *Badger-E* with SRS-1 and SRS-4 ELINT sets seen over international waters on 1st December 1985.

data recorder and cockpit voice recorder). The Air Force representatives claimed that the prescribed take-off procedure had been observed and that the nose gear unit with its tilting bogie feature was the culprit; conversely, the aircraft industry spokesmen blamed the crew.

On 23rd August 1957 M-4 c/n 5302023 crashed near Omsk in West Siberia, killing the crew of eight. Again, debates raged as the Air Force and the aircraft industry hurled accusations at each other, one side claiming the hydraulic control actuators had jammed and the other side stating pilot error was the cause, but the truth was never established.

By the end of 1957 the Myasishchev OKB apron at Zhukovskiy was clogged with up to 30 M-4s requiring modifications for flight safety reasons. The situation was so grave that on 30th December 1957 the Council of Ministers issued grounding orders for the M-4 until all defects had been rectified.

Still, attrition continued. On 18th March 1958 the final production M-4 (c/n 6303235) was lost during a training sortie at Zhukovskiy. The aircraft was taking off in manual control mode (with the hydraulic control actuators disabled); as it became airborne the wind suddenly changed. The rudder trim tab deflected almost fully, causing an uncommanded rudder hardover which the pilots were unable to counter; the aircraft executed an uncontrollable turn to port and crashed. Six of the seven crew members died in the blaze; only the radio operator survived.

It should be noted that, while the Myasishchev OKB had taken precautions

This Tu-16R photographed on 3rd December 1984 has SRS-3 ELINT pods under the wings and an SPS-151 active jammer in a UKhO fairing supplanting the tail turret.

against the unreliability of the day's hydraulic control actuators by incorporating the manual control mode, flying the M-4 in this fashion was no easy task. Even after the surviving *Bisons* had undergone a mid-life update in 1957-58 to facilitate flying in manual mode, the forces on the aileron control wheels at 450-500 km/h (280-310 mph) exceeded 40 kg (88 lb).

The upgraded 3M was no better than the M-4 from a flight safety standpoint. The first *Bison-B* to be lost (c/n 6320303) crashed on 22nd November 1957 when the crew attempted to take off with the flight controls locked; there were no survivors. The second major accident occurred on 14th February

Tu-16Rs normally operated in pairs.

The fuel tanks of a Tu-16R are filled, using gravity refuelling.

A Tu-16SPS active ECM aircraft takes off.

Technicians at work on the rear end of a Tu-16.

A Tu-16 taxies past a sister aircraft being refuelled.

A pair of Tu-16s make a low pass during a demonstration for some civil or military top brass.

A Tu-16 Yolka passive ECM aircraft.

1958 during state acceptance trials when the wheel brakes of 3M c/n 7300704 overheated during taxying, causing the hydraulic fluid to catch fire. Despite the efforts of the fire crews, the entire airframe structure aft of the wings burned out before the blaze could be extinguished. Nevertheless, it was decided to rebuild the bomber completely; the trials continued with a replacement aircraft.

On 20th September 1958 the first production 3MS (c/n 7300901 or 8300901) was ground-running its engines when a compressor blade failed. The resulting fire destroyed the aircraft completely and at least one person died from burns.

According to the Air Force, *Bison* accident attrition was mostly caused by serious design flaws which came to light in the course of operational service. True, the Myasishchev OKB did its best to improve the operational safety and reliability by making changes to the flight control system, the gust locks, the fire suppression system, the ejection seats and by improving the crews' working conditions.

As the 1950s drew to a close, certain factions in the Air Force and in the Ministry of

This Tu-16SPS was caught on camera on 16th March 1983.

Seen from a sister aircraft, a Tu-16Z tanker passes over a 'hostile' missile submarine during an exercise.

Aircraft Industry (MAP – *Mini**ster**stvo aviatsi**on**noy pro**mysh**lennosti*) grew increasingly vocal, questioning the advisability of having two heavy bomber types in the inventory, especially now that the Tu-95K missile carrier was available. This sparked the decision to convert a large proportion of the *Bison* fleet into IFR tankers which would support the operations of the Tu-95K and the remaining 3MS-1 and 3MN-1 strike aircraft. The conversion programme proceeded as a joint effort by aircraft factory No. 23, the Air Force's ARZ No. 360 (***a**viare**mont**nyy za**vod*** – aircraft repair plant) at Dyagilevo AB near Ryazan' and the technical staff of the bomber division based at Engels-2 AB which operated the 3Ms. The conversions were irreversible – the IFR probe was removed and the bomb bay was partially faired over, leaving only small clamshell doors for the hose drum unit.

The tankers showed an adequate flight safety record and fairly high performance – they could transfer up to 46 tons (101,400 lb) of fuel while having a combat radius of 5,500 km (3,420 miles). The converted *Bisons* made up the backbone of the Soviet Air Force's tanker element until the advent of the Il'yushin IL-78 *Midas*.

Indeed, tanker operations were so intensive in those days that the aircraft industry could not supply enough replacement fuel transfer hoses which had a limited service life. The Air Force command had no choice but to extend the hoses' service life; occasionally this led to the hoses snapping in the middle of the refuelling sequence.

DA crews had a bit of trouble mastering the probe and drogue IFR technique. The *Bison* tanker featured an HDU with a long hose terminating in a stabilising drogue with a locking mechanism; the receiver aircraft had a telescopic probe tipped with a special adapter; to

A Tu-16R *Badger-E* with an SPS-151 jammer seen in 1987.

A Tu-16 Yolka ECM aircraft over the sea.

facilitate contact the probe was 'fired' pneumatically into the drogue like a harpoon. However, the apparently simple procedure turned out to be not so simple after all. Bomber crews returned to base without making contact, reporting at the debriefing that they had followed the prescribed 'approach, point and shoot' procedure but the probe would not lock up. Careful analysis of the missions, however, showed that the pilots had been over-cautious, 'firing' the probe at excessively long range. Small wonder it did not lock into place!

In the autumn of 1960 OKB-23 formally ceased to exist as a result of changing government policy towards aviation in general, becoming the Experimental Machinery Plant (EMZ – *Eksperimen**tahl'**nyy mashinostro**it**el'-*

Different kinds of intruders? A Grumman A-6E of VA-95 wards off an inquisitive Tu-16R.

'44 Red', an early Tu-95M. The large tactical codes on the nose soon disappeared from the Tu-95s.

Tu-95M '42 Red' escorted by two MiG-17s took part in the 1961 air parade in Tushino.

A Tu-95A takes off, showing the white-painted undersides.

*nyy za**vod***). Yet its progeny continued flying and scaring the Soviet Union's 'potential adversaries'. 3MS-1s and 3MN-1s flew long-range reconnaissance missions over international waters on a regular basis, shadowing NATO warships, and participated in all manner of military exercises right up to the top level (those commanded by the Soviet Minister of Defence). To fool the West into thinking the Soviet Air Force had more *Bisons* than it actually had, the bold tactical codes carried on the fin and the nose gear doors were changed from time to time. In reality, however, the Long-Range Aviation suffered from a severe shortage of these heavy aircraft.

In 1962 the Air Force inventory included seventy-eight 3M strategic bombers and 25 M-4-2 tankers – that is, 103 of the 116 production *Bisons*. Most of these aircraft had by then been in service for more than six years, exceeding their provisional 1,000-hour service life limit. On 15th April 1962 Pyotr V. Dement'yev, Chairman of the State Committee for Aviation Hardware (GKAT – *Gosu**dar**stvennyy komi**tet** po aviatsi**on**noy*

The nose of Tu-95M '57 Red' (c/n 8800605) as seen by the pilot of a NATO fighter.

A view from the other side: an RAF Lightning F.6 seen from the Tu-95's flight deck.

Here, a Tu-95A is intercepted by a USAF McDonnell F-4E in early air superiority grey colours.

One more view of the same *Bear-A*.

Last-minute instructions are given to the crew of a Tu-95. Note the boarding ladder (crew access is via the nosewheel well).

***tekh**nike*, as the former MAP was known in 1957-62), reported to the Communist Party Central Committee: *'...due to the Air Force's demands to ensure the operational safety of these aircraft up to 1970 it is advisable to perform certain design work and modifications aimed at keeping the 3M and M-4 aircraft up to current operational and tactical standards. To this end the KB-201 design bureau responsible for the 3M and M-4 aircraft has now been formed at the branch office of OKB-52. The plant named after [Mikhail V.] Khrunichev* (the former plant No. 23 – *Auth.*) *has been assigned responsibility for all manufacturing work associated with 3M and M-4 operations and conversion to refuelling tankers.'*

Starting in the summer of 1962, the surviving M-4s had their outer wings reinforced as a precaution against fatigue cracking. The design work was performed by a team of ten KB-201 employees. (Consider that the new '*Bison* bureau' had only 30 people on its payroll.) Obtaining an M-4 airframe, TsAGI held a new series of static tests, while the Siberian Aviation Research Institute (SibNIA – *Si**beer**skiy na**ooch**no-is**sled**ovatel'skiy insti**toot** avi**ah**tsii*) in Novosibirsk consecutively tested three *Bison-B* airframes at loads gradually approaching the actual operational loads. Together with the Air Force the TsAGI and SibNIA engineers set up a system of monitoring the current condition of operational M-4s and 3Ms, detecting fatigue cracks as they appeared. The tests were backed by theoretical research which made it possible to pinpoint the locations which were most prone to fatigue damage during lengthy operation; this

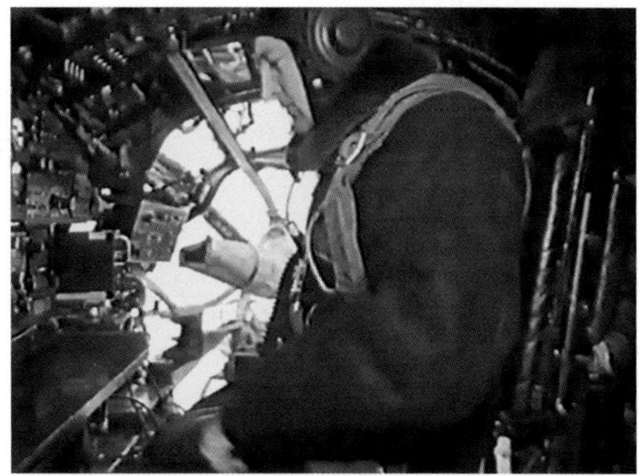

The navigator of a Tu-95 *Bear-A* at his workstation.

The captain of a Tu-95. The port windshield panel appears to be obstructed with something.

allowed the *Bison's* service life to be appreciably extended in the long run. Later, Vladimir M. Myasishchev and his team were awarded honorary medals for this research effort.

The notorious shootdown of Francis Gary Powers' Lockheed U-2A spyplane (56-6689) by an S-75 SAM (NATO codename SA-2 *Guideline*) near Sverdlovsk on 1st May 1960 had made it patently clear that strategic bombers were no longer invulnerable at high altitudes. The USA quickly devised an 'anti-SAM tactic' – from 1962 onwards the B-52s

An F-4N of VF-21 (USS *Coral Sea*) inspects a 'visiting' Tu-95M.

A Tu-95A begins its take-off run.

A fine study of a Tu-95MR (note the lateral dielectric blisters).

Unlike the example in the upper picture, this Tu-95MR is equipped with an IFR probe.

were supposed to penetrate the enemy's air defences at low altitude where the missile guidance radars could not track them. The Soviet Union answered in kind; in January-August 1964 a research programme was held to investigate the possibility of maximum-range flights by Tu-95 and 3M bombers at altitudes of 50-200 m (164-660 ft) in daytime and 200-300 m (660-980 ft) at night. This tactic greatly increased the chances of air defence penetration by single aircraft (formation flying in this case was ruled out for safety reasons). However, operational use of this tactic required the aircraft (including the 3M) to be modified in order to withstand the turbulence at low altitude. MAP declined to undertake this work, which eventually was performed by the Ministry of General Machinery (the agency responsible for the Soviet space and missile programmes). The Council of Ministers tasked V. N. Boogaiskiy, who headed Branch 1 of OKB-52, with getting the 3M low-level combat operations programme included into the task list of KB-90 headed by V. Goosarov; the work was to proceed in January-February 1966. The bomber's range on a 'hi-lo-hi' mission profile decreased dramatically, but this was an acceptable price for the reduced vulnerability during air defence penetration.

By the late 1960s new versions of the Tu-95 had taken over the 3M's role as a strike aircraft. Sometimes, however, the trend was reversed. For instance, during the Afghan War the Long-Range Aviation was tasked with suppressing the resistance of the Mujahideen rebels with conventional bombs to pave the way for Soviet ground troops. The 3M bombers of the 1096th and 1230th TBAPs based at Engels-2 were also prepared for the mission along with other types; the tankers had to be temporarily reconverted by replacing the bomb bay tanks with cassette racks for 52 FAB-250s or 28 FAB-500s.

The Dobrynin-powered versions of the 3M were phased out in the 1980s, though a few aircraft were placed in flyable storage. The remaining 3MS-2 tankers powered by low-time RD-3M-500As were combined in a single regiment – the former 1230th TBAP, which was redesignated the 1230th APSZ (*avia**polk*** *samo**lyo**tov-za**prav**shchikov* – Aerial Refuelling Regiment). After the break-up of the Soviet Union the Russian Air Force was left with just 20 modern IL-78/IL-78M tankers (a large proportion of the *Midas* fleet remained in the Ukraine), which meant the 3MS-2 could not be retired just yet. Still, the Soviet Union had pledged to scrap a substantial number of these bombers under the SALT 2 arms reduction treaty – even though the Soviet Air Force had much fewer heavy bombers than the USAF.

The last 3Ms soldiered on until mid-1994 when the units at Engels had mastered the state-of-the art Tu-160 *Blackjack* swing-wing supersonic bomber. The final sortie took place on 23rd March 1994; in August 1997 the remaining aircraft were struck off charge.

Now we come back to the Tu-16 and its service with the Long-Range Aviation. The first production Tu-16 bombers were delivered to the Soviet Air Force in February-March 1954. The first proof of this came during the May Day parade in Moscow when a formation of nine Tu-16s passed over Red Square.

As mentioned earlier, the first DA air regiments to be equipped with the Tu-16 in early 1954 (and subsequently the Tu-16A) were the 402nd TBAP based at Balbasovo AB near Orsha and the 203rd TBAP at Baranovichi (both Belorussia), which were part of the 45th TBAD. Subsequently production examples entered service with the air regiment based at Engels-2 AB. Concurrently, several were supplied to the special Long-Range Aviation unit based at Bagherovo AB near Kerch on the Crimea Peninsula, the Ukraine, which was involved in the nuclear weapons development programme.

The units of the 13th TBAD (the 185th, 202nd and 226th Heavy Bomber Regiments) began their conversion from the Tu-4 to the Tu-16 in January 1955 pursuant to the Minister of Defence's order No. 00230-54. The command staff, pilots and ground crews took their training at plant No. 22 in Kazan' (the first manufacturer of the *Badger*), while the other personnel was trained on site or at the DA's 43rd Combat Training & Aircrew Conversion Centre (TsBP i PLS – *Tsentr boye**voy** podgo**tov**ki i pere**oo**chivaniya* ***lyot**novo sos**tah**va*) in Ryazan'. The conversion of the 13th Division was completed in 1956 with the following numbers of crews being trained:

• 185th TBAP – 24 crews rated for daylight-only flying and 20 crews rated for night flying;

• 202nd TBAP – 27 day-rated crews and 20 night-rated crews;

• 226th TBAP – 27 day-rated crews and 22 night-rated crews.

In 1956-57 the 185th and 202nd TBAPs took delivery of their Tu-16s and the flight and ground crews were properly trained in the use

A Tu-16R *Badger-E* with SRS-1/SRS-4 ELINT sets.

of nuclear weapons. Between 1956 and 1961 the regiments the 13th TBAD each had a flight of nuclear-capable bombers on full-time quick-reaction alert. In August 1956 the crews started mastering the wingtip-to-wingtip in-flight refuelling technique, working with Tu-16Z tankers; this effort was successfully completed at the end of 1958. The crews also became proficient in poor-weather instrument landing approaches in daytime and at night, in taking off in the prescribed weather minima and in operations from unpaved tactical airstrips.

The Tu-16 served in roughly equal numbers with the Long-Range Aviation and the Naval Air Arm. By the early 1960s the Tu-16 completely replaced the Tu-4 in DA service.

In 1962 the 13th TBAD started training its aircrews to attack maritime targets in the open sea, despite not being a Naval Aviation outfit. By 1963 all of the division's aircrews were able to fly daytime and night sorties radius in visual and instrument meteorological conditions (VMC and IMC) against targets lying within the Tu-16's maximum combat radius. Within the 1957-63 timeframe, the crews logged an average 124-132 flight hours per annum.

In 1964-69 the airmen of the 13th Division continued polishing their combat skills, flying reconnaissance sorties, in-flight refuelling training sorties and other types of missions. In August 1969 the 226th TBAP was transformed into a specialised ECM regiment and placed outside the control of the 13th Division as the 226th OAPREB (*ot**del'**nyy **avia**polk **rah**dioelek**tron**noy bor'**byy*** – Independent ECM Air Regiment), re-equipping with Tu-16P active ECM aircraft and Tu-16 Yolka passive ECM aircraft. In 1973 the 185th TBAP transitioned to the new Tu-22M2 *Backfire-B* third-generation long-range supersonic bomber in keeping with General Headquarters directive No. 314/6/00366 dated 25th January 1973.

The introduction of the Tu-16 necessitated changes in the fundamentals of the Long-

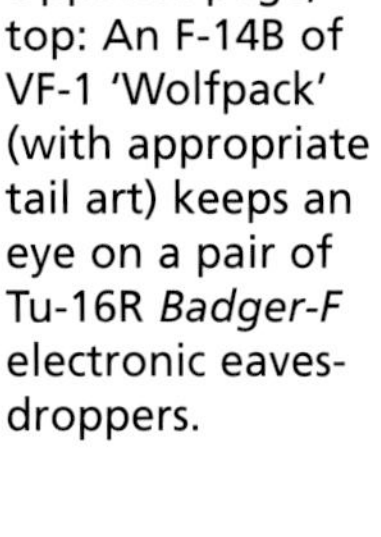

Opposite page, top: An F-14B of VF-1 'Wolfpack' (with appropriate tail art) keeps an eye on a pair of Tu-16R *Badger-F* electronic eavesdroppers.

A Tu-16RR *Badger-K* radiation reconnaissance aircraft equipped with RR8311-100 air sampling pods. Note the mission equipment operator's entry hatch amidships.

Range Aviation's operational training and radical improvements to its airfield network and supply system. The significant differences between the Tu-4 and the Tu-16, particularly as regards ramp weight and field performance, called for runway extension and resurfacing/strengthening at existing airbases. Thus, all airfields used by the Long-Range Aviation were

Below: This Tu-16P has additional ventral ECM blisters.

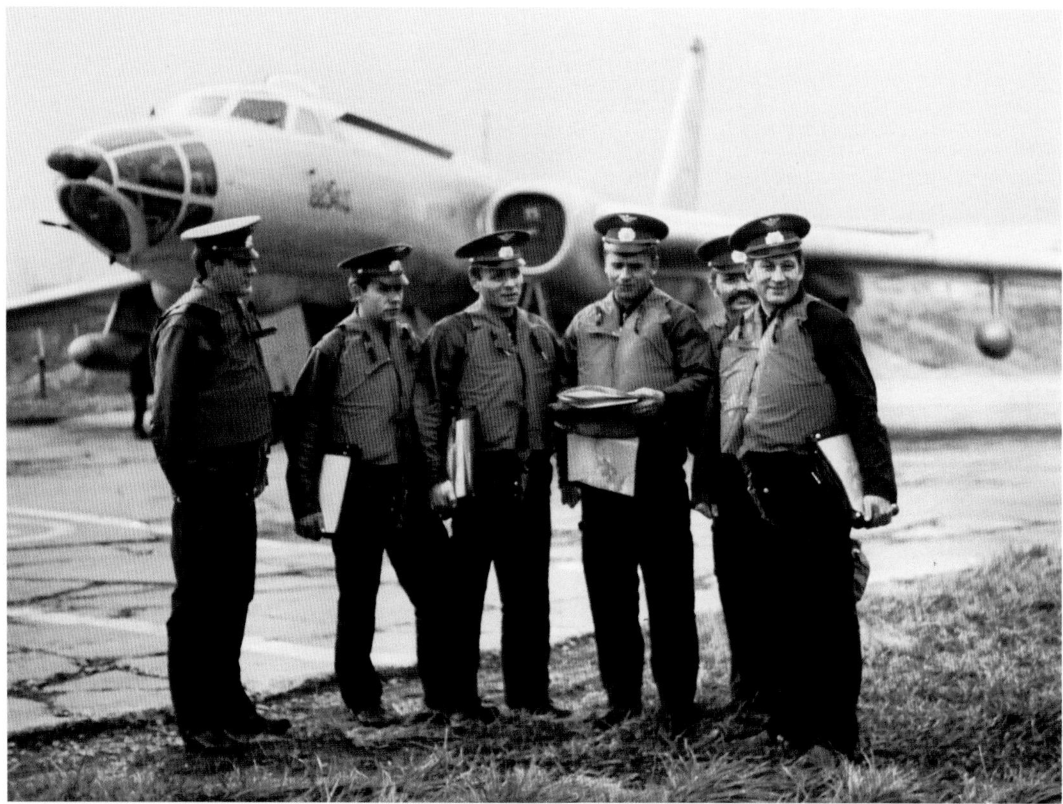

For overwater operations the crews of DA aircraft, such as this *Badger-F*, were issued life vests.

A mix of Tu-16 versions was often operated by the same unit. Here the nearest three aircraft are a Tu-16K-11-16 missile carrier, a basic bomber and a Tu-16E Azalia ECM aircraft.

Tu-16R *Badger-F* '41 Red' (c/n 1883504) tracks the movements of a NATO naval group.

upgraded to 1st class (with a runway length up to 3,250 m/10,660 ft), and often to an even higher grade suitable for practically any type of aircraft (including the Tu-95). The airbases were provided with new radio communications systems and navigation aids. Civil airfields equipped to these standards did not come into being until the end of the 1950s.

Aircraft parking areas and taxiways had to be reorganised. Previously, heavy bombers were parked in long rows on the flight lines. The Tu-16 gained the distinction of being the DA's first type to use dispersed parking in earthen revetments (which were sometimes covered with camouflage netting) to minimise vulnerability to air raids and missile strikes. New fuel dumps were built to cope with the large quantities of kerosene required to operate the jet bombers.

Full-scale production of the Tu-16 began in the mid-1950s, and by the end of the decade the Tu-16 had become the DA's standard

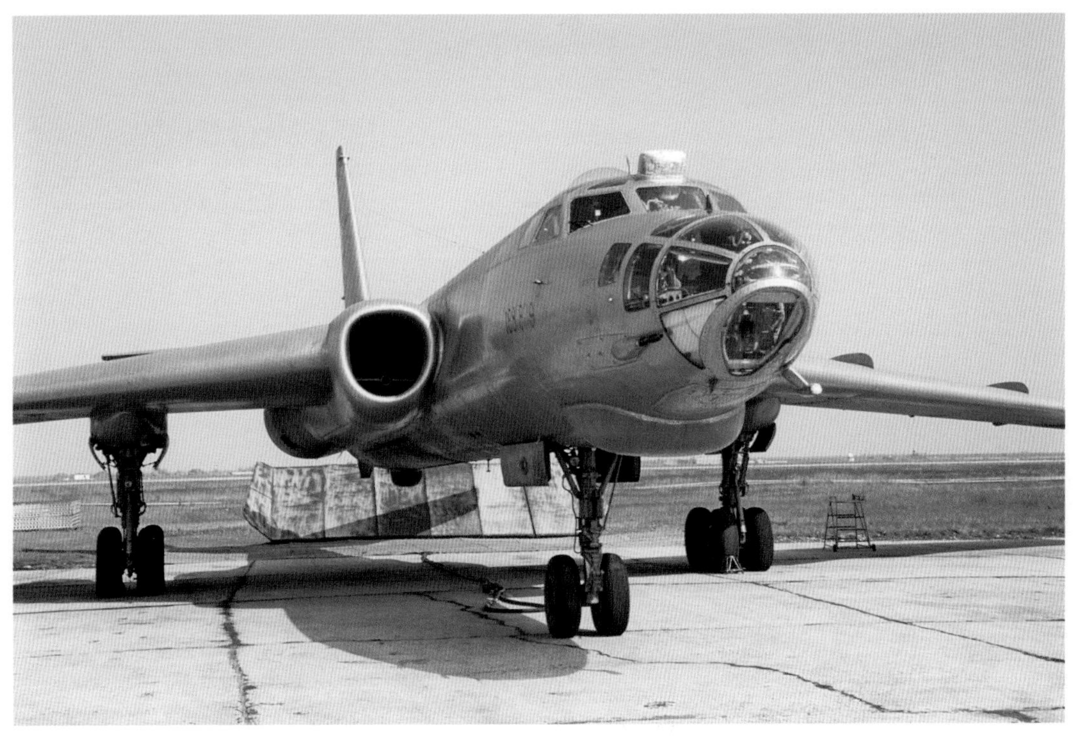

This Tu-16R is fitted with ECM equipment for self-protection.

Tu-16A '15 Black' (c/n 7203907)

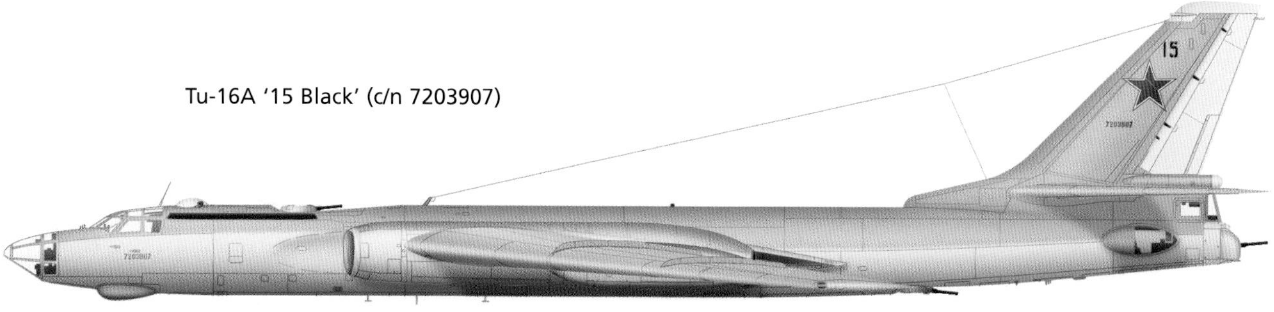

Tu-16R-2 '50 Red' (c/n 1880302)

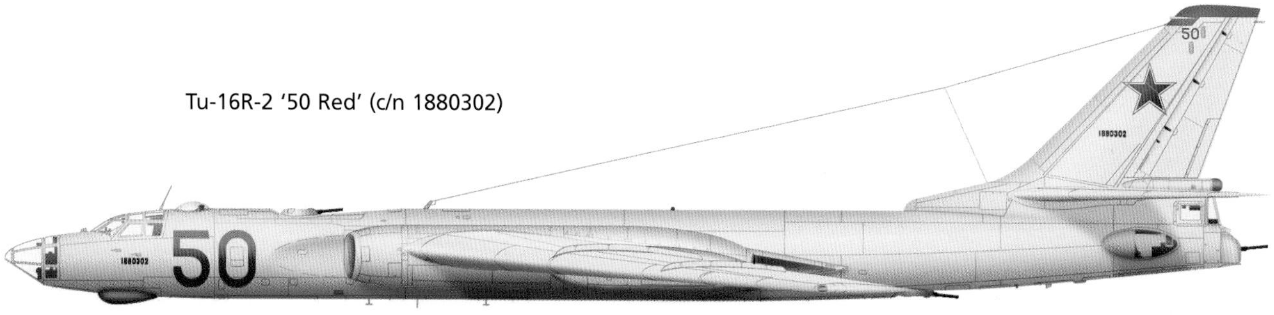

Tu-16R *Badger-E* '30 Red'

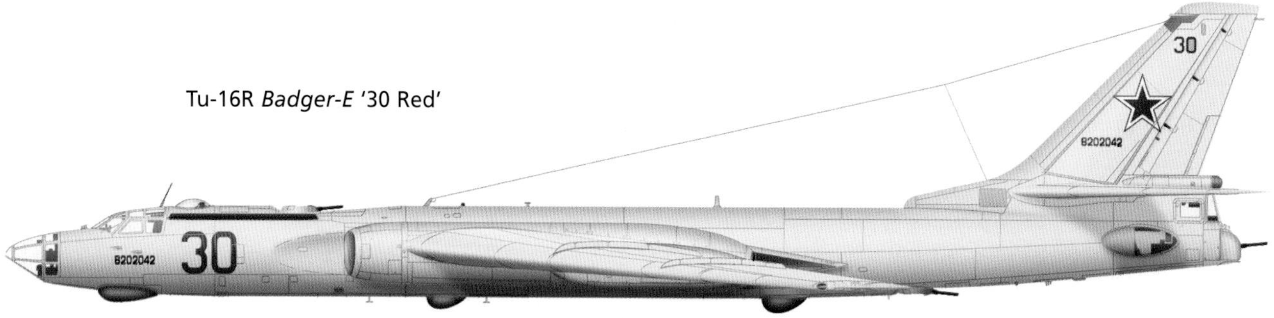

bomber type. It retained this position until the mid-1980s when it was gradually replaced by the Tu-22M. The Tu-16 remained in service until 1994. Several air regiments equipped with the Tu-16 never made the transition to the Tu-22M after the disintegration of the USSR in late 1991.

The Tu-16 was induced into squadron service rapidly and without major trouble thanks to the thought which had gone into its design and the shrewd choice of stability and handling attributes under different flying conditions. At cruising speeds the gradient of stick forces was within the acceptable limits for heavy aircraft (30-100 kg/66-220 lb). At high Mach numbers they increased more steeply: at an altitude of 10,000 m (32,810 ft) with a speed of Mach 0.9 and a centre of gravity at 21% MAC the stick forces reached 120-130 kg (264-286 lb) and handling became more difficult. The Tu-16 was stable up to Mach 0.83, with some instability, but not causing too much trouble, appearing at speeds of Mach 0.83-0.87. At Mach 0.87 the aircraft became stable once again – in fact, significantly more stable than at lower speeds.

The aircraft's highest Mach number determined by its longitudinal stability and controllability was limited to 0.9 at altitudes up to 10,000 m. Higher speeds below this altitude gave rise to an inadmissible increase in all control forces and the machine became to all intents and purposes uncontrollable. The Tu-16 could only exceed Mach 0.9 in a dive from 10,000-13,000 m (32,810-42,650 ft) in order to evade SAMs.

In its forty years of service the Tu-16 equipped many air regiments of the Soviet Air Force and the Soviet Navy. Most of these units had previously operated piston-engined aircraft, but some were newly organised as jet bomber unit. In the course of the Tu-16's service career some of the units operating it were disbanded, others re-equipped with new air-

The badge of the Guards units – the elite of the Soviet Armed Forces.

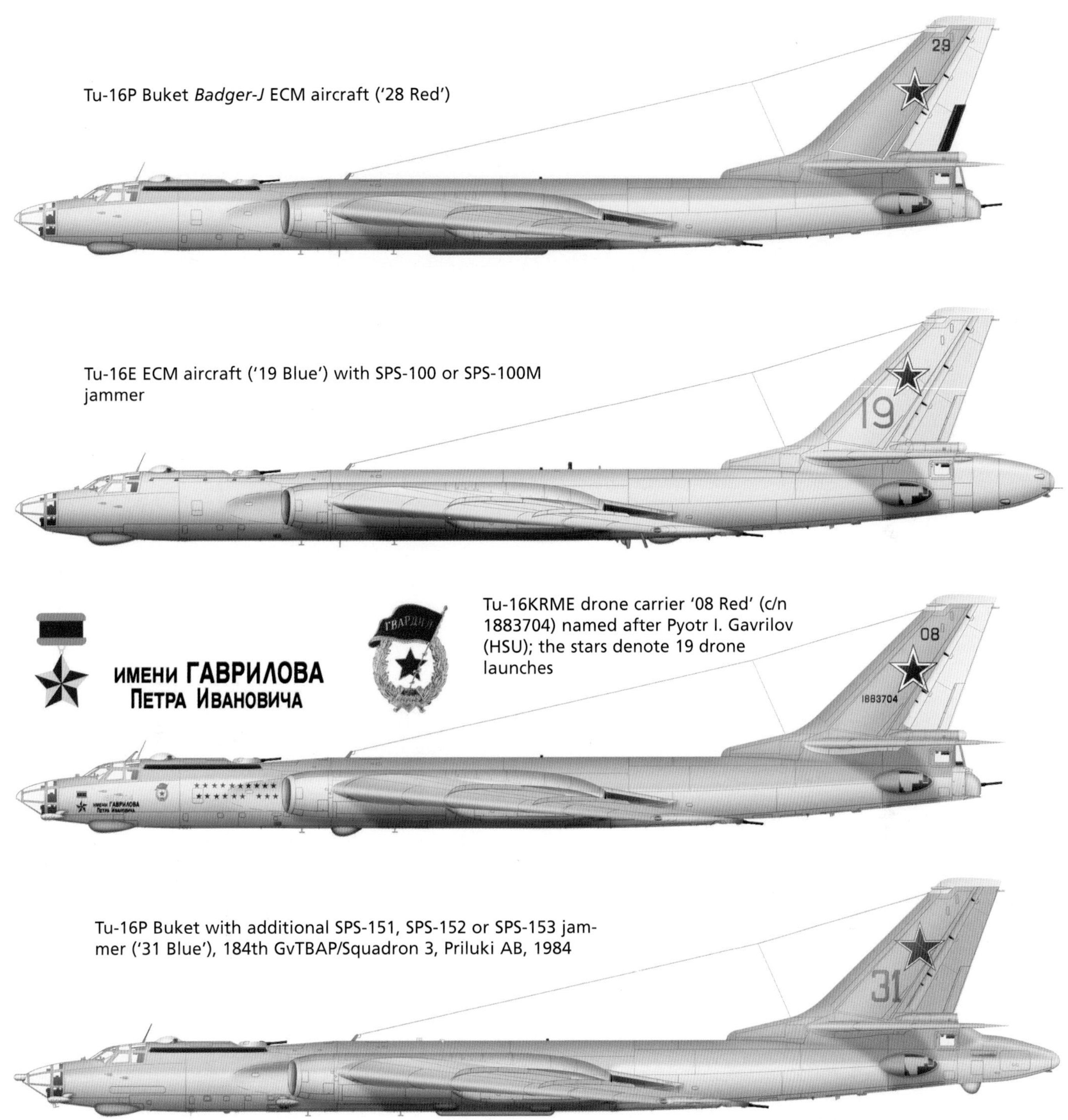

Tu-16P Buket *Badger-J* ECM aircraft ('28 Red')

Tu-16E ECM aircraft ('19 Blue') with SPS-100 or SPS-100M jammer

Tu-16KRME drone carrier '08 Red' (c/n 1883704) named after Pyotr I. Gavrilov (HSU); the stars denote 19 drone launches

Tu-16P Buket with additional SPS-151, SPS-152 or SPS-153 jammer ('31 Blue'), 184th GvTBAP/Squadron 3, Priluki AB, 1984

craft, and there were some which reverted to the Tu-16 after operating more modern machines for a while.

During the 1960s some of the Long-Range Aviation's bomber regiments converted to ASM carrying versions of the Tu-16 for operations against ground targets of strategic importance in the European, Asian and Pacific theatres. Later, the availability of more modern versions of the Tu-16 with more sophisticated and powerful ECM equipment (such as the Tu-16P) enabled the Long-Range Aviation to maintain an effective strike presence on the most important sectors of potential theatres. The Tu-16 kept its functions in this respect virtually until the end of the 1980s.

At various times, the following Tu-16 regiments were based at the following locations:

• in the western and north-western regions of the USSR: at Tartu in Estonia (Baltic Military

A Tu-16 on a training sortie over the sea.

District), at Sol'tsy near Novgorod (Leningrad MD), Shaikovka AB near Kaluga and Migalovo AB near Kalinin (now Tver'; both Moscow MD); at Baranovichi, Bobruisk (two regiments), Machoolishchi AB near Minsk and Zyabrovka AB near Gomel' (all in the Belorussian MD);

- in the south-west: at Belaya Tserkov', Nezhin, Priluki, Poltava (two regiments), Ozyornoye AB near Zhitomir, and at Stryy (all in the Ukraine);
- in the eastern regions of the USSR: at Belaya AB in the Irkutsk Region (Transbaikalian MD, two regiments), Zavitinsk in the Amur Region, Spassk-Dal'niy and Vozdvizhenka AB near Ussuriysk (all Far Eastern MD).

In addition to the airfields listed above, Tu-16 units were based at various times at Mozdok (Chechen-Ingush Autonomous SSR, North Caucasian MD), Engels-2 AB (Volga MD), Skomorokhi AB, Oktyabr'skoe

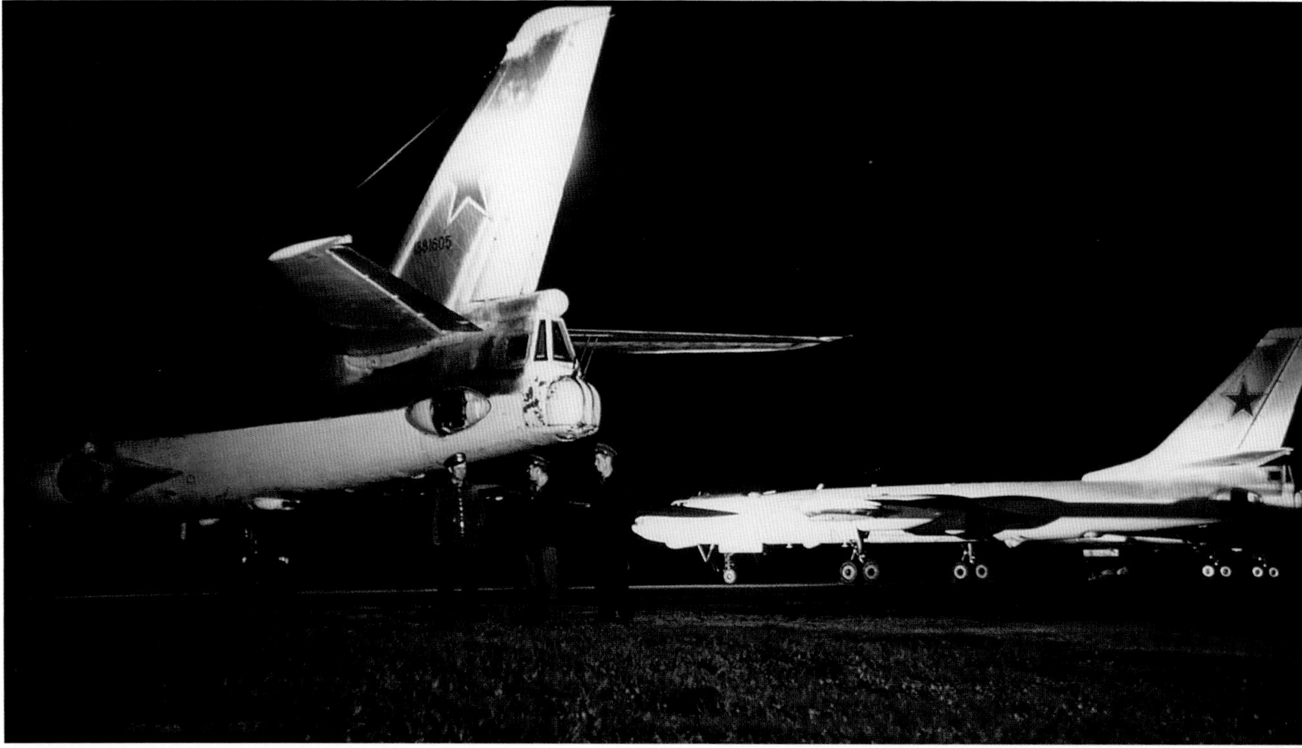

Night scene at a base hosting *Badgers*, including Tu-16 Yolka '23 Blue' and Tu-16R '33 Blue'.

A Tu-16Z refuels a Tu-16R *Badger-F* over mountainous terrain.

AB, and Vesyolaya AB, as well as at other locations.

The Tu-16 was also used by two of the Soviet Air Force's training establishments: the Chelyabinsk Military Navigator College, operating from Kamensk-Ural'skiy, Shadrinsk and Kustanai (the latter location is in Kazakhstan), and the Tambov Military Pilot College. It was also used extensively by research and development establishments: the main facility of the Soviet Air Force Research Institute (GK NII VVS) at Vladimirovka AB near Akhtoobinsk, MAP's Flight Research Institute (LII) and the Tupolev OKB at Zhukovskiy. After their retirement from service, Tu-16 aircraft were kept at the Air Force's storage depot in Chagan near Semipalatinsk, Kazakhstan.

A Tu-16 regiment usually consisted of three squadrons, equipped at first with the Tu-16 and Tu-16A. When the Tu-16KS naval missile

An atmospheric shot of a Tu-16R about to 'hit the tanker' on the evening of 1st December 1985.

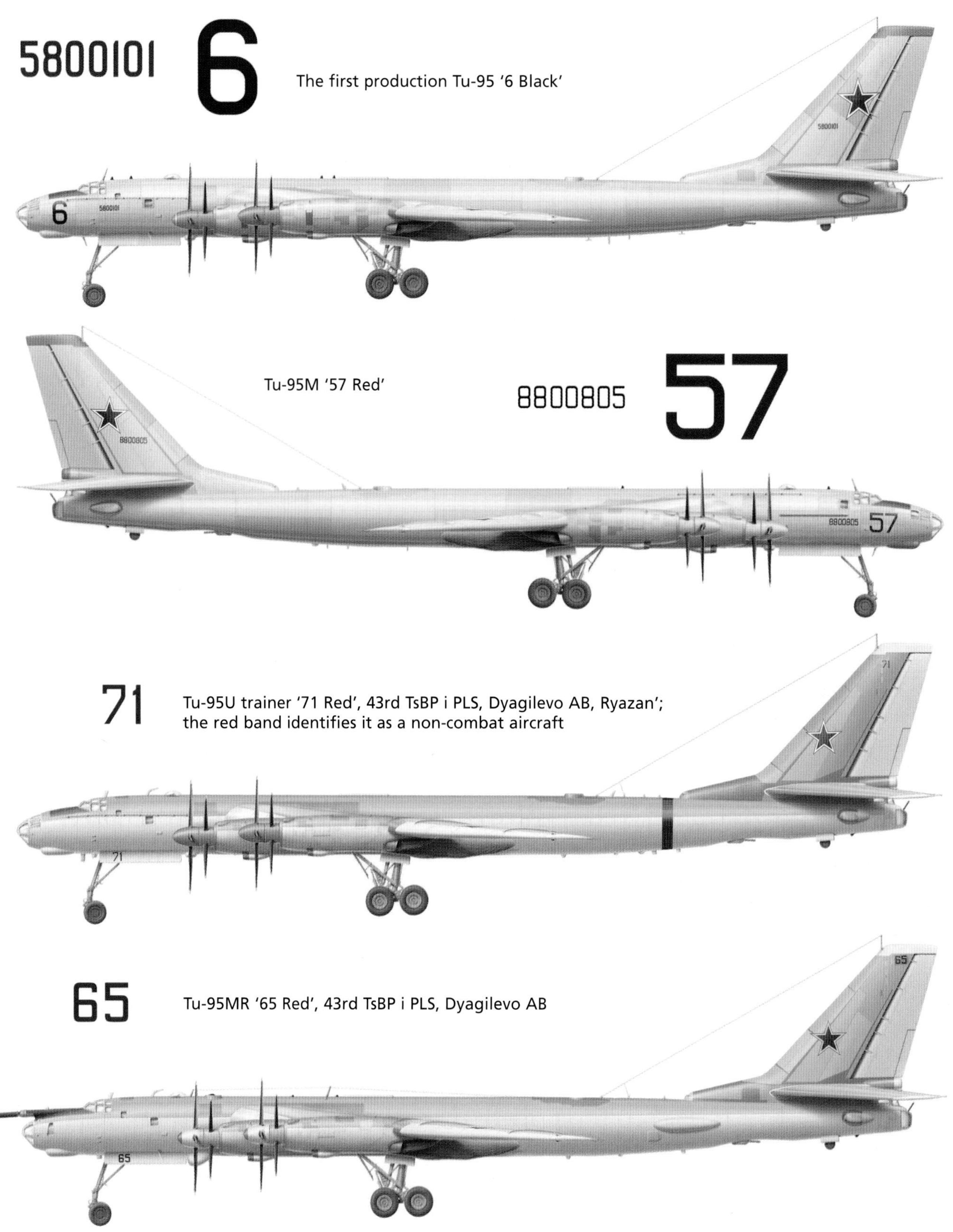

The first production Tu-95 '6 Black'

Tu-95M '57 Red'

Tu-95U trainer '71 Red', 43rd TsBP i PLS, Dyagilevo AB, Ryazan'; the red band identifies it as a non-combat aircraft

Tu-95MR '65 Red', 43rd TsBP i PLS, Dyagilevo AB

carrier entered service, a regiment could be equipped solely with this version or comprise one Tu-16KS squadron and two squadrons of bombers. The number of versions in a regiment rose with the advent of in-flight refuelling. Normally the first two squadrons flew bomber or missile strike versions, including those with IFR capability, while the third oper-

An encounter between a probe-less Tu-95MR reconnaissance aircraft and a McDonnell Douglas F/A-18A from VFA-133 on 18th March 1985.

ated Tu-16Z tankers. With the appearance of ECM versions, these were usually flown by the third squadron, tankers by the second squadron and combat versions by the first. Sometimes the third squadron comprised tankers with ECM capability while the first two squadrons flew combat versions.

In the early 1970s the number of Tu-16Z tankers in squadron service declined as the requirement for wing-to-wing refuelling vanished and the aircraft reached the end of their service lives. Most of the tankers were converted into ASM carriers. A whole series of regiments lost their tankers, despite the fact that almost all combat versions of the Tu-16, as well as reconnaissance and ECM versions, were IFR-capable. One regiment at Poltava, the 226th OAPREB, consisted solely of ECM versions – the Tu-16E and various versions of the Tu-16P, including several with the Cactus active jamming system. In 1986 this regiment was disbanded, leaving a single ECM squadron. Independent reconnaissance air regiments operated tankers and ECM versions in addition to reconnaissance machines. The Tu-16N single-point tanker using the probe and drogue IFR system equipped one squadron (the fourth) in the 200th GvTBAP based at Bobruisk and later at Belaya Tserkov'.

The Combat Training & Aircrew Conversion Centres bore the main responsibility for preparing aircrews. In the Long-Range Aviation such a centre was established in Ryazan' (the 43rd TsBP i PLS at Dyagilevo AB). It was supplied with early production examples of the Tu-16 for aircrew training. At first the specially converted Tu-4UShS navigator trainers fitted with Tu-16 sighting and navigation equipment were used for navigator training. Several regiments had this machine and it remained in service until the early 1960s.

When Long-Range Aviation units converted to the bomber or missile carrier versions of the Tu-16, crew commanders (captains) were

Here, Tu-95MR '46 Red' is intercepted by an RAF F-4K in 1984.

This shot shows the camera ports in the *Bear-E*'s belly and the ventral ELINT blisters.

appointed and trained from the following personnel:

• captains of Tu-16 crews;

• pilots of Il'yushin IL-28 *Beagle* tactical bombers trained in all-weather day and visual flight rules night flying;

• co-pilots who had qualified on the Tu-16 with no less than 150 hours' flying time;

In the late 1980s and early 1990s the Tu-16's designated service life was 35 years, but this was later extended to 38 years. In 1990-91 a number of machines dating from 1955-56 were refurbished and converted to M-16 remote-controlled target drones at the MoD's ARZ No. 12 in Khabarovsk. The last conversion work took place in 1992 when five Tu-16s built in 1957 were modified as target drones. After the dissolution of the USSR, there were no funds available to maintain old hardware, let alone replace it.

The Tupolev OKB kept an eye on all Tu-16 aircraft during the first phase of their squadron

Tu-95MR '65 Red' on the flight line at Dyagilevo AB.

The starboard side of the Tu-95MR's nose, showing the fuel line conduit running back from the IFR probe.

service. The slightest fault with the airframe or its systems, or with its equipment, was rectified and, if necessary, the findings applied to aircraft in service and on the production line. The initial period of squadron service was almost trouble-free, and the few accidents that did occur were investigated and the causes discovered; measures were then taken to ensure that they did not recur in future. Some of the typical and serious accidents are detailed below.

The first loss of an operational Tu-16 took place even before the aircraft was officially included into the Air Force inventory. On 6th April 1954 Tu-16 c/n 4200202, a 402nd TBAP aircraft, crashed near its home base of Balbasovo; the cause was an uncommanded deflection of the elevator trim tab. On 30th January 1955 the nose gear unit of Tu-16 c/n 4201302 collapsed on landing at the GK NII VVS airfield in Akhtoobinsk. On 19th August 1955 a Tu-16 crashed at the airbase in Poltava when the AP-5-2M autopilot failed.

On some occasions, a thoughtless or downright stupid order given by command staff on the ground was the potential cause of an accident. Before the 1954 May Day flypast, test pilot Mikhail A. Nyukhtikov was ordered to descend after passing over the History Museum at the entrance to Red Square and pass the Lenin Mausoleum *at the same height as the saluting stand* before climbing away steeply over St Basil's Cathedral (!). This manoeuvre was clearly impossible – there

An overall view of the Tu-95MR at Ryazan'.

A fine shot of a low-flying 3MS-2 tanker.

A 3MS-2 retracts the landing gear after take-off.

simply wasn't enough room; yet Nyukhtikov had no alternative but to obey the order. He resolved the dilemma by losing height very slightly and then accelerating away at around 1,000 km/h (621 mph) with a roar of engines. The effect was so dramatic that no one remembered to ask why the pilot had not carried out his order to the letter.

Test pilots managed to save the Tu-16 on more than one occasion. In the mid-1950s a test crew from plant No.1 in Kuibyshev was ordered to determine the maximum permissible G load for the Tu-16. At the time, the methodology for this lagged behind the skills in handling the aircraft itself and on reaching the prescribed G load the aircraft stalled,

The crew of a 3MD bomber captained by A. N. Markov.

The captains of two 3M bombers at work.

entering a spin. The aircraft captain lost his nerve and ejected ahead of the other crew members, but was killed immediately afterwards when he was struck by a hatch cover released by another member of the crew as he exited the aircraft. Co-pilot Aleksandr Kazakov, on the other hand, kept his self-control and managed to recover from the spin, exceeding all speed and G load limits in the process. He had thus unwittingly tested the airframe's strength.

Special tests were carried out on a number of examples. In 1956 Lt.-Col G. Yaglov landed a Tu-16 for the first time on an unpaved runway, after which operations from unpaved airstrips were made on a regular basis, using sparsely equipped auxiliary airstrips in the tundra and on the Arctic ice without any adverse consequences.

In the mid-1950s only a few airfields in the Soviet Arctic, such as Amderma, Severomorsk, Chekoorovka, Wrangel Island and one or two others, were suitable for heavy bombers. A special operations group was formed in the early 1960s to co-ordinate the work of the sixteen airfields in the High North. In addition to these, tactical airfields with hard-packed earth runways and ice runways were set up, though these were not intended for heavy bomber operations; on take-off and landing, clods of earth or chunks of ice could be ingested by the aircraft's engines, damaging them.

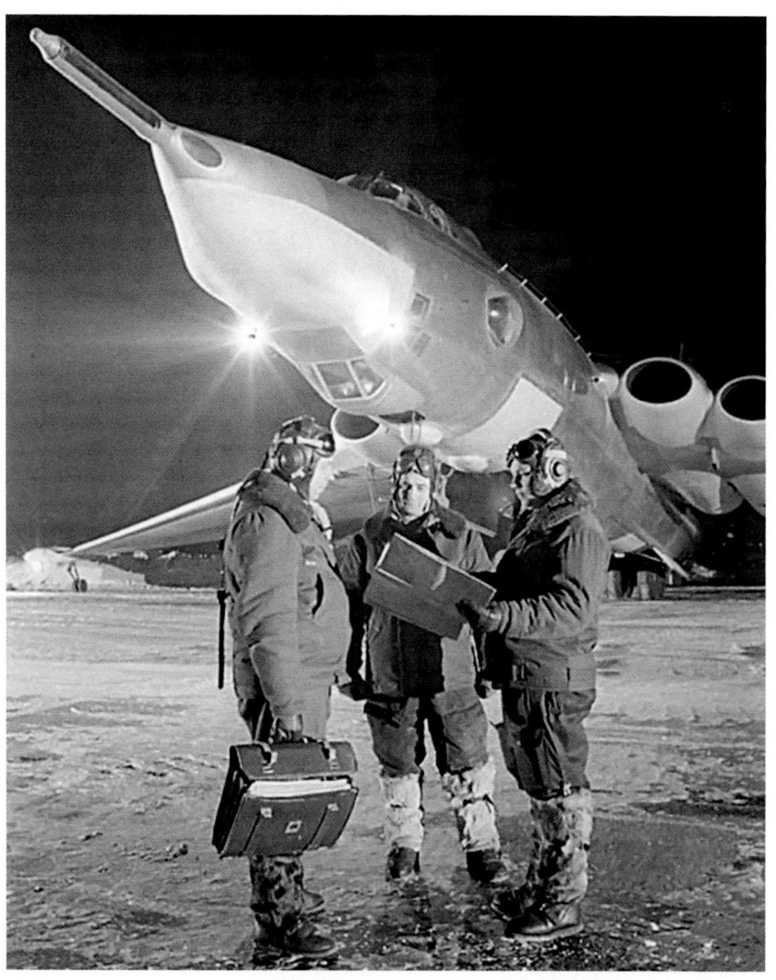

In the second half of the 1950s it was decided to use ice floe airfields in the Arctic to increase the operational capabilities of the Long-Range Aviation. This turned out to be no easy matter since the landing weight of loaded strategic bombers was around 70-95 tonnes (154,320-209,435 lb). While the bomber's weight could not break the ice, which was many metres thick, the aircraft could skid off the runway when it braked on landing Added to this, the ice's high salt content made its surface friable, and the vibration induced on take-off and landing was so violent that it was impossible to read the instruments properly.

One such landing on an ice floe on 26rd April 1958 ended in an accident, making it impossible to fly the bomber back home. For almost a year (until 16th April 1959) the Tu-16 drifted through the Arctic Ocean, accompanied by the staff of a Soviet polar research station and the technician left to guard it. Meanwhile, the ice floe kept crumbling and by April 1959 it was only half its original size. When strong winds and currents began to carry the drifting research station towards the Greenland Sea, the decision was taken to destroy the aircraft to prevent it from falling into the hands of the 'potential adversary'. As early as September 1958 the Tu-16 had been spotted by a Royal Canadian Air Force recon-

A typical Soviet-era publicity shot: the pilots of a 3MD consult a map produced by the navigator, his 'brainbag' hanging open. Imagine that in real life!

Opposite page: More night views of the *Bison-C*.

A 3MD is refuelled by a TZ-22 fuel truck. Note the buried lights flanking the IFR probe; these illuminate the tanker's drogue at night.

naissance aircraft and the Western press began to make noises about the setting up of Soviet strategic bases on neutral territory relatively close to the American continent.

While stripping the Tu-16 of all salvageable items, the technical crew had to use an inflatable dinghy to reach it due to the melting ice. Once the engines and equipment had been recovered, the airframe was doused with kerosene and set alight. The personnel from the drifting polar station, the technician and the dismantling crew were evacuated to the mainland. For his 'lengthy secondment' technician R. Kagilov was given a substantial reward and leave. After this, no more landings by the Tu-16 were made on ice strips in the Arctic, although for various reasons some unplanned landings on the ice did take place.

Ten Tu-16s were lost in fatal and non-fatal crashes between 1954 and 1956. The worst attrition in the Tu-16's service career was between 1957 and 1960 when about ten machines were lost each year. Then the accident rate fell sharply; in the 1960s and 1970s the average annual attrition was one or two. On 15th July 1964 a Tu-16R crew reported sighting an American carrier group 200 km (124 miles) to the east of the Japanese coast. After this, nothing more was heard from the aircraft; there were no survivors among the crew of seven. On 25th May 1968 another Tu-16R reconnaissance aircraft was lost near Newfoundland after overflying the aircraft carrier USS *Essex*. There was suspicion that the aircraft had been shot down by the US Navy air defences immediately after reporting the location of an American destroyer, but this allegation was refuted by the Americans. Wreckage from the aircraft collected during the ensuing search and rescue operation was transferred to a Soviet Navy destroyer.

By the end of 1981, 106 examples of the Tu-16 had been lost for various reasons, including 72 Air Force (DA) aircraft. In the early years the share of fatal and non-fatal accidents caused by hardware failures was fairly high; as the bomber's assemblies and components were developed and improved this was reduced to almost zero, and it was the errors of the flight and ground crews that became the major culprits.

Not all such incidents ended badly for the Tu-16, though. In the early 1980s a Tu-16 on patrol over the Atlantic was intercepted by three of the latest American carrier-based fighters, the McDonnell Douglas F/A-18A Hornet. Trying to scare the Soviet aircraft off

Three views of a Myasishchev 3MD

its intended course, the fighters performed dangerous manoeuvres, including head-on passes. This cat-and-mouse game ended in tragedy when two of the 'attackers' collided directly above the Tu-16 and exploded; one pilot was killed, the other managed to eject. The flying debris damaged the Tu-16 but the latter managed to limp back to base thanks to the courage and skill of its crew.

In the course of its service career the Tu-16 was called upon to carry some unusual civilian passengers. In 1957, when it was vital to summon the First Secretaries of the regional and district Communist Party committees for an extraordinary convention to support Nikita S. Khrushchov against an 'anti-Communist opposition group' within the Soviet government, Marshal Gheorgiy K. Zhookov used his power as Defence Minister to arrange for the necessary Party bosses to be flown in by Tu-16 bombers. Khrushchov was thus able to convoke a plenum quickly and gain the necessary number of votes. In this way the Tu-16 played a crucial part in the power struggle among the political leaders of the USSR in the second half of the 1950s.

The Tu-16 in its various versions formed the backbone of the Long-Range Aviation for a considerable time. From the late 1950s, when the Tu-22 *Blinder* supersonic long-range bomber entered service, several DA regiments at Baranovichi, Machoolishchi, Zyabrovka, Ozyornoye and Nezhin began converting to the new type. However, the Tu-22 was not a completely successful aircraft, accident-prone and complicated to operate. Production of the Tu-22 was terminated at the end of the 1960s. The bomber regiment at Vozdvizhenka AB took delivery of several new machines initially, but then passed them on to other regiments and reverted to the Tu-16.

The service debut of the Tu-22 in the 1960s hardly diminished the role of the Tu-16 in the nation's defence. Firstly, there were far fewer regiments equipped with the Tu-22 than with the Tu-16; secondly, the Tu-16 was the more versatile machine with a significantly wider range of applications; thirdly, at its subsonic cruising speed the Tu-22 had no advantages in performance over the Tu-16; finally, the K-26 weapons system with the KSR-5 missile was at least equal, and in some aspects superior, to the K-22 system.

During the 1970s more modern types of bombers and missile carriers, the Tu-22M2 *Backfire-B* and later the Tu-22M3 *Backfire-C*, began to enter service with the DA and the AVMF. In 1974 the 185th TBAP at Poltava was the first to receive the Tu-22M2, followed by the unit at Sol'tsy AB, both regiments at Belaya Tserkov', the regiment at Shaikovka AB and so on. The regiment at Priluki re-equipped with this type in the 1980s. But even when full-scale production and delivery of the Tu-22M2

The upper surface of a production 3MD.

A special 'cherry picker' truck is used to inspect the 3M's tail.

The nose of a 3MD bearing the legend Otlichnyy (Excellent); the 'Excellent aircraft' badge was not yet in use then.

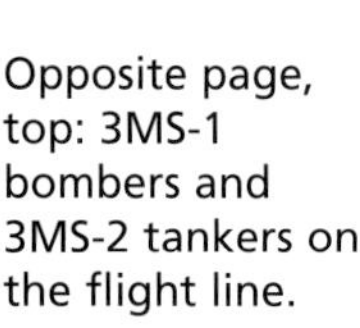

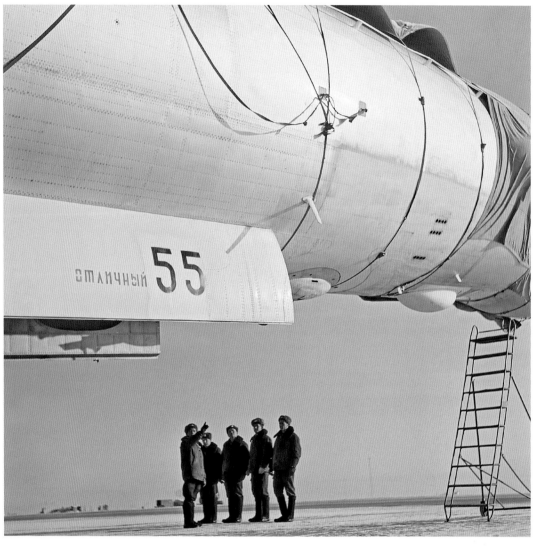

Opposite page, top: 3MS-1 bombers and 3MS-2 tankers on the flight line.

Opposite page, bottom: A technician installs the intake blanks of a 3MD with the engine numbers painted on them.

and Tu-22M3 got under way in Kazan', the Tu-16 remained in service with the overwhelming majority of Long-Range Aviation regiments. The numbers of the Tu-16 versions in service with the DA as of 1st January 1979 are given on the opposite page.

At the end of 1981 the Long-Range Aviation had 487 Tu-16s and the Naval Air

A 3MD is readied for a sortie on a bright and sunny winter day.

Arm had 474. A further 156 were in service with other elements of the Soviet Armed Forces and the defence industry. MAP documents also listed 106 examples as 'not current' by then (this included both aircraft written off due to technical condition and accident attrition). The remaining machines, apart from those exported, do not appear in the statistics for some reason.

The scales began to tip in favour of the Tu-22M in the 1980s after the Tu-16 had been taken out of service in large numbers. At the end of 1990 there were 173 Tu-16s remaining in the European part of the USSR, of which 81 were in Long-Range Aviation service. The DA's Tu-16s served with the 251st UAP (*oo**cheb**nyy* ***avia**polk* – Training Air Regiment) at Belaya Tserkov' (40 aircraft), the 260th TBAP at Stryy (23 aircraft) and the 200th TBAP at Bobruisk (18 tankers).

The last Long-Range Aviation regiment to fly the Tu-16 was the Independent Long-Range Reconnaissance Air Regiment based at Spassk-Dal'niy. After the unit had re-equipped

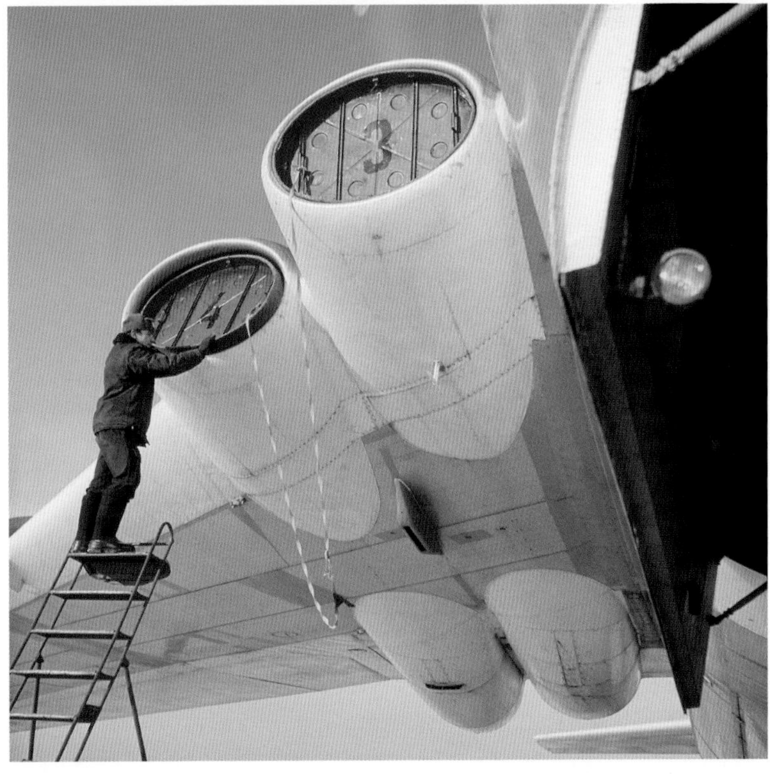

The Long-Range Aviation's Tu-16 fleet (by version) as of 1st January 1979

Year of manufacture	Tu-16	Tu-16A	Tu-16Z	Tu-16N	Tu-16R	Tu-16KSR	Tu-16 'Yolka'	Tu-16P 'Buket'
1954	–	3	–	–	–	17	–	–
1955	8	5	5	–	–	99	8	25
1956	4	9	15	2	–	52	27	44
1957	10	21	–	8	14	38	4	27
1958	1	–	–	–	8	5	29	8
Total	23	38	20	10	22	211	68	104
Grand total	496							

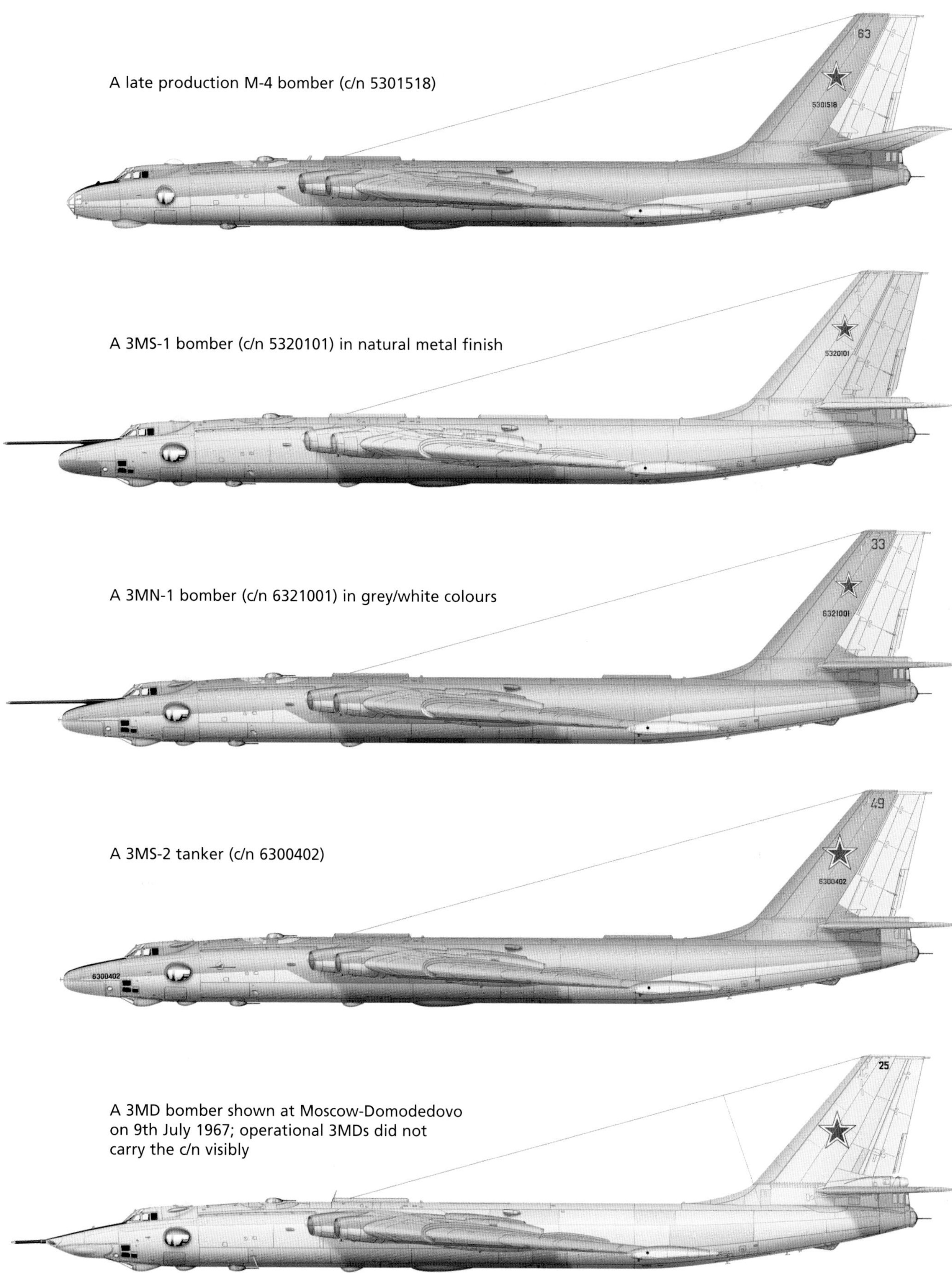

A late production M-4 bomber (c/n 5301518)

A 3MS-1 bomber (c/n 5320101) in natural metal finish

A 3MN-1 bomber (c/n 6321001) in grey/white colours

A 3MS-2 tanker (c/n 6300402)

A 3MD bomber shown at Moscow-Domodedovo on 9th July 1967; operational 3MDs did not carry the c/n visibly

with the Tu-22M, the remaining reconnaissance and ECM versions were ferried to Belaya Tserkov' AB for mothballing. Sadly, no money could be sourced for even placing the aircraft in storage; the remaining Tu-16s in Russia were scrapped.

At the Chagan storage depot in Kazakhstan, some 100 examples of assorted Tu-16s stood rusting away for a long time. After their 'privatisation' by Kazakhstan, they soon became non-airworthy. A similar fate befell the Ukrainian machines after the disintegration of the USSR.

The Tu-95 first entered service as a strategic bomber during April 1956. The first division to operate it was the 196th TBAD based at Uzin AB in the Ukraine. The first regiment was under the command of Col. Nikolay N. Kharitonov (who, during 1958, became chief test pilot for the Tupolev OKB). The next division to receive the Tu-95 was based in Semipalatinsk in Kazakhstan.

Flight crews and maintenance personnel quickly grew familiar with the new bomber. Underscoring this rapid integration of the type into the operational inventory was a group of Tu-95s making a flypast at the traditional Aviation Day air event at Moscow-Tushino in 1956.

In fact, the first Tu-95s suffered from a fair number of problems. The initial production version of the NK-12 engine, for instance, was equipped only with a manual propeller feathering system, which soon proved to be inadequate. On 24th November 1956, Tu-95 c/n 5800310 suffered an engine failure. Because of the crew's inability to feather the massive contra-rotating propellers on the affected engine in timely fashion, the aircraft lost speed, stalled, and crashed, killing all aboard.

Partly as a result of the accident, an automated feathering system was rapidly developed. By the end of the decade all Tu-95s were equipped with NK-12M engines and AV-60N propellers featuring an automated feathering system. This proved a vital device in emergencies and the system is credited with saving many lives.

As it was, the massive reduction gearbox of the NK-12 turboprop required a very efficient lubrication system. During the notoriously cold Russian winters, frozen oil in the engine gearboxes was not an uncommon occurrence. Special heating systems were required to keep the oil in a fluid state and the engine and ground support systems were designed to accommodate this.

3MS-2 tankers in service with the 1230th APSZ at Engels.

This pre-heating process impacted the Tu-95's combat readiness, often requiring some three to four hours to accomplish. At auxiliary airfields that lacked proper heating equipment, the Tu-95s had to run up the engines every three to six hours (depending on the ambient temperature) in order the keep the oil from congealing. When the engines were shut down they were wrapped in thermal insulation covers. Besides the waste of time and energy, such cycling of the engines led to additional maintenance problems and impacted the engine life which was too low as it was. The oil problem eventually was solved by the development of a new formula that remained functional down to –25°C (+13°F).

Despite the numerous difficulties related to keeping the Tu-95 combat-ready, flight crew transition proved relatively easy. By the end of the 1950s, two Long-Range Aviation regiments were fully equipped with the *Bear*. Concurrently, the DA began setting up tactical airfields in tundra areas around the North Polar region. Such facilities placed the bombers within practical striking distance of strategic US targets. Accordingly, within the context of

Another view of a 3MS-2 on a rain-soaked hardstand.

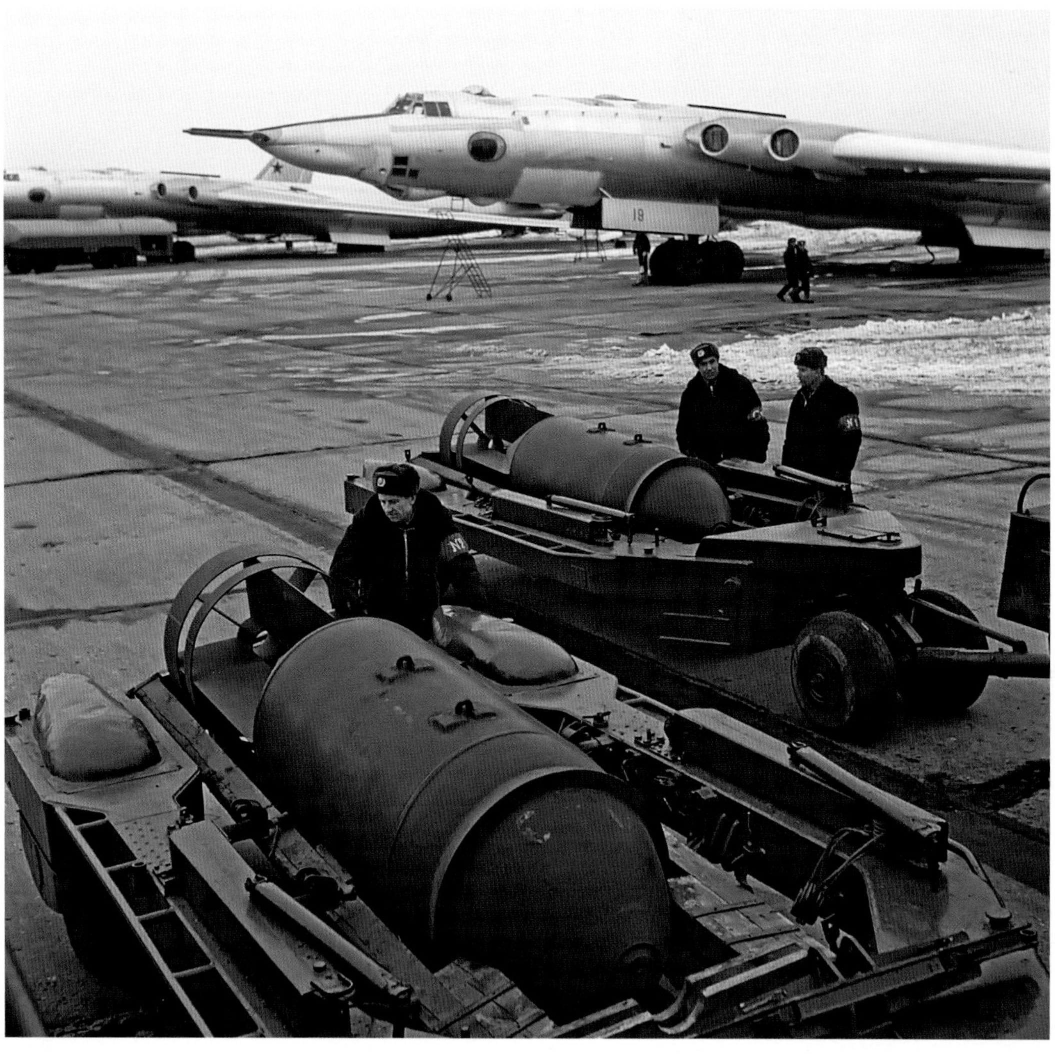

FAB-3000M54 HE bombs are prepared for loading into 3MD bombers.

Opposite page:

Top: CCCP H-1139 (that is, SSSR N-1139), a Tu-4 used as a transport by the Polar Aviation, served to explore the possibility of operating heavy bombers from ice airfields in Arctic.

Bottom: Tu-4 operations in the Arctic; the crew takes measurements (left) and cooks food (right) on board the aircraft.

training to attack such targets, Tu-95/Tu-95M aircraft were operated from packed snow runways in the High North. The width of those runways was only slightly more than the aircraft's wingspan.

Low-altitude as well as high-altitude penetration of the potential adversary's air defences was refined during the early 1960s, using *Bear-As*. Flights of single bombers and bomber formations were undertaken at altitudes that often did not exceed 200 m (650 ft).

The Tu-95s and Tu-95Ms were later modified to accommodate conventional warfare scenarios in addition to nuclear ones. Reviewing conflicts in such areas as the Middle East led to the conclusion that a conventional warfare capability was desirable. Long-range Aviation commanders eventually concluded that the aircraft should be modified for such missions and accordingly, a system allowing the Tu-95 to carry up to 45 250-kg (551-lb) HE bombs was introduced. The mission in this configuration was to destroy enemy airfields and runways.

Tu-95MR reconnaissance aircraft routinely flew reconnaissance missions over US Navy aircraft carrier groups in the Atlantic Ocean. This was initiated in the early 1960s during what later became known as the Cuban Missile Crisis.

The reconnaissance mission was usually conducted with Tu-95s flying in pairs. One aircraft was often a Tu-95K or Tu-95KM missile carrier and the other a Tu-95MR doing the actual reconnaissance role. The missile carrier was used to locate the NATO ships, using its powerful radar. After that, the Tu-95MR overflew the ships and took detail photographs.

During the 1970s and 1980s, the Tu-95MRs generally flew their reconnaissance missions independently. These flights gave Soviet military commanders fresh information concerning the movements of US Navy ships in the Atlantic. This information, when coupled with data being generated by the rapidly developing Soviet space reconnaissance capability, provided a considerable amount of data for use by military planners.

3 Operations in the Arctic

The 'Cold War' was getting hotter, and an armed conflict between the Soviet Union and the USA was becoming increasingly probable. The Soviet and US Armed Forces were facing the same task – wiping out targets in the other nation's territory. However, to engage the targets you needed to reach them first, and this was no easy thing, considering that the two principal Cold War adversaries lay in different hemispheres. The shortest route for Soviet strategic bombers tasked with attacking the continental USA would lie across the North Pole. Yet this route, too, was by no means easy to use because of inclement weather and navigational complications – magnetic compasses were unreliable in the Arctic and there were no landmarks.

A military doctrine including cross-Polar flights was developed in the USA in the late 1940s. First, the Americans set up the drifting research stations Alpha, Bravo and Charlie in the Arctic Ocean; apart from their

A Tu-4 shares the airfield of a drifting Arctic research station with a Mil' Mi-4 helicopter.

primary scientific mission, they performed a military function and the personnel included USAF and US Navy representatives who did their own research. As early as 1946, USAF B-29 bombers regularly flew weather reconnaissance missions over the Arctic and searched for suitable locations where *ad hoc* ice airstrips could be constructed. The USAF also started building airbases in north-western Greenland and setting up early warning radar barriers on the island.

The Soviet Union had begun actively exploring the Arctic Ocean and the vast expanse of the country's High North regions back in the 1930s. These research efforts had been interrupted by the war but resumed in the late 1940s; moreover, in the new Cold War conditions they had assumed strategic importance. The Soviet government decided to establish a defensive line along the northern coasts as a protection against a possible American aggression.

The tail of Tu-4 CCCP H-1139 bearing a Polar Aviation pennant.

On 23rd April 1948 an aircraft delivered the personnel of the SP-2 (***Sev**ernyy **po**lyus* – North Pole) Arctic expedition to the Pole. As distinct from the pre-war Arctic expeditions, which were widely publicised and a matter of national pride, this one was cloaked in secrecy, and with good reason. Codenamed *Vysokoshi**rot**naya-70* (the name means 'high-latitude'), the expedition involved not only the Polar Aviation (a civil aviation branch supporting polar research) but also the Air Force – military airlift, heavy bomber and fighter units.

Leonid N. Ageyev (HSU), an Air Force navigator involved in the SP-2 expedition, recalls these events as follows:

'The activities of the US Air Force and the US Navy in the Arctic caused the Soviet military to undertake a thorough research of the Central Polar basin. The Soviet Arctic exploration programme was revived. On 23rd April 1948 pilot Ivan Cherevichnyy delivered the SP-2 Arctic expedition to the North Pole. The Soviet flag was hoisted above the Pole. The research station worked amid great secrecy and was codenamed Location 36.

The expedition Vysokoshirotnaya-70 [...] involved the Air Force working alongside the Polar Aviation. The Polar Aviation detachment was commanded by Cherevichnyy; it operated [Lisunov] Li-2 [transports], [Douglas] C-47s, [Consolidated PBY-6] Catalinas and even a captured Focke-Wulf Fw 200 Condor. The

One more view of CCCP H-1139 on the Arctic ice; the bomb bays used as cargo bays are open for unloading.

The crew of a Polar Aviation Tu-4.

The crew and Arctic researchers pose with the Tu-4. Note the cargo glider in the background.

latter aircraft captained by pilot Rodnykh was used for delivering fuel supplies.

The Long-Range Aviation seconded two Tu-4s captained by Vaganov and Simonov. The former of these crews was tasked with the primary mission of finding suitable locations for airstrips long enough for DA aircraft in the Arctic Ocean basin. The other crew flew a refuelling tanker.

I was included into Vaganov's crew as an operator/researcher, working the Kobal't radar. My mission was to describe the ocean and the coastline, the way they were depicted on the radarscope, and assess the possibility of using the Kobal't radar for navigation and landing approach to the ice airstrips. We also explored the possibility of bombing targets on the ice during this expedition.

Gen. Serebrennikov was in overall command of the [expedition's] aviation element; V. M. Lavskiy was the chief navigator.

Generally the missions were flown as follows. Cherevichnyy would fly a Li-2 to the assigned area north of 86° N, find an area suitable for landing and land a support team there. The team would proceed to check the [strength and evenness of] the ice, mark the landing strip and give the go-ahead for the Long-Range Aviation's Tu-4s to use this strip.

We would take off from Tiksi Bay and set course for Temp Bay (Cape Anisiy), then turn towards the ocean and land on the ice airstrips. We used our celestial compasses and the radio beacon on Cape Barrow (Alaska, USA) to navigate. Our radio operator Konstantin Malkhas'yan would always give us accurate bearings on this beacon.

Landing on the ice airstrip of the SP-2 drifting research station was a highly complex job. The ice was 1.2 m [3 ft 11¼ in] thick, and when the Tu-4 touched down with a landing weight of 54 tons [119,050 lb], it sent fountains of water gushing from the many holes drilled in the ice for research purposes. It was a fascinating sight, but it was rather scary, too. Incidentally, later the runway at SP-2 broke up into several small ice floes.

[Lavochkin] La-9 and La-11 fighters also landed on the ice airstrips.

After the expedition I filed a report for the Soviet Council of Ministers.

[...] This was how we got the knack of flying in the Arctic.'

By the early 1950s the Soviet Arctic coast had been explored and equipped to such an extent that even the Myasishchev M-4, the heaviest Soviet strategic bomber at the time, could operate from the newly built airfields in those parts. Further airfields were under construction; some of them had strong concrete runways and hardstands, while others were hard-packed earth or ice airstrips. Powerful radio beacons were also put into operation. A Soviet airbase in the High North was normally organised as follows:

- a base commander (usually one of the pilots);
- a headquarters and a control tower;
- an aircraft maintenance department;
- a transport aviation unit equipped with Antonov An-2 *Colt* utility biplanes, Li-2 *Cab* and Il'yushin IL-14 *Crate* transports, and helicopters.

A Long-Range Aviation Tu-4 about to touch down at an Arctic base.

The Tu-4 taxies in. Note the smoke flare indicating the wind direction.

Polar Aviation Tu-4 CCCP H-1139

This organisation allowed the base to cater for the combat operations of any bomber regiment, obviating the need for the bomber units to bring their own maintenance personnel and radio navaids during temporary redeployments.

Quite a few airfields were built beyond the Arctic Circle – at Vorkuta, Noril'sk, Tiksi, on Sredniy Island ('Middle Island'), on Graham Bell Island (part of the Franz-Joseph Land archipelago), at Anadyr', Chekoorovskaya AB, Olen'ya AB and so on. This was no small achievement, considering the difficulty of construction work in the Arctic regions. The airbase organisation and military commandant's offices set up at the airfields allowed any Air Force regiment to operate from these locations. The airbases and military commandant's offices were organised into the Arctic Operations Group (OGA – *Opera**tiv**naya **groop**pa v **Ark**tike*) headquartered at Tiksi; Lt.-Gen. L. D. Reino was appointed Commander of the OGA.

The introduction of jet and turboprop-powered bombers boosted the Soviet Ministry of Defence's interest in the Arctic airfields considerably. Taking off from Tiksi, an M-4 or a Tu-95 could reach US territory fairly quickly by heading across the North Pole. However, the same was true for the USA, which also had jet bombers that could launch a strike at the USSR across the Pole. Therefore, Soviet Arctic expeditions built auxiliary airfields for the bombers on the pack ice so as to have additional bases available, should the main ones be put out of action.

The drifting polar research station SP-6 was inaugurated on 19th April 1956, remaining in existence until 14th September 1959. Working at such research stations was a job for the tough – the conditions were extreme, with a long Polar night, ambient temperatures down to –50°C (–58°F) and frequent blizzards in the winter with wind speeds in excess of 15-20 m/sec (30-40 kts). The cracking and shifting of the ice fields represented the greatest danger,

This Tu-4 lacking defensive armament was used for ice reconnaissance in the Arctic.

Tu-4s, such as '08 Red' (c/n 226002) shown here, had no difficulty operating from ice and snow airstrips.

with gaps of water and ice hummocks forming around the stations; SP-6 was surrounded by three lines of hummocks up to 20 m (65 ft) tall. The ice thickness varied from 6 to 13 m (from 19 ft 8 in to 42 ft 8 in). In the summer the top layer of ice melted and the water could be up to 2.5 m (8 ft 2 in) deep. The personnel worked in shifts which were relieved annually, and by the spring of 1958 the SP-6 was manned by its third crew of researchers under the supervision of S. Serlapov.

By the spring of 1958 the Long-Range Aviation's 52nd TBAP had prepared five Tu-16As and six crews (one was a reserve crew) for operations in the Arctic. All six crews were qualified for night flying and operations in instrument meteorological conditions. Here it is worth mentioning that one of the persons who contributed a lot to the mastering of Arctic operations by the DA in the 1950s was Guards Col. Anton A. Alekhnovich (HSU). This distinguished military pilot was transferred to Baranovichi in 1956 to become CO of the 45th TBAD, which included the 52nd TBAP.

In early 1956 the personnel of SP-6 received orders from Moscow to prepare the runway urgently for incoming heavy aircraft. The type of aircraft was not specified. Throughout April all of the station's personnel not immediately involved in scientific experiments were busy with just one thing – building up a strong runway which had to be huge by local standards. As they shovelled snow and rolled it down to create an even, hard surface, the men kept guessing what sort of aeroplane it was to require so large an 'airport'. Building the runway was a back-breaking job, and one of the men had a bright idea about how to speed up the work – an idea which, in the long run, proved fatal. He suggested drilling holes in the ice to admit sea water which would flood the runway and freeze; the resulting 'ice arena' was then covered with a layer of snow which, it seemed, was packed hard enough. It turned out that it was not.

Meanwhile, on 21st April 1958 the United Nations Security Council held a session with one item on the agenda: urging the USA to discontinue the provocative 'harassment' flights of USAF aircraft along the northern borders of the Soviet Union. Just three days later, on 24th April, Col. Anton A. Alekhnovich assembled the crews of the five Tu-16As earmarked for the Arctic mission at Tiksi-Tsentral'nyy airfield and, for the first time, briefed them fully on the upcoming assignment. First, three Tu-16As were to head for the ice floe where the SP-6 was located; the lead aircraft wearing the tactical code '04 Red' would be captained by Alekhnovich himself, who would thus assume full responsibility for the success of the mission. The lead aircraft was to land on the ice airstrip, then make a U-turn and take off again immediately; this procedure would be repeated by the other two bombers. Next, two Tu-4R reconnaissance aircraft from the 121st RAP (*razvedyvatel'nyy aviapolk* – Reconnaissance Air Regiment) were to land on the ice floe, offload supplies and depart for Tiksi as well. After that, it would be possible to report all the way up to Moscow that the objective had been completed successfully and the strategic forward airfield on the drifting ice was in operation.

Yet, as an old Russian soldiers' song goes, 'On the map there were no hitches, // Alas! forgotten were the ditches // That we would have to cross'. At first, everything seemed to be going nicely. The morning of 26th April at SP-6 was bright and sunny, just as the local weatherman had forecast. In strict accordance with the plan the aircraft took off one by one and climbed into the frosty Arctic sky. The navigators found the drifting research station unerringly. Receiving the go-ahead from the improvised 'tower' at SP-6, Alekhnovich came in to land. The touchdown and the landing run seemed to go normally. Then Alekhnovich turned the heavy bomber in the opposite direction, lining up for take-off; receiving permission, he revved up the engines and released the brakes. Then the catastrophe occurred. After a run of some 500 m (1,640 ft) the 70-ton (154,320-lb) bomber suddenly veered to port, running off the runway into the soft snow and bearing down on a parked IL-14D transport. The wheel brakes were useless on the ice, and the pilot attempted to avert a collision by using differential thrust. Still, the Tu-16 struck the IL-14 with the starboard wingtip and then hit a stack of 200-litre

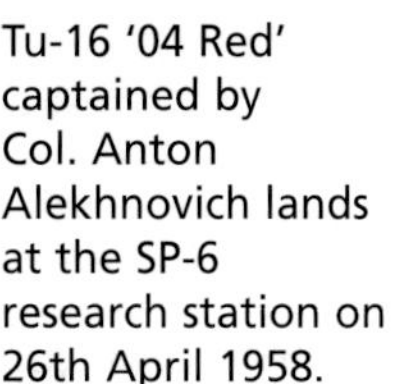

Tu-16 '04 Red' captained by Col. Anton Alekhnovich lands at the SP-6 research station on 26th April 1958.

(55-gallon) fuel drums, sending them rolling in all directions. As the bomber came to a halt, fuel poured from the damaged port wing.

At Alekhnovich's orders all six crewmembers vacated the aircraft promptly. Luckily there was no fire. Nor were there any major personal injuries, save for co-pilot Maj. Bazarnyy, who gashed his forehead on the instrument panel shroud, and the navigator, whose legs were badly bruised. The ATC officer forbade the other two Tu-16s to land, and they headed back to Tiksi after circling the station once. Next, the two Tu-4Rs were coming up; they were captained by Alfyorov and Guards Maj. Aleksey Akulov. The crews were quick to realise something was wrong when, descending to 400 m (1,310 ft), they saw an aircraft stuck in a strange position on the verge of the airfield. Alfyorov requested permission to land and received the OK, whereupon both aircraft landed normally.

As the Tu-4 crews climbed out, Col. Alekhnovich slowly walked up to them, waved a hand in a gesture of dismay and said in a strangely flat voice, 'Well, guys, that's it. So much for my flying career.' He was well aware

A Tu-16A being serviced at a snowbound airbase in the High North.

that in the Khrushchov era, the Soviet leader's attitude to aviation being the way it was, not even a Hero of the Soviet Union like him would be pardoned for a flying accident. It hurt him all the more because it was the sole accident in his long and distinguished flying career. Alekhnovich made the trip back to Tiksi as a passenger.

After this accident neither the Soviet Air Force nor the USAF tried operating jet bombers from ice airstrips ever again. Later, when the ice runway was examined, it turned out that the luckless bomber's port main gear bogie had hit a pothole filled with salt water that had not frozen properly, and the resulting jerk was enough to throw the machine off course. Added to this, there was a strong crosswind at the time. Thus, the crew was blameless – but the top brass did not care in the least.

Attempts to repair the damaged bomber on site were unsuccessful. Eventually, when the ice floe started drifting too close to the 'potential adversary', the machine had to be destroyed to prevent capture.

Accidents with DA aircraft in the High North were not limited to ice airstrips. Lt.-Col. M. A. Mironets (Retd.), who was an inspector pilot with the 201st TBAD in the 1950s, recalled: *'...the division's aircrews operated from the airfields at Vorkuta, Noril'sk, Tiksi, Sredniy Island, Graham Bell, Nagoorskoye (on Franz-Joseph Land), Anadyr', Chekoorovka, Olen'ya... I had occasion to land at all of these airfields. There we would top up our tanks and continue our flight "around the corner" towards American shores or northward, towards the Pole. The harsh climate of the North and the condition of the airfields were against us occasionally.*

In 1957 an M-4 captained by Kireyev and co-piloted by instructor Stepanov overran the runway on landing, sinking into the deep snow. It took the enlisted men 24 hours to dig it out of the snow, shovelling like mad. Later, Col. Ivanov ferried the machine to Engels.

In 1972 a 3M captained by Maj. Bondarenko struck a snow berm with the port wingtip while taking off from Vorkuta. The aircraft rolled over and crashed inverted, killing the entire crew.'

Using the auxiliary airfields beyond the Arctic Circle, the Long-Range Aviation operated successfully in the High North and over the North Pole right up to the collapse of the Soviet Union. This, in February and March 1961, sorties were flown in the Arctic regions under a plan codenamed *Sputnik* (Satellite); similar flights were undertaken in 1962 under a plan codenamed *Globus* (Tabletop globe), involving 12 crews. The intensity of the combat training can be judged by the fact that just one heavy bomber regiment performed 43 flights along designated routes in the Arctic and 17 aircraft captains and 16 navigators were trained for such missions in 1962. In 1971, 12 crews made 38 landings at airfields in the tundra (eight at Chekoorovka and 30 at Vorkuta), logging a total of 147 flight hours.

Opposite page, left and right: Soviet nomenclature of air-dropped nuclear weapons was quite wide and included the SK-1 Skal'p anti-submarine atomic bomb.

Below: Technicians unwind the fuel transfer hose of a Tu-16Z tanker for maintenance purposes.

4 The Long-Range Aviation's Involvement in Nuclear Testing

Many crews from first-line units of the Long-Range Aviation had a chance to use nuclear weapons – albeit not in anger. They were involved in the nuclear test programme, either performing the actual drops of nuclear bombs or flying air sampling missions to measure radiation levels in the wake of the explosion.

On 22nd November 1955 at 0947 hours Moscow time, the world's first-ever hydrogen bomb test took place. The 1.6-megaton RDS-37 H-bomb was dropped by a Tu-16A at the Semipalatinsk test range. This was the Soviet Union's 24th test of a nuclear device.

The RDS-37 was manufactured in Arzamas-16, a secret nuclear research centre and weapons manufacturing facility; it utilised a completely new structural layout and laid the foundation for the development of further thermonuclear devices in the Soviet Union. After being released by the Tu-16 the bomb detonated at 1,550 m (5,085 ft) above ground level; the tremendous blast yielded a wealth of important research data. However, an unwelcome side effect was that several buildings and other objects outside the test range were affected by the blast. As a result, all subsequent testing of thermonuclear

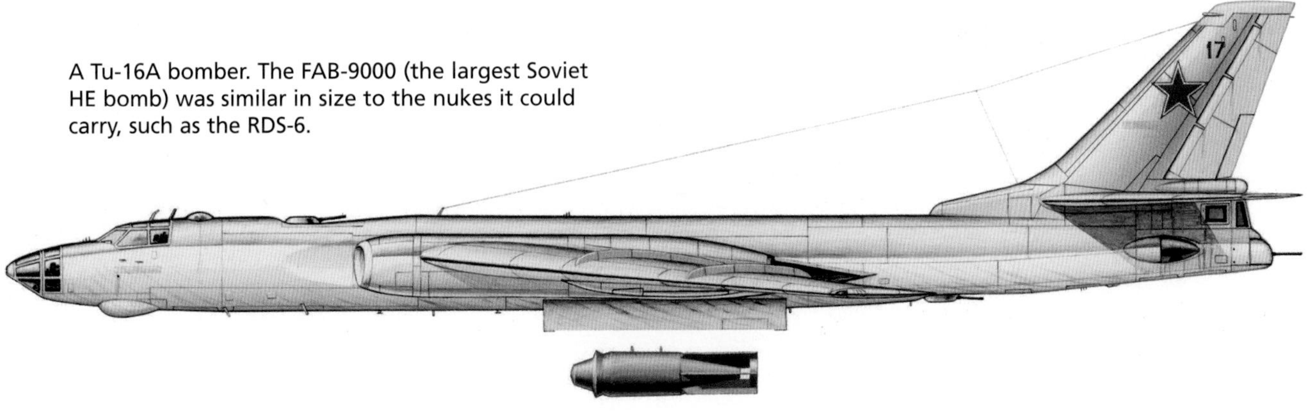

A Tu-16A bomber. The FAB-9000 (the largest Soviet HE bomb) was similar in size to the nukes it could carry, such as the RDS-6.

The globular RDS-1, the first Soviet experimental atomic bomb. The sensor 'eyes' give it a weird look.

This cover at the back of the RDS-1 encloses a connector used for arming the bomb before take-off.

devices having a similar or higher yield was transferred to a new location meeting the safety criteria more fully.

By decree of the USSR Supreme Soviet' Presidium (the highest government authority) Maj. F. P. Golovashko, who had captained the Tu-16 during that historic test mission, was awarded the Hero of the Soviet Union title for his bravery and heroism.

In 1957 a 73rd TBAD/79th TBAP Tu-16A dropped a nuclear bomb at the new test range on Novaya Zemlya ('New Land') archipelago. The bomber's crew was captained by Capt. G. A. Kirpichnikov and included navigator/bomb-aimer D. A. Khokhlov. Another pair of Tu-16s operated by the 34th OTBAE (*ot**del'**naya tya**zhol**aya bombardi**rov**ochnaya **a**viaeskad**ril'**ya* – Independent Heavy Bomber Squadron) of the 6th OTBAK (*ot**del'**nyy tya**zhol**yy bombardi**rov**ochnyy **a**via**kor**pus* – Independent Heavy Bomber Corps) flew weather reconnaissance and radiation intelligence (air sampling) sorties.

In 1958 a group of four 34th OTBAE Tu-16s was involved in a similar test mission at the same location. Seven crews captained by Adamovich, Baranov, Titarenko, Didenko, Shavtel'skiy, Volokhov and Yepishev took turns flying the bombers.

In 1961 several Long-Range Aviation detachments took part in nuclear tests at Novaya Zemlya. These were:

- a detachment of Tu-95s from the 106th TBAD captained by Ye. A. Moornin, A. Ye. Doornovtsev and V. M. Troobitsyn;
- a detachment of Tu-16s captained by Pronchatov, Tropynin and Loman;
- two detachments of Myasishchev 3M heavy bombers from the 201st TBAD captained by Skalenko, Kireyev, Kazantsev, Borisov, Silant'yev, Pronevich and Myamlin;
- a detachment of Tu-16As from the 13th TBAD/226th TBAP captained by N. I. Nichepurenko, I. F. Stepanov and N. M. Antipov;
- a detachment of Tu-16As from the 326th TBAD captained by M. A. Arkatov, A. I. Sal'nikov and Rudenko;
- a Tu-16A from the 326th TBAD/840th TBAP captained by V. Ye. Protsenko.

Also in 1961, five Tu-16s from Long-range Aviation units participated in nuclear weapons trials at the Semipalatinsk range. They were captained by I. K. Nikolaichuk, G. D. Dikusar, L. T. Khoodoseyev, I. D. Tret'yakov and S. S. Chobotov.

In 1962, the nuclear tests at Novaya Zemlya again involved a large number of *Badger* and *Bear* detachments put up by the Long-Range Aviation:

- a detachment of Tu-16s from the 6th OTBAK/34th OTBAE captained by N. A. Katyurgin, P. P. Yepishin, G. A. Rychkov, V. P. Shavtel'skiy, P. M. Protsenko, V. N. Maratayev, V. Ye. Blinov, V. I. Kornyakov and N. T. Yakimov;
- two Tu-16As captained by V. N. Lazarev and B. I. Korovkin;
- the unique Tu-95V (Tu-95-202) H-bomb carrier from the 106th TBAD captained by A. Ye. Doornovtsev;

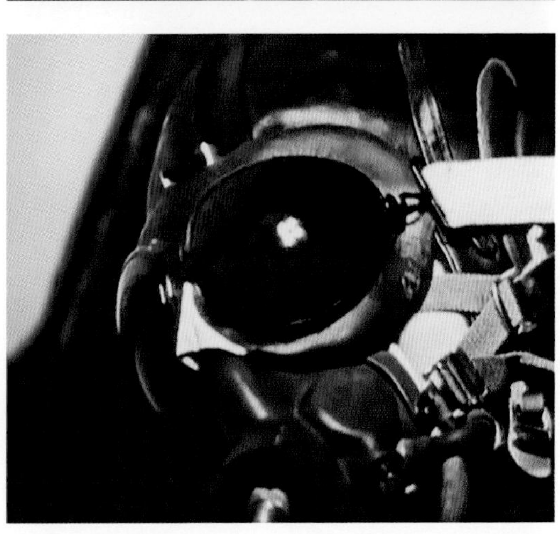

Left column:

Nuclear bombs are delivered to the aircraft on covered dollies.

The covers are removed, revealing the RDS-37 H-bomb.

The RDS-37 is prepared for loading into the Tu-16V.

The area around the bomb bay was curtained off to prevent unauthorised personnel from seeing the bomb.

Right column:

The Tu-16V carrying the H-bomb taxies out. Note the special probe on the nose.

The bomber takes off, heading for the test range.

The pilot donned special dark goggles immediately before the explosion.

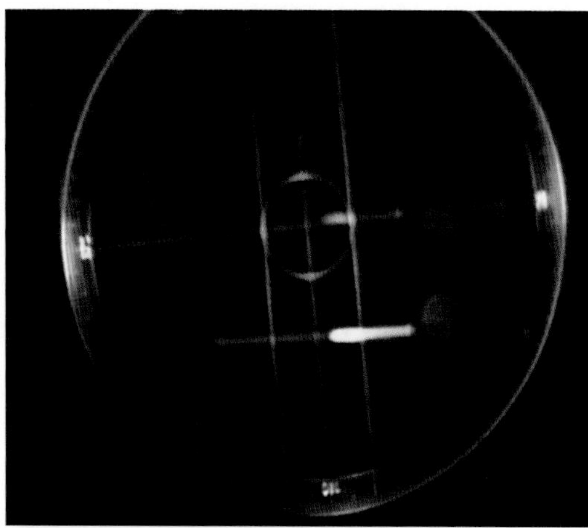

The radarscope of the Tu-16V showing the target during the test drop of the RDS-37.

The mushroom cloud of the nuclear explosion breaks through the overcast.

Seen from ground level, the fully developed mushroom cloud looked pretty scary.

Here the cloud has broken up and is borne on the wind, contaminating everything in its path.

- a 3M heavy bomber from the 201st TBAD captained by N. A. Belenko;
- a detachment of Tu-16As from the 13th TBAD captained by D. A. Lysakov, V. G. Avdeyev, A. A. Popov, N. I. Fomin, D. M. Klimachenkov and P. M. Antimonov;
- a detachment of six Tu-16As captained by Rymar', T. Yu. Koondich, A. A. Zhdanov, V. S. Nikitin, Ye. S. Nikolayev and V. P. Razdobreyev;
- a detachment of six Tu-16As captained by K. P. Il'yin, V. A. Polozhentsev, A. I. Goorov, V. A. Lazin, M. F. Puchkin and P. K. Yakushin;
- a detachment of three Tu-95s from the 106th TBAD captained by A. A. Plokhov, Loginov and Stepanov;
- a detachment of three Tu-95s from the 79th TBAD captained by V. M. Bezbokov, L. I. Agurin and I. F. Shepotenko;
- a detachment of 3M heavy bombers;
- a detachment of 12 Tu-16As from the 13th TBAD/185th TBAP which participated in a tactical exercise involving live drops of nuclear weapons.

That same year six Tu-16As captained by M. P. Shastin, P. V. Kalmykov, M. T. Kryukov, A. S. Darmayev, V. I. Yenushevskiy and V. Ye. Sadovyy participated in the nuclear test at Semipalatinsk.

The *Bear-A* and *Bison-B* strategic bombers dropped their first nuclear weapons in 1958 and 1962 respectively. On 7th October 1958 a Tu-95M captained by S. V. Seryogin (the crew included navigator/bomb-aimer F. S. Chernyshov) dropped a 1.5-megaton atomic bomb at the Semipalatinsk test range. The 3M 'joined the club' on 27th February 1962 when a 1096th TBAP aircraft dropped a 320-kiloton bomb; the aircraft was captained by N. A. Belenkov, with A. Ye. Mitin as navigator/bomb-aimer. Yet the world's most powerful air-dropped nuclear munition was tested in the Soviet Union in 1961, using a specially modified Tu-95. This event warrants a more detailed description, since it was one of the 'hottest' episodes of the Cold War.

During the autumn of 1954, the Soviet Union started work on an aircraft-deliverable H-bomb rated at 100 megatons. It quickly became apparent that the Tu-95 was the only viable delivery option for this proposed behemoth.

Initial bomb studies called for a gross weapon weight of 40 tons (88,180 lb), but Tupolev engineers said no. This weight amounted to 20% of the maximum take-off weight and would have imposed unacceptable

The RDS-4, the first Soviet operational nuclear bomb, had a fairly conventional appearance.

penalties on the Tu-95's performance – in fact, the bomber would have been unable to reach the test site, never mind America. Therefore, a smaller super-weapon was developed. While still packing a formidable 50-megaton punch, the bomb had a gross weight of 20 tons (44,090 lb). This was a much more feasible figure for the Tupolev engineering team, amounting to 12% of the MTOW.

The new H-bomb had the official name Vanya or Ivan. Accordingly the Tu-95 version optimised to carry it was designated Tu-95V. The designation Tu-95-202 has also been quoted; the '202' is a reference to *izdeliye* 202, as the bomb was designated.

During the first quarter of 1955, technical specifications for the Vanya weapon were provided to Tupolev so that work could begin on the redesign of the Tu-95's bomb bay. It was decided to install a beam-type bomb rack similar to the BD-206 used on the Tu-95K missile carrier for hooking up the Kh-20 missile). The model fitted to the Tu-95V was designated BD7-95-242 (aka BD-242); it incorporated three Der 5-6 bomb shackles rated at 9,000 kg (19,840 lb) each.

The BD-242 fitted quite nicely into the bomb bay; the only tricky moment was the installation of the rearmost bomb support positioned at right angles to the fuselage axis. The BD-242 was attached directly to the longitudinal load-bearing beams which flanked the bomb bay. The bomb bay aperture was 7.15 m (23 ft 5½ in) long and 1.78 m (5 ft 10⁵⁄₆₄ in) wide.

The bomb shackle system passed its bench test series without difficulty. Subsequently Tu-95 c/n 5800302 was converted into the Tu-95V prototype by Tupolev. Following manufacturer's tests at Zhukovskiy it was formally accepted by the Air Force in September 1959.

Front and rear views of the RDS-4. Again, the bomb has an arming connector at the rear.

In the meantime, the super-bomb (known as *izdeliye* 202 in its definitive form) had grown in weight to 24 tons (52,910 lb) and a 800-kg (1,763-lb) parachute retarding system had been added as well. The weapon's diameter, too, was bigger than originally estimated; hence the Tu-95V's bomb bay doors had to be removed for the weapon to be carried in a semi-recessed position.

The aircraft was now cleared to drop the world's most powerful nuclear weapon. Yet, actual tests of the Tu-95V dropping a live nuclear weapon were halted for political reasons. The Soviet leader Nikita S. Khrushchov was due to visit the USA and it was deemed inappropriate for such a massive weapon to be tested while the Soviet leader was on American soil.

As a result, the one-off Tu-95V was delivered to the airbase in Belaya Tserkov' ('White Church') in the Ukraine. For more than two

The RDS-6 nuclear bomb; note the brake petals incorporated into the stabiliser.

years it was used as a crew trainer by the resident 200th TBAP, since the specially configured bomb bay rendered it unusable for any other role.

In 1961, as the Cold War began to intensify again, the Tu-95V was 'restored to active duty' and ferried to Olen'ya AB in the North, where a functional nuclear bomb was mounted in its bomb bay. The tests were supervised by N. I. Pavlov representing the Ministry of Medium Machinery (this strange-sounding name referred to the agency responsible for the Soviet nuclear programme), Lt.-Gen. N. I. Sazhin representing the Air Force and Maj.-Gen. V. A. Chernorez (the chief of the 71st Test Range located on the mainland).

The parachute retarding system of the *izdeliye* 202 hydrogen bomb.

On 30th October 1961 the Tu-95V departed Olen'ya AB and flew non-stop to Novaya Zemlya. (Some sources say the flight was made from Vayenga airfield near Murmansk.) The aircraft was captained by Lt.-Col. A. Ye. Doornovtsev (he had been promoted to Lieutenant-Colonel immediately before the mission), co-pilot Capt. M. K. Kondratenko, navigator/bomb-aimer Maj. I. N. Kleshch, senior systems operator Lt. (SG) A. S. Bobikov, radar operator Capt. A. F. Prokopenko, Flight engineer Maj. G. M. Yevtushenko, chief gunner Capt. V. M. Snetkov and gunners/radio operators Lt. (SG) M. P. Mashkin and Private First Class V. L. Bolotov.

Izdeliye 202 had been developed and manufactured by the Arzamas-16 nuclear research centre in the Urals. The huge bomb measuring 8 m (26 ft) in length and 2 m (6 ft 7 in) in diameter weighed 26 tons (57,320 lb). This figure included a parachute retarding system giving a 3.5-minute delay, enabling the aircraft to get clear before the bomb detonated; the system comprised an extractor parachute with an area of 0.5 m^2 (5.38 sq ft), a second extractor parachute with an area of 5.5 m^2 (59.2 sq ft), three auxiliary parachutes with an area of 45 m^2 (484.38 sq ft) each and a 1,600-m^2 (17,222-sq ft) main canopy.

The Tu-95V headed east towards Novaya Zemlya, with a Tu-16 captained by Lt.-Col. V. F. Martynenko as a chase plane; the drop sequence would be filmed from this aircraft. The route of the two aircraft took them from Olen'ya to Cape Kanin Nos, Rogachovo and finally Par'kova Zemlya Island where the actual test range was situated. The target, which was located near Matochkin Shar Strait, was codenamed D-2 in paperwork.

Doornovtsev and his crew released their enormous bomb. The Tu-95V was 40 km (24.85 miles) away and the chase plane 55 km (34.18 miles) away, heading back to Olen'ya AB, when the bomb detonated as 4,000 m (13,120 ft).

After the explosion, radio communication with the crews was knocked out for 40 minutes. A flash of untold brightness lit up the Novaya Zemlya archipelago; irregularities were observed in the aurora borealis, which became rather chaotic for a while. A huge mushroom cloud rose over the archipelago, standing 60-65 km (37.28-40.39 miles) high and measuring

A mock-up of the 50-megaton *izdeliye* 202 hydrogen bomb; the hollow core of the stabiliser houses the parachute system.

90-95 km (56-59 miles) in diameter; the foot of the 'mushroom' was some 26-28 km (16.16-17.4 miles) in diameter. The cloud was visible from a distance of up to 800 km (496 miles)!

The shock wave of the explosion caught up with the aircraft, hitting it several times (they say this wave travelled around the globe three times!). The explosion created a tsunami all

The actual 100-megaton 'Vanya' H-bomb dropped on 30th October 1961.

An RDS-6 bomb is wheeled out of the storage bunker.

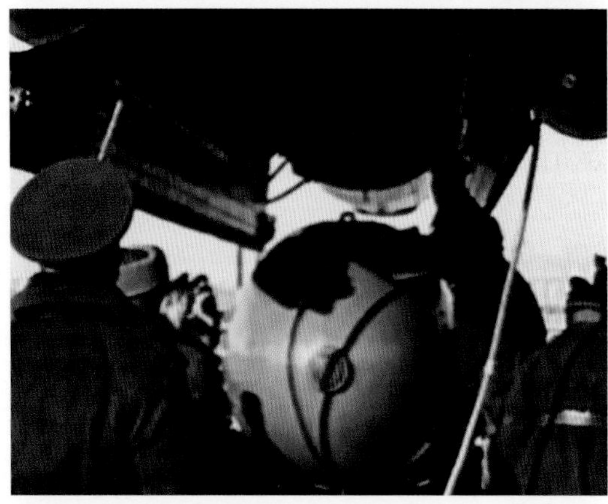
The dolly with the bomb is in position below the bomb bay of a Tu-16A.

Here the bomb is hoisted slowly into the bomb bay.

The RDS-6 inside the Tu-16A's bomb bay.

along the northern coastline of the Soviet Union and the coasts of the Scandinavian countries; seismic stations all around the world recorded a seismic wave which travelled around the globe.

For their part in the testing of this monstrous bomb Lt.-Col. A. Ye. Doornovtsev, Lt.-Col. V. F. Martynenko and Maj. I. N. Kleshch were awarded the HSU title on 7th March 1962.

Lt.-Gen. A. A. Plokhov (HSU), who was acting Commander of the 106th TBAD in 1960-63, recalled this unforgettable event as follows:

'Long before the drop of this most powerful nuclear bomb I got a phone call from [Air Marshal Vladimir A.] Soodets, the Commander of the Long-Range Aviation, who instructed me to pick an aircraft and a crew for the mission. We had a Tu-95 languishing at the end of the runway, away from the parking area; no one would fly this particular aircraft. We sent this machine to Kazan' for modifications; there the bomber was fitted with new engines and a recess was cut in the fuselage [underside]. When the bomb was hooked up to the aircraft, it was semi-exposed.

The drop of the most powerful nuclear bomb took place on 31st October 1961. This test had to be performed earlier than originally planned; the reason was that a Communist Party convention opened [in Moscow] and Khrushchov, speaking at the convention, stated that the Soviet Union would hold tests of an extremely powerful weapon in the next few days. That's when all hell broke loose. I came home [from the airbase] for lunch at 2 PM. Then the phone rang; it was Soodets.

"Have you heard Khrushchov's speech?"

"Yes, I have."

"Well, he has mixed everything up. And this means now we have to get ready [for the test] urgently."

After this phone call intensive preparations for the test mission began, lasting some eight hours without let-up. According to the original plan, Doornovtsev (who was a squadron commander at Uzin AB) was the captain of the reserve crew; Yevtushenko was his flight engineer and Kleshch was his navigator. Then the [bomb's] designers phoned me, asking how qualified Kleshch was; I replied that he could place the bomb with a circular error probable of 200 m [440 ft]. The bomb's design yield was 50 megatons, but the actual yield proved to be higher. According to the designers' estimates, the shock wave would catch up with the Tu-95

Left column:

The crew of the Tu-95V is ready for the mission.

The Tu-95V starts its engines…

…and takes off with the huge *izdeliye* 202 H-bomb semi-exposed.

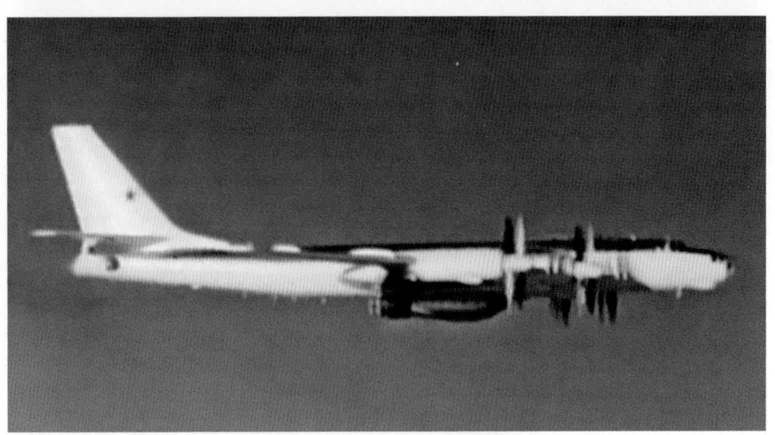

Right column:

The Tu-95V climbs away.

The Tu-95V en route to Novaya Zemlya with a Tu-16 flying chase.

A. Doornovtsev in the captain's seat of the Tu-95V.

The huge bomb falls away from the Tu-95V; the extractor parachute is already deployed.

Here the main retarding parachute has opened.

The first moments after the explosion. A huge fireball rises...

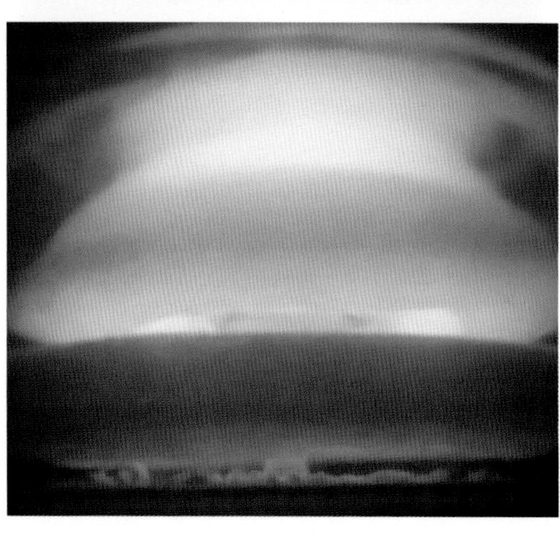

...and develops into a multi-layer mushroom cloud.

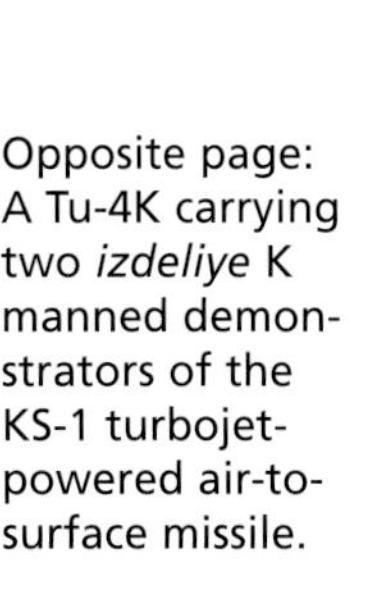

Opposite page: A Tu-4K carrying two *izdeliye* K manned demonstrators of the KS-1 turbojet-powered air-to-surface missile.

at a distance of 60 km [37.28 miles] from the epicentre; in fact, it caught up when the aircraft was only 45 km [28 miles] away. There were four blast waves, and the first three hit the aircraft real hard; the fourth one was not so bad. Doornovtsev suffered a quadruple engine flameout and lost all flight instruments; the aircraft started losing altitude rapidly but remained controllable. The crew had no choice but to sit and wait for what would come next. At 7,000 m [21,965 ft] Yevtushenko managed to restart one engine; another engine came alive at 5,000 m [16,400 ft]. The aircraft came home on three engines – the fourth one refused to restart. Afterwards, it turned out that all electric wiring on the aircraft was charred ('fried' by the electromagnetic pulse of the explosion – *Auth.*) *After the tests there was a lot of arguments on how to split the money rewards. Rewards of up to 40,000 roubles were allocated; this kind of dangerous and high-priority work was well rewarded and paid for.*

There were plans to drop one more bomb, with a yield of 100 megatons, but the aircraft turned out to be unsuitable for carrying it. Hence the 'hundred' was never tested.

In the autumn of 1962 I had a chance to participate in nuclear weapons tests myself. I was the flight leader of a detachment of Tu-95s. We took off from Olen'ya airfield, returning there after the mission. The mission was to pass within 80 km [49 miles] of the mushroom cloud. We approached from the south and circled the cloud, watching as it developed into a ball; the cloud rose and pulled everything up together with it. 15-20 km [9.3-12.4 miles] above the ground the 'ball' burst and deflated, travelling on the wind. Being the division's commander, I was obliged to inform the aircrews of the division's regiments of what I had seen. Doornovtsev and Kleshch received the HSU title; the other crew members were awarded the Red banner Order.

Gunner/radio operator Pavlenko died three or four months after the 1961 nuclear test. He was the leading gunner/radio operator in the division. The other crew members, too, died one by one. Kleshch lived for a few more years. My family and the Doornovtsevs were neighbours – our apartments were on the same staircase. Before the mission Doornovtsev was promoted to Lieutenant-Colonel – but that was as far as he went in the Air Force. His wife kept nagging me because of this. Later, the Doornovtsevs moved to Kiev where this courageous pilot passed away.'

5 Soviet Air-Launched Missile Systems

In the early 1950s the principal mission of the Long-Range Aviation – to nail the USA – was pretty much a Mission Impossible because the DA's then-current aircraft simply lacked the performance required to reach the North American continent and penetrate the potential adversary's air defences. Even the Myasishchev M-4 jet bomber brought out in the mid-1950s did not have the necessary range; it could reach the USA and (hopefully) unload its bombs on the target but had no chance of coming back. Also, the rapid development of western air defence systems during the 1950s made Soviet bombers much too vulnerable.

Ways and means were sought to tackle this problem. One way of extending a strategic aircraft's radius of action was to use stand-off weapons – air-to-surface missiles (ASMs) carried under the fuselage or wings. These could be launched from way outside the range of the enemy's air defences. In that case, however, the drag created by the external stores would eat up a considerable part of the aircraft's own range; the long-range air-to-surface missiles of the day were much too bulky to permit internal carriage.

Nevertheless, the Soviet designers kept working in this direction. The first tangible result of this work was the *Ko**met**a* (Comet) weapons system with a launch range of 90 km (56 miles) – the first of its kind in the world to reach the practical stage. It could be used against both maritime and ground targets.

Development of the Kometa weapons system comprising the Tu-4K carrier aircraft (the K denoted Kometa), the KS-1 air-to-surface missile and the Kometa-1 and Kometa-2 guidance systems began pursuant to a Council of Ministers directive dated 2nd August 1948. The KS-1 (NATO codename AS-1 *Kennel*) was developed by the OKB-155 design bureau under Artyom I. Mikoyan and Mikhail I. Gurevich – or rather a section of it led by Aleksandr Ya. Bereznyak and tasked with designing air-to-surface missiles (which subsequently became a separate enterprise). Therefore it is hardly surprising that the missile resembled a scaled-down MiG-15*bis*P (*izdeliye* SP-1) – an experimental interceptor version of the MiG-15*bis* *Fagot-B* fighter – minus cockpit canopy. The KS-1 was powered by a 1,590-kgp (3,505-lbst) RD-500 centrifugal-flow turbojet, the Soviet copy version of the Rolls-Royce

A production KS-1 missile on a ground handling dolly.

Derwent V; it had mid-set swept wings, a swept cruciform tail unit and a nose air intake with a guidance antenna radome on top.

The guidance systems were products of OKB-1 then headed by Sergey L. Beria – the son of the infamous Minister of the Interior Lavrentiy P. Beria. The Kometa-2 guidance system included the Kometa-M search/target illumination radar (a version of the Tu-4's Kobal't-N modified for working with the missiles; N stood for *no**sit**el'* – [missile] carrier) in a retractable radome; hence the crew included a weapons system operator (WSO). (After Stalin's death in 1953 and the subsequent arrest and execution of L. P. Beria, Sergey Beria was removed from office and replaced by Konstantin Patrookhin.)

Overall co-ordination of the Kometa project was the responsibility of the Third Main Directorate of the Soviet Council of Ministers. The whole programme was shrouded in utmost secrecy and only a few people had access to it.

The task of Andrey N. Tupolev's OKB-156 was to equip a Tu-4 bomber with the Kometa-2 guidance system and a pair of BD-KS pylons under the wings for carrying KS-1 missiles. The advanced development project of the Tu-4K (also called Tu-4KS) was ready in 1949; the missile pylons were to be mounted between the inner and outer engines.

State acceptance trials of the Kometa weapons system began in July 1952, continuing until January 1953. During one of the live launches a single hit of a KS-1 missile with its 500-kg (1,102-lb) warhead proved enough to sink the target, a decommissioned light cruiser sailing in the Black Sea about 100 km (54 nm) from Feodosia. The trials were deemed successful and the Kometa system was included into the Soviet Naval Aviation (AVMF – *Avi**ah**tsiya vo**yen**no-mor**sko**vo **flot**a*) inventory for use against large surface ships.

The KS-1 missile entered production at Plant No. 207 in Doobna, Moscow Region. The aircraft itself, on the other hand, was not

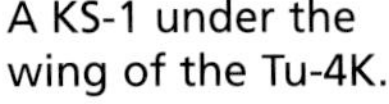

A KS-1 under the wing of the Tu-4K.

A production-standard Tu-4K with a full complement of missiles.

built as such; about 50 bombers were converted to Tu-4K (Tu-4KS) standard by Plant No. 22 in Kazan' and Plant No. 23 in Moscow. The type saw service with two regiments (one in the North Fleet Air Arm, the other in the Black Sea Fleet Air Arm) until the mid-1950s.

Yet, the Tu-4 was clearly outdated as a missile platform. Thus the introduction of turbojet- and turboprop-powered aircraft in 1956-60 came as a true revolution for the Long-Range Aviation. These aircraft extended the reach of air-launched missiles a great deal;

Here, a KS-1 is hoisted into position under the port wing of a Tu-16KS.

A KS-1 is manually wheeled into position under the wing of a Tu-16KS.

A technician adjusts the electric connectors of the KS-1 suspended from the pylon.

moreover, the ASMs could be fitted with nuclear warheads as well as conventional high-explosive ones. Hence the nation's political and military leaders reviewed once again the significance of the Long-Range Aviation and its mode of operation in a future war; new directives controlling the DA's operations were prepared and published. Military academies and research institutions conducted research in the field of strategy and tactics development.

The new generation of bombers and missile carriers featured a much more comprehensive fit of electronic equipment and a much higher degree of systems automation. This included the provision of short-range and long-range radio navigation systems. A gun ranging radar at the tail gunner's station gave timely warning of impending fighter attack from the rear; once an enemy fighter attack had been repelled, the pilots were able to make a rapid dive to ultra-low altitude in order to take cover thanks to the provision of accurate radio altimeters. Once the objective had been completed, the radio navigation systems would guide the bomber back to base and enable a safe landing approach.

The service entry of the Tu-16 immediately offered a missile platform able to reach high subsonic speeds, an altitude of 12,000-13,000 m (39,370-42,650 ft) and possessing a large combat radius. The bomber was immediately adapted to take the Kometa system; the resulting aircraft received the designation Tu-16KS (referred to in paperwork as *izdeliye* NKS) and the NATO reporting name *Badger-B*.

The Tu-16KS was intended for attacking radar-defined maritime and land targets within a maximum combat radius of 1,800 km (1,118 miles); it had a cruising speed of 800-850 km/h (496-528 mph) and an all-up weight of 72,000 kg (158,730 lb) with two missiles. Targets could be detected at a distance of 150-180 km (93-111 miles) and the KS-1 was launched at an altitude of 4,000 to 5,000 m (13,120-16,400 ft) some 70-90 km (43.5-56 miles) from the target, approaching it at an altitude of 400 m (1,310 ft). Production examples of the Tu-16KS had the improved Kobal't-P radar.

The 90-km range of the KS-1 and its subsonic speed soon ceased to satisfy the Soviet Air Force which needed a new supersonic missile with a range of up to 150 km. In the autumn of 1958 two examples of the Tu-16 were fitted with the Rubicon guidance system; one carried the old KS-1 missiles and the other

A Tu-16KS in flight with a single missile.

was armed with KSR rocket-powered missiles. Tests at altitudes of 4,000-10,000 m (13,120-32,810 ft) showed that the new KS-PM guidance radar could detect a ground target at ranges up to 200 km (124 miles) and provide stable tracking over distances of 160-180 km (99-111 miles). When the missile came within 13-15 km (8.0-9.3 miles) of the target, its own homing radar took over for terminal guidance. In launches against maritime targets, detection and acquisition range depended on a number of factors, including the type of target and the angle of approach. The results of these tests formed the basis for the development of new aircraft/ASM combinations and for the K-11 and K-16 weapons systems with their different guidance systems.

The KSR-2 missile (NATO AS-5 *Kelt*), a production derivative of the KSR, was carried by the Tu-16 equipped with the Rubicon system as part of the K-16 system for use against surface ships, bridges, dams, power stations, factories, railroad junctions, airfields and other targets of importance. In May-July 1957 a production Tu-16KS was converted into the first experimental carrier aircraft for the K-16 system as the Tu-16KSR-2. The successful trials of the system prompted GKAT to suggest to the Soviet Ministry of Defence that 100 Tu-16KS missile carriers and 300 Tu-16A bombers should be converted to Tu-16KSR-2 configuration. It was also suggested that the viability of adapting the Tu-22 supersonic bomber to carry the KSR-2 missile should be explored.

The KSR-2 was a conventional mid-wing monoplane with swept wings and tail surfaces. It was powered by an Isayev S5-6 twin-chamber rocket motor burning TG-02 hypergolic (self-igniting) fuel and AK-20F nitric acid oxidiser which provided up to 1,200 kgp (2,650 lbst) initial thrust and up to 700 kgp (1,540 lbst) at normal cruising speed. An 850-kg (1,874-lb) high-explosive warhead was fitted, but provision was made for fitting a nuclear warhead. Production KSR-2s were 8.62 m (28 ft $3\frac{3}{8}$ in) long, with a wingspan of 4.52 m (14 ft $9\frac{61}{64}$ in) and an all-up weight of 4,077-4,100 kg (8,988-9,040 lb). A maximum speed of 1,260 km/h (782 mph) was reached over a flight distance of 120-140 km (74.5-87

Many Tu-16KSs were later converted to carry rocket-propelled KSR-2 missiles like this one.

A KSR-2 is hooked up to a Tu-16KSR-2 during an exercise. Note that the personnel are wearing gas masks.

miles). One or two KSR-2s could be carried and launched either simultaneously or individually. Preparations for launch were the responsibility of the navigator, the automated processes carried out by the Rubicon system making the provision of a WSO (as on the Tu-16KS) unnecessary. The Tu-16KSR-2 was codenamed *Badger-G* by NATO.

The Rubin-1K radar making up the core of the Rubicon system could detect and select a target at a range of 300-350 km (186-217 miles). It then passed the information to the missile's own KS-PM radar which had been locked on to the target prior to launch. Once the KS-PM was receiving a clear signal from the target, the navigator switched over to the missile's own tracking and homing system. Missiles were launched at altitudes between 4,000 and 10,000 m at speeds between 700 and 800 km/h (435-496 mph). After launching its missiles, the Tu-16KSR-2 could turn away from the target, thus reducing its vulnerability to enemy anti-aircraft defences. No IFR system was fitted initially.

In parallel with the modification of the Tu-16KS and IFR-capable Tu-16KS (ZA) missile carriers into the Tu-16KSR-2, refits of the Tu-16A and Tu-16 (ZA) bombers were also carried out. The *Badger-As* thus modified retained their capability to carry free-fall nuclear bombs; in this respect the Tu-16KSR-2A (converted from the Tu-16A) differed from the Tu-16KSR-2. Comparatively few Tu-16As (155 examples) and Tu-16KSs were converted to *Badger-Gs* in the early 1960s due to the decision to develop the K-11-16 combined system able to use the KSR-2 ASM with active radar homing and the broadly similar KSR-11 with passive radar homing. In the 1970s the Tu-16KSR-2s and Tu-16KSR-2As were again refitted as the Tu-16KSR-2-5 *Badger-G* Mod as part of the K-26 ASM system.

As mentioned above, initially the Tu-16KSR-2 could not carry bombs. However, after modifications, free-fall bombs could be carried in the bomb bay, just like on the Tu-16KSR-2A, and the two sub-variants became identical in their capabilities. The Tu-16KSR-2A was able carry a limited bomb load internally, but it was further modified to carry bombs externally on the wing pylons, bringing its maximum bomb load to 10,000 kg (22,045 lb).

In the early 1970s some Tu-16KSR-2s were fitted with active ECM equipment to prevent detection by enemy radars – either for individual protection, using the SPS-5 *Fasol'* (String bean) jammer, or for operations as a group,

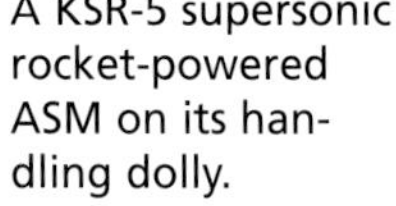

A KSR-5 supersonic rocket-powered ASM on its handling dolly.

A production Tu-16KSR-2 with a single missile intercepted by the Swedish Air Force.

using the SPS-100 *Rezeda* (Mignonette) jammer. The latter was housed in an ogival fairing known as UKhO (*oonifi**tsee**rovannyy khvos-to**voy** ot**sek*** – standardised tail compartment) supplanting the tail gun barbette, reducing the defensive armament to four cannons in the dorsal and ventral barbettes. Aircraft equipped with these UKhO fairings were designated Tu-16KSR-IS.

This rather grubby Tu-16K-11-16 carries two missiles. Note the refuelling receptacle under the port wingtip.

Work on the K-11 weapons system was carried out in parallel with the K-16, the KSR-2 being given a passive radar homing system for use against the enemy's ground or shipborne radars and becoming the KSR-11 anti-radar missile (ARM). The design work on the K-11 system took two years. By the end of 1959 the basic issues of radar detection and target indication, as well as passive homing, had been solved (the former by the Ritsa system named after a lake in the Caucasus region) and the first models of the entire system were ready for testing. Two examples of the Tu-16 were adapted at the Kazan' aircraft factory and designated Tu-16K-11.

The K-11 was the first Soviet air-to-surface missile with passive radar homing for use against enemy radars, radar-controlled anti-aircraft defences and surface-to-air missiles. The Tu-16K-11 modified from production Tu-16A and Tu-16ZA bombers could, like the Tu-16KSR-2, also be used as a bomber. It was outwardly identifiable by an inverted T-shaped direction finder aerial on the extreme nose (on the navigator's station glazing frame). In order

Another Tu-16K-11-16 over international waters.

A Tu-16K-26 modified with a Rubin-1M radar under the wing centre section (*Badger-G Mod*).

to accommodate the Ritsa radar detection/homing system, save weight and keep the CG within prescribed limits the PU-88 fixed forward-firing cannon installation and the PKI gunsight were removed. The KSR-11 hardly differed from the KSR-2 in its design and carried a high-explosive or explosive-fragmentation warhead. At 4,000 kg its all-up weight was 100 kg less than the KSR-2's due to its lighter guidance system (a 2PRF-10 passive homing radar in a nose radome which increased the missile's length to 8.6 m (28 ft) and an AP-72-11 missile autopilot which maintained course between launch and impact). The missile was launched once its radar had locked-on. After launch and ignition, the KSR-11 climbed to the same height as the Tu-16 and maintained that altitude

before finally entering a 30° dive to impact. The Tu-16 could carry out any manoeuvre after launch, including U-turns; the target tracking information was retained by the KSR-11.

The K-11 weapons system had a 2,000-km (1,242-mile) combat radius with the aircraft flying at altitudes between 4,000 and 11,000 m. Missile launch at 10,000 m was effected at a cruising speed of 750-800 km/h. The radar detection range was 270-350 km (167-217 miles), with the KSR-11 having a range of 160 km (99 miles) and a 'kill' probability of 80-90%. The missile had a 'heading memory' feature, which allowed it to close in on the enemy radar and destroy it even if the radar was switched off after the missile had locked on.

A Tu-16K-26 *Badger-G* with a chin-mounted RBP-4 radar...

...and a modified Tu-16K-26 *Badger-G Mod* with a Rubin-1M radar. Flights with just one missile were common practice.

Although the K-11 was accepted, it was decided to use the combined K-11 and K-16 weapons systems for operational use.

The high degree of commonality between the KSR-2 and KSR-11 missiles suggested that

This *Badger-G Mod* carries a KSR-2 to port and a KSR-5 to starboard.

they could be fitted to the same carrier. Therefore, in 1962 the K-11-16 weapons system was accepted for operational use, its Tu-16KSR-2-11 carrier aircraft (equipped with Rubicon and Ritsa guidance systems) carrying either two KSR-2 active radar-homing ASMs or two KSR-11 ARMs, or one of each type. The maximum range of the KSR-11 was 85 km (52.8 miles) if launched from 4,000 m (13,120 ft) and 120 km (74.5 miles) if launched from 10,000 m (32,810 ft), with detonation between 4 and 12 m (13-39 ft) above the target. The KSR-2 was fitted with either a conventional (high-explosive) or a nuclear warhead; it had a maximum range of 150 km (93 miles) if launched from 10,000 m and a minimum range of 70 km (43.5 miles). The Tu-16KSR-2-11 had an operational radius of 2,050 km (1,273 miles).

155 Tu-16A and Tu-16A (ZA) bombers were converted to Tu-16KSR-2-11 configuration and the Tu-16KSR-2As were modified. 15 Tu-16KS missile carriers and a number of Tu-16KSR-2s, as well as some Tu-16S maritime search and rescue aircraft which lacked bomb-carrying capability, were also upgraded to Tu-16K-11-16 standard under the terms of 'order 497' (or 'order 497E' if they carried KS-1 missiles). Initially their ability to carry bombs was not restored, but this was subsequently done on many of these aircraft. In such cases, the underside of the machine was painted white either completely or partly. Conversion of the Tu-16KSR-2 into the Tu-16K-11-16 entailed installation of the Ritsa radar homing system and removal of the nose gun turret and gunsight. The missile pylons could be used for either KSR-2 ASMs or KSR-11 ARMs. Outwardly the Tu-16K-11-16 differed from the Tu-16KSR-2 in having extra skin panels on the weapons bay doors closing the access hatch to the former WSO's cabin and the cutout for the deleted Kobal't-P radar. In addition, the undersurfaces of the machines lacking bomber capability were natural metal,

A Tu-16K-26 touches down.

Front view of a Tu-16K-26, showing the inverted-T aerial of the Ritsa homing system on the extreme nose.

not white. The designation Tu-16K-11-16KS was also sometimes used where the conversion had been from a *Badger-B*.

A total of 441 Tu-16A, Tu-16 (ZA), Tu-16KS and Tu-16S aircraft were refitted to take the K-16 and K-11-16 weapons systems. Of these, 211 aircraft served with the Air Force. The Tu-16K-11-16 was equipped with SPS-5 and SPS-100 active jammers. Refits to this configuration were done at the MoD's aircraft repair factories in the 1960s. Later, in the 1970s, the Tu-16K-11-16 was modified yet again to Tu-16K-26 configuration.

The performance of the Tu-16K-11-16 barely differed from the Tu-16KSR-2, although the need to carry two guidance systems increased the former aircraft's empty weight to 40,600 kg, necessitating a reduction of the fuel load to 29,000 kg. The Tu-16KSR-2-11 and Tu-16K-11-16, as well as the Tu-16KSR-2, were all known by the NATO reporting name *Badger-G*.

At first the Tu-16K-11-16 lacked bomber capability, but after modification under the terms of 'order 684/2' it could carry a full bomb load of up to 13,000 kg (28,660 lb) comprising forty FAB-100 or FAB-250 bombs, or twenty-six FAB-500s, or four FAB-1500s, or two FAB-3000s, or eight torpedoes (four in the bomb bay and four on underwing pylons).

Design work on the new K-26 air-to-surface missile system built around the improved Rubin-1KV radar and the new KSR-5 ASM was initiated by Council of Ministers directive of 11th August 1962. The system was to comprise either the Tu-16K-26 or Tu-16KSR-2-5 or Tu-16KSR-2-5-11 as a carrier, two KSR-5 (with conventional or nuclear warheads), KSR-2 or KSR-11 ASMs, and the Vzlyot (Take-off) guidance system.

The KSR-5 (NATO codename AS-6 *Kingfish*) was developed by OKB-2-155 (the missile branch of the Mikoyan OKB) during the late 1950s and early 1960s; its design benefited from the experience gained with the KS-1, KSR-2 and KSR-11 missiles, as well as with the Kh-22 (AS-4 *Kitchen*) for the supersonic Tu-22K. It was devised as a highly accurate delta-wing 'fire-and-forget' missile for use against ground or maritime targets. The missile was powered by an S5.35 three-chamber rocket engine designed by the Isayev OKB and equipped with a VS-K active radar homing system, proving superior to all preceding Soviet air-to-surface missiles. With a length of 10.56 m (34 ft 7¾ in), a wing span of 2.6 m (8 ft 6$\frac{23}{64}$ in) and a launch weight of 3,900 kg (8,600 lb), the KSR-5 had a maximum speed of 2,500-3,000 km/h (1,552-1,863 mph) and a flight altitude of 22,000-25,000 m (72,180-82,020 ft). Its range from a low-altitude launch was 200-240 km (124-149 miles), increasing to a maximum of 500 km (310 miles) if launched at a higher altitude. The KSR-5 could carry either a high-explosive warhead with an impact fuse or a nuclear warhead detonating at a preset height. Later developments included the

Three views of the Kh-20 missile developed for the Tu-95K.

An early probe-less Tu-95K carrying a Kh-20 missile makes a flypast at an air event.

Close-up of the semi-recessed Kh-20, showing the retractable fairing closing the air intake.

A Tu-95KM carrying no missile is examined by a Grumman F-14A from VF-111, NAS Miramar.

KSR-5P, KSR-5M, KSR-5B and KSR-5N, as well as the D-5NM (MV) target drone.

The K-26 system was accepted by the Long-Range Aviation and Naval Air Arm pursuant to Council of Ministers directive No. 882-315 of 12th November 1969. The Tu-16K-26, Tu-16KSR-2-5 and Tu-16KSR-2-5-11 were all known by the NATO reporting name *Badger-G Mod*.

Fifteen examples of the Tu-16K-11-16KS were modified into Tu-16K-26 missile-carriers under the terms of 'order 386'. In service they were referred to as *izdeliye* NK-26 or *izdeliye* NK-4. The Tu-16K-26 differed from the Tu-16K-11-16 only in its new missiles and the equipment required for carrying them. The Tu-16K-26 could carry one or two KSR-2, KSR-5 or KSR-11 ASMs, or a single missile plus

a conventional bomb or nuclear weapon load up to 4,000 kg. Modernised versions of the *Kingfish* were later used on upgraded versions of the *Badger-G Mod*: the KSR-5M on the Tu-16K-26M (K-26M weapons system; M = *moderni**zee**rovannaya* – updated), the low-level KSR-5N on the Tu-16K-26N (K-26N weapons system; N = ***niz**kovy**sot**naya* – low-altitude) and the KSR-5NM low-altitude target drone (***niz**kovy**sot**naya mi**shen'***).

125 examples of the Tu-16KSR-2-11 (which retained bomber capability) were equipped with the K-26 system in a similar way to the Tu-16K-26, becoming Tu-16KSR-2-5-11. These aircraft carried a pair of KSR-2, KSR-11 or KSR-5 missiles of various subtypes (except the

Another *Bear-C* escorted by USN McDonnell F-4Js.

A Tu-95KM is chased by a BAC Lightning F.6 near British shores.

Two views of a probe-less Tu-95K '32 Red' was used as a trainer by the 43rd TsBP i PLS at Dyagilevo AB.

passive radar homing KSR-5P). Outwardly they differed from the Tu-16K-26 in lacking the panels on the rear sections of the bomb bay doors and the white-painted undersurfaces. This modification became one of the standard missile-carrying versions of the Tu-16.

110 examples of the Tu-16KSR-2A were similarly converted for the K-26 system under the terms of 'order 386A'. The Rubin-Ritsa link equipment was not fitted. The Tu-16KSR-2-5 could be used as a bomber and carried two KSR-2 or KSR-5 missiles of various subtypes (including the KSR-5NM target drone). Unlike the two preceding versions, the Tu-16K-26 and Tu-16KSR-2-5-11, it was not equipped to

Looking a bit tatty but sporting an 'Excellent aircraft' badge, Tu-95K '61 Red' was also operated by the 43rd Centre.

Tu-95K '34 Red' rests between flights at Dyagilevo AB.

carry the KSR-11 or KSR-5P anti-shipping missiles.

The equipment fitted to the Tu-16KSR-2-5 differed from that on the Tu-16K-26 in that it included a PKI reflector sight, an SP-50 blind landing system, and later an active ECM suite consisting of SPS-5M and SPS-151/152/153 jammers from the Siren' (Lilac) series. But the reconnaissance, and target-indicating equipment and the bombsight were omitted

A Russian Air Force Tu-95K seen a second after becoming airborne.

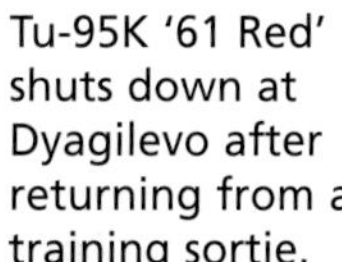

Tu-95K '61 Red' shuts down at Dyagilevo after returning from a training sortie.

(although some retained their OPB-112 bombsight which came back into use when they were reconverted to bomber capability under the terms of 'order 684/2'). The version had the same defensive armament as the Tu-16A.

Externally the Tu-16KSR-2-5 differed from the Tu-16KSR-2-5-11 in lacking the Ritsa radar homing system's inverted-T aerial on the navigator's station glazing and in having a PU-88

Old but well kept: Tu-95K '33 Red' sports the 'Excellent aircraft' maintenance award badge.

Another view of sister ship '32 Red'.

As a Tu-95K taxies to the hardstand after landing, the outer engines are shut down early to save fuel and conserve engine life.

A Tu-95KM has just launched a Kh-20M missile.

Here a *Bear-C* is escorted away from US shores by a pair of Convair F-102A Delta Daggers, including 56-1321

nose gun mounting. It also differed from the Tu-16K-26 in lacking the panels on the bomb bay doors. It also had a different kind of aerial above the pilots' cockpit from that on the Tu-16KSR-2A.

From 1973 onwards some Tu-16KSR-2-5-11s were fitted with the Rubin-1M combined radar and optical sighting system. This was an upgraded version of the Rubin-1KV with a greater detection range. It was therefore quite

The crew of a Tu-95MS missile carrier reports mission readiness to the unit CO.

Tu-95K-22s often carried air sampling pods for RINT duties.

different in appearance from the other Tu-16 missile-carrier versions, being readily identifiable by the large teardrop radome under the centre fuselage and the lack of the usual chin radome whose position was faired over. This was because the Rubin-1M was too large and heavy and would have caused CG problems if installed under the nose. The new radar instal-

A Tu-95K-22 minus air sampling pods shows off its arrow-like shape.

lation necessitated the removal of the No. 3 fuel tank, causing a reduction in the fuel capacity by 3,150 litres (693 Imp gal), but the range of the KSR-5 ASM was increased to 450 km (279 miles). On this version the PU-88 nose gun installation was deleted.

The Tu-16KSR-2-5 with the Rubin-1M did not carry Ritsa radar homing equipment and therefore could not use anti-radar missiles. Externally it differed from the version detailed above in lacking ARM compatibility and hence the distinctive inverted-T aerial on the nose glazing. Like the Tu-16K-26 'Rubin-1M', it lacked the nose gun installation.

In the late 1970s the KSR-5 ASM was updated as the KSR-5M or KSR-5B with new guidance systems designed to strike smaller targets. Several Tu-16K-26s were modified for this weapons system, known as the K-26M. Aircraft brought up to K-26PM standard and carrying KSR-5M and KSR-11 missiles were designated Tu-16K-26PM and were equipped with the AMP-M communicator linking the aircraft and missile radars.

Another *Bear-G* takes off; the missile pylons are just visible under the wing roots.

A Kh-22M missile on the port pylon of a Tu-95K-22.

Now let's turn our attention to the Tu-95 strategic bomber. Having the longest range among contemporary Soviet bombers and a large payload, the *Bear* was a prime candidate for 'missilisation'. By virtue of its conventional tricycle landing gear the Tu-95 was much better suited for carrying a large air-launched weapon than the competing Myasishchev M-4 *Bison-A* and 3M *Bison-B* bombers, which had a bicycle landing gear and consequently a much smaller ground clearance.

As early as 11th March 1954 the Council of Ministers tasked the Tupolev OKB with developing a missile strike derivative of the Tu-95M armed with the Kh-20 supersonic ASM. The aircraft was designated Tu-95K and the entire weapons system was called K-20. Development of the missile was entrusted to the specialised Section K of the Mikoyan OKB led by Mikhail I. Gurevich. Dubbed AS-3 *Kangaroo* by NATO, the Kh-20 was of the Mikoyan I-7U experimental swept-wing fighter; it had a design launch range of 350-800 km (217-496 miles) and could be equipped with a conventional or a nuclear warhead. The guidance system would be developed by the Ministry of Electronics' OKB-1 under B. M. Shabanov.

The Tu-95K and the Kh-20 missile entered flight test in 1956. The aircraft was equipped with a YaD twin-antenna search/guidance radar in a distinctive 'duck bill' radome and the missile was carried in a semi-recessed position in the bomb bay until immediately before launch. On 9th September 1960 the Council of Ministers issued a directive officially including the K-20 weapons system into the operational inventory of the Soviet Air Force. The Tu-95K received the reporting name *Bear-B*.

Besides carrying missiles, the Tu-95K could be used as a conventional bomber. To this end two large cigar-shaped bomb dispensers could be suspended under the centre fuselage.

Bear-B production continued until 1962; apart from the two prototypes, 47 new-build aircraft were manufactured (three in 1958, 17 each in 1959 and 1960, and the final ten in 1961). Later, 28 Tu-95Ks (27 production aircraft and one prototype) were updated to Tu-95KM standard (see below). The remaining 20 *Bear-Bs* stayed in service until the early 1980s. At the end of their service career some of them were modified for the training role as Tu-95KUs and served as such into the early 1990s.

The Tu-95K achieved initial operational capability during late 1959. One regiment

The UKhO rear ECM fairing was another distinctive feature of the Tu-95K-22.

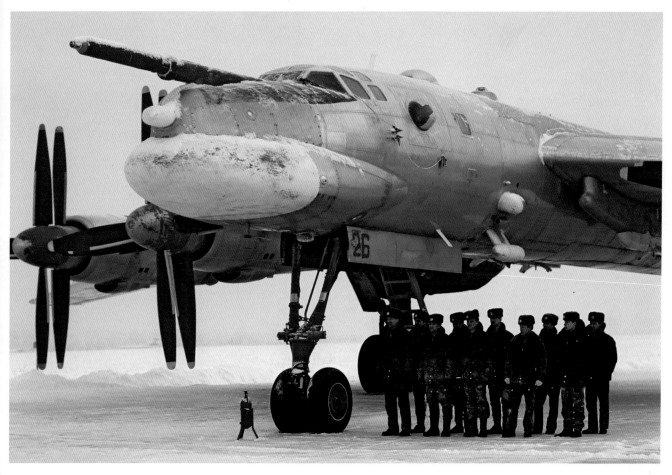

from the 106th TBAD based at Uzin AB became the first to receive the aircraft. During the early 1960s, the Tu-95K was introduced into the heavy bomber regiment in Mozdok (North Caucasus). As a result, the Long-Range Aviation took on the task of getting the missile-carrying variants of the Tu-95 up to fully operational status. From January to October 1962, nineteen Kh-20 missiles were launched from Tu-95Ks in the Mozdok regiment. Fifteen of these missiles effectively destroyed their theoretical targets. This was considered a good record in light of the fact that the Kh-20 missile and its associated transport and target-

The crew of this *Bear-G* is ready to fly but the aircraft needs a bit of cleaning!

A typical Tu-95K-22.

A *Bear-G* comes home after a training sortie.

Rear view of the Tu-95K-22. The small pods on the fuselage house data link antennas.

ing systems were still new and effectively untried.

The Tu-95K was the first version that demonstrated the need for in-flight refuelling, the missile carrier's range being inferior to that of the basic bomber. The range penalty, in fact, was 4,200 km (2,608 miles). To remedy this, on 2nd July 1958 the Council of Ministers issued a directive tasking the Tupolev OKB with giving the Tu-95K IFR capability.

In May 1961 a production Tu-95K was set aside at factory No. 18 in Kuibyshev for modification with the probe-and-drogue IFR system. This aircraft was designated Tu-95KD (***dahl'****niy* – long-range). Up to 50 tons (110,230 lb) of fuel could be transferred in a single refuelling session.

Stage A of the Tu-95KD's state acceptance trials took place between 5th July and 8th September 1961. Eighteen flights were con-

ducted with an average duration of 38 hours. Stage B of the trials followed between 17th October 1961 and 30th January 1962. A Myasishchev M-4-2 was the tanker in all cases. The tests were successful and the aircraft was recommended for production. However, the Tu-95KD remained a one-off because more changes were incorporated before the IFR-capable version went into production, which led to a change of designation.

In 1962 the Kuibyshev aircraft factory launched production of the upgraded missile

A Tu-95K-22 fitted with RR8311-100 air sampling pods takes off on a routine sortie.

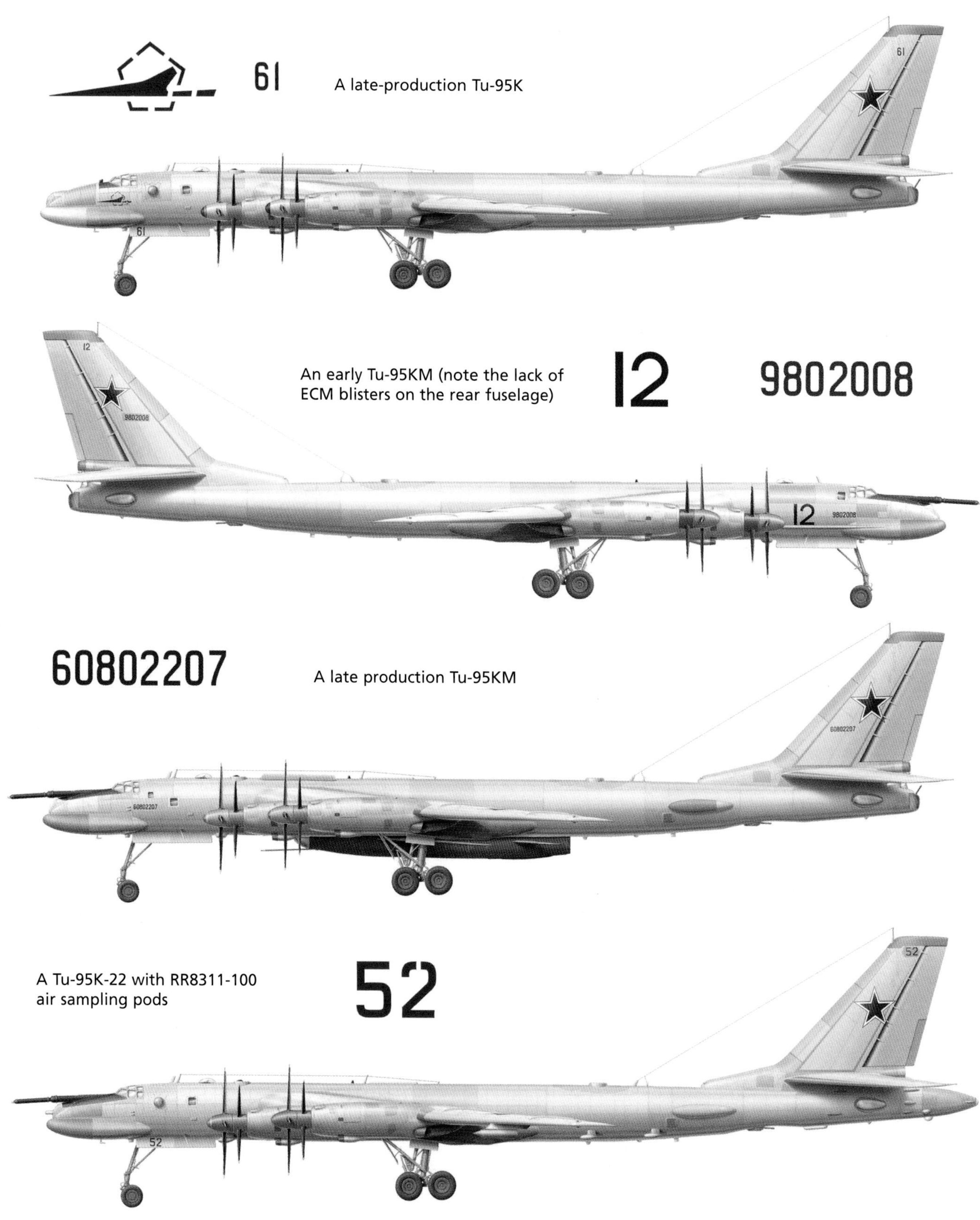

A late-production Tu-95K

An early Tu-95KM (note the lack of ECM blisters on the rear fuselage)

A late production Tu-95KM

A Tu-95K-22 with RR8311-100 air sampling pods

carrier version designated Tu-95KM (*modernizeerovannyy*, upgraded); it was identifiable by the ECM blisters on the rear fuselage sides. Concurrently, the Mikoyan OKB upgraded its Kh-20 missile; the version used on with the Tu-95KM was designated Kh-20M.

The upgraded weapons system comprising the Tu-95KM, the Kh-20M missile and its K-20

guidance system was designated Tu-95K-20. The Tu-95KM's combat radius varied between 6,340 and 8,250 km (3,937 and 5,123 miles) and the Kh-20M's launch point-to-target-range of was 450-600 km (270-373 miles). The aircraft, however, had to be within 260 and 380 km (161 and 236 miles) of its target. These figures were deemed palatable by the Air Force during the 1960s. It should also be noted that the Kh-20 definitely wasn't a 'fire and forget' weapon; the weapons systems operator in the *Bear* had to maintain guidance contact with the Kh-20 until just before the missile scored a hit, which increased the aircraft's vulnerability to enemy action.

In all, 23 Tu-95KMs were built as such – ten in 1962, eight in 1963, four in 1964 and one in 1965. Besides, as noted earlier, 28 Tu-95Ks were upgraded to this standard. Thus, 51 missile strike aircraft were equipped with the refu-

An F-14A from VF-51 maintains an interest in a visiting *Bear-G*.

A Tu-95K-22 cruises high over shredded clouds on 15th July 1976.

Five Tu-95MS missile carriers on the flight line.

elling system and known to the West as the *Bear-C*. The total number of Tu-95K/Tu-95KM missile carriers completed was 71.

In due course the aircraft were retrofitted with a new ***Too**cha* (Storm cloud) weather/navigation radar. In the late 1960s several Tu-95KMs were equipped with two RR8311-100 air sampling pods on underwing pylons for radiation reconnaissance (RINT) duties. This system was developed specifically to explore the results of above-ground nuclear testing, primarily in China.

The development of western air defences during the late 1960s and early 1970s meant that the Tu-95KM had little chances of delivering its missile to a target. Hence in February

A Tu-95MS approaches an IL-78 tanker.

1973 the Council of Ministers made the decision to undertake a further upgrade of the Tu-95KM. It involved integration of a new weapons system – the K-22 which included the more advanced Kh-22 missile (AS-4 *Kitchen*) developed for the Tu-22K *Blinder-B*. This was no longer a warmed-over fighter but a purpose-built aerial vehicle with delta wings and a rocket motor. Two such missiles were suspended on pylons under the wing roots. The reconfigured aircraft was designated Tu-95K-22 and the weapons system as a whole received the designation K-95-22.

Starting in 1981, a number of Tu-95KMs was upgraded to the new standard at the Kuibyshev plant. The Tu-95K-22 entered service with the same units that had operated the *Bear-B/C*. Following introduction of the type into the operational inventory during 1987 it became an important weapons system in the Soviet Air Force. The new version received the NATO reporting name *Bear-G*.

Like the precursor, some Tu-95K-22s were modified to carry RR8311-100 air sampling pods for monitoring nuclear tests. The type's service career proved to be brief; starting in the mid-1990s the Tu-95K-22s were progressively retired and scrapped in keeping with START-1 (Strategic Arms Reduction Treaty).

A high-flying Tu-95MS leaves contrails across the sky.

A McDonnell Douglas F-15A from Eglin AFB escorts a Tu-95MS away from Alaskan shores.

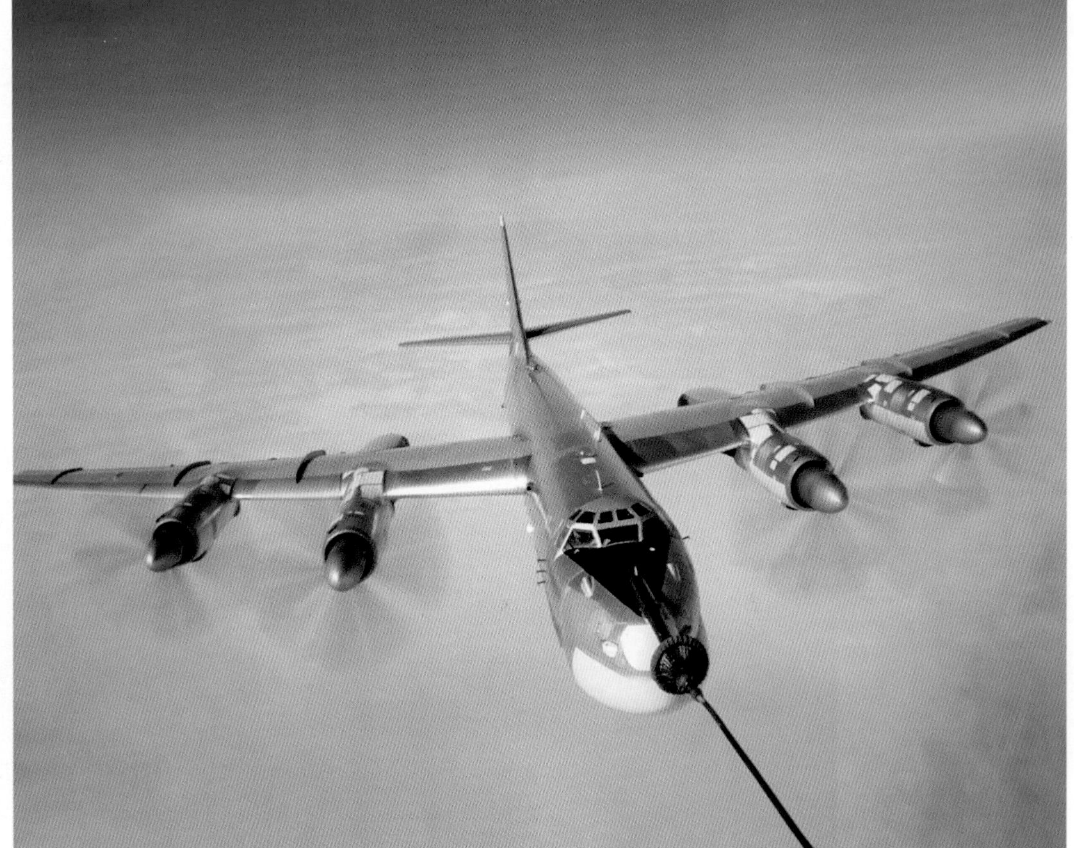

A *Bear-H* is refuelled over heavy overcast. The curvature of the wings is a trick of the wide-angle lens.

Tu-95MS operations at the 43rd Training Centre in Ryazan'.

The wing underside and main gear fairings of the Tu-95MS are blackened with exhaust.

In the mid-1970s an acute need arose to re-equip the Long-Range Aviation units with modern weapons systems. This meant first and foremost introduction of air-launched cruise missiles (ALCMs) that were compact enough to permit internal carriage of several missiles and capable of ultra-low-level terrain-following flight over a range of 2,500-3,000 km (1,552-1,863 miles). Such a missile was developed by the ***Ra****duga* (Rainbow) design bureau as the Kh-55 (RKV-500A).

Accordingly the Tupolev OKB began adapting the venerable *Bear* to take the new armament. Designated Tu-95MS, the new cruise missile carrier was derived from the radically reworked Tu-142 *Bear-F* anti-submarine warfare aircraft, featuring the latter's new wing structure (with integral fuel tanks instead of bladder tanks) and more spacious flight deck.

Development of the Tu-95MS began in July 1977. First, a test aircraft known as the Tu-95M-5 and armed with two Kh-22 ASMs in similar manner to the Tu-95K-22 was further converted to tackle the problems associated with the Kh-55 cruise missile and appropriately redesignated Tu-95M-55. Only a single missile pylon was installed initially, but as work progressed it was decided to incorporate an MKU-6-5 rotary launcher permitting the carriage of six missiles internally. The conversion was completed at the Kuibyshev factory in July 1978. Equipment to accommodate the new *Doob* (Oak) pre-launch system associated with the Kh-55 was installed, as well as electro-hydraulic rotary launcher controls, test instrumentation and a new flight avionics/navigation suite integrated with the new weapons system.

The Tu-95M-55 entered flight test on 31st July 1978. During the following four years, many different Kh-55 missiles were tested in both dummy and live configuration. The results of these tests proved instrumental in the final design both of the missile and the proposed production version of the Tu-95MS. Sadly, on 28th January 1982 the aircraft crashed on take-off at Zhukovskiy, killing the entire crew captained by N. Ye. Kool'chitskiy.

The first prototype Tu-95MS was converted from a production Tu-142MK *Bear-F Mod 3* at the Taganrog aircraft factory manufacturing this version, utilising documentation prepared by the Tupolev OKB. The conversion began in 1978 and was completed in September 1979, the Tu-95MS making its maiden flight in the same month.

Among the most significant changes were a new nose configuration to accommodate a new *Ob**zor*** (View, or Perspective) target illumination/guidance radar and miscellaneous new systems associated with the Kh-55 cruise missiles. The new radar was enclosed by a 'duck bill' radome reminiscent of the Tu-95K/Tu-95KM but rather smaller and neater. The new installation caused the fuselage to be shortened somewhat for CG reasons.

The weapons system included an MKU-6-5 rotary launcher. New communications and ECM suites complemented the new radar package. The four NK-12MV turboprops were replaced with the more powerful NK-12MP version offering improved performance and constant-speed drives for powerful AC generators. The crew was reduced to seven (captain, co-pilot, navigator, second navigator, flight engineer, systems operator and tail gunner).

Following two years of flight testing and modification, Tu-95MS production was initiated at the Taganrog factory in 1981 and transferred to Kuibyshev in 1983. The *Bear-H*, as the type was codenamed by the NATO, was built in two versions: the Tu-95MS-6 and the Tu-95MS-16. The former carried six Kh-55 missiles internally, while the Tu-95MS-16 had four pylons with multiple ejector racks for carrying an additional ten missiles under the wings. The inboard pylons were mounted between the inner engines and the fuselage, carrying three missiles abreast; the outboard pylons (each with two missiles side by side) were located between the inner and outer engines.

The defensive armament was also updated. A new UKU-9K-502 tail turret with two 23-mm (.90 calibre) Gryazev/Shipunov GSh-23

A Tu-95MS at a tactical airfield in the High North.

A fine in-flight study of the Tu-95MS.

A typical *Bear-H* with an 'Excellent aircraft' badge.

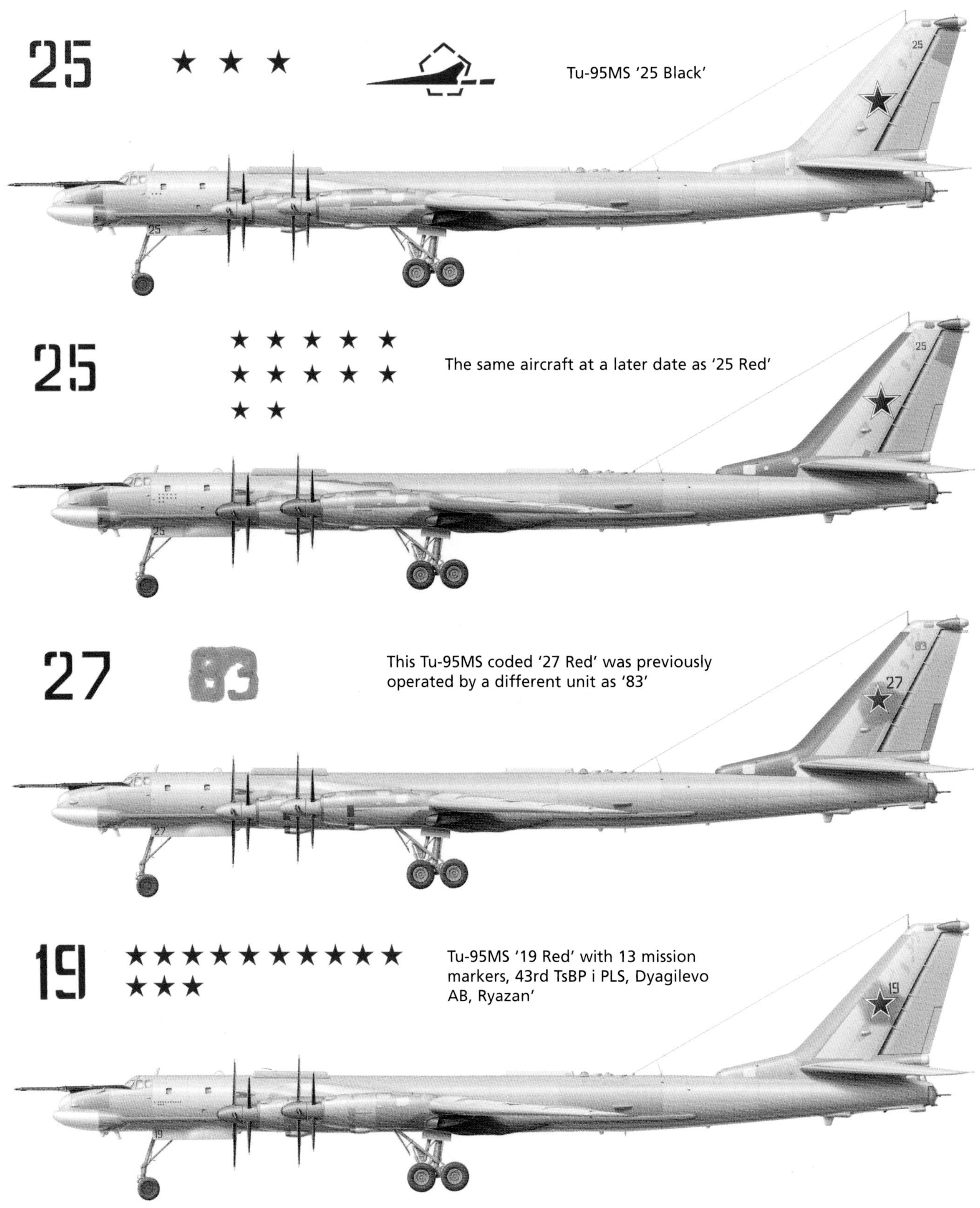

Tu-95MS '25 Black'

The same aircraft at a later date as '25 Red'

This Tu-95MS coded '27 Red' was previously operated by a different unit as '83'

Tu-95MS '19 Red' with 13 mission markers, 43rd TsBP i PLS, Dyagilevo AB, Ryazan'

double-barrelled cannons was installed, replacing the original turret with two AM-23 cannons. The cannons were trained by means of a PRS-4 Krypton radar.

A total of 88 *Bear-Hs* were built – 31 Tu-95MS-6s and 57 Tu-95MS-16s. The latter, however, eventually had their underwing missile pylons removed under the terms of the

START-1 treaty (Strategic Arms Reduction Treaty) which limited the number of nuclear warheads to be carried by a single delivery vehicle. As a sort of compensation, MKB Raduga developed the Kh-55SM, a longer-range version of the missile equipped with jettisonable conformal fuel tanks.

By early 1991 the Soviet Union's long-range bomber arm was equipped with 84 Tu-95MSs. Over the years this figure declined, not least because the Ukraine, after gaining independence in 1992, took possession of a number of *Bear-Hs* based on Ukrainian soil. They were placed in storage, together with the similarly acquired Tu-160 bombers, as the Ukraine actually had no need for this kind of weaponry. At the end of 1999 Russia and the Ukraine reached an agreement under the terms of which three Tu-95MSs and eight Tu-160s were transferred to Russia as debt payments.

Together with the Tu-160, the Tu-95MS remains the primary strike asset of the Russian Air Force's Long-Range Aviation.

The Tu-95MS entered service with regiments of the Soviet Union's Long-Range Aviation branch during 1982. A unit based in Semipalatinsk was the first to receive the aircraft. It was officially declared to be operational at the end of 1982.

During 1985 the Long-Range Aviation unit in Uzin converted to the Tu-95MS, and during 1987 the regiment at Mozdok also was so equipped. Concurrent with delivery of the type to these units they were perfecting the launching of the Kh-55SM missile, and getting to grips with in-flight refuelling techniques.

During 1986, the Tu-95MS demonstrated its capabilities and the level of crew readiness that had been achieved to that point. Utilising IFR, aircraft of the Uzin regiment flew around the perimeter of the Soviet Union. At the same time, aircraft from Semipalatinsk flew from their home base, across the North Pole, and on to the Canadian border. These missions verified the Tu-95MS's ability to deliver weapons over intercontinental ranges.

Missile carriers in Long-Range Aviation service

In 1954-55 the Long-Range Aviation established its first missile carrier division – the 116th TBAD whose first commander was Air Maj.-Gen. V. P. Dragomiretskiy. The division comprised the 12th and 685th TBAPs flying Tu-16KS missile carriers and an independent air squadron equipped with MiG-15SDK cruise missile simulator aircraft (these were fighters equipped with the KS-1 missile's guidance system, allowing the Tu-16KS crews to practice missile launches without wasting actual missiles). The customary abbreviation TBAP was actually more of a cover-up to conceal the two regiments' true role and armament. All three units were based at Ostrov AB near Pskov in north-western Russia, not far from the Finnish border. The base was shrouded in secrecy and heavily guarded, with stringent security measures and a system of special passes; a special storage depot for nuclear munitions was located nearby, and the personnel avoided mentioning it if at all possible.

The flight crews of the 116th TBAD were sourced from many Long-Range Aviation units, all with a wealth of combat experience in the Great Patriotic War. The division's personnel received higher pay, quicker promotions and other incentives.

In 1954 Maj.-Gen. Dragomiretskiy became one of the division's first crews to master the launch of KS-1 missiles. Live weapons training

A Tu-95MS on final approach.

A standard Kh-55 cruise missile with everything deployed in front of a Tu-95MS.

A group of Tu-16KSR-2s in echelon port formation.

took place at the Air Force's target range No. 77 on the Caspian Sea. An average 'kill' rate of 81% was achieved during these practice launches; most of these were performed by single aircraft cruising at 3,000-4,000 m (9,840-13,120 ft), with a launch range of 60-65 km (37.2-40.3 miles).

In 1959-60 the 116th TBAD and 685th TBAP were disbanded. The 12th TBAP and Ostrov AB were transferred to the Naval Aviation.

The late 1950s were characterised by large-scale introduction of missile systems in all arms and services of the Soviet Armed Forces, including the Long-Range Aviation. In 1958 the Soviet Union's first missile divisions armed with nuclear-tipped surface-to-surface ballistic missiles were formed. Originally they were part of the Air Force, reporting to the DA's 43rd and 50th Air Armies. On 31st December 1959, however, the Council of Ministers issued a directive, singling out these units into a separate armed service – the Strategic Missile Forces (RVSN – *Ra**ket**nyye voy**ska** strate**gich**eskovo nazna**chen**iya*); the 43rd and 50th VA were transferred to the new service, becoming missile armies. Accordingly the Long-Range Aviation was reformed once again in 1960 – the Air Armies gave place to three Independent Heavy Bomber Corps: the 8th OTBAK originally headquartered in Blagoveshchensk (Far East) and, from 1965 onwards, in Irkutsk (East Siberia), the 2nd OTBAK headquartered in Vinnitsa (the Ukraine) and the 6th OTBAK headquartered in Smolensk (western Russia). This order of battle persisted until 1980.

In 1961 the aircrews and ground crews of the 402nd and 200th TBAPs took conversion training for the K-16 weapons system, mastering the Tu-16KSR-2. Two years later, a special technical service responsible for mission preparation of the missiles was set up in the DA's missile carrier units. In April 1963 the 184th and 185th TBAPs started converting to the Tu-16KSR-11-16 armed with KSR-2 ASMs and KSR-11 anti-radar missiles; a crew captained by Lt.-Col. Marin performed the first practice launch of a KSR-2 missile in November 1964.

Also in 1964, the 52nd, 132nd, 840th and 111th TBAPs began theoretical training in the course of conversion to the K-16 weapons system, while the 402nd and 200th TBAPs became fully proficient in the combat use of the KSR-2. In 1965, four such missiles were launched at maritime targets (each of the two units made two launches); in the 402nd TBAP the honour of making the first launch fell to the crew of the unit's CO Col. V. P. Yakovlev, with Lt. Col. V. P. Galaninskiy as navigator.

In 1966 the 132nd TBAP took theoretical training for the K-16-11 weapons system; the 52nd, 111th, 200th, 402nd and 840th TBAPs followed suit in 1967. These latter units were rated for day and night use of KSR-2 ASMs against ground and maritime targets; the 132nd TBAP was similarly qualified to use both the KSR-2 and the KSR-11 missiles. This included live missile launches at weapons ranges.

The reader may be interested to learn some statistical data on how the Long-Range Aviation units gained their practical skills of using ASMs in the 1960s and 1970s.

In 1968 the DA's missile carrier regiments made eight live launches of KSR-2s and KSR-11s (of these, four KSR-11 ARMs were launched by the 132nd TBAP, while the 402nd and 200th Regiments each made two KSR-2 launches). Also, the 52nd TBAP completed theoretical training for the K-16-11 weapons system.

In 1969 the DA units launched nine KSR-2s; the 840th TBAP completed theoretical training for the new K-26 weapons system. All regiments equipped with missile-toting Tu-16s

A Tu-16K-26 with a Rubin-1M radar carries two KSR-5 missiles over the Baltic Sea.

Two of the many Tu-16K-11-16s intercepted by the Swedish Air Force. '02 Blue' carries a single KSR-2 missile while '55 Blue' (c/n 7203820) has none.

now had some experience of live missile launches.

In 1970 the Long-Range Aviation units launched three KSR-2s and a single KSR-5. The following year they made three KSR-2 launches, one KSR-11 launch and one KSR-5 launch.

No data are available for 1971 and 1972. In 1973 the 52nd TBAP launched five KSR-11s; the 200th TBAP chalked up two launches of KSR-2Ms, while the 840th TBAP made five KSR-5 launches.

In 1974 the 45th and 52nd TBAPs made one KSR-5 launch each; the 132nd TBAP launched one KSR-11. The 200th and 402nd TBAPs were credited with four and three KSR-2 launches respectively.

This is very probably the same '02 Blue' as shown above, now carrying a KSR-5 on the port wing pylon.

Judging by the jacks placed under the port wing, Tu-95K '32 Red' is due for maintenance.

In 1975 the 200th TBAP launched as many as 12 KSR-2 missiles at practice targets. The 402nd TBAP fired seven such missiles, while the 840th TBAP made two KSR-5 launches.

1976, by comparison, gave meagre results. Only four missiles were launched – two KSR-5s and one KSR-11 by the 132nd TBAP plus one unspecified missile by the 840th TBAP

In 1978 the 402nd TBAP launched a single KSR-2; the 200th TBAP fired one KSR-5 and the 132nd TBAP launched one KSR-5P and one KSR-11. The latter regiment completed the transition to the KSR-5P missile that year, while the 200th Regiment became fully proficient with the K-26 weapons system.

In 1979 the 402nd Regiment made three KSR-2 launches; the 200th and 132nd TBAPs fired two and three KSR-5s respectively. The 200th Regiment had now mastered the K-26 weapons system completely, while the 402nd TBAP had only just begun the transition to the same system.

The captain of an early-model Tu-95 immediately after a sortie.

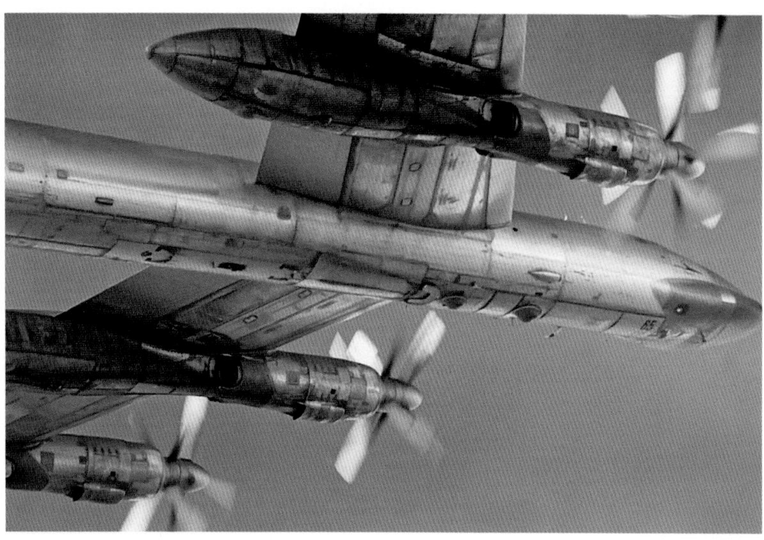

This picture taken on 14th July 1987 shows very well the undersides of a Tu-95K.

By the end of 1980 all units of the 6th Independent Heavy Bomber Corps were ready to wage war, using conventional and nuclear-tipped missiles. All of them had practical experience of missile launches.

The Tu-95K missile carrier – the 'longest-legged' aircraft in the DA – joined the operational inventory in late 1959. During the early 1960s, the Long-Range Aviation began building up the numbers on the *Bear-B*. Between January and October 1962, nineteen Kh-20 missiles were launched by 182nd TBAP Tu-95Ks based at Mozdok in what was then the Chechen-Ingush Autonomous Soviet Socialist Republic. Later, the first-generation Tu-95K regiments had little difficulty upgrading to the improved Tu-95KM. In the 1980s, these units transitioned to the further upgraded Tu-95K-22.

Concurrently with transitioning to new hardware the *Bear* units were getting to grips with in-flight refuelling techniques. This was a major challenge. On early Soviet hose-and-drogue tankers the refuelling drogue weighed more than 200 kg (440 lb) and was rather unstable, swaying crazily in the slipstream; hence making contact with the tanker required good flying skills. Besides, the refuelling process took some 20 minutes because of the low fuel transfer rate and other reasons, and keeping formation with the tanker for so long took a lot of effort; the pilots of the receiver aircraft would lose a couple of pounds in the process!

Some serious accidents with near-disastrous consequences happened during in-flight refuelling. On at least two separate occasions (in 1973 and 1983) the tanker's hose broke and became entangled around the receiver aircraft, nearly causing it to lose control. There was a case when the drogue was ingested into the propeller of a Tu-95KM, ruining it completely; the bomber barely made it back to base. On another occasion the receiver aircraft overshot and collided with the tanker, losing part of the vertical tail and seriously damaging the tanker; luckily, both aircraft landed safely.

Other problems unique to the missile carrier version were associated with hooking up the missile. When the Kh-20 was wheeled in under the bomber on its ground handling dolly, the extremely limited clearance would often cause the missile's fin to strike the bomber's belly, obliterating the data link receiver antenna on the fin top. Moreover, at the start of the Tu-95K's service career the arming procedure took 22 hours (!); in due course this was shortened to four hours.

When intercontinental ballistic missiles (ICBMs) were assigned the task of destroying targets of importance in the continental US, US Navy carrier groups and NATO convoys in the Atlantic and Pacific gradually became the Tu-95K-22's primary targets. The *Bear-G* proved the most suitable platform for this mission, since it was equipped with the advanced Kh-22 air-to-surface missile. And, given proper guidance, the Kh-22 was a potent weapon; its shaped-charge conventional warhead could tear a gaping 12-m (40-foot) hole in a ship's side.

'I'll eat you.' The Tu-95K was intimidating enough in 'life', but this stripped-out hulk looks like some Martian monster.

In November 1993, the Russian MoD daily ***Kras**naya zvez**da*** (Red Star) published an excerpt from a Russian Armed Forces' General Headquarters message that described a typical operational scenario for the Tu-95K-22 attacking US Navy ships. It ran as follows:

'On 18th July 1993, units of the US Navy Pacific Fleet ([headquartered at] San Francisco) formed a multi-purpose carrier task force (CTF)

A Tu-95K-22 commences a training sortie.

A badge marking the 40th anniversary of the Long-Range Aviation in 1982. The aircraft is an IL-4 and the original acronym ADD is used.

An anniversary badge of the 46th (Strategic) Air Army of the Supreme High Command (established 1942) listing its consecutive names.

headed by the nuclear-powered aircraft-carrier USS Abraham Lincoln *in order to relieve the aircraft carrier USS* Nimitz *on combat duty in the Persian Gulf zone.*

The transfer of responsibility from one carrier to the other was done under the protective umbrella of optical and electronic camouflage and under complete radio silence. In order to detect the location and configuration of the carrier group, the Commander of the Russian Air Force's Long-Range Aviation decided to undertake aerial reconnaissance via a group of four Tu-95K-22 strategic aircraft.

Two pairs of missile-carriers took off from an airfield in the Far East at 18:03 GMT on 28th July. The aircraft crossed the Kurile Archipelago and, five hours later, radar signals from the CTF were intercepted at a distance of 1,400 km [869 miles] from the shore line. Turning towards this source, the bomber crews discovered they were 220 km [137 miles] from the task force [...] which consisted of six ships. As they approached the CTF, the bomber crews noted, at a distance of 3 km [1.86 miles], that there were four ships in a tight formation. The carrier was 140 km [87 miles] behind.

The bombers then turned on a heading of 190° magnetic and reduced their speed to 120 knots. The first pair of missile-carriers descended to 500 m [1,640 ft] and made their photo runs across the task force's path. A pair of F/A-18 fighters (each with two Sidewinder air-to-air missiles) were launched to intercept the bombers following their second pass. The fighters came within 200 to 300m [660 to 990 ft] of the bombers within a few minutes after take-off. Thirty minutes later, two more fighters came up from behind the bombers on the right. These approached to within 100 m [330 ft]. Meanwhile, the second pair of Tu-95K-22s located their target. At the same time, they discovered and photographed a supply ship which was sailing separately from group.

Thus the assignment concerning detection of this US combat fleet at sea was successfully accomplished.'

The growing power of the Long-Range Aviation and the proficiency of its aircrews were repeatedly proved in the course of such Cold War-era Soviet Armed Forces exercises as *Dnepr*, *Dvi**na*** (the names of Russian rivers), *Oke**an*** (Ocean) and *Yoog* (South).

A case is on record when the Tu-95M and the Tu-95K were used in a rather unconventional way. This episode merits a more detailed description.

In February 1972 the Soviet missile submarine K-19 was returning to base from a solo voyage. 30 minutes before the sub was due to surface from great depth, a violent fire erupted in Bay 9 where the crew sleeping quarters were located. The seaman on duty managed to wake the men, who evacuated from the bay, and alert the conning tower. When the submarine surfaced, it found itself in the middle of a raging storm and with no propulsion. Bays 8 and 9 were on fire, bays 6 and 7 were filled with poisonous fumes and smoke; the air temperature in Bay 7 exceeded 100°C (212°F). The men who had taken refuge in Bay 10 were trapped: any attempt to reach the conning tower would be sheer suicide.

To save the crew, it was necessary to deliver rescue equipment urgently to the stricken submarine, which was still very far from native shores. The only vehicle that could perform the mission rapidly enough was the Tu-95 strategic bomber. The Commander of the Long-Range Aviation Col.-Gen. Vasiliy V. Reshetnikov ordered the Commander of the 106th TBAD to pick the two best-qualified crews for a mission of national importance. Maj.-Gen. Boris I. Artem'yev, who was then an assistant navigator in the rank of captain in the 1006th TBAP, recalls the events as follows:

'...Late in the afternoon I was urgently summoned to the Division's headquarters. As I walked in, I saw that several flight crews were already there. The division's command staff was poring over a map. The secure link telephones kept ringing; one had scarcely put down the receiver when the next call was coming in. From the tense atmosphere I gathered that an important mission was cooking. A few minutes later the division's Commander assigned two crews – a Tu-95K crew captained by Mel'nikov, with navigator Artem'yev, and a Tu-95M from the 409th TBAP. His briefing was succinct: "One of our submarines is in distress at such-and-such location (the Commander stated the coordinates and pointed to a spot on the map). You are to depart immediately for Severomorsk airfield (a major North Fleet Air Arm base near Murmansk in the High North – *Auth.*)*. There, a payload will be hooked up which you are to drop at the stated location. Good luck!"*

From the HQ we drove straight to the airfield. The aircraft were all ready and awaiting take-off.

At Severomorsk the payload packed into KAS-90 [paradroppable rescue] capsules was loaded into our machines; the location of the

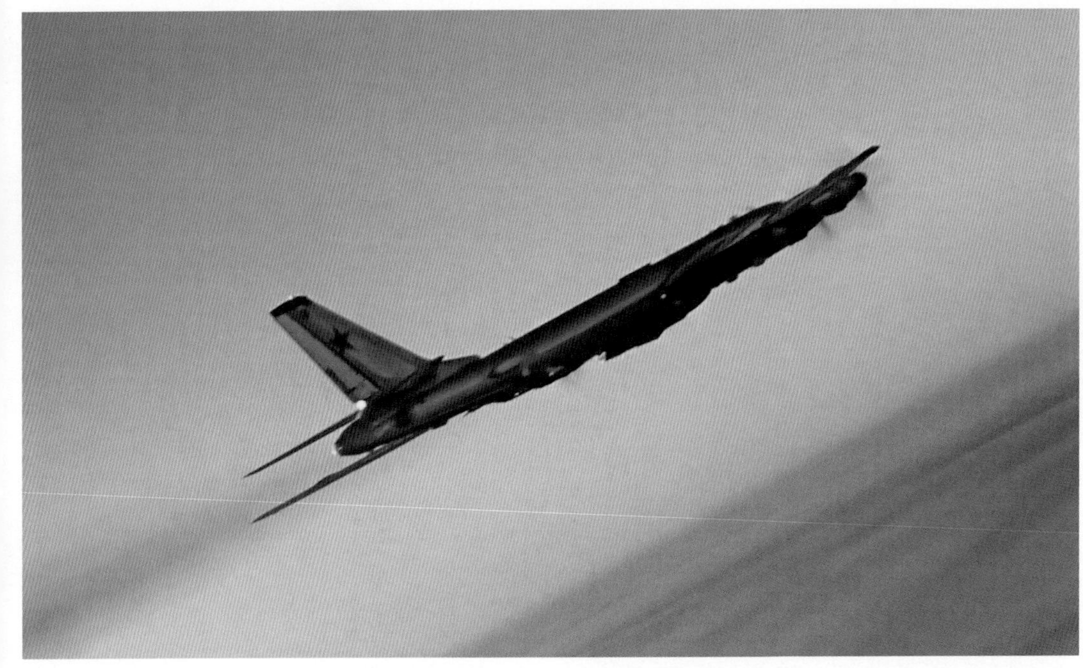

A Tu-95K-22 carrying a single Kh-22M missile cruises at high altitude.

submarine in distress was given more specifically, we were given the radio call signs of [Soviet] Navy ships [participating in the search and rescue operation] and a weather bulletin. The weather was extremely adverse: there was solid overcast above the area, with the top of the clouds at 11,000 m [36,090 ft] and the cloudbase at 150 m [490 ft]; the sea state in the drop area was 5 to 6 on the Beaufort scale. As we departed the last bit of home ground on the Kola Peninsula, we were aware that there would be no alternate airfields for us. Our aircraft was the flight leader. Knowing all too well that all responsibility for guiding us to the are of the maritime disaster rested with me personally, I pulled myself together and began my navigational calculations.

A while after passing the shores of Ireland we got the ships on our radars. We took the decision to descend below cloudbase while maintaining formation. When we broke through the clouds, we had the ships right ahead of us. As we descended to 150 m, we saw the ocean below us; it was choppy, in a sea state of 5 or 6. The submarine was straight ahead of us, with a [Soviet] ASW cruiser next to it, and US Navy ships were swarming all around like birds of prey. Moreover, when we opened our bomb bay doors, a US Navy [Lockheed P-3] Orion maritime patrol aircraft

The same aircraft silhouetted against the late afternoon sky.

The qualification badges issued to Soviet military pilots (1st, 2nd and 3rd Class; the unnumbered version is the lowest grade).

pulled in close and positioned itself right beneath my bomb bay. I already had some experience with the Americans, our crew having flown reconnaissance missions over their carrier task forces in the Atlantic Ocean many times, and I knew how insolent they could get. We had to do a bit of evasive manoeuvring in formation at ultra-low level and eventually did deliver our cargo. Then we climbed all the way back through the clouds and returned to Severomorsk. There, a new payload was hooked up, and after a short turnaround another stress-filled 15-hour mission to the disaster area began.

We were to learn later that 12 of the submarine's crew, including officer B. Polyakov who was in charge, were trapped in Bay 10 for 23 days. The rest of the crew communicated with them on a telephone whose design dated back to 1916. This telephone did not require batteries – all you had to do was spin the handcrank of a magneto to keep it working.

Our ships approached the submarine; men from another sub acted as the rescue team. The rescue vessel Altai *took the submarine in tow, and she was escorted by a picket of our ships.*

On 18th March the rescue vessel and the submarine reached the home base. The sub's captain Captain 1st Grade Kulibaba, senior political officer Verem'yuk and boatswain Krasnikov refused to leave the sub, staying on onboard throughout the journey home. The seamen trapped in Bay 10 had to be blindfolded before they could be led out into the open, supported by other men, and some had to be carried on stretchers; they had spent the 23 days in pitch darkness in a bitterly cold bay, hoping all the while they would be rescued. Having flown two sorties, our two crews returned to Uzin. Despite the classified nature

A Tu-95MS blends with the thick cloud cover on a bleak day.

of our mission, the people in the garrison had learnt how dangerous the mission was. The Air Force Commander-in-Chief thanked all the crewmembers involved for their service. I was given a valuable gift (a portable radio) on his behalf for my good airmanship...'

The 1980s saw the introduction of yet another missile carrying version – the Tu-95MS – into the operational inventory of the Soviet Air Force. The type attained IOC in 1982; the Long-Range Aviation's 1223rd TBAP in Semipalatinsk was the first to receive the aircraft. During 1985 the 409th TBAP at Uzin AB re-equipped with the Tu-95MS, the 182nd TBAP in Mozdok following suit in 1987. Concurrently with the transition to the type to these units were perfecting the launching of Kh-55 cruise missiles. The Tu-95K-22s were then concentrated in the 79th GvTBAP at Ookraïnka AB in Eastern Siberia near Lake Baikal. There, the aircraft replaced the Myasishchev 3M bomber fleet, which was ageing rapidly.

By the mid-1980s the Tu-95MS had ousted the Tu-95K/Tu-95KM almost completely and complemented the Tu-95K-22 in the 1006th, 182nd and 1226th TBAPs (the latter was based at Uzin AB). By the early 1990s the *Bear-Hs* equipped four complete regiments forming part of the 37th (Strategic) Air Army of the Supreme High Command.

During 1986, the Tu-95MSs of the Uzin regiment demonstrated their capabilities by flying around the perimeter of the Soviet Union, utilising in-flight refuelling. At the same time aircraft from Semipalatinsk flew from their home base across the North Pole and onward to the Canadian border. These missions proved the *Bear-H*'s ability to deliver weapons over intercontinental ranges.

Similar qualification badges were issued to the navigators/ bomb-aimers.

In response to the American deployment of Pershing II intermediate-range ballistic missiles (IRBMs) in Western Europe, in 1968-89 the Tu-95MSs patrolled the international waters in the vicinity of American and Canadian shores on a regular basis. Such missions were flown from auxiliary airstrips beyond the Arctic Circle and supported by 3MS-2 tankers. During this 26-month period of constant duty the aircraft of the 37th (Strategic) Air Army logged a total

A Tu-95MS seen from a sister ship during group operations.

A fine lower view of a Tu-95MS taken from an intercepting NATO fighter.

time of 1,224 hours flown by the missile carriers and 755 hours flown by the tankers. The *Bear-Hs* would loiter in the designated areas for 16 hours or more.

The service introduction of new air-launched missile systems based on the Tu-22M and Tu-160 supersonic 'swing-wing' aircraft in the 1970s and 1980s gave another major boost to the DA's importance in the defence of the Soviet Union. (These aircraft are dealt with in the next chapter.) Armed with long-range cruise missiles, these aircraft were able not only to deal actual missile strikes against targets anywhere in the world but also to 'project force' without having to fire in anger. This turned out to be an effective deterrent and an important instrument in maintaining strategic parity between the Soviet Union and the USA.

To sum up this chapter, we have to mention that virtually every sortie outside Soviet airspace flown by Long-Range Aviation aircraft involved encounters with NATO aircraft. Usually these were NATO or Japanese Air Self-Defence Force fighters operating from shore bases, or US Navy and Royal Navy fighters launched from aircraft carriers to ward off the uninvited guests.

Opposite page: A Tu-22KD missile carrier in a winter setting.

As a rule, the western 'inspectors' maintained the same altitude and a separation of between 100 m (330 ft) and 2-3 km (1.24-1.86 miles). Occasionally they would manoeuvre all around the Soviet bomber, the fighter pilots taking pictures in the process. On very rare occasions the fighters would come dangerously close (within 10-30 m/33-100 ft). When the Cold War was at its hottest, NATO fighters would go so far as to position themselves ahead of the bomber and engage their afterburners, causing one of the engines to flame out. A case is on record when the pilot of a US Navy McDonnell F-4 Phantom II misjudged the distance and collided with the Tu-16 he was intercepting, tearing a gash in the wing with the fighter's fin and only narrowly missing the fuel tanks; luckily the incident had no disastrous consequences. Generally, however, there was an unwritten rule that neither aircraft was to use the other as a practice target during such encounters, since the price of an accidental shootdown provoked by the actions of some hothead could be all too steep. Hence the tail guns of the Soviet bombers would be in the fully up position as a sign that the crew had no hostile intentions.

6 Beyond the Sound Barrier

In spite of the high priority allocated to missile systems in the Soviet Union in the late 1950s and early 1960s, aircraft design was not altogether neglected and progress was being made. The principal Soviet long-range jet bomber – the Tu-16 – was in need of a replacement, a supersonic aircraft that would be equally suitable for the bomber, reconnaissance, missile carrier and ECM roles. The Tupolev OKB took on the task, and the result was the Tu-22 ('aircraft 105A'); powered by two Dobrynin VD-7M afterburning turbofans, the first Soviet supersonic bomber entered flight test in 1958, attaining a top speed of 1,600 km/h (994 mph) and a range of 5,800 km (3,603 miles). Tu-22 production took place at the Kazan' aircraft factory No. 22 in 1960-69, the production run amounting to 311 aircraft in reconnaissance, bomber, missile carrier, ECM and trainer versions. More than 50% of the Tu-22s left the factory with an IFR probe allowing them to work with 3MS-2/3MN-2 and Tu-16N hose-and-drogue tankers.

In 1961 the Soviet government took the decision to hold a major air parade at Moscow-Tushino in July; the participating aircraft were to include the first ten Tu-22s. However, by the spring of 1961 only five Tupolev OKB pilots and another three test pilots at GNIKI VVS had received their type ratings on the bomber; therefore it was decided to train three Long-Range Aviation pilots to fly the type as a matter of urgency. In May 1961 Lt.-Col. V. S. Vakhnov (the DA's Senior Inspector of Combat Training), Maj. V. S. Nikerin (the Senior Instructor Pilot of the DA's 43rd Combat Training & Conversion Training Centre) and Col. A. I. Bolysov (deputy CO of the 203rd TBAP). Since the Tu-22U conversion trainer (*oo***cheb***nyy* [*samo***lyot**] – trainer) did not exist at the time, an unusual technique was chosen: after a series of ground training sessions in the cockpit the pilots would fly solo straight away, while the instructor would fly chase in a fighter throughout the sortie and give them instructions on the radio as required. Test Pilot 1st Class Eduard V. Yelian was the main coach of the first Long-Range Aviation pilots transitioning to the Tu-22. Bolysov made his first solo flight in the Tu-22 on 18th May 1961, followed a day later by Vakhnov and Nikerin.

The training proceeded quickly and was completed in time for the first ten production Tu-22s to appear over Tushino on 9th July. Merited Test Pilot Aleksandr D. Kalina flew the lead aircraft; it was followed by three vics of three bombers. Of these, the first three aircraft were flown by other Tupolev OKB test pilots, the second trio by GNIKI VVS test pilots and the final trio by DA pilots. After this the Tu-22 received the NATO reporting name *Blinder*.

A fine study of an IFR-capable Tu-22RD reconnaissance aircraft.

For the successful mastering of the Tu-22 and their participation in the 1961 Tushino flypast Vakhnov, Bolysov and Nikerin were awarded the Red Star Order; their navigators/radar operators received the Combat Service Medal.

The Tu-22's service introduction was difficult and required a lot of hard work. Lots of design flaws and manufacturing defects surfaced in the course of evaluation, causing flight operations to be suspended frequently – sometimes for lengthy periods, while the problem was identified and eliminated. For example, in 1965 the Tu-22 fleet was grounded almost throughout the year while modification work was in progress; in the meantime, the crews had to fly the old Tu-16s in order to maintain proficiency.

Early operational experience with the Tu-22 in first-line units showed that it was impossible to do without a dual-control trainer version. The Tupolev OKB accelerated the development of the Tu-22U *Blinder-D* trainer; in the meantime a specialised design bureau in Leningrad created the KTS-22 flight simulator (***kom**pleksnyy trena**zhor** samo**lyo**ta* – integrated aircraft simulator).

The first Tu-22 *Blinder-A* bombers and Tu-22R *Blinder-C* reconnaissance aircraft were delivered to the Long-Range Aviation's operational units in 1962. The bomber units operating the type included the 203rd TBAP in Baranovichi, Belorussia, which had the distinction of being the first service unit to operate the *Blinder*.

A Tu-22KD is refuelled by a Tu-16N tanker.

This view of a *Blinder-C* shows well the Tu-22's sleek lines and area-ruled fuselage.

New operational techniques were developed and tested in parallel with the type's service introduction. On 14th June 1963 a Tu-22 flown by Merited Military Pilot Col. V. S. Vakhnov made the first experimental bomb drop at supersonic speed. Subsequently this bomb delivery technique was included into the combat training plan of first-line units.

The Tu-22R saw service with the DA's independent long-range reconnaissance regiments – the 121st ODRAP (*ot**del'**nyy **dahl'**niy raz**ved**yvatel'nyy **a**via**polk***) at Machoolishchi AB near Minsk, the 290th ODRAP at Zyabrovka AB (both in Belorussia) and the 199th GvODRAP at Nezhin (the Ukraine). Re-equipment was hampered by slow deliveries, and the 290th ODRAP's Tu-16Rs were finally phased out only in 1965. The 199th GvODRAP commanded by Guards Col. A. S. Yerokhin began training in July 1964 and completed conversion to the Tu-22R by early 1967.

On 14th October 1964 a 'quiet *coup d'état*' took place in the Soviet Union; at a session of the Communist Party Central Committee the Soviet leader Nikita S. Khrushchov was divested of his power as First Secretary of the Central Committee. Instead,

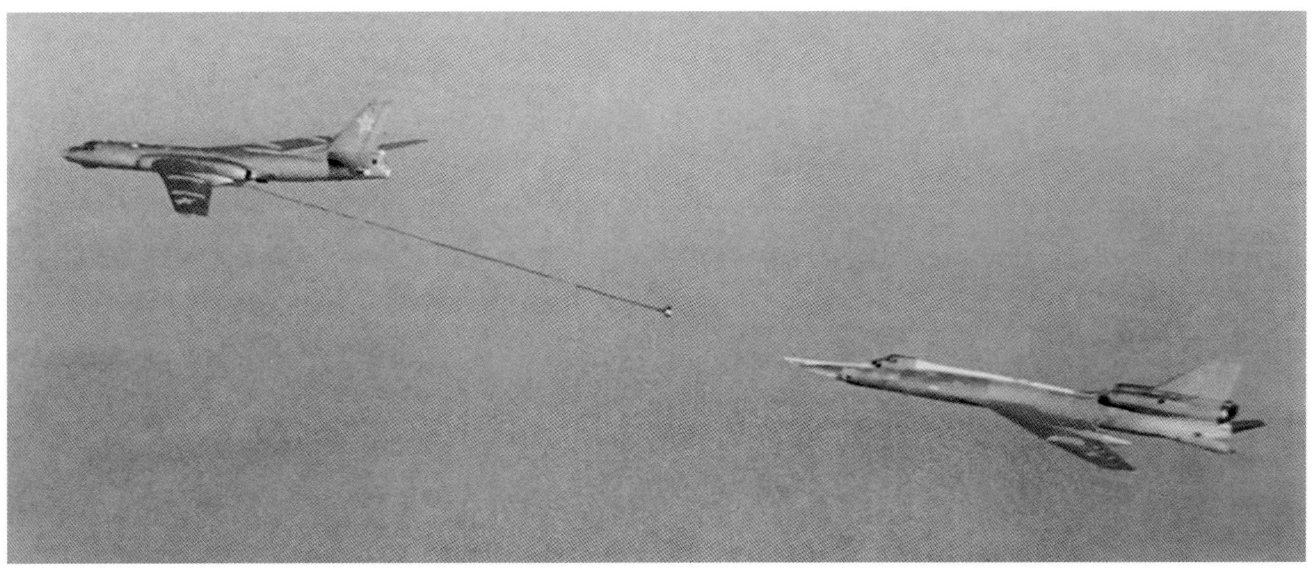

A Tu-22UD trainer approaches a Tu-16N tanker.

The nose of an upgraded Tu-22RDK. Note the K-22 ejection seats which act as crew lifts for embarkation and disembarkation.

The same Tu-22RDK undergoing maintenance. The cheek fairings characteristic of this version house SRS-10 Koob-3 ELINT gear, hence the K suffix.

Leonid I. Brezhnev was elected First Secretary (later becoming General Secretary). He pursued a more hard-line course than his predecessor, and a strong military lobby came to power together with him. This inevitably brought about a change both in the Soviet Union's foreign policy, which became tougher and more warlike, and in the government's attitude towards the nation's armed forces – including the Air Force. An era of unlimited military spending began.

In the second half of the 1960s the regiments operating bomber and recce variants of the *Blinder* began receiving the Tu-22K missile strike version carrying a single Kh-22 (AS-4 *Kitchen*) ASM with a launch range of 310 km (192 miles). In so doing the 121st ODRAP changed its specialisation in 1966, becoming the 121st DBAP and passing on the Tu-22Rs to Zyabrovka and Nezhin. Apart from the above-mentioned units at Baranovichi and Machoolishchi, the Tu-22K saw service with

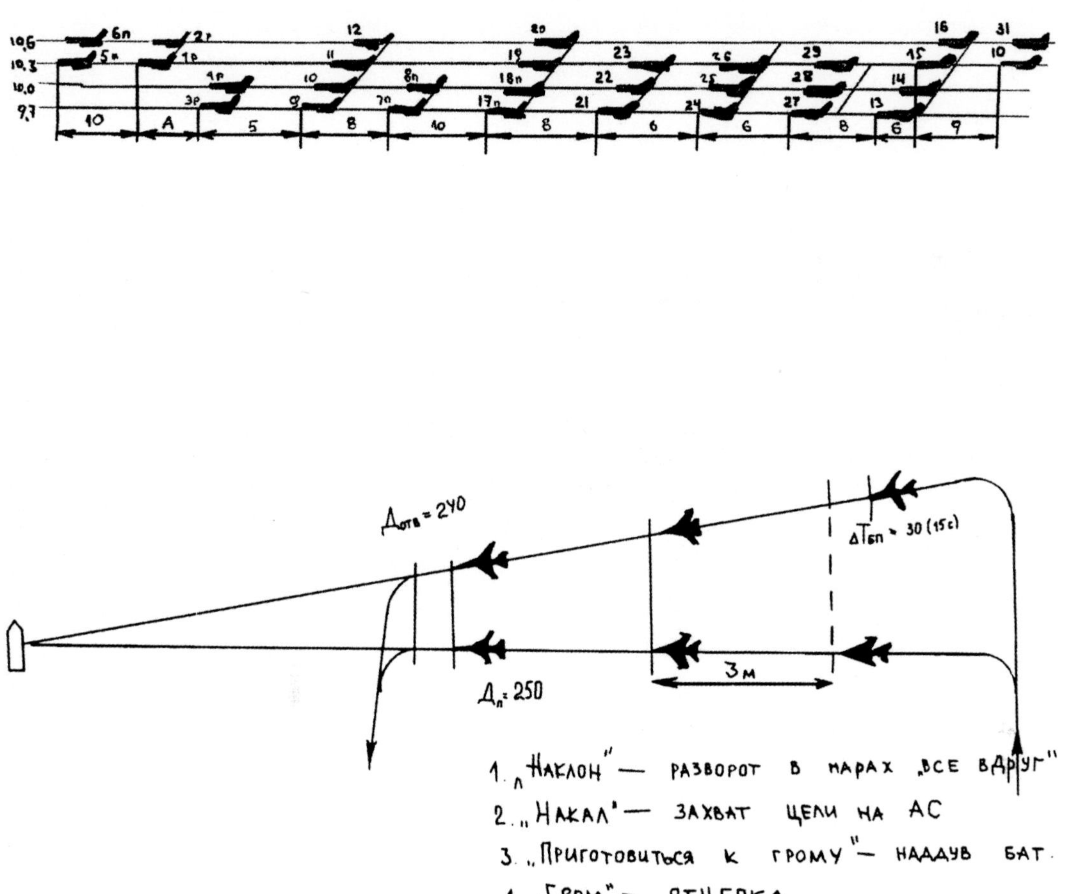

This drawing shows how a regiment of Tu-22Ks was to attack a NATO carrier group. Four strike groups (including recce and ECM aircraft) plus two pairs of aircraft decoying the air defences were to fly at varying altitudes (9,700-10,600 m/31,820-34,880 ft) with time intervals of 3 minutes. Coded commands were transmitted: *Na**klon*** (Tilt) for the pairs of bombers to turn simultaneously onto the target heading; *Na**kal*** (Incandescence) for target lock-on; *Prigo**tov**it'sya k **gro**mu* (Prepare for thunder) for pressurising the Kh-22 missile's DC batteries (which was part of the pre-launch procedure) and *Grom* (Thunder) for the actual launch. After launch the Tu-22Ks would turn away while 240-250 km (150-155 miles) from the target.

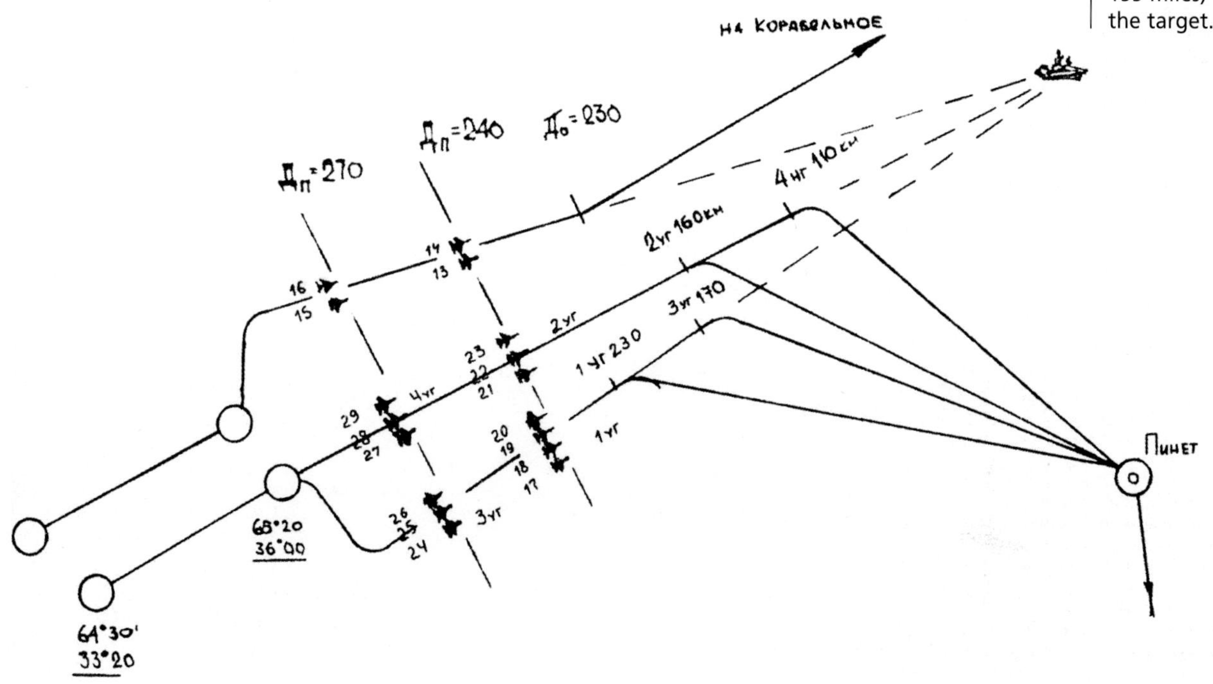

A Tu-22RD cruises at high altitude.

Maintenance in progress on a Tu-22PD ECM aircraft. The dragon nose art is noteworthy.

A pair of Tu-22RDs in echelon port formation.

the 341st TBAP at Ozyornoye AB near Zhitomir in the Ukraine, which re-equipped in 1968.

In addition to two squadrons of Tu-22K (Tu-22KD) missile carriers, each regiment had a squadron of Tu-22P (Tu-22PD) *Blinder-E* aircraft equipped with various ECM suites; their mission was to provide collective ECM cover for missile carrier formations. Each squadron usually had 10 to 12 aircraft, later augmented by a pair of Tu-22U/UD trainers. Some of the Tu-22RD reconnaissance aircraft were refitted with more up-to-date mission equipment in the early 1980s and redesignated Tu-22RDM. Other updated examples were designated Tu-22RK (Tu-22RDK); here, the K did not mean ***kom****pleks* [*vo'oru****zhen****iya*] (weapons system), as in the case of the missile carriers, but alluded to the SRS-10 *Koob-3* (Cube) ELINT suite.

A Tu-22RDM completes the landing run, showing the ventral equipment pannier.

A Tu-22RDM takes off in full afterburner.

A standard Tu-22R in flight.

A Tu-22PD ECM aircraft takes off past several sister ships.

In 1967 a formation of Tu-22Ks carrying Kh-22 missiles represented the Long-Range Aviation at the grand air show staged at Moscow-Domodedovo airport on 9th July. The lead aircraft escorted by six Mikoyan/Gurevich MiG-21 *Fishbed* fighters was piloted by Gen. I. V. Gorbunov, Commander of the 2nd OTBAK. It was followed by more *Blinders* representing the 203rd TBAP (commanded by Lt.-Col. A. N. Volkov) and the 341st TBAP (commanded by Lt.-Col. V. V. Chesnokov).

By late 1967 the Tu-22 was fully operational, with 145 aircraft in service with the DA – nearly twice as many as operated by the Soviet Navy. Tu-22s served alongside Tu-16s rather than replacing them – both types soldiered on side by side into the early 1990s. As of 1967, DA *Blinders* were based as follows:

A Tu-22RDM with a UKhO tail fairing housing ECM equipment at Dyagilevo AB, Ryazan'.

Day PHOTINT cameras fitted to a Tu-22R (front to rear: two AFA-42/20s, two AFA-42/75s and two AFA-42/100s).

Long-Range Aviation Tu-22 fleet in 1967

Base	Aircraft on strength
Baranovichi	30
Zyabrovka AB	24
Machoolishchi AB	24
Dyagilevo AB (training)	7
Nezhin	24
Ozyornoye AB	31
Vozdvizhenka AB	5

The Far East Military District got 'left out' when it came to distributing the *Blinders*. A handful of bomber crews from Vozdvizhenka AB headed by V. V. Gonchenko took their training at Kazan' and proudly flew five Tu-22s back home. But in the late 1960s the top brass in Moscow decided it was more expedient to keep the type on the European theatre of operations, and the bombers were taken away, forcing the units stationed in the Far East to make do with old Tu-16s.

As of 1st January 1969, 257 of the 295 Tu-22s completed by then were in service, including 114 Tu-22Rs, 66 Tu-22Ks, 22 Tu-22P-1s, and 33 Tu-22P-2s and Tu-22Us. Of this total, 179 aircraft were operated by the DA. 24 aircraft had been written off in

A pair of Tu-22KD missile carriers taxies out for take-off.

accidents and 14 more were in use as ground instructional airframes.

In the spring of 1968, disillusionment with the communist regime had led to unrest in Czechoslovakia. As it had done 12 years earlier in Hungary, the Soviet government chose to stomp out the mutiny by military force before the country had a chance to break away from the Soviet bloc, and a Soviet military task force took control of Czechoslovakia. The Long-Range Aviation participated in the invasion as well; no bomber sorties were flown but the 226th OAPREB equipped with Tu-22PD ECM aircraft gave ECM support to the operations of other military units.

Experiments with new operational techniques continued. On 21st November 1968 a Tu-22 with a 43rd Training Centre crew captained by Col. V. S. Vakhnov made the first take-off using jet-assisted take-off (JATO) boosters at Dyagilevo AB. The four SPRD-63 solid-fuel boosters (***star****tovyy* *porokho***voy**

A Tu-22KPD is prepared for a mission, with a Kh-22 missile in the process of being hooked up.

Front view of a Tu-22UD trainer.

*ra**ket**nyy **dvig**atel'*) suspended under the wings were ignited halfway through the take-off run, shortening it considerably; the terrific flames produced by the boosters left a lasting impression on everyone involved in the tests. After burnout the boosters were jettisoned over the designated area. A second rocket-boosted take-off followed on 11th December. Lt.-Gen. S. K. Biryukov, the training centre's Deputy Chief (Combat Training), was in charge of the test programme.

After a brief pause the tests resumed in January 1969. The objective was now to check the take-off performance with two JATO boosters instead of four and determine the peculiarities, if any, of the landing procedure with the boosters in place, should they fail to separate after burnout. After one such flight with two boosters the test commission discovered with dismay that a skin panel adjacent to a flexible fuel tank had burned clean through. It turned out that the igniter of the port booster had popped like a cork from a champagne bottle and the escaping powder gases had burned through the wing skin; only sheer luck had averted an in-flight fire. The commission ruled that all SPRD-63 boosters were to be checked and modified to prevent a recurrence; using them in as-was condition was out of the question. Thus the idea of using JATO boosters on the Tu-22 (and on other heavy aircraft, for that matter) was abandoned.

Also in January 1969, Col.-Gen. Vasiliy V. Reshetnikov was appointed the new Commander of the Long-Range Aviation.

When IFR-capable versions identified by the D suffix reached the operational units, Tu-22 pilots were in for a hard time when it came to learning in-flight refuelling techniques. 'Hitting the tanker' demanded excel-

Another aspect of the same trainer, showing the stepped-tandem cockpits. Note the nose art.

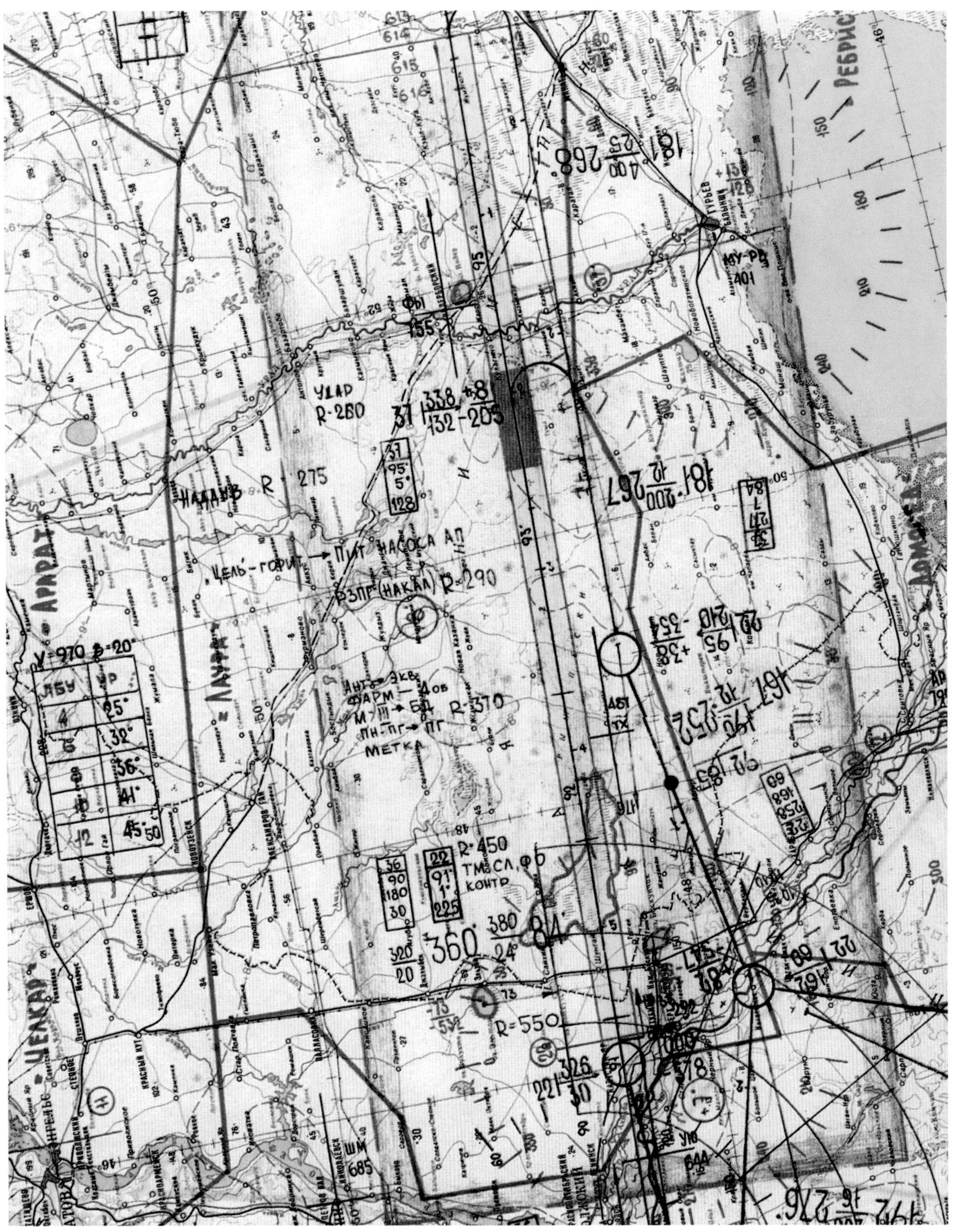

A typical tactical map showing the area where a Tu-22K unit is to perform a live missile launch at a training range (in this case, Range 600 in Kazakhstan).

lent airmanship and called for a lot of training. A typical IFR session looked like this. A probe-equipped Tu-22 flying at 5,000-8,000 m (16,400-26,250 ft) and maintaining a speed of 600 km/h (372 mph) assumed line astern formation with a Tu-16N, coming within 50 m (164 ft) of the tanker. Then the *Blinder* slipped back, and when the horizontal separation increased to 150 m (490 ft) the pilot started the run-in, trying to spear the tanker's drogue with his probe. Trying to execute this operation as cleanly as possible, the Tu-22 pilot often inadvertently opened the throttles, increasing the closing speed. The last 10 m (33 ft) or so before contact was made were a nerve-racking experience as the pilot watched the black blob of the drogue growing rapidly before his eyes, seemingly about to hit him in the face. Lack of concentration and/or a steady hand meant the Tu-22 would overshoot and it was necessary to take urgent evasive action, turning right and diving to avoid to avoid hitting the tanker literally, then start all over again. 'Green' Tu-22 pilots required as much as 400-450 km (250-280 miles), or even more, to complete the refuelling, and some would not manage to make contact at all, which meant the mission had to be aborted.

In the 1970s a more effective technique was devised in the 199th ODRAP, then commanded by V. L. Konstantinov. Assuming echelon starboard formation with the Tu-16N, the aircraft would move into line astern formation so that the probe would be almost even with the drogue and about 5 m (16 ft) to starboard of it. The Tu-22 pilot would equalise the speed and reduce the lateral separation with the drogue to 1.5-2 m (5-6.5 ft). Maintaining this position relative to the drogue, he would then radio to the tanker pilot, 'I'm making contact'. Increasing power, the Tu-22 pilot then began a gentle side-slip; when the drogue was straight ahead of him he would 'fire' the telescopic probe and make contact, allowing fuel transfer to begin.

As of 1st January 1975, the Tu-22 force had shrunk only slightly, with 221 in service. That year 12 Tu-22Rs were converted to Tu-22B bombers and exported to Iraq, along with a couple of Tu-22UDs; another squadron of second-hand bombers was supplied to Libya in 1976.

About 200 *Blinders* remained active in the 1980s, but the numbers dwindled steadily. 196 Tu-22s of all models were still airworthy in 1986, 195 in 1987, 190 in 1988, 187 in 1989, 182 in 1990 and 181 in 1991 when the Soviet Union ceased to exist. As of 1st January 1992, the Tu-22 fleet in the CIS republics (excluding the naval examples) looked like this:

CIS Tu-22 fleet as per 1st January 1992

Unit	Location	On strength
199th GvODRAP	Nezhin, Ukraine	26
341st TBAP	Ozyornoye AB, Zhitomir, Ukraine	30
290th GvODRAP	Zyabrovka AB, Gomel', Belorussia	30
203rd TBAP	Baranovichi, Belorussia	32
121st TBAP	Machoolishchi AB, Minsk, Belorussia	34

In early 1992 the Tu-22 units based in Belorussia were placed under Russian jurisdiction. That same year the 290th GvODRAP received all of the Baltic Fleet's remaining Tu-22Rs as the 15th ORAP operating them re-equipped with Su-24MR *Fencer-E* tactical ELINT aircraft. (It may be mentioned that two years later the units at Zyabrovka, Machoolishchi and Baranovichi were disbanded and the aircraft moved to the DA's air maintenance unit at Engels-2 AB for storage and eventual disposal.

The Tu-22R quickly earned the nickname ***sheelo*** (Awl) because of its sharply pointed silhouette. Flying the *sheelo* turned out to be a challenge, as take-off and approach speed was greater than the Tu-16's and cockpit visibility was poor. The very basic KTS-22 simulator was of little help since it could not simulate take-off and landing – the hardest part of the job. The Tu-22U took some time coming; the 199th GvODRAP received its trainers when the crews were already well versed in flying techniques.

At first the Tu-22 was definitely not a 'pilot's airplane' and called for a lot of muscle. Two sorties a day were more than enough for even the brawniest pilot if you flew manually (without engaging the autopilot). Holding the control wheel with one hand was out of the question – the stick forces were just too high.

Landing was a rather complicated procedure. The flight manual strictly forbade lowering the approach speed below 290 km/h (180 mph), otherwise the aircraft would pitch up sharply into a vertical position and do a tail-slide – with fatal results. Also, the Tu-22 was notoriously prone to bouncing on landing when one of the main gear bogies would start

A navigational chart showing the routes flown by 290th ODRAP Tu-22Rs from Zyabrovka AB over the Black Sea. Note the clearly marked boundary of Turkey's coastal waters.

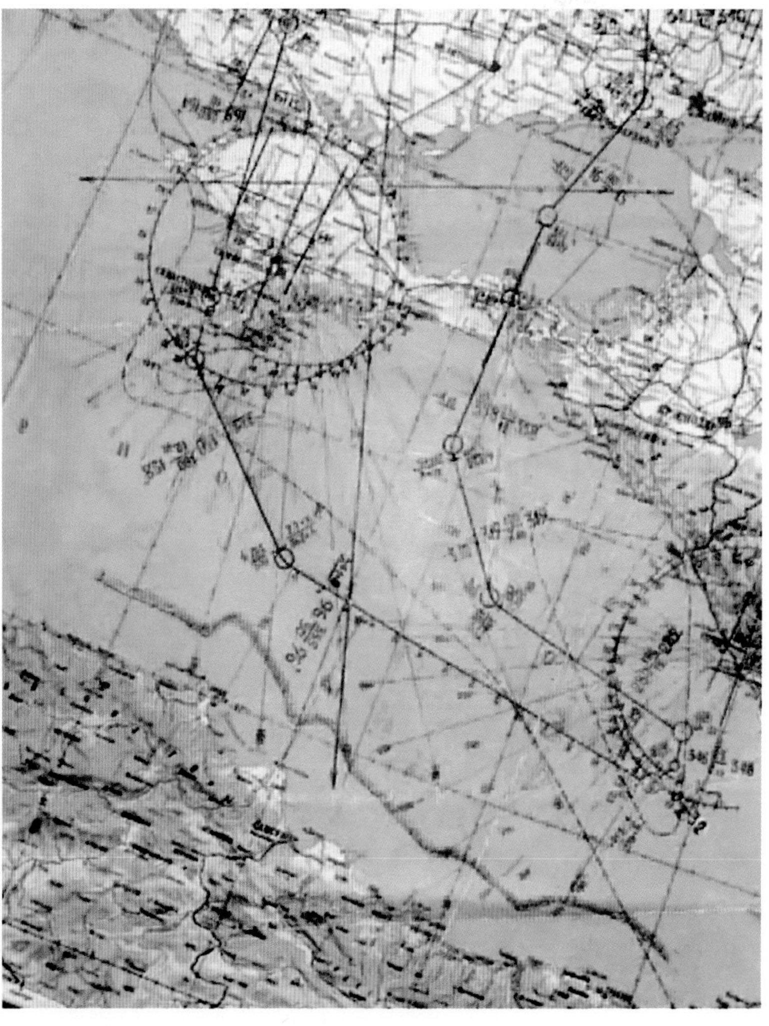

Three-quarters rear view of a Tu-22UD, which had neither a tail barbette nor an UKhO ECM fairing.

'galloping' – rocking wildly to and fro, making contact alternately with the front and rear wheels. This caused violent vibration and sometimes the affected main gear unit would collapse. The aircraft then slewed off the runway and the nose gear collapsed, causing the fuselage nose to cave in. Usually only the navigator got hurt in such crash landings – unless, of course, the aircraft collided with buildings or parked aircraft.

Cockpit ergonomics were poor, and reaching the necessary switches could be a problem in the cramped cockpits. The pilot's seat was slightly offset to port, affording the pilot pretty good downward visibility in the left front quadrant. However, in a left crosswind when the aircraft had to crab into the wind during approach, the pilot found that the canopy frame blocked his forward view entirely. Hence inexperienced Tu-22 pilots were barred from

Four stored Tu-22Rs and Tu-22RDs at a dispersal area.

An elderly Tu-22 is broken up with the help of a special cutter.

flying in crosswinds in excess of 12 m/sec (24 kts). The navigator's field of view was also extremely limited, while the gunner had to rely entirely on his radarscope. Thus, the Tu-22's NATO reporting name *Blinder* was oddly appropriate.

Generally the Tu-22 flew well; it was stable almost throughout its flight envelope and CG range. Still, there were some handling peculiarities which the pilot had to keep in mind. The aircraft displayed reverse roll reaction at speeds above Mach 1.1 (applying right rudder would cause the aircraft to roll left instead of right). Above Mach 1.4 the Tu-22 tended to drop a wing, which had to be compensated by aileron input. Since early aircraft suffered from aileron reversal at Mach 1.4, this was the maximum speed allowed in service until changes were made to the control system. At low speed the Tu-22 would pitch down sharply when engine power was increased because of the high thrust line. All this called for new

Row upon row of retired Tu-22s sit at a storage depot, awaiting scrapping.

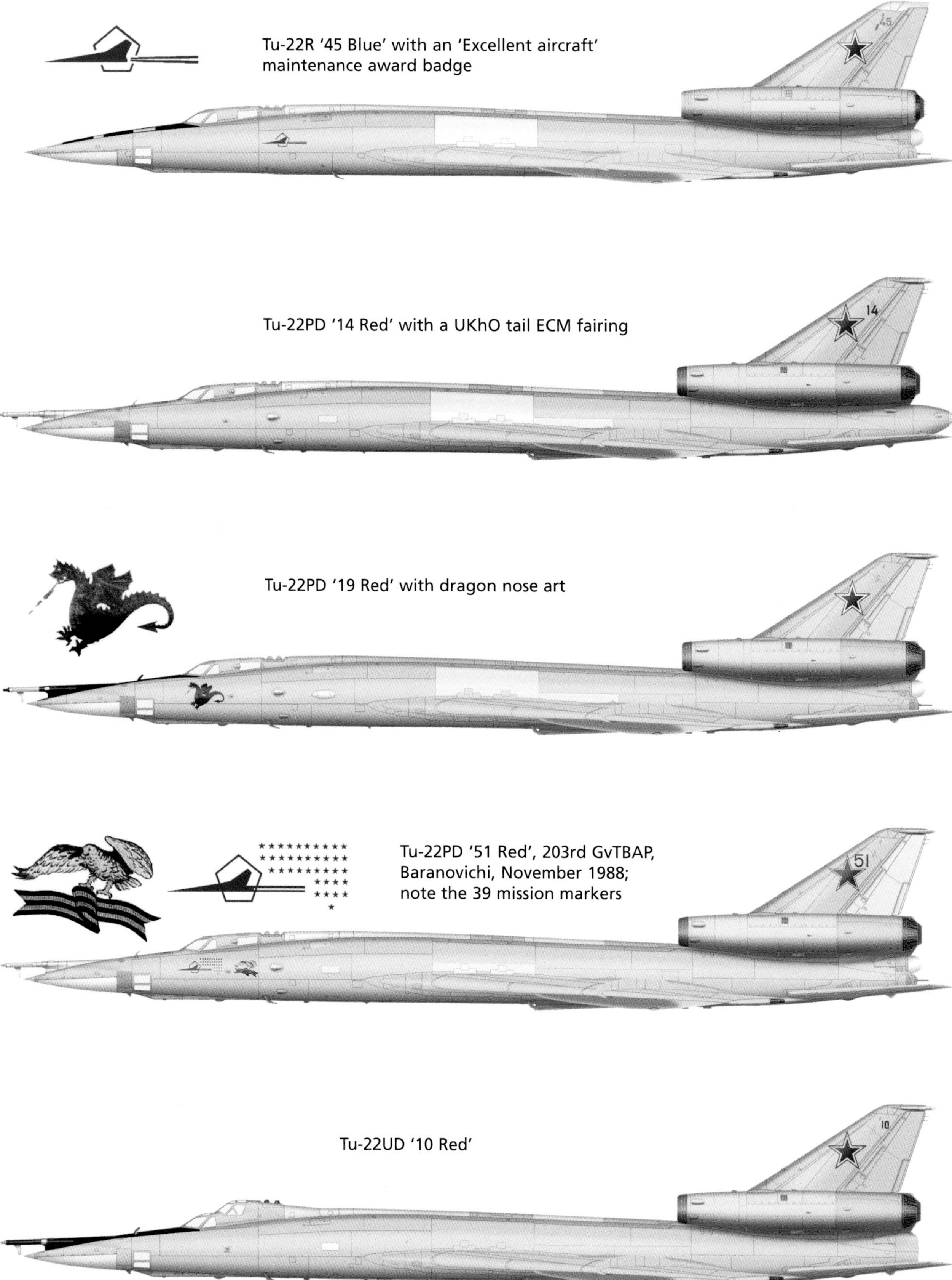

Tu-22R '45 Blue' with an 'Excellent aircraft' maintenance award badge

Tu-22PD '14 Red' with a UKhO tail ECM fairing

Tu-22PD '19 Red' with dragon nose art

Tu-22PD '51 Red', 203rd GvTBAP, Baranovichi, November 1988; note the 39 mission markers

Tu-22UD '10 Red'

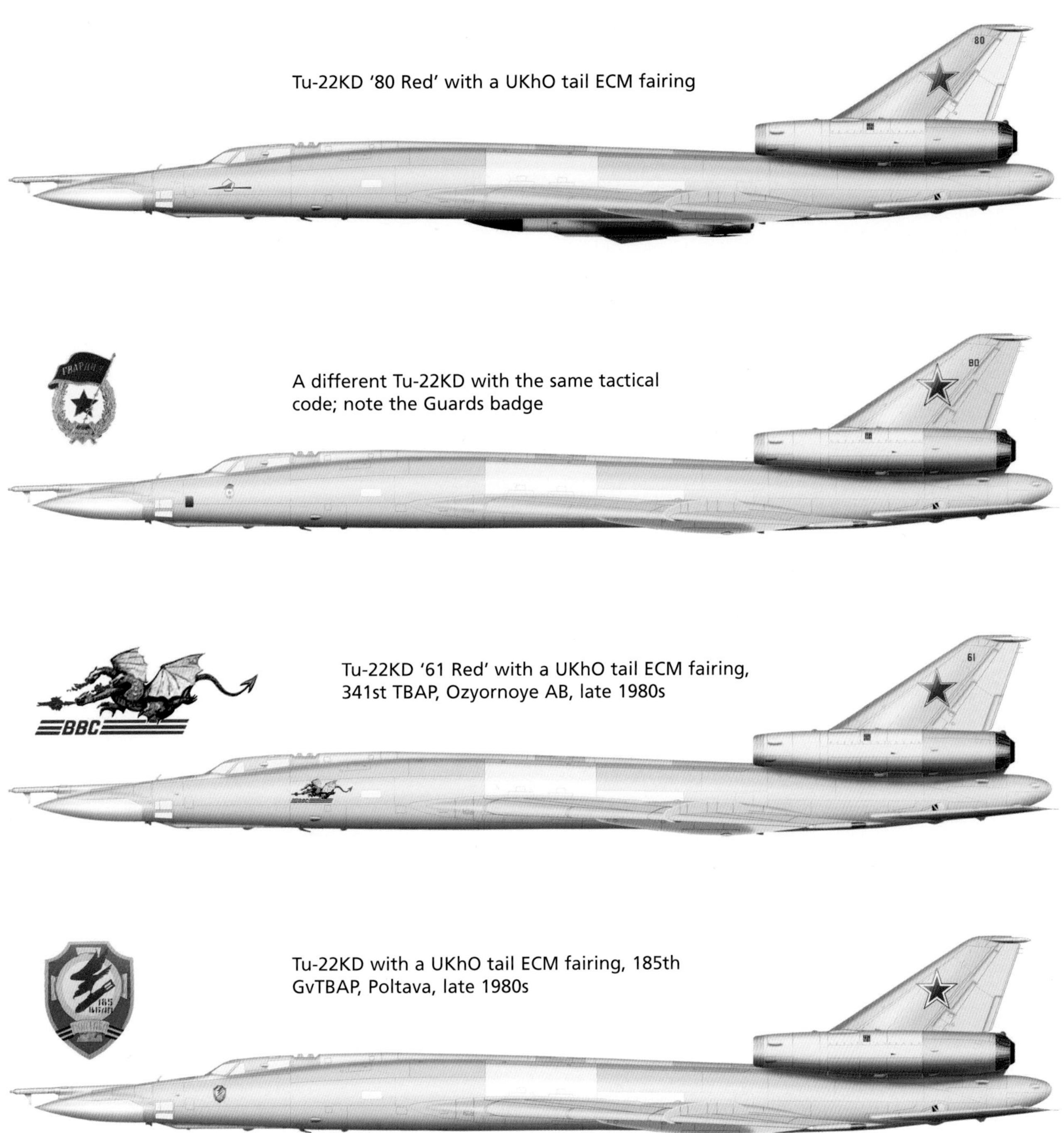

Tu-22KD '80 Red' with a UKhO tail ECM fairing

A different Tu-22KD with the same tactical code; note the Guards badge

Tu-22KD '61 Red' with a UKhO tail ECM fairing, 341st TBAP, Ozyornoye AB, late 1980s

Tu-22KD with a UKhO tail ECM fairing, 185th GvTBAP, Poltava, late 1980s

training techniques and great care in flying the aircraft.

The *Blinder* gave the technical staff a tough time, too. For one thing, bases had to be rebuilt (especially parking areas had to be expanded), and new ground handling and support equipment that went with the Tu-22 had to be mastered. For another, the Tu-22 was maintenance-heavy and the multi-point gravity refuelling procedure used originally was extremely troublesome. Improvements introduced during the type's service career, including single-point pressure refuelling, eased the maintenance workload.

The numerous problems associated with the type's service introduction and the frequent (and sometimes critical) systems failures caused the Tu-22 to be regarded as a royal pain in the butt by its aircrews and ground crews at the opening stage of its career. Eventually, however, the persistent work of the Tupolev OKB, the manufacturers and the Air

Force bore fruit. Reliability was improved dramatically and many typical defects eliminated, and the Tu-22 became more like the deadly weapon it was meant to be.

Between 1969 and 1991, 56 Soviet Air Force Tu-22s were written off in accidents. Most of the accidents occurred during the first 10 to 15 years of service. Some aircraft were lost by sheer bad luck or due to the negligence of ground personnel. For example, in August 1966 a fighter landing at Ozyornoye AB veered off the runway, crashing into a parked Tu-22, and both aircraft were destroyed by the ensuing fire.

Being designed as a day bomber, originally the Tu-22 lacked equipment for night flying. Yet night sorties were part of the plan. Sometimes the risk paid off; sometimes it didn't. In July 1969 two 199th GvODRAP Tu-22Rs collided in mid-air over their home base as they came in to land after a night training sortie. The crew of the lead aircraft ejected safely, as did the pilot of the other bomber (the navigator and gunner/radio operator were killed as the uncontrollable aircraft dived into the ground). Left to its own devices, the lead aircraft proceeded towards the city of Nezhin. Fighters were scrambled to intercept and destroy the runaway Tu-22 but no one would give the order to fire, fearing that the aircraft would drop on a heavily-populated area. Finally, 52 minutes later the machine fell into a swamp without causing any further damage.

Some accidents happened for seemingly no logical reason. In April 1976 one of six FotAB-250-215 flare bombs exploded in the bomb bay of a Tu-22RD as it was dropped, causing the aircraft to break in two. The crew ejected but the navigator lost his life, ejecting below minimum altitude; he had released his seat belts in order to be more comfortable using the bombsight, and it took him too long to refasten them. Test drops were made at GNIKI VVS to investigate the matter. Tragically, one of these resulted in an identical accident when the bombs blew the aircraft apart, and the controversial flare bomb was promptly withdrawn.

The Tu-22 proved to be a fairly rugged machine and could take a lot of punishment during high-speed low-level sorties – and that means the extra stress and strain on the airframe, as well as battle damage. In January 1984 a Tu-22R reached a speed of 1,000 km/h (621 mph) at 150 m (490 ft), exceeding all possible limits – and came home none the worse for wear.

Tu-22 crews averaged up to 100 flying hours per year; each crew had to log at least two hours of supersonic flying annually. Usually the Tu-22 cruised below Mach 1, making only a 10-minute supersonic dash over the

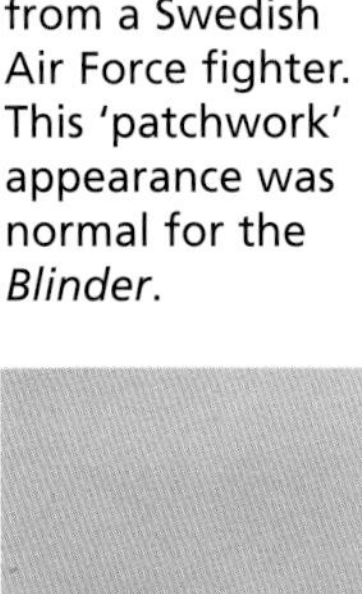

A Tu-22RD seen from a Swedish Air Force fighter. This 'patchwork' appearance was normal for the *Blinder*.

A pair of Tu-22KDs carrying Kh-22 missiles.

target; this included 60° rolls and bomb drops or missile launches.

For structural integrity reasons the Tu-22 was not allowed to go supersonic at low altitude; however, low-level flights at speeds close to Mach 1 were standard operational procedure. These sorties were a sore trial for the pilots since the Tu-22 was not equipped for automatic terrain following. The result was sometimes tragic; in April 1978 a Tu-22R flew into high ground at the Polesskoye training range during a low-level dash.

To avoid angering law-abiding citizens, supersonic flying was restricted to high altitude and sparsely-populated areas. Generally shock waves produced by high-flying supersonic aircraft die down before reaching the ground; one occasion in the early 1970s, however, made short work of this theory. There was some sort of atmospheric anomaly that

This Tu-22KD survived long enough to see Russian Air Force service.

A pre-production Tu-22M1 is refuelled by a 3MS-2. Note the multiple ejector racks with bombs on the wing hardpoints.

A probe-less Tu-22M2 formates with a tanker in a simulated refuelling.

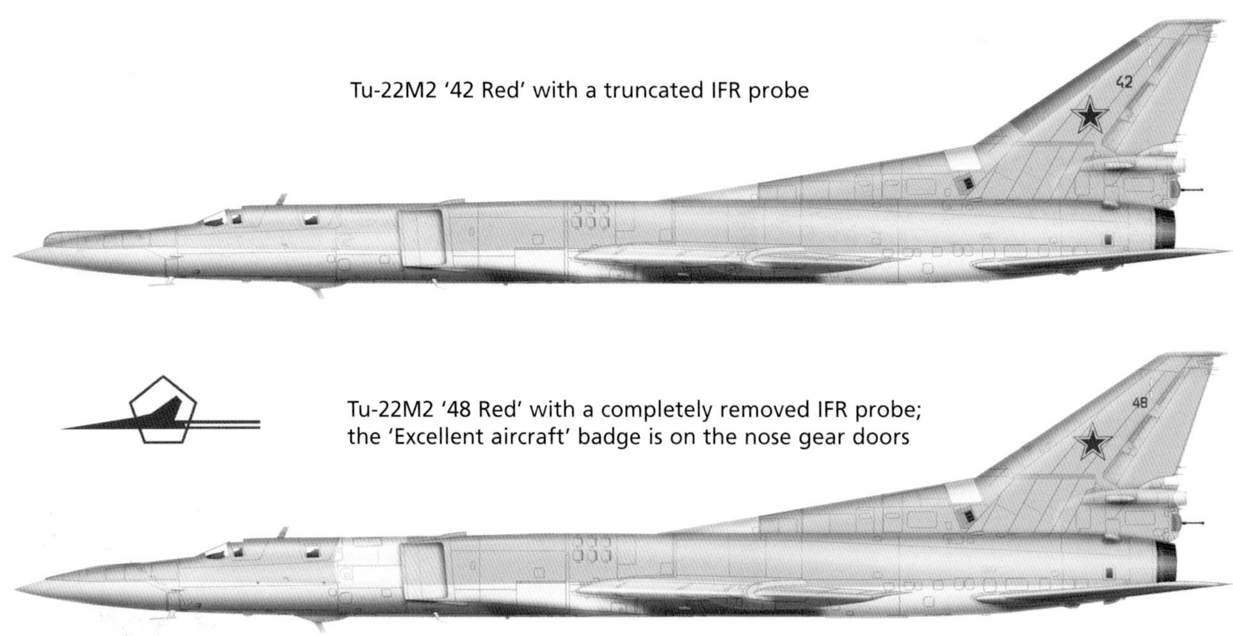
Tu-22M2 '42 Red' with a truncated IFR probe

Tu-22M2 '48 Red' with a completely removed IFR probe; the 'Excellent aircraft' badge is on the nose gear doors

day, and when a 199th GvODRAP Tu-22R overflew the Ukrainian city of Soomy at 11,000 m (36,090 ft) it created a tremendous sonic boom that shattered windows all over town. The place looked like a war zone!

Blinder units were assigned specific targets. In the event of war, Tu-22Ks supported by Tu-22P ECM aircraft were to take out NATO bases in Europe and US Navy 6th Fleet warships. In anti-shipping strike missions the bombers were to reach the Mediterranean flying over the Balkan Peninsula. Anti-shipping strike training was performed at a missile range in the north-eastern part of the Caspian Sea, using decommissioned warships as targets.

A Tu-22M2 with the wings at minimum sweep. Only one MER is fitted.

A *Backfire-B* is escorted by a US Navy F-14A.

Here a Tu-22M2 carrying a single Kh-22M is escorted by a Royal Norwegian Air Force F-16A.

Another view of the same aircraft, showing the missile more clearly.

The DA's Tu-22Rs were to reconnoitre NATO air defences, C³I (command, control, communications and intelligence) facilities and other land targets, track enemy warships and supply convoys, and perform damage assessment. The 199th GvODRAP was tasked with strategic reconnaissance in the West European theatre of operations (West Germany and Austria), South-Western TO (Greece, the Bosporus and the Marmara Sea) and Southern TO (the Black Sea, Turkey and Iran). The 290th ODRAP at Zyabrovka covered the Baltic Sea, the North-Western TO and even above the North Sea and Atlantic Ocean. The two units also flew training sorties in an easterly direction towards the Volga River and the Caspian Sea; geographically they were a 'mirror image' of 'the real thing'.

Missile strikes against carrier groups were considered the most dangerous of the wartime missions. Such a mission involved at least four Tu-22Rs, up to a regiment of Tu-22Ks and one or two squadrons of escort fighters. The Rs came first, identifying the aircraft carrier in the group. As they approached the target, two of them stayed at high altitude, jamming enemy radars and relaying intelligence until the strike group (including ECM aircraft) came up.

The other two descended and pressed on towards the target, skimming the sea at 100 m (330 ft) and trying to come within visual range of the target (10-15 km/6.2-9.3 miles). On sighting the carrier they radioed its coordinates to the Tu-22Ks which launched their missiles. Then things really got ugly for the Tu-22Rs, as they had to dodge anti-aircraft fire, not to mention the carrier's fighters. If the incoming Kh-22 missiles had nuclear warheads, getting far enough before the blast became a major problem. In a nutshell, it was *very* long odds for the Tu-22R crews.

In peacetime the mission was limited to photographing NATO ships and tracking their movements. NATO fighters scrambling to intercept the snoopers went to great lengths to drive the Russians off. A typical tactic was to come up underneath and obstruct the Tu-22's cameras' field of view. Sometimes the fighters would make dangerous manoeuvres, risking a mid-air collision.

The Tu-22R typically used a 'pin-prick technique', heading straight for the border and provoking the enemy air defences into revealing themselves. Having caused a commotion and recorded the radar and radio frequencies, the ferret aircraft made a U-turn some 20 km (12.3 miles) from the border and made for home.

Tu-22Rs were also used to 'harass' Soviet air defences during exercises. On one occasion in the late 1980s, a group of *Blinders* staged a major 'NATO air raid from bases in Turkey', following 16 predetermined avenues of approach to cover all of the Ukraine. The aircraft flew at low level, following rivers and the Black Sea coastline to escape radar detection. The result was shocking. Some aircraft slipped through unnoticed, others were 'destroyed' but not before they had penetrated deep into Soviet territory and 'done great damage'. Reprisal was swift: the chiefs of the southern air defence districts were removed.

The more difficult tasks facing Tu-22R crews included checking the tactical camouflage of own forces, the observability of camouflaged ICBM launch control centres and other military installations. For example, they searched for RS-12 ***Top****ol'* (Poplar; NATO SS-20) ICBMs on transporter/erector/launcher vehicles in the Ukraine and Belorussia and on 'Hell's Train' ICBM launchers disguised as boxcars in the suburbs of Moscow.

However, even though the Tu-22 remained in service long enough to see the demise of the Soviet Union, as early as the end of the 1960s it was obvious that the *Blinder* would not be able to replace the legendary *Badger* completely. Quite apart from the Tu-22's

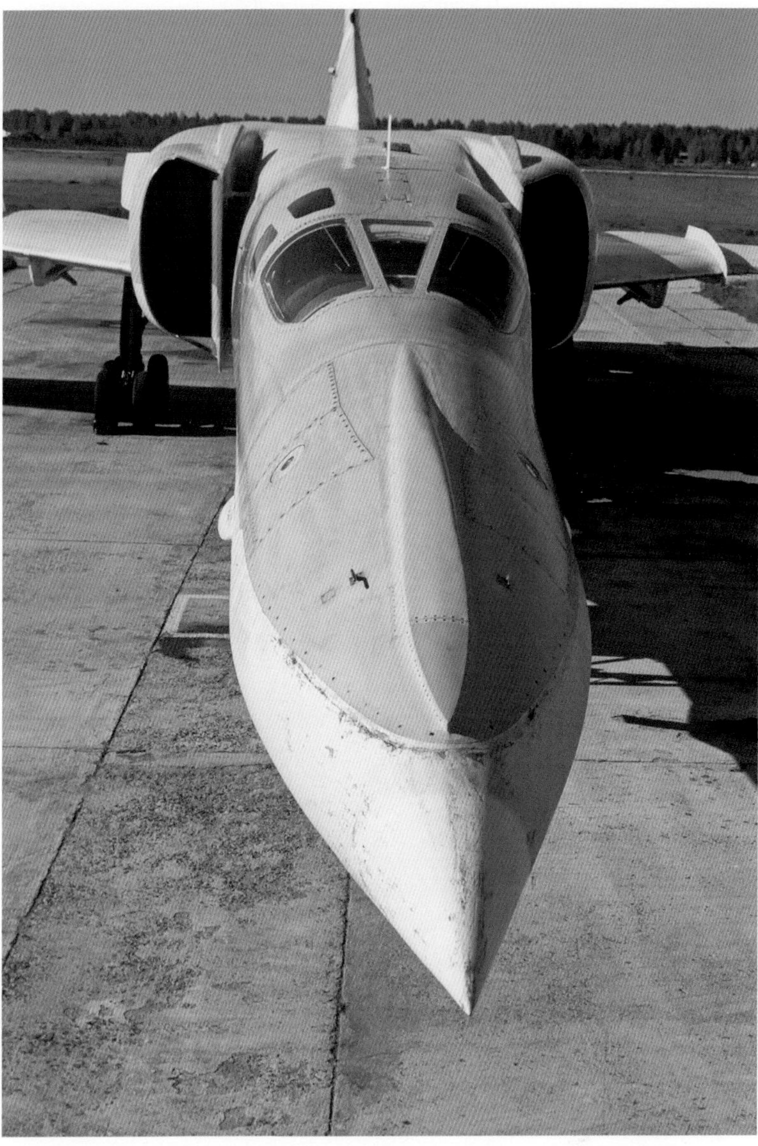

The shallow bulge on the nose of this Tu-22M2 is all that's left of the deleted IFR probe.

The Tu-22M2 often carried MERs under the air intake trunks. This is a 52nd GvTBAP machine at Shaikovka.

A rather weathered Tu-22M2; the paintwork on the cockpit section has not faded thanks to being under wraps most of the time. Note how the the stabilators assume a fully nose-down position when hydraulic power is off.

initially poor reputation caused by low reliability and high accident rate, the aircraft did not live up to the customer's expectations. The Air Force wanted higher performance and a true multi-mode aircraft able to operate efficiently at both subsonic and supersonic speeds.

The Tupolev OKB solved the problem by developing a long-range bomber with variable geometry wings and modern fuel-efficient afterburning turbofans. The original project ('aircraft 145') was derived from the Tu-22 ('aircraft 105A'), and even though the project was totally reworked in the course of development and the end result had virtually nothing in common with the *Blinder*, the new bomber was designated Tu-22M for political reasons (in order to win government support). The first of ten Tu-22M0 *Backfire-A* prototypes made its maiden flight on 30th August 1969; the other nine were manufactured by plant No. 22 in Kazan' in 1970-71. These aircraft and the nine Tu-22M1 pre-production machines (likewise known as the *Backfire-A*) built in 1971-72 with various improvements were used in the trials programme.

In particular, the DA's 43rd Combat Training & Aircrew Conversion Centre at Dyagilevo AB took delivery of two Tu-22M0 prototypes in February 1973, thus marking the beginning of the *Backfire*'s operational career. Incredibly perhaps, the aircrews and ground crews at Dyagilevo received their type ratings in just 20 days, though this was helped a lot by prior training at the Tupolev OKB, LII and the Kazan' plant.

Neither variant was found acceptable, and it was only the further improved third version, designated Tu-22M2 and codenamed *Backfire-B*, that entered mass production and service with the Long-Range Aviation. Powered by two Kuznetsov NK-22 afterburning turbofans, the Tu-22M2 could be used either as a bomber carrying up to 24 tons (52,910 lb) of free-fall bombs or as a missile carrier armed with up to three Kh-22M ASMs. Depending on the type of guidance system, the Kh-22M had a launch range of 310 to 500 km (192-310 miles). The Tu-22M2 had a maximum speed of 2,120 km/h (1,317 mph) and a range of 5,800 km (3,604 miles) on internal fuel, which could be extended by topping up the tanks from a 3MS-2 or Tu-16N tanker.

Incidentally, it was this IFR capability that triggered a major political crisis in the late 1970s when the second Soviet-US Strategic Arms Limitation Treaty (SALT 2) was being drafted. On learning of the *Backfire-B*'s IFR capability, US defence experts concluded that, with several fuel top-ups, the bomber was capable of reaching the USA and listed it as a strategic bomber, trying to have it included into the list of weapons systems subject to restrictions under the SALT treaty. Not wishing

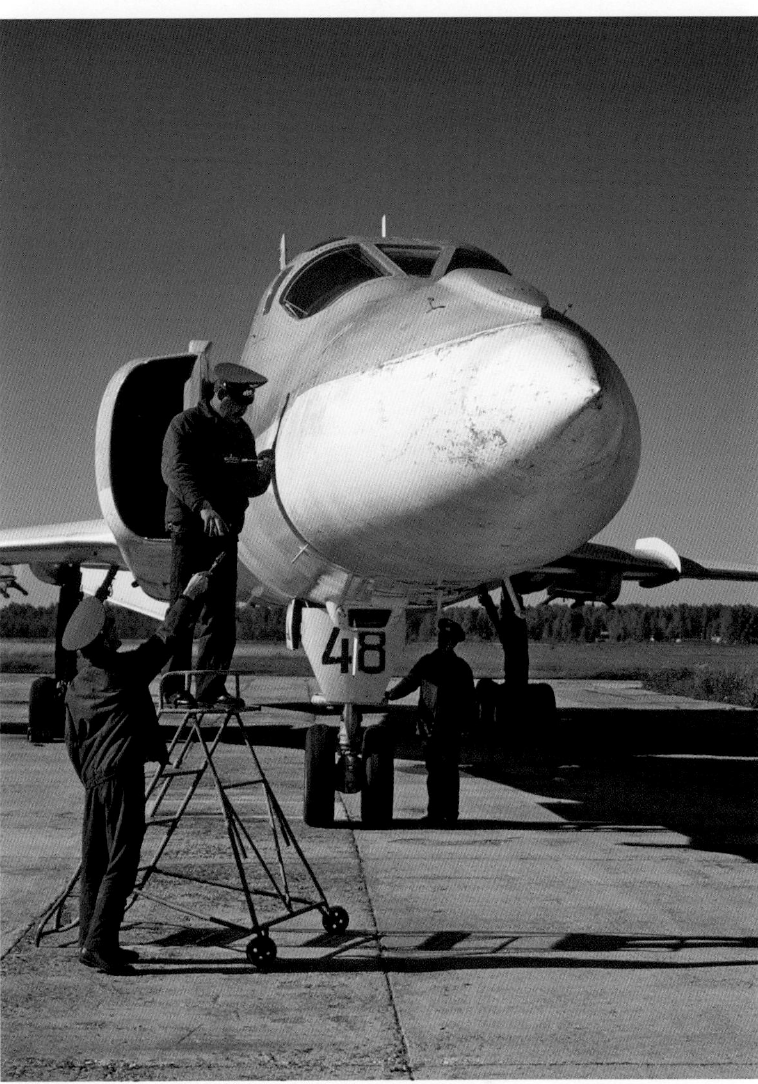

Minor maintenance of the same aircraft.

Side view of the *Backfire-B*'s ogival nose.

Another 52nd GvTBAP Tu-22M2 with the wings at maximum sweep.

Front view of the same aircraft.

The Tu-22M series had four upward-ejecting seats accessible through individual canopy doors and requiring tall platforms for boarding.

A Tu-22M2 in a snow-covered hardstand with canvas covers over the intakes.

to have unnecessary restrictions imposed on the number of Tu-22M2s, which were long-range bombers but not true strategic aircraft by any means, the Soviet side took the unconventional step of removing the IFR system from all operational *Backfires*. Little good did it do, though; the Americans insisted on having the Tu-22M included in the SALT 2 treaty.

Tu-22M2 production in Kazan' took place between 1973 and 1983; a total of 211 were built, serving with both the Air Force and the Navy. In the Long-Range Aviation, the first production-standard Tu-22M2s were delivered to the 43rd TsBP i PLS in the spring of 1974; a month later one of the Centre's crews made the first launch of a Kh-22 missile.

The first operational unit to receive the type was the 185th GvTBAP based at Poltava (the Ukraine) and operating the Tu-16. The unit's CO was none other than Lt.-Col. Pyotr S. Deynekin, who eventually rose to Colonel-General and became Commander of the DA and, later still, C-in-C of the Russian Air Force. The transition to the *Backfire* took place in 1974; the first two 'swing-wing' bombers arrived in July and three more in September, and conversion training went ahead quickly. In 1976 a group of 185th GvBAP Tu-22M2s

A Tu-22M2 at the training centre at Dyagilevo AB, Ryazan.

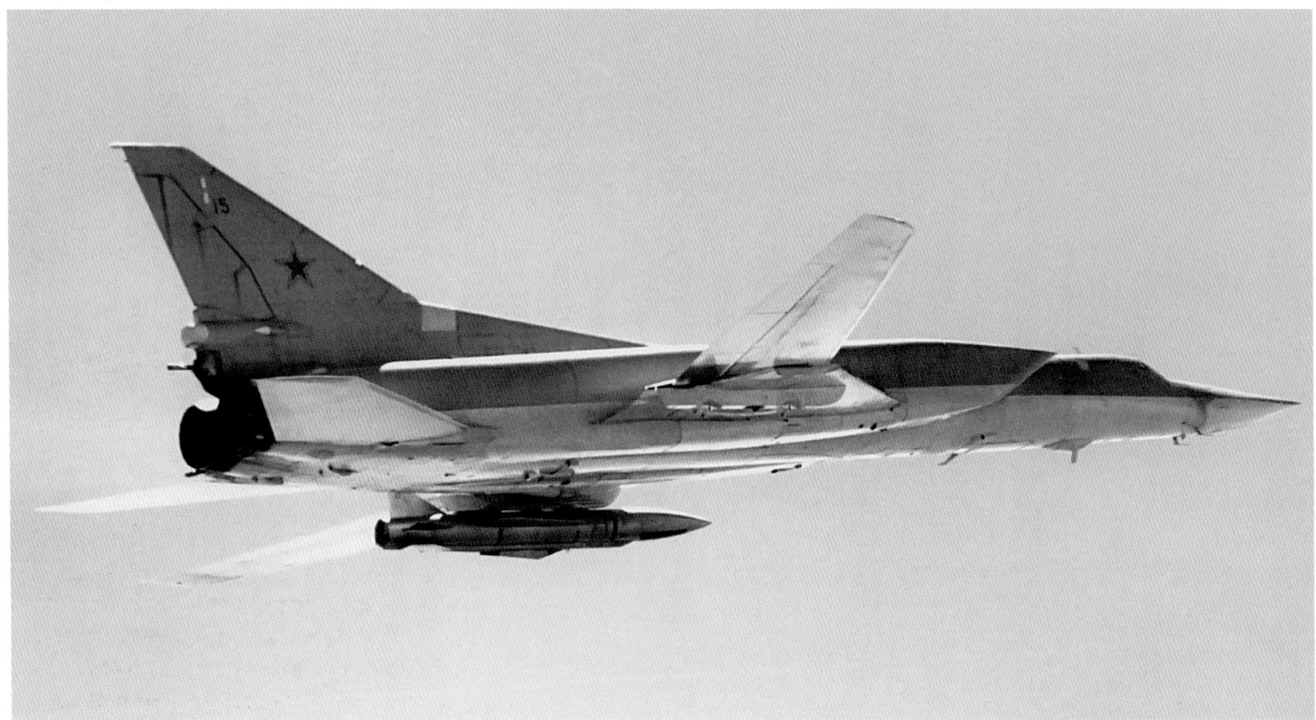

A Tu-22M3 with a single Kh-22PG missile under the port wing.

These *Backfire-Cs* each carry a single Kh-22MA.

demonstrated the type's capabilities in low-level high-speed formation flight.

The 840th TBAP based at Sol'tsy AB near Novgorod (north-western Russia) and commanded by Col. V. M. Mazalov was next, converting to the Tu-22M2 in 1976; two regiments based at Belaya AB near Irkutsk in East Siberia (the 1225th and 1229th TBAPs) followed suit in 1982. These three regiments had likewise operated various versions of the Tu-16.

Because of the SALT 2 treaty the period of the Tu-22M2's in-flight refuelling operations was very brief. In June 1984 the 31st TBAD was tasked with mastering the IFR procedure on the new bomber. The training took place at Belaya AB. It involved the division's best and most experienced pilots with polished flying skills – the

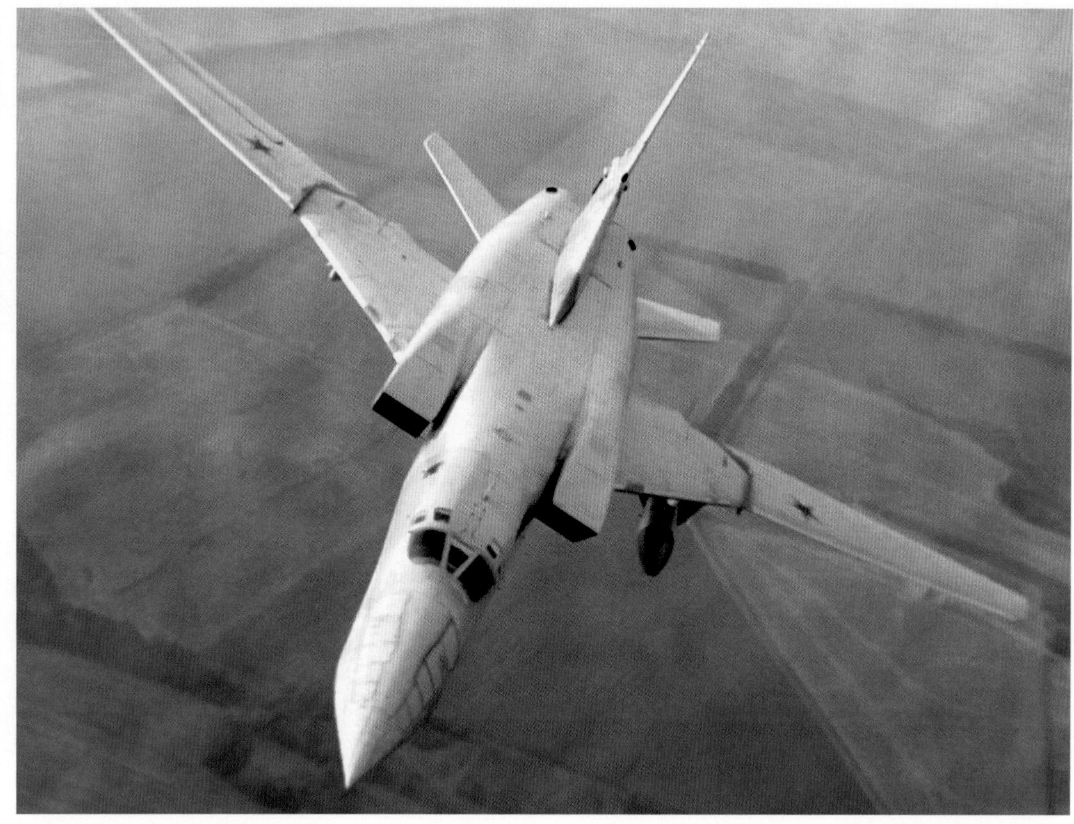

A Tu-22M3 formates with the tanker in a simulated refuelling session.

31st TBAD CO Col. G. P. Treznyuk and Deputy CO Col. V. V. Rodionov, the 1225th TBAP CO Col. B. M. Karpovskiy, the 1229th TBAP CO Col. V. F. Sookhorev and their deputies. Several Tu-16N tankers from the 251st TBAP at Belaya Tserkov' in the Ukraine were deployed to Belaya AB for the occasion; their crews had received prior training at the 43rd TsBP i PLS. The team of instructor pilots was headed by Col. A. D. Pechonkin from the combat training department of the Soviet Air Force's Main HQ.

The Tu-16N was the optimum tanker for the Tu-22M2 as far as the speed was concerned. The refuelling was to take place at 550-600 km/h (341-372 mph). The fuel was supplied from the transfer tanks which, like

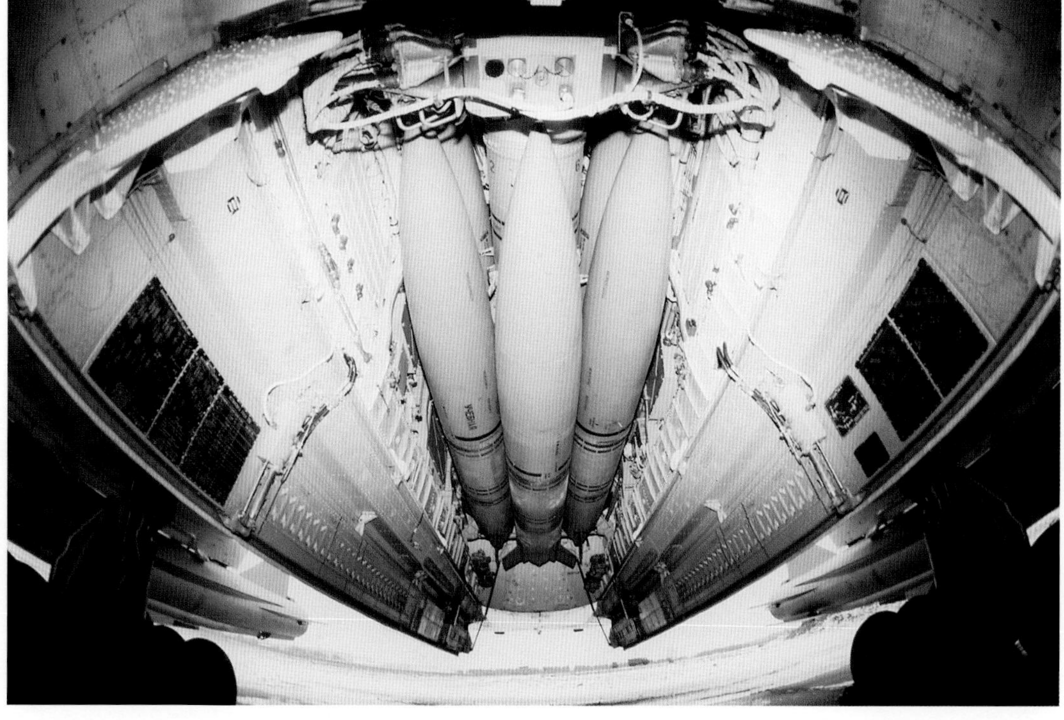

The bomb bay of a Tu-22M3 with six Kh-15 missiles on an MKU-6-5 rotary launcher. Note the two Kh-22Ms on the wing pylons.

This view shows the Tu-22M3's redesigned air intakes.

the hose drum unit, was located in the tanker's bomb bay. The *Backfire-B* could receive 15 tons (33,000 lb) of fuel in a single refuelling session; with a fuel transfer rate of 1.6-1.8 tons (3,530-3,970 lb) per minute, the session lasted nine or ten minutes.

The training proceeded according to the following pattern:

- 'dry runs' (contact with the drogue without any fuel being transferred) – three flights (familiarisation flight, check-up flight and solo flight);

Front view of a *Backfire-C*. The fixed IFR probe was to have been located at the tip of the nose.

The active radar homing Kh-22MA on the wing and centre-line stations of the Tu-22M3.

• actual refuelling with 10 tons (22,000 lb) of fuel being transferred (check-up and solo flights);

• actual refuelling with 15 tons of fuel being transferred (credit and solo flights).

The training sessions took place close to the airbase, allowing the flight time to be used with maximum efficiency. The Tu-16N took off first, climbing to 5,000-7,000 m (16,400-22,965 ft) and maintaining a speed of 600 km/h. As the tanker approached the base's inner marker beacon the receiver aircraft lined up for take-off, commencing the take-off run after receiving radio confirmation that the tanker had passed the IMB. As a result, by the time they reached the outer marker beacon at the other end of the runway the aircraft were already in line astern formation. The instructors and the trainees

A Tu-22M3 armed with two Kh-22MAs at Machoolishchi.

A pair of armed *Backfire-Cs* represents the DA at an air event.

The unit badge of the 185th TBAP based at Poltava.

were all seasoned pilots, and the training went without a hitch and right on schedule. The training mostly took place in daytime, but a few crews were permitted to practice night refuelling.

The crews took care to fly the IFR training sorties below the clouds in order to avoid detection by US surveillance satellites; the radio communication was coded to prevent electronic eavesdropping. At the time the US-Soviet negotiations on the SALT 2 treaty were in progress and the Tu-22M2 was listed as a long-range bomber (that is, it did not fall into the strategic category as regards range). At about the same time Tupolev OKB test pilot Boris I. Veremey made a non-stop flight in a Tu-22M2 from central Russia to the Soviet Far East and back with several fuel top-ups. Apparently the US intelligence agencies had got wind either of this flight or of the training

Parked Tu-22M3s with the special boarding platform beside the nearest aircraft.

A Tu-22M3 takes off; the nose gear unit is fully stowed while the main units are just beginning to retract.

sessions at Belaya AB, and the US delegation at the SALT negotiations raised the issue of transferring the *Backfire-B* to the strategic bomber category. As a result, the Long-Range Aviation HQ immediately issued an order banning all further IFR operations on the type, and the IFR probes were subsequently removed from all Tu-22M2s. Still, many DA pilots had taken the opportunity while it lasted, gaining invaluable experience.

In the 1970s the Long-Range Aviation's supersonic missile carrier crews intensively practiced missile launch techniques. Initially the Tu-22K/Tu-22KD was used. Thus, four Kh-22 missiles were launched in 1970; in 1974 the 121st TBAP launched a single Kh-22PG passive radar-homing missile and the 203rd TBAP launched three Kh-22Ms. The latter unit launched two missiles in 1975 and three in 1976. In 1978 the 121st, 203rd and 840th

A Tu-22M3 shares the flight line at Ryazan' with two Tu-22s.

A Tu-22M3 makes a high-speed pass with the wings fully swept back.

TBAPs launched one Kh-22M missile each; the 840th TBAP crew captained by G. P. Treznyuk (then in the rank of Lieutenant-Colonel) had the distinction of being the first operational Tu-22M2 crew to do so. By the end of 1980 all Long-Range Aviation units constituting the 6th OTBAK were proficient in using cruise missiles with conventional and nuclear warheads.

Tu-22M3 '35 Red' in factory finish

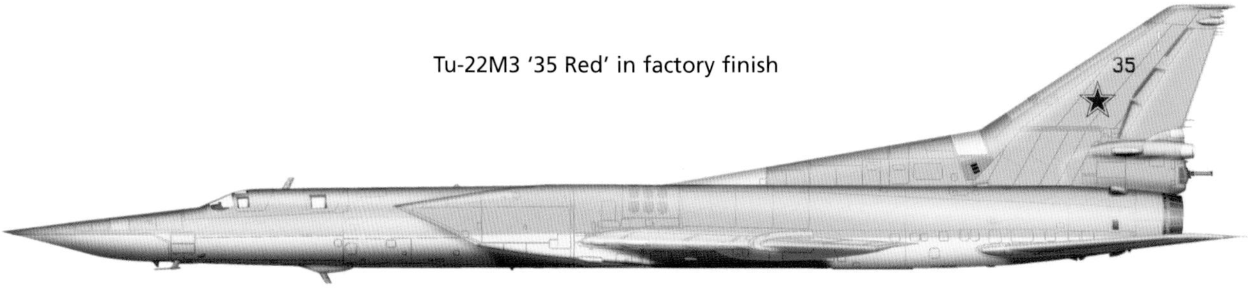

'33 Red', a Tu-22M3 operated by a Guards unit

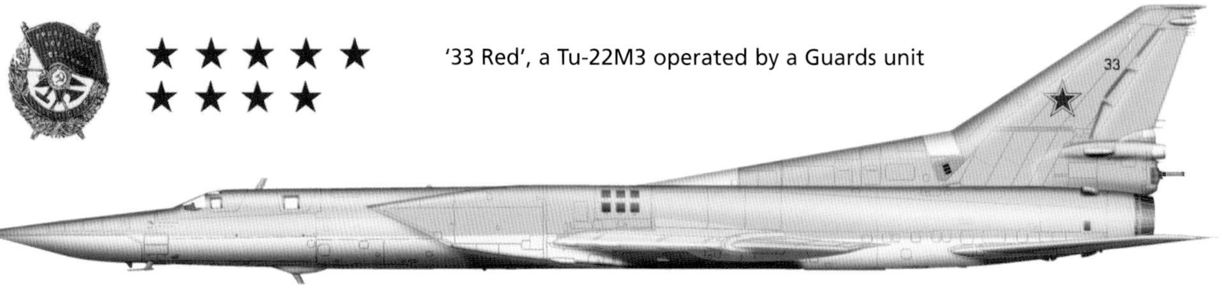

Tu-22M3 '03 Blue' with 37 mission markers

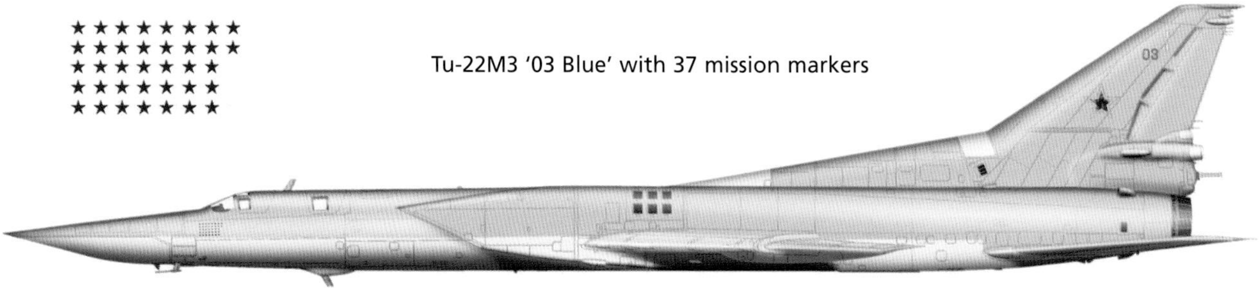

Tu-22M3s and IL-78M tankers on the flight line at Engels-2 AB.

Since, unlike the *Blinder*, the Tu-22M had no dedicated trainer version, from 1982 onwards *Backfire* pilots took their training on the Tu-134UBL *Crusty-B* (*oo**cheb**no-boye**voy** dlya **lyot**chikov* – combat trainer for pilots), a purpose-built derivative of the Tu-134B short-haul airliner. Such aircraft were based at Engels, Tambov and Priluki. The navigators were trained in Voroshilovgrad on the older Tu-134Sh-1 *Crusty-A* (***shtoor**manskiy*), a navigator trainer based on the Tu-134A and featuring the ability to carry practice bombs (see Chapter 10).

To save wear and tear on the new bombers, the units converting to the Tu-22M2 initially retained a single squadron of Tu-16 missile carriers for proficiency training. New mission types were included in the training routine to reflect the greater capabilities of the *Backfire*. These included long-range missions using the navigation suite, high-speed/low-level missions and weapons training.

A *Backfire-C* tucked in for the night, with a canvas cover on the canopies.

The combat standard of the 184th TBAP.

The Tu-22M2's service entry was less troublesome than that of the *Blinder* because its systems, particularly the control system, had many of the predecessor's bugs designed out of them. However, the beginning of its career was marred by a poor reliability record. The *Backfire*'s systems were fairly complex and had their share of problems. Ground crews, too, often made mistakes at the beginning of the learning curve, damaging the aircraft. The result was one of the lowest mean time between failures (MTBF) rates in the Soviet Air Force, which earned the Tu-22M2 the uncomplementary nickname of *vsepo***god***nyy defekto***nos***ets* – 'all-weather defect carrier'.

Engine life was initially a mere 50 hours and the manufacturer was forced to impose a limit on exhaust gas temperature, thus limiting the NK-22's thrust. The engine was also plagued by excessive vibration which occasionally led to failures. Leaky hydraulics were another source of annoyance; often the Tu-22M2 returned to base with the aft fuselage covered in hydraulic fluid. Rivets began popping and fatigue cracks appeared after low-level high-speed missions.

Avionics failures and electromagnetic compatibility problems were common in the early days. The automatic flight control system sometimes failed, leaving the pilots no choice but to fly manually all the way home. If a Kh-22 missile was carried on the centreline hardpoint the co-pilot had to check with the WSO that the missile was in the fully up position before cycling the undercarriage, otherwise the main gear doors would damage the missile's wings.

A minor inconvenience was associated with the landing gear itself. The mainwheel brakes had electric cooling fans using three-phase AC. This could only be supplied by the auxiliary power unit and the crew had to remember to start up the APU before landing.

Gradually the Tu-22M2 took up residence both sides of the Urals Mountains, replacing the Tu-16 and Tu-22 in front-line service.

The badge of the 326th *Tarnopol'skaya* TBAP established in 1943.

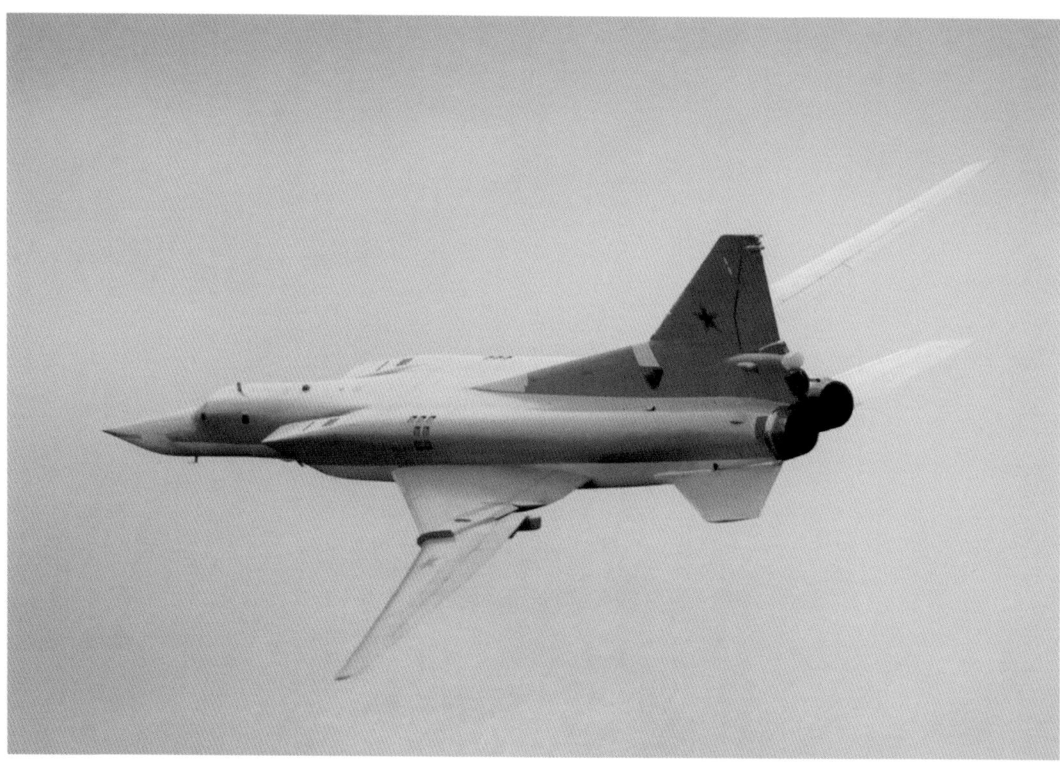

A Tu-22M3 makes a low turn with the wings at minimum sweep.

Winter operations of a Tu-22M3.

Despite the initial bugs, the type was well liked by the aircrews; besides, Tupolev, Kuznetsov and other bureaux involved with the *Backfire* worked hard to eliminate the shortcomings and the aircraft kept improving.

The further improved Tu-22M3 *Backfire-C* featuring new Kuznetsov NK-25 afterburning turbofans, redesigned air intakes, a new electric system and other changes first flew on 20th June 1977. Production started in 1978, increasing gradually, and the new version shared the Kazan' production line with the Tu-22M2 before finally taking over completely in 1984; a total of 268 had been built when production ended in 1992. The Tu-22M3 passed its state acceptance trials and attained

One more view of '47 Red' being refuelled in its earthen revetment by a TZ-22 articulated fuel bowser.

The first operational Tu-160s in service with the 184th GvTBAP.

A Kh-55SM long-range cruise missile (note the external tanks) with wings and tail surfaces folded.

More views of the first operational Tu-160s at Priluki AB.

IOC in 1981, but it was not until five years later that it became fully operational.

According to official sources, 257 *Backfire-B/Cs* were stationed in the European part of the Soviet Union in 1990, serving with 12 DA and Navy units (four regiments in Russia, five in the Ukraine, two in Belorussia and one in Estonia). Sixty more aircraft (including one regiment at Belaya AB) were based east of the Urals Mountains. The Tu-22M2 remained in Long-Range Aviation service until the mid-1990s, whereupon the aircraft were trans-

Tu-160 '03 Red' taxies at Engels.

Tu-160s on the flight line at Engels.

ferred to the Air Force reserve and mothballed. The Tu-22M3 became the main bomber type in the DA inventory, which had shrunk appreciably. Only Russia and the Ukraine retained the *Backfire* in post-Soviet times (the Tu-22Ms stationed in Belorussia moved to Russia).

The 43rd TsBP i PLS received its first Tu-22M3s in March 1981. That same year the type attained IOC with the 840th TBAP, followed shortly by the 185th GvTBAP; in both cases it replaced the Tu-22M2. In 1985 the 185th GvTBAP's pilots gave a startling demonstration of the bomber's defence penetration capabilities, flying a high-speed low-level mission in tight formation. Several more Long-Range Aviation regiments re-equipped with the Tu-22M3 in the mid-1980s; these were based at Shaikovka AB near Kaluga (Russia), in Priluki (the Ukraine), Orsha (Belorussia) and Tartu (Estonia). Two other regiments at Bobruisk (Belorussia) and Stryy (western Ukraine) followed shortly afterwards.

New tactics increased the Tu-22M's combat potential. Covertly approaching the target at ultra-low level, the bombers would receive guidance from Il'yushin/Beriyev A-50 *Mainstay*

AWACS aircraft and airborne command posts, with Sukhoi Su-27 *Flanker-B* and MiG-31 *Foxhound* interceptors flying top cover.

The *Backfire-C* turned out to be far less troublesome than its precursor, earning a good reputation with the crews. It also proved to be a rugged aircraft. In September 1986 a Tu-22M3 on short finals had a malfunction causing uncommanded retraction of the flaps at 30 m (100 ft). As wing lift suddenly diminished, the aircraft 'fell through' all the way to the ground. Reacting instantly, the captain selected full afterburner and the bomber made an unscheduled but spectacular 'touch and go' short of the runway, ploughing 100-metre (330-foot) furrows in the soft earth. When it landed safely a few minutes later, a wing, a stabilator and the landing gear had been badly bent by the impact, but the aircraft remained flyable and returned to service after the damaged airframe components had been replaced.

The DA's Tu-22 and Tu-22M operators in the European part of the CIS are listed below.

Tu-22/Tu-22M units in the European part of the CIS

Unit	Location	On strength
121st TBAP	Machoolishchi AB, Minsk, Belorussia	34
185th GvBAP	Poltava, Ukraine	22
200th TBAP	Bobruisk, Russia	20
203rd TBAP	Baranovichi, Belorussia	32
260th TBAP	Stryy AB	20
341st TBAP	Ozyornoye AB, Zhitomir, Ukraine	30

In 1984 the 184th TBAP, a Tu-16 operator based at Priluki in the Ukraine, re-equipped with Tu-22M3s. However, they were but a stepping stone to the Tu-160 *Blackjack* which the unit was ultimately to fly. This 'interim type' strategy worked well, easing the transition from Tu-16 to Tu-160, since the *Backfire* and the *Blackjack* have a lot in common, including supersonic speed, VG wings and cockpit layout.

In 1985 the Tupolev OKB brought out the Tu-22M3R reconnaissance aircraft with advanced photo and ELINT equipment intended to replace the outdated Tu-22R/RD/RDM. The prototype first flew on 6th December; however, the programme made slow progress and the production version designated

A Tu-160 taxies at Engels with old (3MS-2) and new (IL-78M) tankers in the background.

Close-up of the Tu-160's all-movable tail surfaces that caused problems in the type's early days.

A pair of Tu-160s with the wings at maximum sweep.

Tu-22MR was built in only a handful of examples. The *Backfire's* ECM versions intended to replace the Tu-22P/Tu-22PD fared even worse – the Tu-22M2P remained a one-off prototype and the projected Tu-22M3P was not built at all.

1984 was the year when the latest Soviet strategic bomber – the Tu-160 *Blackjack* – entered production in Kazan'. Three years later, in April 1987, the Tu-160 achieved IOC with the 184th GvTBAP in Priluki, one of the Soviet Air Force's best bomber units. The first two aircraft were delivered on 17th April 1987, although some sources quote the date as 23rd or 25th April. One of the bombers was piloted by Merited Military Pilot Maj.-Gen. Lev V. Kozlov –

A Kh-55SM in flight configuration with the wings, tail surfaces and engine deployed.

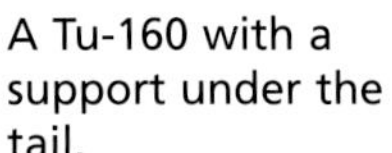

A Tu-160 with a support under the tail.

A Tu-160 pilot looking almost like a spaceman in his special high-altitude outfit.

the then Deputy Commander (Combat Training) of the Long-Range Aviation and the first service pilot to fly the Tu-160. One of them belonged to the second prototype batch while the other was the first production aircraft.

Before the Tu-160 was delivered, the 184th TBAP aircrews took extensive theoretical training at Kazan' and Samara. Tupolev OKB test pilot Boris I. Veremey and the factory test pilots from Kazan' took a leading part in coaching instructor-pilots for the 37th Air Army which included the 184th TBAP. With their assistance, a programme of training flights for the regiment's aircrews was provided.

Mission preparation included clearing away the snow – the old-fashioned way.

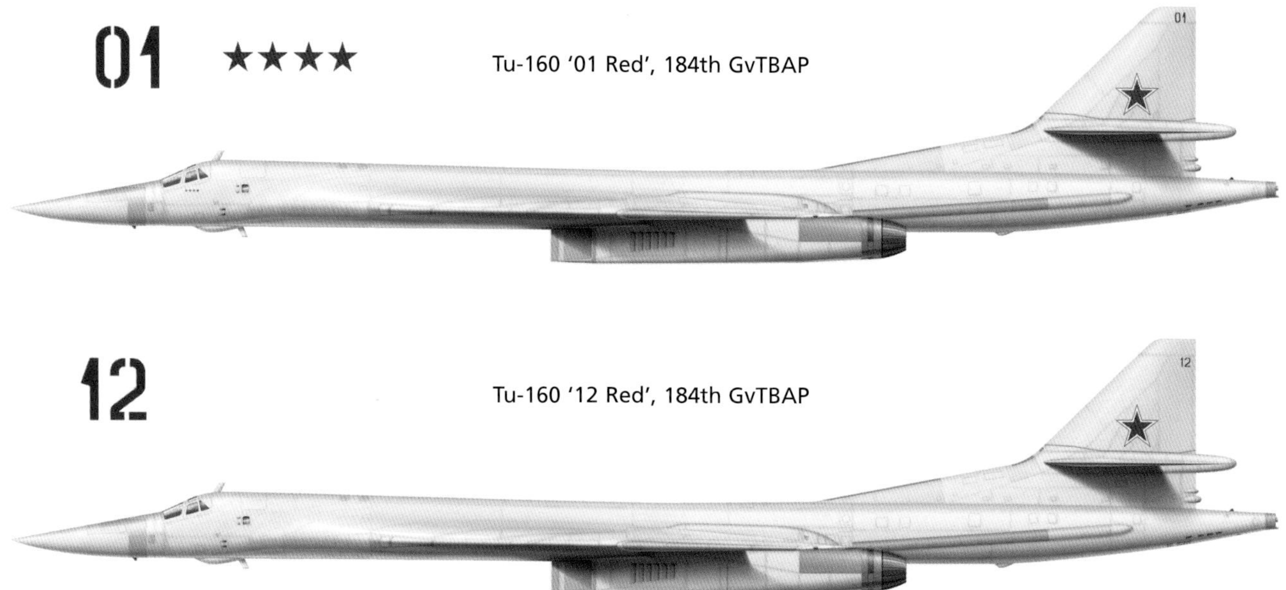

★★★★ Tu-160 '01 Red', 184th GvTBAP

Tu-160 '12 Red', 184th GvTBAP

The first squadron took eight months to be fully trained on the Tu-160, and the regiment underwent an intensive familiarisation programme. Again, Tu-134UBL trainers were used to save the bombers' service life.

The advent of the Tu-160 brought about a major reconstruction of the Priluki airbase. Among other things the runway was reinforced and extended to 3,000 m (9,840 ft).

The personnel of the 184th GvTBAP had to master the Tu-160 while the state acceptance trials were still in progress. This was because the trials looked set to be a protracted affair due to the large scope of the work. The decision to start Tu-160 operations (or, to be precise, evaluation) made it possible to assess the *Blackjack*'s strengths and weaknesses, accumulating first-hand experience which other units slated to re-equip with the type would find invaluable.

On 12th May Kozlov made the first flight from Priluki; on 1st July this was followed by the first sortie of a 184th GvTBAP crew captained by the regiment's CO Lt.-Col. Vladimir Grebennikov. In late July 1987 (some sources state early August) a Tu-160 crew captained by

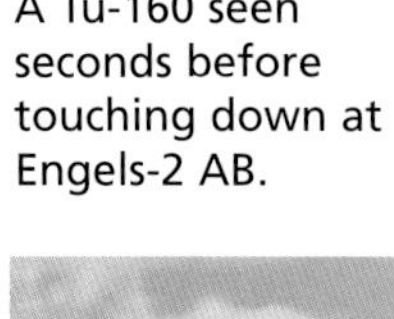

A Tu-160 seen seconds before touching down at Engels-2 AB.

Grebennikov performed the unit's first launch of a Kh-55SM cruise missile with excellent results.

Pilots converting from the Tu-22M found the Tu-160 to be much easier to fly. The bomber was blessed with excellent acceleration and rate of climb (pilots said that the Tu-160 'climbed by itself'); it also exhibited good low-speed handling, which facilitated the landing procedure. The engines' total thrust was tremendous. On one occasion a Tu-160 even managed to become airborne and climb with the spoilers deployed by mistake. The *Blackjack* featured an audio warning system and a stick-pusher which prevented grave piloting errors.

Due care was taken to ensure trouble-free operation. For instance, in the first months of service the crews were expressly forbidden from taxying to the holding point under the aircraft's own power in order to prevent foreign object damage (FOD) to the engines. The engines were started on a special parking stand which had been painstakingly swept clean of all loose objects; then the bomber was towed to the runway with the engines running at ground idle, preceded by a string of soldiers picking up loose stones and twigs.

Still, the Tupolev OKB and the Air Force had to wrestle with the bomber's design flaws and operational problems for many years. Malfunctions occurred in virtually every single flight – primarily in the avionics which were a real pain in the neck. Luckily there were no serious accidents, mainly thanks to the multiple redundancy of the vital systems.

Problems with the powerplant were encountered regularly; engine starting was especially troublesome and the full authority digital engine control (FADEC) system could not cope with it. FADEC failures occurred in flight as well. The petals of the NK-32 turbofans' variable nozzles often failed. On the other hand, the *Blackjack* had adequate power reserves to maintain level flight and even take off with one engine inoperative. Changes had to be made to the air intakes, whose aerodynamic imperfections caused dangerous vibrations, and to the design of the main landing gear units. The excessively complicated initial design led to reliability problems that even caused 184th GvTBAP crews to refrain from retracting the gear for several months in 1988.

The bonded honeycomb-core panels utilised in the bomber's tail unit were not strong enough: they would occasionally crack at high speeds, causing severe vibration, or even fail. Eventually the Tupolev OKB grounded the Tu-160 fleet and undertook an urgent redesign, reducing the horizontal tail span. Now all existing Tu-160s had to be refitted with new stabilators, and an immediate problem arose: the all-movable horizontal tail was a one-piece structure too large to be carried internally by any transport aircraft in Soviet Air Force service. Ferrying the bombers to Kazan' for a refit was ruled out for safety reasons. Hence an Il'yushin IL-76 *Candid-B* transport owned by the Kazan' aircraft factory was modified to carry Tu-160 horizontal tail assemblies piggy-back from Kazan' to Priluki AB where they were replaced *in situ*.

A Tu-160 in high-altitude cruise. It is easy to see why the aircraft was dubbed the White Swan in the Soviet Union.

This Tu-160 has just launched a Kh-55SM missile.

The flight deck ergonomics and equipment earned praise, but also criticism. For instance, originally the main and back-up flight instruments were of different types, which was inconvenient; later the instruments were standardised. The K-36DM fighter-type ejection seats proved uncomfortable on long flights. This was improved by the introduction of a seat cushion which provided pulsing air

A Tu-160 on final approach.

This view shows the Tu-160's wing hinge and the inboard flap segment folding upward to form a wing fence at 65° maximum sweep.

massage. Worse, the seats could be adjusted lengthwise, and it turned out that ejection was impossible with the seat in a certain position. This was an extremely dangerous defect, and NPP Zvezda (the manufacturer of the seat) eventually admitted that the situation was unacceptable and set about modifying the seat.

One more problem was that with the wings at maximum sweep (65°) the CG shifted so far aft that the parked bomber could easily tip over on its tail. Hence the wings had to be left at minimum sweep (20°) on the ground, even though the Tu-160 required a lot more apron space in this configuration. Sometimes a support would even be placed under the tail, just to be on the safe side.

Much aggravation was caused by the state-of-the-art avionics, notably the ESM suite, 80% of which was housed in the aft fuselage. This area was subjected to serious vibration (particularly when the engines were running in full afterburner) and the vibrations ruined the delicate electronics. By the spring of 1990 the ESM suite had worked up an acceptable reliability level, but still malfunctions did occur from time to time.

Even though the Tupolev OKB had taken steps to facilitate the Tu-160's maintenance procedures as much as possible, the *Blackjack* turned out to be extremely 'labour-intensive' – it required 64 man-hours of maintenance per flight hour. Preparing the Tu-160 for a sortie required between 15 and 20 ground support vehicles, some of which were perhaps unique for the type. The technicians were confronted with other problems which were just as serious. When the engines were started the noise and vibration were horrendous; the APU was not very quiet either, to say the least. Instead of the usual oil-based hydraulic fluid the

A Tu-160 flies a training sortie near Engels at dusk.

Two Kh-55SM missiles are prepared for loading into a *Blackjack*'s weapons bay.

Tu-160's hydraulic systems used a highly corrosive fluid. To make matters worse there was an acute shortage of ear protectors, special vibration-damping boots and vibration protection belts for the ground personnel.

A weapons system of this complexity demanded a completely new approach to ground crew training. Suffice it to say that in the first days of Tu-160 operations in the 184th GvTBAP it took up to 36 hours (!) to

Mission preparation at Engels. It takes more than one such fuel bowser to fill the Tu-160's tanks.

prepare the aircraft for a mission. Gradually mission preparation times were reduced to an acceptable level thanks to the persistent work of the unit's technical staff and the immense help of the OKB's operations department.

The bomber's inevitable teething troubles were the subject of close attention from the aircraft industry. The defects discovered were quickly eliminated on both operational aircraft and the Kazan' production line. For instance, the NK-32's service life, which initially was a mere 250 hours, was tripled in due course. The number of auxiliary blow-in doors in the engines' inlet ducts was increased in order to

One more view of a Tu-160 taxying at Engels.

This view shows the antennas of the Tu-160's defensive suite.

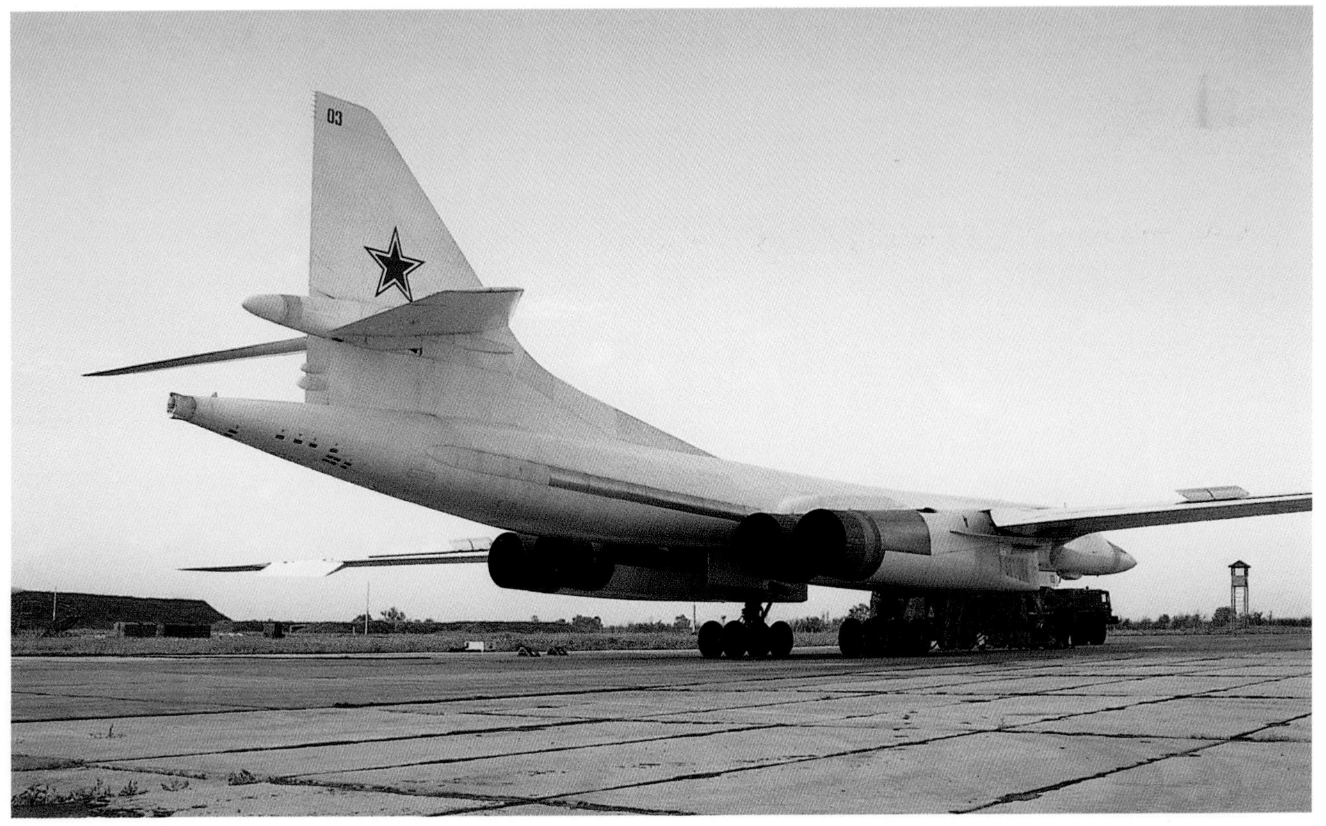

The 'Pilot 2nd Class' qualification badge.

prevent compressor stalls and their control system was simplified. Some honeycomb-core metal panels were replaced by composite panels of a similar design, saving weight and improving fatigue life.

All problems notwithstanding, the 184th GvTBAP's 1st Squadron was fully ready for operational duty with the Tu-160 after an eight-month period. The unit did its best to

The 'Navigator 2nd Class' qualification badge.

overcome the learning curve; average Tu-160 utilisation rose steadily, reaching 100 flight hours per annum. Six-, ten- and twelve-hour missions were flown on a regular basis. Many pilots who transitioned to the *Blackjack* from the Tu-16 or Tu-22M3 said this was the best aircraft they had ever flown.

Some time after service entry the Tu-160 received an avionics upgrade. Improvements were made to the long-range radio navigation (LORAN) system working with ground beacons. The navigation system was augmented by a self-contained celestial corrector which accurately determined the aircraft's position with the help of the sun and the stars; this was a real asset when flying over the ocean and in extreme northern latitudes. The navigators were pleased with the new PA-3 moving map display showing the aircraft's current position. A satellite navigation system with an accuracy margin of 10-20 m (33-66 ft) was also due for introduction on the Tu-160; it worked with several MoD satellites launched into geostationary orbit under a special government programme. The engineers also succeeded in debugging the software of the targeting/navigation avionics suite.

The Tupolev OKB devised and implemented a multi-stage programme aimed at making the *Blackjack* more stealthy. The air intakes and inlet ducts were coated with black graphite-based radar-absorbing material (RAM). The forward fuselage received a coat of special organic-based paint, some engine components were provided with special screens minimising radar returns, and a wire mesh filter was incorporated into the flight deck glazing to reduce electromagnetic pulse (EMP) emissions which could give the bomber away. This filter also helped to protect the crew from the flash of a nuclear explosion.

The persistent efforts of the Air Force and the aircraft industry soon bore fruit; gradually the Tu-160 turned into a fully capable weapons system. Still, many of the planned improvements did not materialise, including the intended upgrade of the navigation/targeting suite (only in the 21st century was this issue taken up again). Unlike their American colleagues flying the B-1B, Tu-160 pilots never practiced ultra-low-level terrain-following flight, and far from all *Blackjack* crews were trained in IFR procedures which gave the aircraft its intended intercontinental range. The Kh-15S short-range ASM was never integrated, leaving the Tu-160 with the Kh-55 cruise missile as its only weapon.

Gradually, as the Soviet Air Force built up operational experience with the type, the range of the Tu-160's missions expanded. The bombers ventured as far as the North Pole, sometimes even across the Pole. The longest sortie lasted 12 hours 50 minutes; the bomber got within 450 km (279.5 miles) of the Canadian coast. NATO fighters often scrambled to intercept the Tu-160s over international waters; the first such occasion was apparently in May 1991.

This is how Distinguished Military Pilot Aleksandr S. Medvedev (dubbed 'Ace

The cover of a 'Military Pilot 2nd Class' qualification certificate. The certificate is an old one, judging by the 'War Ministry' inscription instead of 'Ministry of Defence'.

Medvedev'), a 184th GvTBAP pilot who gained Russian citizenship after the break-up of the Soviet Union and subsequently became a Senior Inspector Pilot with the Combat Training Department of the Long-Range Aviation (the 37th (Strategic) Air Army of the Supreme High Command), describes the *Blackjack*'s service introduction period:

'We first got acquainted with the Tu-160 about a year before the first bombers arrived at Priluki. We visited the factories where the aircraft proper, its engines and avionics were manufactured to study the hardware first-hand. After we had received the Tu-160s flight and combat training got under way. The Cold War was far from over then, and we were tasked with mastering the new aircraft as quickly as possible. Note that we had to do this in the course of service tests, which we had to perform instead of the factory pilots. This is why we got up to 100 systems malfunctions per flight in the early sorties. As we grew familiar with the machine the number of failures decreased, and in due time we came to trust the aircraft.

Where did we fly, you ask? We departed Priluki in the direction of Lake Onega (near Petrozavodsk in Karelia, north-western Russia – *Auth.*), *thence we flew to Novaya Zemlya Island* ('New Land' – *Auth.*), *the Franz-Joseph Land archipelago and onwards, heading towards the North Pole. The guys back at home used to joke that 'the Cowboy* (the Tu-160 was thus nicknamed because it had two 'six-shooters', that is, multiple launchers – *Auth.*) *is studying the States'; indeed, the 'potential adversary' was within easy reach for us. However, over the Pole we would turn and head towards Tiksi* (on the Laptev Sea coast – *Auth.*)*; all the more reason to do so because the terrain there was similar to the coasts of northern Canada. Next thing we would overfly Chelyabinsk* (in the southern part of the Urals mountain range – *Auth.*)*, Lake Balkhash and the Caspian Sea, heading across the North Caucasus back towards Priluki. There was also a route from Priluki to Lake Baikal and back again; I used to fly it with Vladimir Grebennikov. Missiles were launched against targets on a range in Kazakhstan; we would enter the designated launch zone and say goodbye to our missiles. Later we also practiced missile attacks at target ranges in other parts of the USSR.'*

The 'Sniper Pilot' qualification badge.

On some occasions the Tu-160s were escorted by Sukhoi Su-27P interceptors of the Air Defence Force operating from bases near Murmansk and on Novaya Zemlya Island.

A parked Tu-160 with canvas wraps on the flight deck section.

Overwater missions were flown in pairs because this added psychological comfort; if one of the crews had to ditch or eject over water, the other crew could radio for help, indicating the coordinates of the crash site. This was important because Tu-160 crews had nothing except life jackets for such an emergency; heat-insulated waterproof rescue suits were a privilege of Naval Aviation pilots. This situation was caused by the lumbering bureaucratic machine responsible for materiel supplies in the Armed Forces. Fortunately no such emergencies have occurred to date... knock on wood.

One of the reasons why the new strategic bomber became operational very quickly was the targeting and navigation system's high degree of automation. The Kh-55SM cruise missile was guided to the target by a pre-entered programme featuring a digital route map; therefore the WSO's duties basically boiled down to accurately guiding the aircraft to the launch point, monitoring the missiles' systems status and pushing the release button at the right time. The missile was then ejected downwards, deploying its wings, tail surfaces and engine, and followed its pre-programmed course. Meanwhile the launcher rotated, bringing the next missile into position for release.

Towards the end of 1987 the 184th GvTBAP had increased its Tu-160 fleet to ten aircraft; nevertheless, the regiment stuck to its Tu-22M3s and Tu-16P *Badger-J* ECM aircraft to maintain combat readiness during the transition period. Later, as the number of *Blackjacks* grew, the older types were progressively transferred to other units; some of the Tu-16s were scrapped to comply with the Conventional Forces in Europe (CFE) treaty limiting the number of combat aircraft a unit was allowed to have. The strategic bombers themselves were governed by a different treaty, the Strategic Arms Reduction Talks (START) treaty.

As the economic downturn caused by Mikhail S. Gorbachov's *perestroika* got worse, Tu-160 production and delivery rates slowed down somewhat; by late 1991 the 184th GvTBAP had 21 *Blackjacks* in two squadrons. At the beginning of that year the unit's 3rd Squadron had received a small number of Tu-134UBLs. The latter were used for lead-in and proficiency training, saving the bombers' service life and helping to avoid costly repairs.

The Western intelligence community maintained a close interest in the Tu-160, and especially its mission equipment, long before the aircraft entered service. The Soviet KGB counter-intelligence service was extremely alarmed to discover a self-contained signals intelligence (SIGINT) module near Priluki AB in the spring of 1988. Disguised as a tree stump, this unit monitored and recorded air-to-ground radio exchanges and other signals emitted by the aircraft operating from the base.

On the other hand, *perestroika*, *glasnost'* (openness) and the new domestic and foreign policies initiated by Gorbachov removed the pall of secrecy from the Soviet Armed Forces and defence industry, making a lot of previously classified information available via the mass media. Also, in addition to military delegations from allied nations the Soviet Union began inviting high-ranking military officials from countries previously regarded as 'potential adversaries'. New Soviet military hardware was demonstrated to Western experts both at home and abroad during major international airshows and defence trade fairs.

The West got its first close look at the *Blackjack* on 12th August 1988 when Frank C. Carlucci, the then US Secretary of Defense, visited Kubinka AB near Moscow during his Soviet trip. Kubinka had a long history as a display centre where the latest military aircraft were demonstrated to Soviet and foreign military top brass. The aircraft on show included a 184th GvTBAP Tu-160. In an unprecedented show of openness, Mr. Carlucci was allowed to inspect the weapons bays, the flight deck and other details. As he moved about in the flight deck he hit his head on a carelessly positioned circuit breaker panel (which the witty airmen promptly dubbed 'the Carlucci panel'). Incidentally, almost every person making his first visit inside the *Blackjack* bumps his head on it! The US delegation was accompanied by TV crews and press photographers, and soon the first reasonably good pictures of the Tu-160 were circulated in the world media. Also, some performance figures were disclosed for the first time, including an unrefuelled range of 14,000 km (8,695 miles).

The Tu-160's public debut took place on 20th August 1989 when one of the development aircraft from Zhukovskiy made a low pass over Tushino airfield as part of the annual Aviation Day display. The first known display in Zhukovskiy was on 18th August 1991 (one day before the failed hard-line Communist coup which brought an end to the Soviet Union's existence).

By early 1991 the 184th GvTBAP had 19 Tu-160s operated by two squadrons.

Opposite page:

'04 Red' (c/n 1883511), a Tu-16R *Badger-E* with SRS-1/SRS-4 ELINT systems and an SPS-100 jammer in a UKhO tail fairing.

Tu-16R '05 Blue' (c/n 1883405) is a *Badger-F* with SRS-3 underwing ELINT pods.

7 The Long-Range Aviation in Times of Cutbacks

Until the mid-1950s the Long-Range Aviation could not match the capabilities of the USAF's Strategic Air Command for a number of objective reasons. At the time the Soviet nuclear arsenal consisted solely of free-fall atomic bombs; hence for several years the Air Force, with its long-range bomber fleet, held a monopoly for delivering these weapons. The strategic bombers were responsible for destroying nuclear weapon depots, airbases and the nuclear-capable SAC aircraft stationed there, and other targets of importance.

A generation leap in the development of the Soviet Long-Range Aviation came with the introduction of jet bombers – the long-range Tu-16 and the intercontinental Tu-95, M-4 and 3M. The DA started venturing into the Arctic; its aircrews began flying sorties 'around the corner' – this was Soviet Air Force slang for flights out over

'32 Blue' (c/n 1882013), a Tu-16 Yolka passive ECM aircraft, is prepared for a sortie.

the Atlantic Ocean circumnavigating the Scandinavian Peninsula. This was also the time when heavy air-to-surface missiles were developed and units equipped with missile carrier versions of the Tu-16 and Tu-95 became operational. Using stand-off missiles, these units were capable of delivering nuclear strikes at targets of importance without coming within range of the potential adversary's air defence systems. Now the capabilities of the bomber arm were determined not so much by the number of aircraft but rather by the number and calibre (yield) of the bombs and missile warheads, as well as by the ability of the

A Tu-16 drops a stick of bombs.

Long-Range Aviation to deliver the weapons accurately.

In 1955-58, trying to project a more peaceful image of itself on the outside world, the Soviet Union began unilateral arms reductions. This, in 1955 the USSR gave up on its sole Navy base on foreign soil – Porkkala-Udd in neighbouring Finland; Soviet forces were withdrawn from Port Arthur in China and from Austria, where they had been stationed after World War Two. During these four years the personnel strength of the Soviet Armed Forces was slashed by 2,140,000. In January 1960 the Supreme Soviet (= parliament) passed a bill envisaging further cuts – a further 1.2 million servicemen would be discharged from military service and an appropriate number of regiments and divisions would be disbanded.

The Air Force was affected by these cuts, too. In 1956-60 several air regiments and

A Tu-16K-26 carrying a single KSR-5 missile.

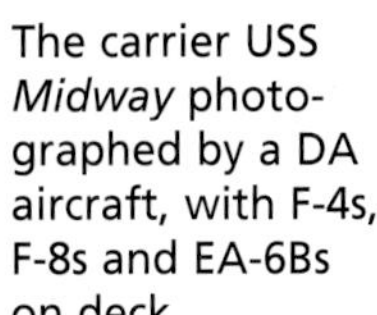

The carrier USS *Midway* photographed by a DA aircraft, with F-4s, F-8s and EA-6Bs on deck.

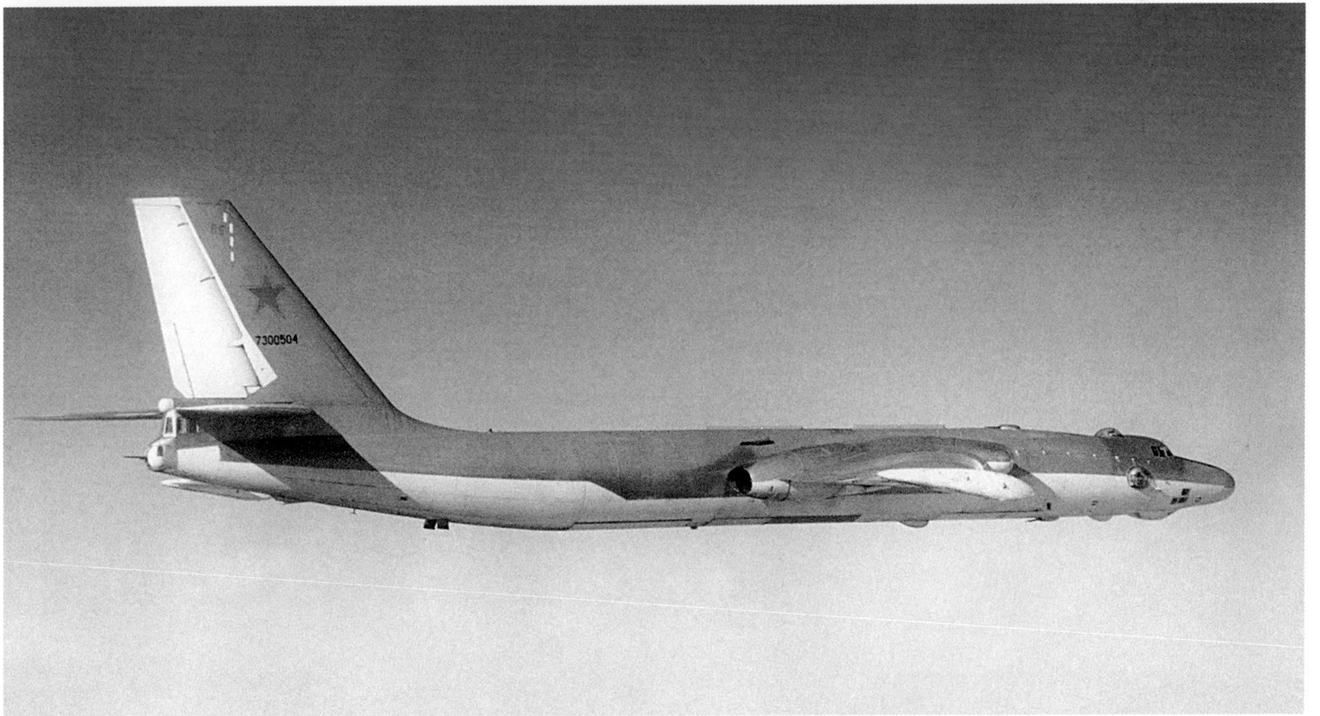

'85 Red', a 3MS-2 tanker, in cruise flight.

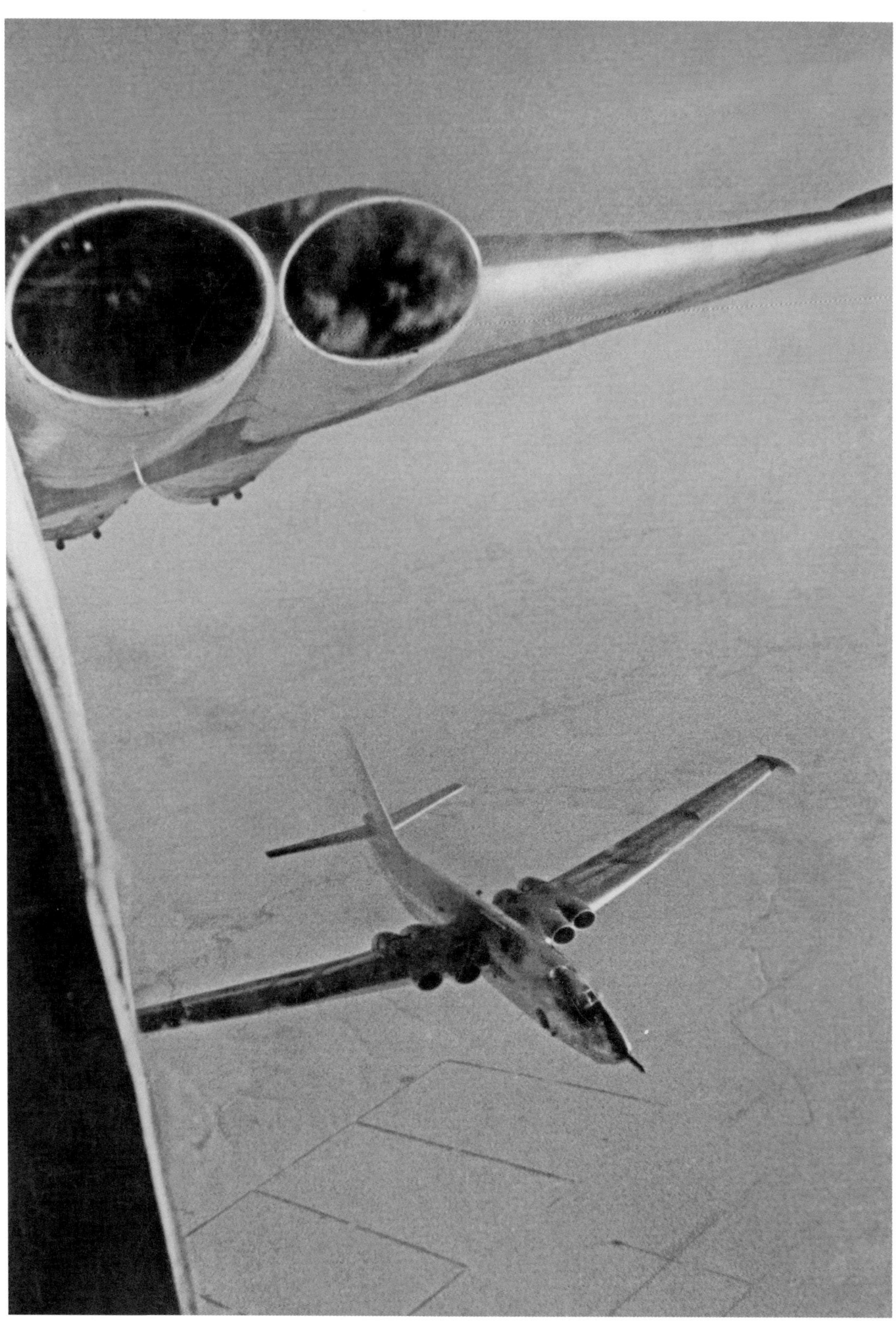

A 3MD *Bison-C* bomber is seen from the port observation blister of an M-4-2 *Bison-A* tanker.

divisions were liquidated; several thousand airmen and aircraft technicians either had to look for new jobs in civvy street or were transferred to the Strategic Missile Forces (RVSN).

The latter, as mentioned previously, had been established in 1959, a fact which led to significant changes in the Long-Range Aviation's order of battle. Pursuant to the Minister of Defence's order No. 00119 dated 31st December 1959 and the General Staff's directive No. 321102 issued on 22nd January 1960 the control of two air armies, several air divisions and 29 air regiments was transferred to the RVSN. These were now to be ballistic missile units; the DA's equipment levels were unaffected, however, as the aircraft were

Here, the same 3MD is seen after making contact with the tanker's drogue.

redistributed among the remaining bomber units. In keeping with the General Staff's directive No. 71154 dated 30th June 1960 and the Air Force Main Headquarters' directive No. 322034 dated 1st July 1960 the command structure of three Independent Heavy Bomber Corps was formed – the 2nd OTBAK in Vinnitsa, the 6th OTBAK in Smolensk and the 8th OTBAK in Blagoveshchensk. The three corps reported directly to the Air Force Commander-in-Chief, who was one of the Minister of Defence's deputies. This command chain existed from 1960 to 1980.

The 50th Air Army of the Long-Range Aviation became the 50th Missile Army of the RVSN. Its constituent units were armed both

Above and below: A 3MD seen from the tanker's tail gunner's station. The bomber is doused with fuel as it breaks contact with the drogue.

Left: A 3MN-1 *Bison-B* bomber is refuelled by a sister ship.

Below left: A pair of 3MS-2s (note the lack of IFR probes) makes an airshow performance.

with missiles having conventional warheads (for fulfilling strategic objectives set by the fronts' commanders) and nuclear-tipped missiles (for fulfilling objectives set by the Supreme High Command on not-too-distant theatres of operations). The 43rd Air Army was similarly transformed into the 43rd Missile Army. As early as 1960 several missile regiments had been brought up to full operational status.

Speaking at a session of the USSR Supreme Soviet in January 1960, Nikita S. Khrushchov said: *'Our nation is in possession of mighty missile systems. At the current stage of military hardware development, the Air Force and the Navy have lost their significance of old. These arms will not be cut back – rather, they will be*

replaced. Military aircraft will be replaced almost entirely by missiles…'

Khrushchov was famous for going to extremes. Less than two years after this speech, however, he changed his mind, deciding that the Air Force and the Navy were necessary after all. Aircraft industry and Air Force experts spared no efforts, trying to get the message across that the performance of combat aircraft and their weapons was rapidly growing and that military aviation should not be killed off, as it could perform certain missions that were beyond the capabilities of the missile forces. The most rational approach was to have the Air Force and the RVSN complement each other.

A fine in-flight study of a Tu-22RD coded '88 Red'.

A pair of high-flying Tu-22RDs approaches a tanker.

An air-to-air of a Tu-16SPS active ECM aircraft.

In 1959 a revolution broke out on Cuba; the dictator Fulgencio Batista was toppled by Fidel Castro Ruz, who became a staunch ally of the Soviet Union. Now the USA, which until then had considered itself largely safe from Soviet missile attack, had serious cause for worry; having a communist regime right on their doorstep did not suit the US government at all. The CIA began preparing a special operation, planning to use the Cuban opposition that had fled to the USA after the revolution to topple Castro and reinstall a friendly regime. Realising this, Castro turned to Khrushchov for assistance, and the Soviet leader said yes. A decision was taken to deploy a Soviet military contingent on Cuba.

Since conventional arms could not inflict sufficiently heavy damage on the USA, Khrushchov decided to deploy nuclear weapons on Cuba. Thus began Operation *Anadyr'* (named after a Russian river) launched in the second half of 1962; Soviet ship convoys set sail across the Atlantic Ocean, carrying missiles and other military hardware to 'Liberty

Seen from a Swedish Air Force fighter, Tu-16 Yolka '15 Red' (c/n 1882017) shows its ventral chaff outlets.

'40 Red' (c/n 8204206), a Tu-16P Buket ECM aircraft.

Island', as Cuba was commonly referred to by the Soviet propaganda.

All Soviet security measures notwithstanding, the Americans were quick to guess the intentions of the Soviet Union, and a major scandal known as the Cuban Missile Crisis erupted. The USA imposed a maritime blockade of Cuba to prevent more military supplies from coming in; the confrontation between the two superpowers reached its peak and the prospect of the Third World War loomed large.

In this situation the Long-Range Aviation, being a component of the Soviet nuclear triad, was placed on 'hot' alert. The crews virtually lived on the flight lines, ready to take off at a moment's notice.

Another *Badger-J* shows the ECM fairing and cooling air scoops.

A Tu-16Z wing-to-wing tanker refuels a Tu-16R.

Luckily the Cuban Missile Crisis was resolved peacefully – Khrushchov and US President John F. Kennedy had the common sense to find a way out of this stalemate. The USA guaranteed non-aggression towards Cuba and removed its missile units from Turkey, while the Soviet Union withdrew the missiles from Cuba. The world – including the DA's aircrews – breathed a sigh of relief; as a Russian saying goes, an uneasy peace is better than a good quarrel.

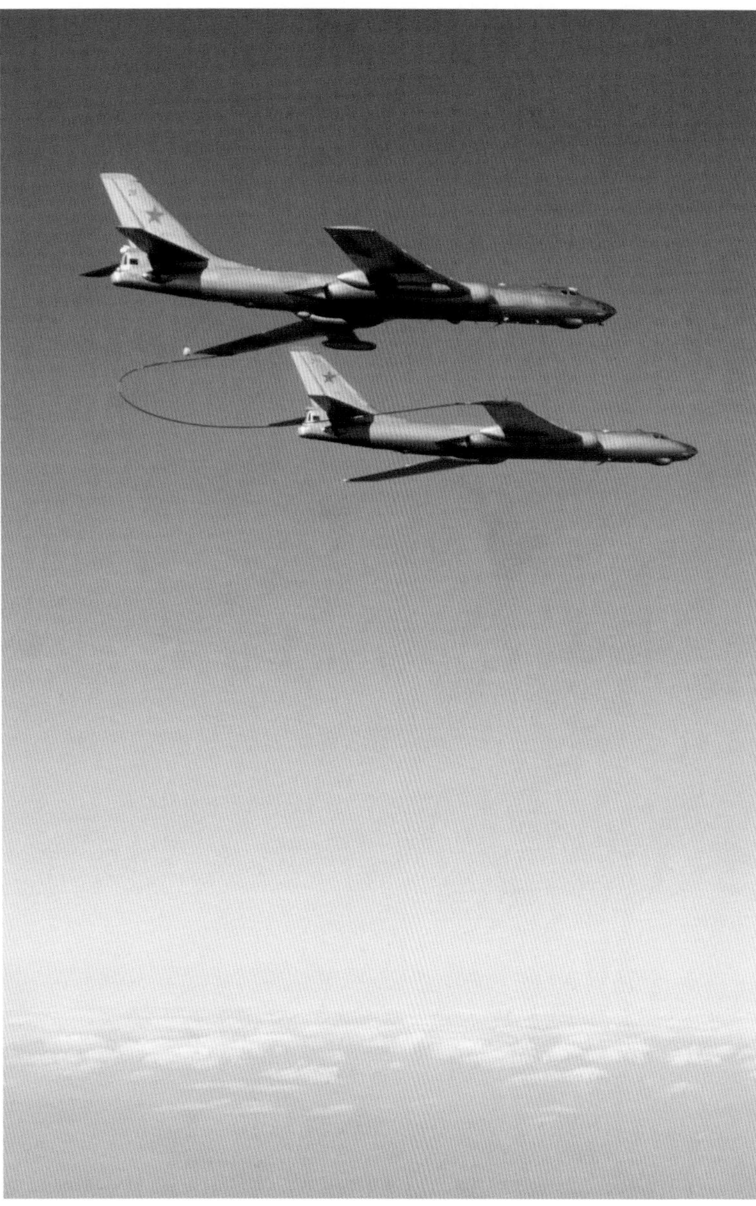

In April 1962 Air Marshal Filipp A. Agal'tsov was appointed the new Commander of the Long-Range Aviation.

In the early 1960s the DA had quite a large aircraft fleet, and flight operations were very intensive. For instance, in the 13th TBAD the average flight time per crew in 1957-63 was about 130 hours per annum. On the other hand, aircraft technology developed so rapidly that the airmen and ground crews were in the middle of a perpetual process of mastering new equipment; hardly had they become proficient on a given model when the next and more sophisticated version was coming in. Besides, new aircraft invariably suffer from teething troubles. All of this took its toll on flight safety, contributing to accident attrition.

In accordance with the Soviet MoD's combat training plans drafted in the early 1960s, the Long-Range Aviation began practice flights of entire regiments including simulated attacks on the USA. Thus, on 1st October 1965 twenty-three Myasishchev 3M bombers of the 79th TBAP laden with HE bombs took off from Ookraïnka AB and headed east. Crossing the Sea of Okhotsk, the bombers topped up their fuel tanks over Kamchatka Peninsula, whereupon the formation descended to 200 m (660 ft) and set course towards the Aleutian Islands. There the bombers made a left turn and headed north, then made another left turn off St. Matthews Island (USA), passed over the Russian cities of Anadyr' and Magadan and finally unloaded their bombs at the Litovka target range not far from their home base. The mission lasted 11.5 hours. The bomber formation was led by 79th TBAP CO Lt.-Col. V. D. Podol'skiy. Thus the Ministry of Defence demonstrated the DA's capabilities to the nation's new leader Leonid I. Brezhnev.

Over the years the airmen of the Long-Range Aviation kept improving their skills. As an incentive to the introduction of new hardware, in 1965 the Council of Ministers established the Distinguished Military Pilot and Distinguished Military Navigator qualification grades; this was followed in 1971 buy the introduction of the Sniper Pilot and Sniper Navigator grades, with appropriate uniform

badges. Qualifying for these grades involved a wage increase, among other things.

In 1965 the HQ of the 8th OTBAK moved from Blagoveshchensk to Irkutsk, which was farther from the state border.

Getting to Grips with In-flight Refuelling Techniques

As mentioned earlier, in 1953 the Soviet Union started work on in-flight refuelling systems as a means of extending the range of heavy

Tu-16Z '30 Black' (c/n 1882801).

A Tu-16R *Badger-F* makes contact with a Tu-16Z.

A 3MS-2 seen from the captain's seat of a Tu-95MS missile carrier.

bombers. The same range problems were experienced by the USAF and the Royal Air Force, and the USA and Great Britain were working on IFR systems as well.

Several IFR systems were tried out. For the Tu-16 jet bomber, the Tupolev OKB chose to use the wingtip-to-wingtip system which was inordinately complicated to use. This system was absolutely unsuitable for the larger Tu-95 and M-4 with their larger wingspan and elastic wings; therefore the probe-and-drogue system was used for these types.

In February 1957 a bomber achieved a non-stop range of 14,000 km (8,700 miles) in a test flight; the mission involved two IFR sessions on the outbound leg and on the return leg. Yet, for first-line pilots, 'hitting the tanker' was one of the most harrowing kinds of combat training. It demanded maximum concentration from the crews of the tanker and the receiver aircraft. Some DA pilots chalked up quite an impressive score in this type of operations; thus, Maj.-Gen. K. K. Subbotin, who served with the division stationed at Ookraïnka AB and rose from detachment commander to division CO, made more than 200 contacts with the tanker during the 13 years when he flew the 3M. It was he who made a non-stop flight lasting nearly 22 hours; taking off from Olen'ya AB in the High North and making contact with a tanker at night, the 3M bomber proceeded to the North Pole, thence to Kamchatka, passed the coast of Japan off Tokyo, then topped up its tanks once again and finally landed at Ookraïnka AB.

Starting in 1958, the DA began converting its M-4 bomber fleet to M-4-2 tankers. The M-4-2 could transfer up to 41,400 kg (91,270 lb) of fuel in a single sortie. It took about 20 minutes to transfer that much fuel, the crews being under considerable stress all the while – it was necessary to keep formation exactly while cruising at high speed.

The Tu-16 crews were even worse off – the wing-to-wing refuelling process was considerably more complex and dangerous. The Tu-16Z tanker would deploy a 40-m (130-ft) hose from the starboard wingtip on a cable of identical length. The receiver aircraft would place its port wingtip over the hose and a fitting on

The last seconds before contact is made; note the reference lights around the drogue's perimeter.

the rear end of the hose would lock into a receptacle; then the cable was rewound and the other end of the hose locked into place on the tanker. Next, the receiver aircraft manoeuvred so that the hose formed a loop, rotating the receptacle and opening a valve, whereupon fuel transfer began. The horizontal separation between the aircraft was a mere 6-8 m (20-26 ft), with the aircraft travelling at 600-800 km/h (372-496 mph). The slightest error on the part of either pilot would result in a collision or cause the hose to snap, striking the wing. To top it all, the pilots could not see the wingtips and had to rely on the senior gunner who sat in the tail, working the ventral cannon barbette; looking out of the port side sighting blister, the gunner would assess the relative position of the aircraft and give instructions to the captain. At night the process was even more complicated, notwithstanding the fact that the aircraft were provided with signal and position lights. As A. A. Belenko (HSU), a pilot with considerable experience of IFR operations on the Tu-16, put it, the procedure was 'akin to holding a tiger by the tail – sheer fear and no pleasure'.

Medics examining the Tu-16 pilots who took part in IFR operations established that the pilot would lose an average 4 kg (8.8 lb) during the mission – so great was the stress. During the refuelling procedure the pilots' pulse rate would go as high as 200 and the blood pressure would rise, too.

The 13th TBAD was the first to commence in-flight refuelling operations on the Tu-16 in

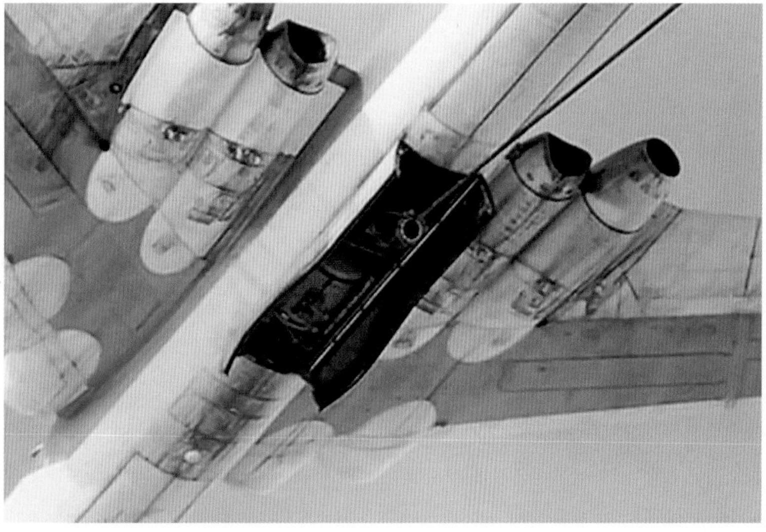

The KAZ hose drum unit and auxiliary tank in the bomb bay of a 3MS-2.

Opposite page, top and centre: 3MS-2 tankers of the 1230th APSZ at Engels-2 AB; the upper machine is retired.

This page and opposite page, bottom: 3MS-2s deploy their triple brake parachutes on landing. Note how the inboard flaps match the shape of the engine housings.

1956. By 1958 several of the division's crews had received their IFR procedure ratings. Also in 1958, a special group was formed in the 184th TBAP to coach the crews in IFR techniques; the coaching was done by instructors seconded from Moscow. The group included highly experienced pilots from various regiments.

Soviet pilots referred to the Tu-16's in-flight refuelling procedure rather mockingly as a 'circus act', yet everyone realised that they would have to master it fully. Therefore the crews had a sense of relief when the Tu-22KD/RD/PD/UD variants equipped with a nose-mounted refuelling probe entered service; wing-to-wing refuelling became much less frequent.

Soviet designers did their best to refine the IFR system and associated equipment, and with good reason – failure to make the rendezvous with the tanker out over the ocean could mean the loss of the aircraft, and possibly the crew as well. Hence in due course all IFR-capable aircraft of the Long-Range Aviation were equipped with the RSBN-2S *Svod* (Dome) and ***Vstre****cha* (Rendezvous) short-range radio navigation systems.

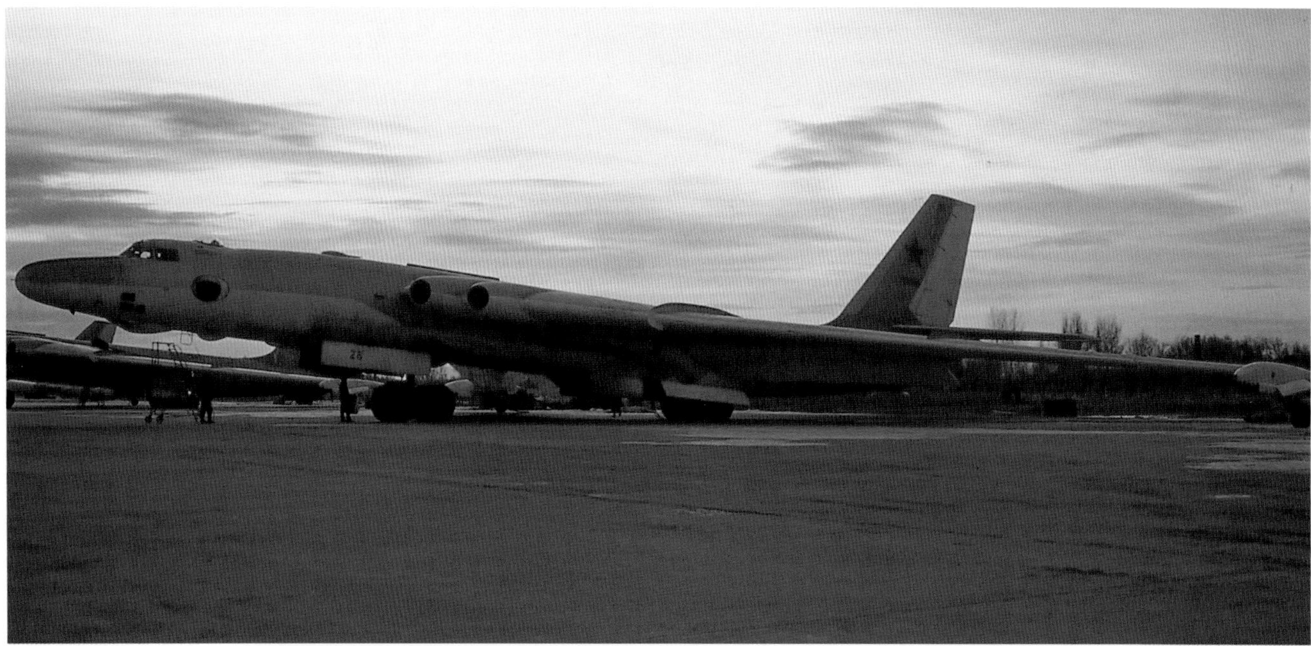

3MS-2 tankers on the flight line at Engels-2 AB.

A winter scene at Engels as a *Bison-B* tanker is readied for a mission.

A trio of Tu-95K-22s cruises in echelon starboard formation at differing flight levels.

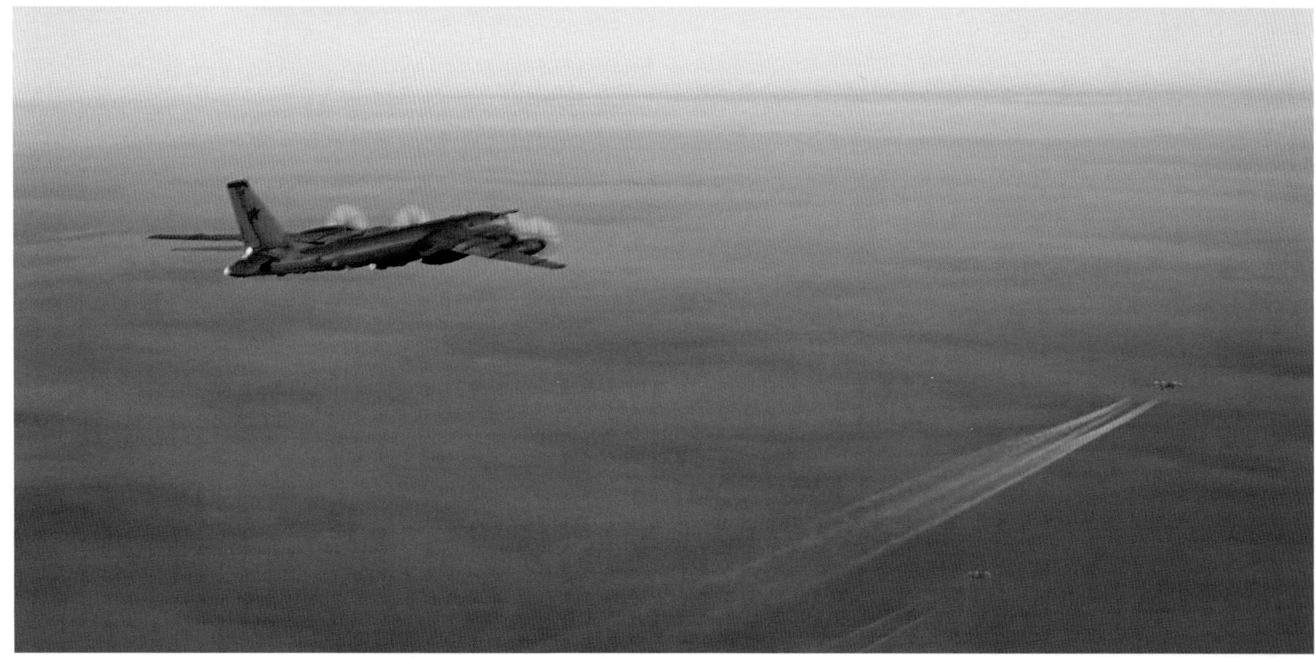

8 In Support of 'Friendly Nations'

The early 1950s were characterised by a boom of national liberation movements and revolutions all over the world. This was due in no small part to the spread of socialist ideas. The Soviet leader Nikita S. Khrushchov actively promoted a friendly policy towards Asian, African and Latin American states in the hope of winning them over into the socialist bloc – and quite often this policy bore fruit. Among other things, this policy included the extension of military aid – the armed forces of the 'friendly nations' would be trained by Soviet instructors and equipped with Soviet hardware. Hence the Soviet military colleges and academies received an influx of unusual cadets coming from Egypt, Iraq, Syria, China, Indonesia and so on. Among other military aircraft, the five nations mentioned here took delivery of Soviet heavy bombers.

Indonesia

In the spring of 1961 the government of the newly independent Indonesia had completed the nationalisation of the Dutch enterprises. However, Holland was not about to let go of its former colony so easily. Pretty soon Holland and Indonesia were at odds over the province of Irian Jaya (West Irian); the tension mounted and things were moving towards a military conflict. The USA, which placed the entire globe within the sphere of its strategic interests, sided with Holland; in turn, the Jakarta government sought assistance from the Soviet Union.

In 1962 the Soviet government took the decision to dispatch a squadron of Tu-16KS missile carriers from the Long-Range Aviation's 56th Breslavl'skaya TBAD, as well as a group of escort fighters, to Indonesia. The group of bombers was commanded by Col. N. I. Korobchak and senior navigator Yu. L. Deryabichev; it was composed of highly experienced crews that were hand-picked on the criteria of both professionalism, moral character and ideological trustworthiness. The crews were captained by Lt.-Col. A. A. Sharlapov, Lt.-Col. B. I. Sharonov, Maj. N. F. Akimov, Maj. N. A. Varlamov, Maj. L. V. Kotov, Capt. V. A. Lyamin, Capt. V. M. Meshkov and others.

On arrival at Jakarta the Soviet airmen made several flights over the capital to make their presence known and started preparing to wage war in Irian Jaya. An *ad hoc* airstrip was set up at Maratam, a coral island 500 km (310 miles) from the disputed province, where the Tu-16s would make refuelling stopovers. A supply of fuel and all necessary equipment to support the operations of the *Badgers* was delivered to Maratam, and three Tu-16KSs maintained a full-time presence at this forward operating location. This show of force was enough to make the Dutch and the Americans back down; the US Ambassador in Jakarta advised the Dutch government to avoid open warfare and transfer Irian Jaya peacefully to Indonesia.

Once the appropriate treaty between Holland and Indonesia had been signed, the Soviet crews were given a new assignment; they were now to act as instructors, training the local airmen to fly the Tu-16s which the Soviet government had decided to transfer to the Indonesian Air Force. This was an extremely complicated job, for the Indonesians had not flown any aircraft of a similar class before; besides, no flight charts and no interpreters proficient in aviation terminology were available initially. Still, these difficulties were overcome eventually. A practice bombing range was set up on Sumatra where the combat training took place. The aircrews of the 56th TBAD spent six months in Indonesia until the local airmen were qualified to fly the *Badger*; the ground crews stayed for another four months until local technicians had been trained.

Many of the Soviet servicemen participating in the Indonesian deployment were awarded the Order of the Red Banner of Combat for this operation.

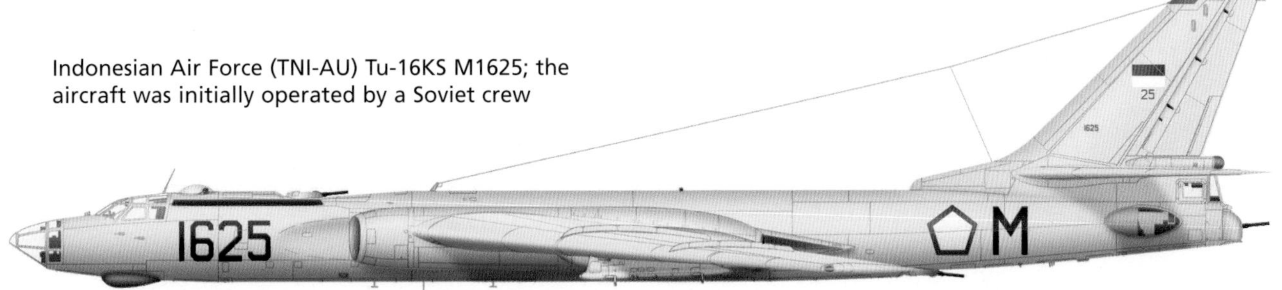

Indonesian Air Force (TNI-AU) Tu-16KS M1625; the aircraft was initially operated by a Soviet crew

M1619, one of the Tu-16KS missile carriers supplied to the TNI-AU. The aircraft were Soviet-crewed initially.

Another Indonesian Air Force Tu-16KS with two KS-1 missiles.

Egypt

On 23rd July 1952 a revolution (or rather military coup) took place in Egypt. The king was deposed and the Arab Republic of Egypt was proclaimed; Gamal Abdul Nasser, the leader of the coup, became Egypt's first President. In 1956 the Egyptian government nationalised the Suez Canal, a vital transport thoroughfare. This triggered the Suez Crisis; faced with the loss of the canal, Great Britain, France and Israel sought to recapture it by force. In the ensuing war, Egypt was backed by the Soviet Union, which had started supplying arms and sending military advisors after the revolution.

As part of the Soviet military aid, 15 Tu-16 crews from the Long-Range Aviation's 56th Breslavl'skaya TBAD/244th TBAP were on temporary deployment to Egypt from October 1962 to February 1963. The group was commanded by the division's deputy CO Col. Sevast'yanov; the crews were captained by:

Captain	Navigator
Lt.-Col. A. S. Shmonov	Maj. V. M. Doobrovskiy
Lt.-Col. Yu. I. Vladimirov	Maj. V. A. Shashkov
Lt.-Col. Ye. N. Kartunovskiy	
Maj. A. N. Volkov	Maj. V. V. Rudenko (became Air Marshal in 1987)
Maj. V. A. Shoyev	Maj. V. O. Zhivitsa
Maj. V. F. Laputin	Maj. V. A. Tkachov
Maj. B. B. Bachoorin	Maj. A. I. Antropov
Maj. A. A. Ternovskiy	Capt. A. V. Vasil'yev
Maj. P. F. Goodkovskiy	Capt. I. T. Bakhtin
Maj. Yu. P. Zakharov	Capt. Yu. V. Zakharov
Capt. A. M. Oseledets	Capt. M. V. Ponomaryov
Capt. V. T. Povedeyko	Capt. V. F. Levkin) *et al*

The Tu-16s were mostly operated by mixed Soviet-Egyptian crews; sorties were flown in large groups up to the bomber's maximum combat radius of 3,700 km (2,300 miles) and at altitudes up to 16,000 m (52,490 ft), and sometimes even higher. Most of the targets were in South Yemen, with an occasional target in Saudi Arabia. In order to hit the enemy vehicle convoys delivering weapons the bombers often had to descend to low altitude. The sorties were mostly flown at night, and when the Tu-16s returned to base in the early morning their fuel tanks were almost empty. Quite often the bomber formation was led by Brigadier Col. Hosni Mubarak, who would later become Egypt's third President.

The working conditions in Egypt were tough; quite apart from the climate, the crews

Libyan Arab Republic Air Force pilots and their Soviet instructors pose in front of a Tu-22 at Zyabrovka AB, Belorussia.

had to be ready to scramble at a moment's notice 24 hours a day. In addition to the 244th TBAP, crews from other DA units were seconded to the Soviet detachment. All of the Soviet airmen displayed excellent combat skill and unyielding discipline. After the Egyptian tour of duty the participating aircrews received Soviet and Egyptian military awards.

In 1967 Israel unleashed what became known as the Six-Day War (5th-11th June), delivering massive air strikes against Egypt, Syria and Jordan. The air forces of these three nations were largely destroyed and the runways at Egyptian, Syrian and Jordanian airfields were cratered. The Soviet Union, which had economic and military assistance treaties with the three Arab nations, took the difficult decision to fulfil its obligations under the treaties and intervene in the conflict. First, a political salvo was fired: in the course of the six-day blitzkrieg the United Nations' Security Council passed a number of resolutions demanding an immediate ceasefire. Israel, however, refused to abide by these resolutions. Then the Soviet Union and several other countries broke off diplomatic relations with Israel, and several Soviet Air Force long-range bomber units were placed on ready alert with the objective of

One more view of Arab trainee pilots and Soviet instructors at the same location.

bombing Tel Aviv and other Israeli targets. Luckily the Soviet units did not have to go into battle, as Israel chose to halt its offensive.

After the cessation of the hostilities, a detachment of six Tu-16T torpedo-bombers arrived from the USSR in September 1967, taking up residence at Cairo-West AB. There, Soviet instructors began training Egyptian crews to fly the type.

When the tension in the Middle East had somewhat subsided, Egypt began rebuilding its Air Force. Accordingly A. S. Shmonov (who by then had been promoted to Colonel and appointed Commander of the 45th TBAD) was tasked with taking delivery of ten brand-new Tu-16s at one of the production plants and ferrying them to Egypt. In April-May 1968 a group of Soviet airmen headed by Shmonov and his deputy Lt.-Col. V. P. Mikhaïlenko arrived in Egypt; it included N. Semenchuk, I. Yupatov, E. Zaïtsev, V. Kurushin and others. The group's primary mission was to demonstrate the capabilities of the Tu-16's reconnaissance and strike versions to the friendly Arab nations in the hope of attracting orders. Additionally, the pilots made a round of the local airfields to see which ones could host the *Badger*. It turned out that most of the Syrian and Egyptian airbases had rather short runways and offered neither the required support equipment nor navigation aids; therefore the Soviet pilots had to resort to their experience when operating into these airfields. The beastly local climate, with day temperatures of up to +50°C (122°F) and *khamsin* sandstorms, did not make it any easier. Once the task had been completed, the Soviet pilots turned the bombers over to the Egyptians and returned home aboard a Soviet Air Force Antonov An-12 *Cub* transport.

Libya and Iraq

The decolonisation of Africa and Asia continued in the late 1960s and the 1970s. On 1st September 1969 the monarchy in Libya was toppled; the country became a republic called the Socialist Libyan People's Arab Jamahiriya. The leader of the rebellion, Col. Muammar Qaddafi, became the nation's new leader and has remained in office ever since. True to type, the Soviet Union supported 'the nation's choice of independence', to use a Soviet propaganda cliché. Hence Qaddafi's government soon began receiving Soviet military aid, including combat aircraft for the Libyan Arab Republic Air Force; these included Tu-22B bombers and Tu-22UD trainers.

Crew training took place at Zyabrovka AB in Belorussia; the training course was completed in 1976. A while earlier, in 1973-74, Iraqi Air Force crews took conversion training for the Tu-22 at the same location under the supervision of Maj. Gen. V. S. Shookshin. The Soviet flying instructors recalled that the trainees took the practical part very earnestly but displayed a total lack of interest for the theoretical course. The language barrier was no problem, since the Iraqis had taken their initial flight training in the USSR and spoke Russian fairly well. Upon completion of the training course the Iraqis were allowed to pick the best of the unit's Tu-22Rs which they flew home after the aircraft had been converted to Tu-22B standard.

Iraqi pilots and Soviet instructors at Zyabrovka upon completion of the Tu-22 conversion training course in 1974.

Opposite page: Tu-22M2 bombers akin to this one were used in the Afghan War. Note the MBD3-U9 multiple ejector racks for bombs.

9 The Long-Range Aviation in the Afghan War

The Long-Range Aviation had a chance to 'fire in anger' during an armed conflict in which the Soviet Union was officially involved, unlike the Middle Eastern deployments – the Afghan War of 1980-89. The main share of the task of destroying the Mujahideen rebels opposing the communist government in Kabul fell to the Tactical Aviation and Army Aviation units seconded to the so-called 40th Army (the limited Soviet contingent in Afghanistan). However, the DA also got its share of the action. Individual crews, squadrons and entire regiments of the 30th and 46th Air Armies of the Supreme High Command flying Tu-16 and Tu-22M2/M3 bombers and Tu-22PD ECM aircraft made more than 1,150 sorties on the Afghan theatre of operations, 'fulfilling their internationalist duty', as a Soviet propaganda catch phrase went.

In the course of 1984 the 132nd TBAP, a single squadron of the 200th GvTBAP (both flying *Badgers*) and six Tu-22M2s from the 1225th GvTBAP pounded Mujahideen targets in Afghanistan with the largest free-fall conventional weapons in the Soviet inventory – 3,000-kg, 5,000-kg and 9,000-kg (6,610-lb, 11,020-lb and 19,840-lb) bombs. The 'veteran' Tu-16 was used in this conflict primary because of its ability to carry a 9,000-kg bomb. A single *Backfire-B* could take as many as sixty-three 270-kg (595-lb) OFAB-250-270 bombs.

The 132nd TBAP made two sorties with its full strength of 17 Tu-16s. In the spring of 1986 several Tu-16s of the 251st GvTBAP were called upon to destroy Mujahideen hideouts hewn out of the living stone or hardened with concrete.

One of the biggest raids on the Mujahideen base took place on 22nd April 1984. Twenty-four Tu-16KSR-2-5s, each carrying either 40 or 25 FAB-250 HE bombs, took part in the raid. The target was located in a mountain valley near Kandahar. Two squadrons from the regiment at Bobruisk and one squadron from the regiment at Belaya Tserkov' were involved; the aircraft flew in echelon formation, one squadron behind the other. The first eight machines were led by Col. Pachin, CO of the 200th GvTBAP.

At first it was planned to deliver the bombs from an altitude of 6,000 m, but the formation flew into cloud on approach to the target, which created the danger of collision since the aircraft were flying in close formation. Under these conditions, the group leader took the decision to climb and the target was approached at an altitude between 8,700 and 9,500 m. The lack of visibility meant that the bombing had to be carried out using LORAN. The first eight machines were greeted with anti-aircraft fire, although they were out of the air defences'

'71 Red' (c/n 7203804), a 251st GvTBAP Tu-16KSR-2-5 from Belaya Tserkov', was one of several operating into Afghanistan, being on temporary deployment (TDY) at Maryy-2 AB in December 1988

Nose art worn by 251st GvTBAP Tu-16KSR-2-5 '71 Red', December 1988.

range. The bombs dropped by the leading squadron neutralised the anti-aircraft defences, so that the other two squadrons carried out their attack unmolested. Gaps in the cloud showed explosions testifying to the accuracy of the bombing. On average each squadron dropped 250 bombs into an area measuring 200 x 300 m (660 x 990 ft).

After the Tu-16s had done their bit, the base was hit by Sukhoi Su-24 *Fencer* tactical bombers and Su-25 ground-attack aircraft. As the Tu-16, Su-24 and Su-25 formations attacked from different directions, the raid was unofficially dubbed a 'star strike' (***zvy-ozd****nyy* *na****lyot*** – an old term for such a tactic dating back to the late 1920s).

After their return to the airfield at Karshi, the Tu-16KSR-2-5s were refuelled and rearmed, and a new raid was carried out four hours later. This time each group of aircraft had its own individual objectives in destroying the remains of the Mujahideen gang who were fleeing in all directions from the devastated area. The bombs were dropped from between 1,500 and 2,000 m with the enemy clearly visible against the snowy background.

A Tu-22M3 in a rarely seen configuration with four MBD3-U9 MERs with nine FAB-250M54 bombs each.

A side view of the same aircraft ('94 Red').

Post-attack reconnaissance was made by a Tu-16R; the photographs showed clearly that the air group had carried out their mission with distinction.

In the autumn of 1988 a special Long-Range Aviation Group was formed in the Central Asian Military District, remaining in existence until the Soviet pullout from Afghanistan. It operated from three airbases – Maryy-1 and Maryy-2 in Turkmenistan and Khanabad in Uzbekistan (near Karshi). Its personnel came from various DA regiments.

On 31st October 1988 the 185th TBAP flew its first sortie over Afghanistan. The mission was led by the unit's CO Valeriy I. Nikitin, with his two deputies Androsov and Parshin as his wingmen. Merited Military Pilot of Russia Maj.-Gen. Pavel V. Androsov, who is the Commander of the Long-Range Aviation – that is, the 37th (Strategic) Air Army of the Supreme High Command – as of this writing, recalls:

'...1988 was a special year in my life; that was when I graduated from the glorious Air

Another aspect of the bombed-up *Backfire-C*.

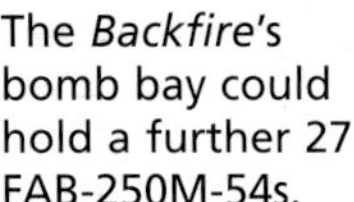

The *Backfire*'s bomb bay could hold a further 27 FAB-250M-54s.

Force Academy in Monino township. You can imagine a young officer's state of mind: there are bright prospects ahead, the wish to be stationed at the designated Air Force unit as soon as possible – and, best of all, training is done and now it's time to fly! Then came the commission assigning the graduates to their units. I could hardly believe my luck – I was assigned to the 185th Kirovogradsko-Budapeshtskiy Guards Heavy Bomber Regiment at Poltava as Deputy CO (Flight Training), and I would be flying the Tu-22M3.

Upon arriving at the airbase in late August I was introduced to the regiment's CO Col. Valeriy I. Nikitin and the division's CO Col. Leonid Ye. Stolyarov. Next, I was introduced to the unit's personnel that would be serving under my command. By the end of September I had brushed up completely my Combat Training Course as regards both daytime and night flying, passing the final check-up in October. The orders in late October 1988 to redeploy to Maryy-2 airfield and prepare for combat on the territory of the Republic of Afghanistan came as a total surprise, it seemed. We had thought that we, the Long-Range Aviation, would be left alone and would not be involved in the war. Yet, the Commander of the DA, Gen. P[yotr] S. Deynekin, had made a firm decision. Thus the Tu-22M3 received its baptism of fire. Accordingly, so did we – the men who flew these excellent fighting machines.

In the wink of an eye the airbase and its garrison had switched to an entirely different rhythm of life. All the experience accumulated during the years of training, flights, and painstaking work done by the regiment's entire personnel, HQ and CO now materialised in the extremely intensive preparatory work that followed the [redeployment] order. The regiment required less than 24 hours to redeploy bodily to a new strategic area of operations. Another 24 hours after the first landing at Maryy-2 the unit was ready to fly combat sorties in full strength. Our target was a concentration of bandits north-east of Kandahar. The first sortie was followed by others which were flown by the entire regiment or by sections. We flew our missions almost daily; from time to time the work was halted for no more than 24 hours in order to inspect the machines and prepare fresh loads of bombs.

FAB-1500 and FAB-3000 bombs waiting to be uncrated at Maryy-2 AB.

185th GvTBAP Tu-22M3s taking off from Maryy-2 in late 1988.

Tu-22M3s drop FAB-1500 bombs on a target in Afghanistan.

It is worth mentioning that the principal bomb calibres we used were 1,500 kg [3,306 lb] and 3,000 kg [6,613 lb]. Imagine what happened on the ground when the entire regiment unloaded their bombs! This means eighteen aircraft carrying eight FAB-1500 high-explosive bombs. The punch we delivered was astounding! Sorties had to be flown both in daytime and at night over virtually all of Afghanistan. As a rule, the targets were assigned in the late afternoon, once the debriefing had been completed, the day's strike results analysed and tomorrow's missions planned. The crews would be briefed on the mission, prepare for it, be checked and, after a short rest, return to the airfield. And off we would go, with nothing but the mountains to be seen underneath – silent, uneasy mountains which seemed about to scrape the aircraft's belly and which almost invariably would grow hideous in the target area, reaching out for our machines with the smoky trails of Stinger missiles.

Among other things, we had to do our job right next to the Afghan-Pakistani border. We had memorised well the lessons taught by the [Pakistan Air Force] F-16 pilots who would strike instantly across the border and return whence they came. [Lt. Col. Aleksandr V.] Rutskoi is the most vivid example; he was shot down while flying a sortie next to the border. (Rutskoi flew a Sukhoi Su-25 *Frogfoot-A* attack aircraft; he survived the shootdown and went on to become a politician after retiring from the Air Force – *Auth.*) *On such missions the close interaction with our fighter units stationed at Shindand and Bagram was a great help. Usually we planned our mission in such a way as to pass close to these airfields. On receiving our commands the fighters would scramble and formate with us, escorting us all the way to the target. While we were bombing the target they would loiter near the border, covering us against a possible F-16 attack; as we headed home, the fighters would cover*

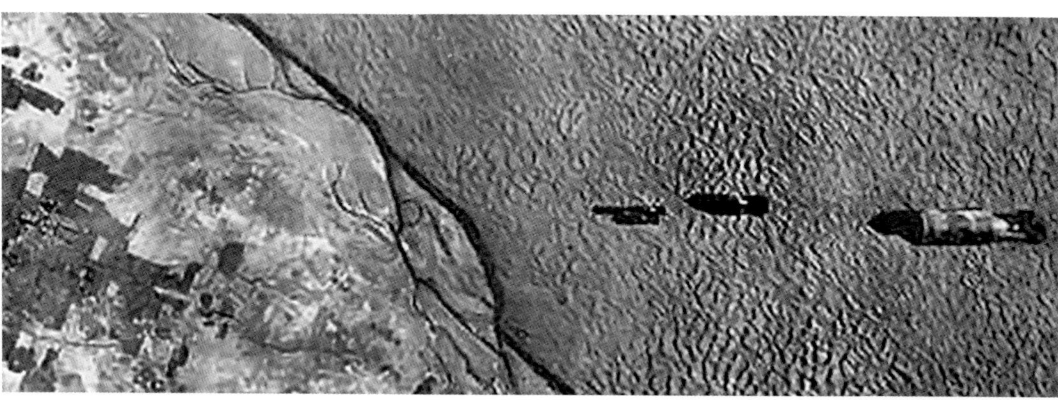
Depicted by the Tu-22M3's strike camera, AB-1500 bombs fall on the bank of the Dori River near Kandahar.

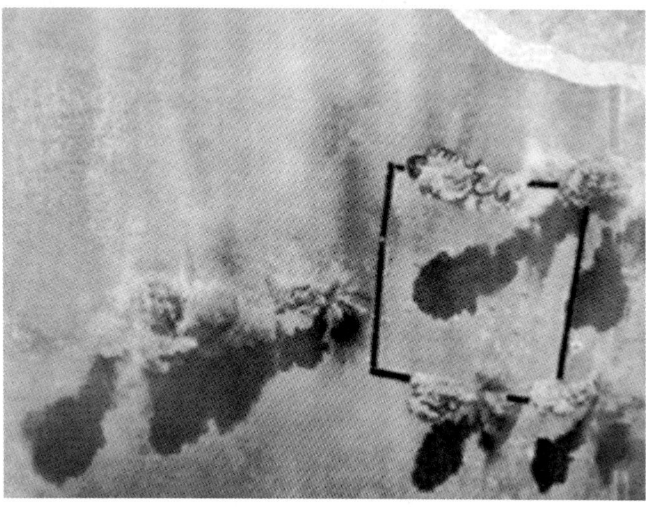
Smoke and debris rise from the target, a Mujahideen stronghold.

Maj. V. I. Bandyukov in his Tu-22M3 at Maryy-2 AB.

our tails. As we passed the fighters' bases we would radio our warmest thanks and proceed northward across 'the ribbon' (Soviet Army/Air Force slang for the Pyandj River forming the border with Afghanistan – *Auth.*), *while they would rock their wings and descent to their airfields in blazing Afghanistan.*

There is one particular sortie which I would like to recall. It occurred when our Afghan tour was drawing to a close. I was preparing my group for the sortie. The aircrews were briefed on the mission, received their sidearms and left to accept the bombers from the ground crews. My crew and I, too, were about to proceed to the aircraft when I was summoned to the control tower by the regiment CO. Telling the crew to go to the hardstand, I climbed the stairs to the control room and reported to the CO. Col. Nikitin asked me if the group was ready for the mission; I answered affirmative. Then Nikitin informed me that there would be a substitute in my crew, gave a few more instructions and dismissed me.

I felt ill at ease as I walked back towards my aircraft. Having a crew member substituted at the last minute is always considered a bad omen – all the more so because we were due to bomb a target located 20 km [12.4 miles] from the Pakistani border and 80 km [49.6 miles] from a Pakistani F-16 base, and I was going to lead the formation. According to the plan we were to drop our bombs at supersonic speed (Mach 1.4), flying at 9,000 m [29,530 ft]; each aircraft was carrying two FAB-3000 bombs. This mission profile was being flown for the first time; bombs of so large a calibre had not been dropped at supersonic speed until then. In a nutshell, this was a highly complex mission requiring high professional skill and good crew resources management, which means the crew had to be your close friends.

'Warm greetings to Ahmad-Shah [Massoud, one of the Mujahideen leaders]', says the inscription on this FAB-3000. The airmen are Maj. Troosov, Capt. Rekalov and Capt. Mochalov.

A Tu-22RD over the snow-covered mountains of Afghanistan.

Yet, we had to obey orders. I accepted the aircraft from the ground crew; the regiment's Chief Navigator Nikolay Simakov and I climbed into the cockpits and waited. Minutes before we were due to start up the engines the regiment CO's staff car pulled up beside the aircraft; the Commander of the 326th TBAD and the division's Chief Navigator Col. Peshkov stepped out of it. They climbed into the seats of the co-pilot and the weapons systems operator respectively.

The group took off and the mission began. The objective was completed successfully – the ground forces confirmed the destruction of the target. After the sortie, standing beside the aircraft, the Commander of the 326th TBAD thanked me for the flight and for the opportunity to examine the war zone. This commander was none other than Djokhar Musayevich Dudayev. Little did anyone know at the time that this man would later be the President of Ichkeria – now ex-President... (The 'Chechen Republic of Ichkeria' was the name under which Chechnya, run by Gen. Djokhar Dudayev as self-appointed President, tried to secede from Russia in 1993-94. Now it

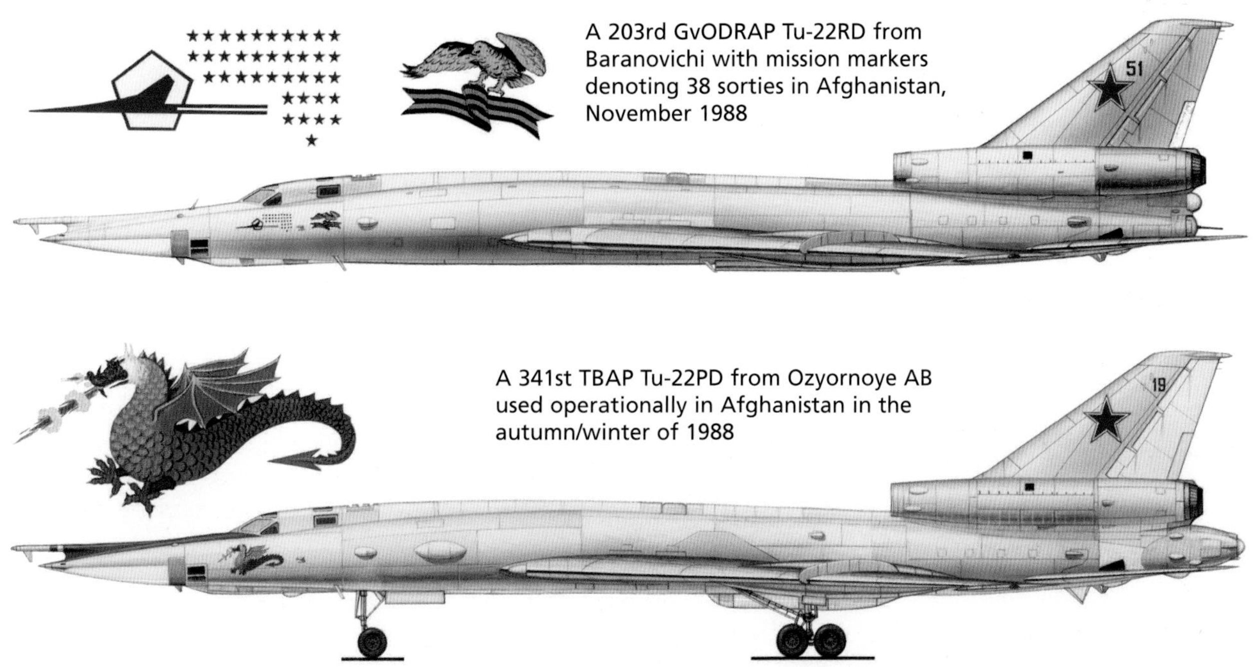

A 203rd GvODRAP Tu-22RD from Baranovichi with mission markers denoting 38 sorties in Afghanistan, November 1988

A 341st TBAP Tu-22PD from Ozyornoye AB used operationally in Afghanistan in the autumn/winter of 1988

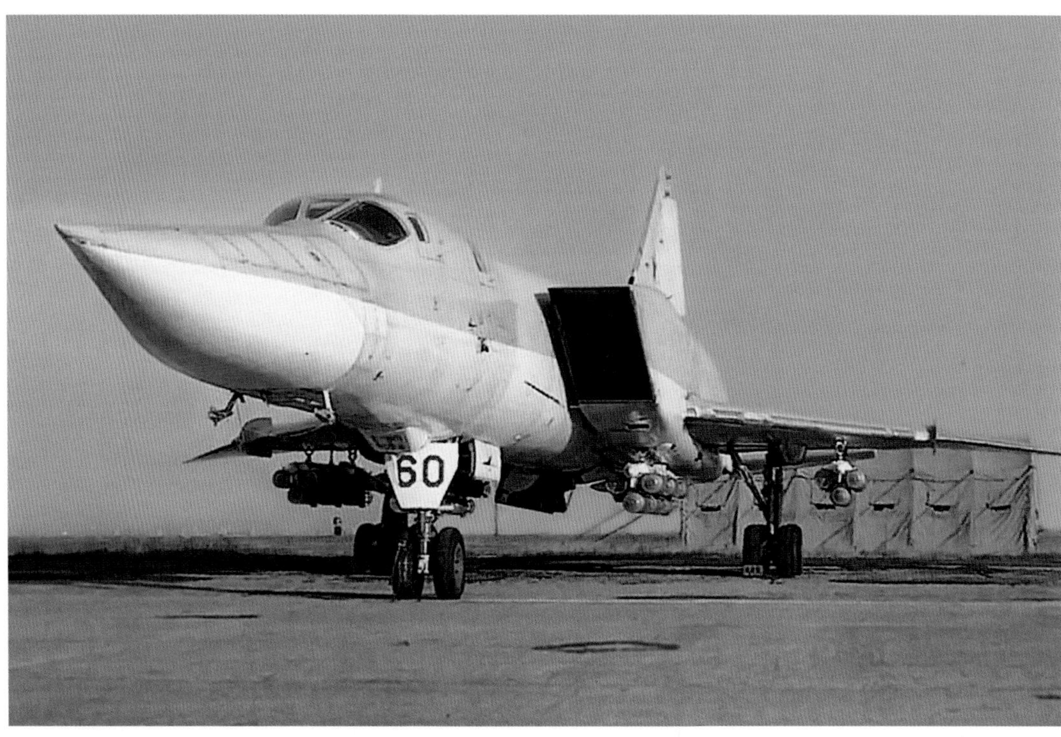

A Tu-22M3 with a full load of bombs awaits the next mission.

is officially called the Chechen Republic and is a constituent republic of the Russian Federation – *Auth*.)

During the deployment each and every member of the flying personnel had a chance to experience the atmosphere and mood of real-life combat at least once. Psychologically these missions took a fairly heavy toll on everyone; each man went through his first combat sortie in his own way. Gradually the men got the knack of it and became battle-hardened, acquiring that special state of mind of an air warrior which the former DA Commander Col.-Gen. V[asiliy] V. Reshetnikov, a Great Patriotic War veteran, so magnificently described in his book. The active work of the regiment's chief political officer Lt.-Col. I. F. Losenkov [aimed at boosting the crews' morale] deserves special mention in this respect. Credit is also due to the unit's tech staff commanded by Lt.-Col. R. A. Sirayev. Thanks to the care they took of our aircraft, the machines never let us down. God only knows when the technicians managed to grab some sleep. Boy, you should have seen the beaming face of our crew chief when he painted another mission marker on the side of our aircraft. Our logistics officers, signals officers and command post crews also gained a lot of practical experience. It has to be said that generally all of the unit's departments coped with their tasks well enough. Our regiment completed all missions without drawing criticism from the bomber division's command.

In late December 1988 our Afghan tour came to an end. The instructor pilots remained at Maryy-2 [to take care of the next 'shift']. We waited around until our colleagues from the 402nd TBAP arrived from Orsha and passed on our experience to them. We gave them a few familiarisation rides over Afghanistan and showed how we used our combat skills in practice.

Soon afterwards we redeployed back to Poltava. I am lost for words to describe how good it felt to see our families and friends again. The Afghan tour made the unit more mature and improved the crews' skill level. A check-up of our Air Army at large and our bomber division and regiment in particular by the MoD's Chief Inspectorate a year later was

Armourers hook up cluster bombs to the port outboard MER of a *Backfire*.

ample proof of this: our regiment was the only one in the Air Army to receive good grades...'

The Tu-16's typical bomb load in the Afghan War consisted of twelve 500-kg (1,102-lb) FAB-500 bombs. Sometimes, in special circumstances, larger or smaller calibre bombs of the M-54 or M-46 series – 250 kg (551 lb), 1,000 kg (2,204 lb), 3,000 kg, 5,000 kg and even 9,000 kg. The latter calibre was used by the aircraft of the 251st GvTBAP. The FAB-9000 could give the terrain a 'working over', levelling hills and high ground and producing craters so that the terrain resembled a lunar landscape. On occasion this was because the bombs were nearing the end of their storage life and had to be disposed of.

Bombing raids were carried out during daylight hours, using optical bombsights. The bombers were supported by Tu-16P ECM aircraft with 'Buket' sets to jam the Pakistani air defence radars, and also to counter the Pakistani Air Force fighters which often intervened and posed a serious threat to the Soviet bombers.

The aircraft flew from Soviet territory in small groups: a flight of three or four or a squadron of eight to ten machines. Only experienced aircrews trained in formation flying were chosen, and the overall standard for aircraft captains and navigators had to be no lower than Pilot (or Navigator) 2nd Class.

Bombing operations over Afghan territory were carried out by almost all air regiments operating the Tu-16 in the European part of the USSR. The most active was the Belaya Tserkov' regiment. The missions were flown from Central Asian airfields, particularly from Maryy in Turkmenia and Karshi in Uzbekistan. From here the crews made training flights over the desert and practised bombing with the aid of LORAN.

The badge of Maryy airbase.

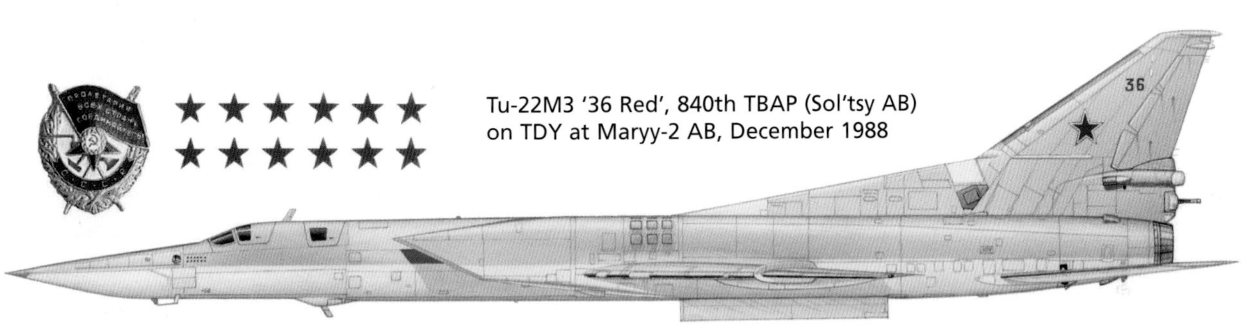

The Tu-22M3s bombed not only rebel fortifications, bases and materiel dumps but also mountain passes and any avenues of approach which the enemy could have used, causing numerous avalanches and rendering the roads impassable. 500-kg (1,102-lb) GP bombs were followed by 1,500-kg and 3,000-kg bombs which, as eyewitnesses recounted, 'flattened the mountains completely'.

Night sorties were also flown to keep the Mujahideen guerrillas from regrouping and

Tu-22M3 '36 Red', 840th TBAP (Sol'tsy AB) on TDY at Maryy-2 AB, December 1988

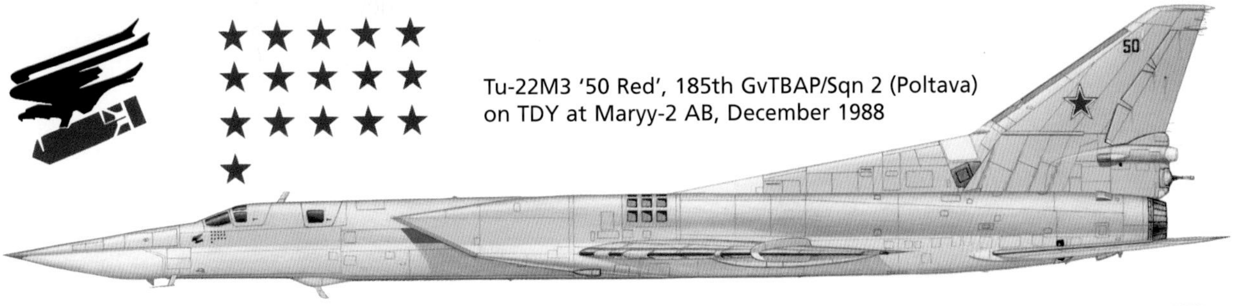

Tu-22M3 '50 Red', 185th GvTBAP/Sqn 2 (Poltava) on TDY at Maryy-2 AB, December 1988

Another 185th GvTBAP Tu-22M3 ('50 Red') Maryy-2 AB, December 1988

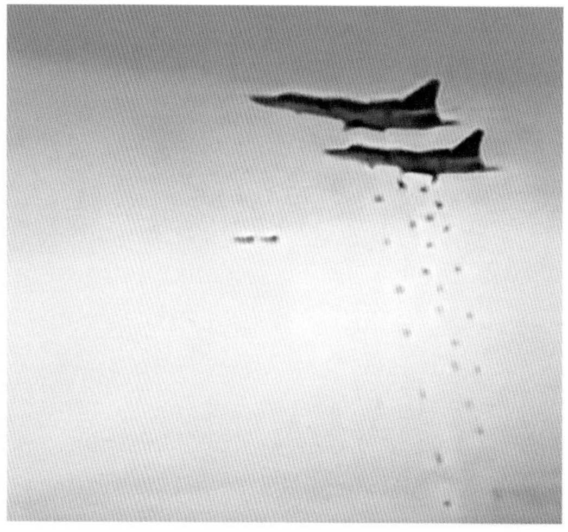

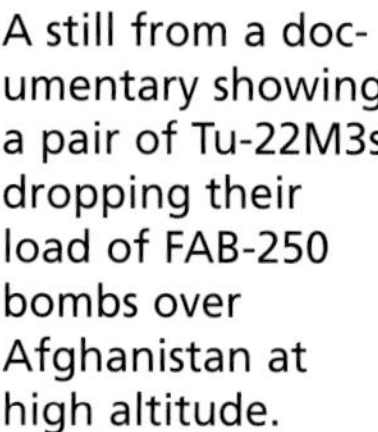

A still from a documentary showing a pair of Tu-22M3s dropping their load of FAB-250 bombs over Afghanistan at high altitude.

A Tu-22M3 dropping FAB-1500 bombs on Afghanistan.

A fiery explosion as the bombs find their mark.

Opposite page: A production B-4 (Tu-4) bomber at the factory airfield in Kazan'.

preparing for strikes against the leaving Soviet troops. The bombers also hit supply convoys coming in from Iran and Pakistan. Night missions involved carpet bombing; one such mission resulted in the total destruction of the city of Gerat. The Tu-22M3's final missions in Afghanistan were flown in January 1989 around the notorious Salang pass, the scene of bitter fighting throughout the war where many Russian soldiers died.

The Tu-22M3 typically carried two FAB-3000s or eight FAB-1500s in Afghanistan. Some of them were delayed-action bombs with time fuses set to detonate within six days.

As mentioned above, in December 1988 the 185th TBAP was relieved in Afghanistan by the 402nd TBAP (commanded by Lt.-Col. Yanin) and by the 840th TBAP of the 326th TBAD. The latter regiment flew 71 missions in Afghanistan, dropping a total of 122 FAB-3000 bombs on the Mujahideen. The division's commander Gen. Djokhar M. Dudayev made several more sorties during this period – combat sorties this time, earning the Order of the Red Banner of Combat.

The bombers flew high enough to keep out of range of Mujahideen air defences, especially Stinger man-portable SAMs, and not a single Tu-22M3 was lost or damaged during the war. In recognition of their services, many of the *Backfire* crews taking part in the Afghan tour received combat orders and medals.

Soviet Air Force *Blinders* saw action during the closing stage of the Afghan war. In October 1988 four 341st TBAP Tu-22PDs were detached to Maryy-2 airbase to provide ECM support for the 185th TBAP's Tu-22M3 bombers from Poltava in the Ukraine. The *Backfires* operating out of Maryy flew bomb strike missions against Mujahideen rebels in the areas adjacent to the Afghan-Pakistani border, including Khost province. Pakistani Air Force F-16A Fighting Falcons were becoming increasingly active in the area and Raytheon HAWK radar-guided surface-to-air missiles were also considered a distinct threat, forcing the VVS to take preventive steps.

The Tu-22PDs stayed until January 1989 when they were replaced by four sister ships from the 203rd TBAP. By then, however, the fighting had largely moved to areas within the country, notably the Salang pass. Mujahideen air defences were not so sophisticated there and ECM support was no longer a priority task, so the Tu-22PDs returned home by February.

The 199th ODRAP was also due to fly missions in Afghanistan. On 3rd November 1988, three of its Tu-22R reconnaissance aircraft were deployed from Nezhin to Mozdok in the then Checheno-Ingush Autonomous Republic (southern Russia). A week later, however, they returned to Nezhin without making a single combat sortie.

The final sortie of a DA aircraft in the Afghan War was flown on 14th February 1989 (some 'Valentine card', indeed). On 13th March all the bombers returned to their home bases.

10 The Aircraft of the Long-Range Aviation

The following is a brief description of the aircraft that saw service with the Long-Range Aviation in Soviet times. The development history of each type is given, but only the versions operated by the DA are listed (naval and experimental versions are excluded).

Tupolev Tu-4 *Bull* long-range bomber

By the beginning of 1945 it became clear that, due to the comparatively retarded level of Soviet aviation technology, the work on the 'aircraft 64' long-range bomber under development at the Tupolev design bureau would take longer than expected. This meant that in the very near future the USSR would lack a strategic bomber – and by the time the development problems had been overcome it might be too late, considering that the USA already had nuclear weapons. Bearing this in mind, the Soviet government took the unprecedented decision: to copy and series-produce the Boeing B-29 Superfortress long-range bomber. This was made possible by the fact that three B-29s which had force-landed in the Soviet Far East after carrying out raids on Japan had been interned by the Soviets in late 1944 in keeping with the non-aggression pact with Japan of May 1941.

The task of reverse-engineering the B-29 was given to Tupolev, and on 6th June 1945 the State Defence Committee issued its Directive No. 8934 for the organisation of series production of the B-4 (the Soviet designation given to the B-29) at Factory No. 22 in Kazan'.

The three airworthy B-29s were flown to Moscow. One was transferred to the Flight Research Institute (LII) for examination and compilation of an operating manual; another was placed at the disposal of the Tupolev OKB for dismantling, study, copying and the preparation of production documentation, and the third retained as a reference. After examining the machine, Andrey N. Tupolev assessed the time needed as three years, basing his estimate on the supposition that US technology surpassed Soviet technology not only as regards aviation but other related fields as well. The Soviet leader Iosif V. Stalin replied by offering Tupolev carte blanche but reduced the time allowed to two years. Some 900 enterprises and organisations were involved in the work on the B-4.

Tupolev began by creating a 'think tank' comprising the heads of the OKB's departments, with Dmitriy S. Markov in overall charge. As early as the summer of 1945, an operations group was organised to draft the aircraft's main assemblies. It soon became obvious that success could not be achieved without radical changes in the manufacturing technology and, above all, in the Soviet metallurgical industry. New structural materials had to be

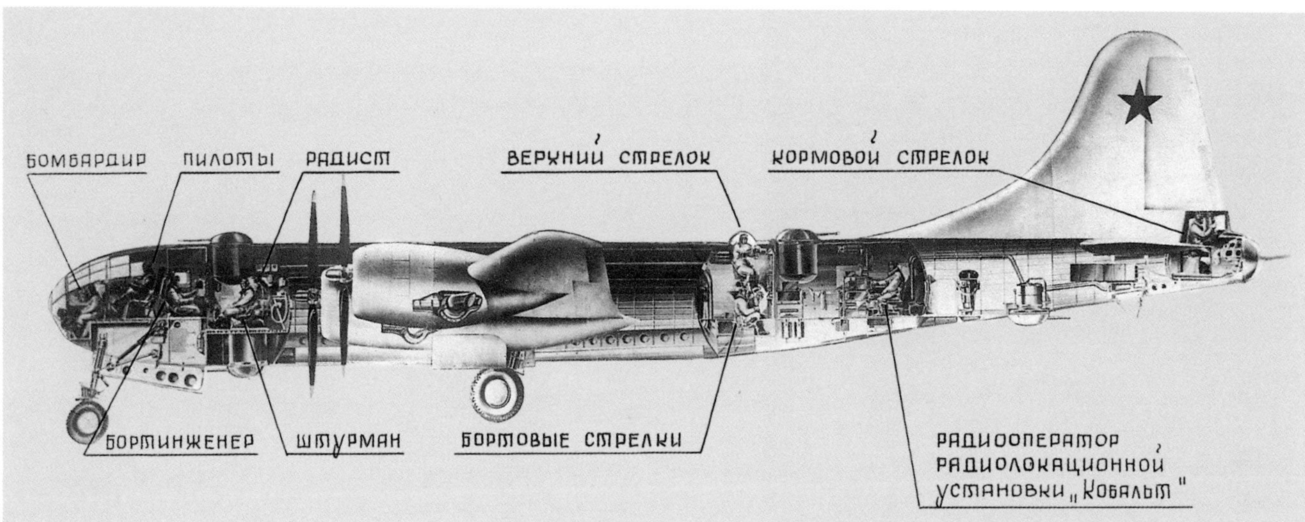

A drawing from the Soviet documents showing the Tu-4's internal layout.

developed, and more capable aircraft equipment and systems components had to be placed in production.

The Tupolev OKB strictly observed Stalin's dictum that the American original was to be copied exactly, since any deviation from the prototype on the part of the design bureaux could cause additional complications and adjustments, possibly leading at best to failed deadlines and at worst the to the failure of the entire project. The work of the OKB's structural strength analysts headed by Aleksey M. Cheryomukhin is a case in point. Together with the technologists, they had to work out the requirements for the Soviet equivalents of American structural materials. The structural strength department had to solve a difficult 'reverse' task – determining the dimensions of a real part in the B-29's structure after having studied the properties of the American material from which the part was made. They then passed the requirements for the new alloy to the metallurgists.

The task of stripping down the aircraft and making the manufacturing drawings was completed in March 1946, generating 40,000 pages of A4 size drawings. The aircraft's equipment was sent to specialised design bureaux for examination and copying.

The issue of engines for the B-4 was solved comparatively easily, as the aero engine design bureau led by Arkadiy D. Shvetsov had been working on derivatives of Wright radials built under American licence since the 1930s. In the late 1930s/early 1940s the Shvetsov OKB had developed the M-71 and M-72 14-cylinder radials which were similar in design and performance to the Wright R-3350-23A engines powering the B-29. Therefore, the American engine was not copied; the supercharged

Front view of a production Tu-4.

2,000/2400-hp ASh-73TK entered production instead. However, the supercharger and its control system, the magneto and the heat-resistant bearings used on the American engine were copied.

Another difference from the American bomber was the heavier defensive armament. The B-29's 12.7-mm machine-guns were replaced at first by 20-mm Berezin B-20 cannons and then by 23-mm Nudelman/Rikhter NR-23 cannons with the American armament control system retained.

In the spring of 1947, less than two years after work had begun, the first production B-4 was completed at Factory No. 22, and on 19th May 1947 a test crew led by Nikolay S. Rybko

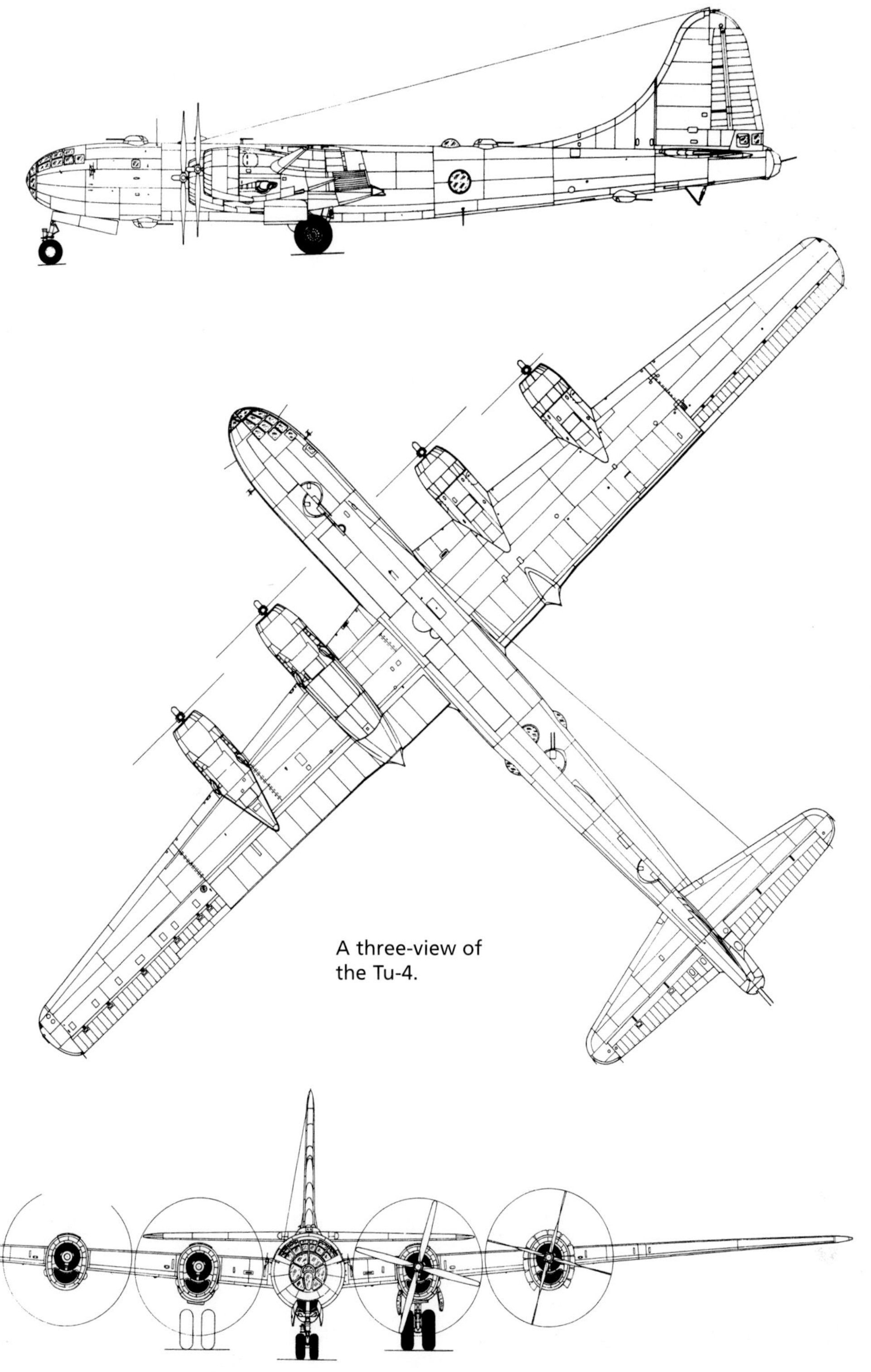

A three-view of the Tu-4.

An unserialled early production Tu-4s seen during pre-delivery tests.

made the first flight. The second and third examples were test flown by Mark L. Gallai and Aleksandr G. Vasil'chenko. By the end of the year twenty B-4 bombers had been built on which test and development work was carried out for almost two years.

A board headed by Soviet Air Force C-in-C Air Chief Marshal Aleksandr Ye. Golovanov and Deputy Minister of Aircraft Industry Pyotr V. Dement'yev was formed to oversee the flight test programme. Representatives of the organisations and ministries working on the aircraft's equipment frequently attended its meetings, with Dmitriy S. Markov as the permanent representative of the Tupolev OKB. Joint manufacturer's/Air Force trials were immediately conducted on the first batch of twenty aircraft, thus facilitating the maximum opportunity for rapid development and the aircraft's introduction into squadron service. In the course of its tests the aircraft was given the new official designation Tu-4 (*izdeliye* R).

Tests continued until 1949, the order for them to be held being signed by Stalin himself, a unique event in the history of Soviet aviation. Finally, on 11th May 1949 the Tu-4 was officially included into the Soviet Air Force inventory.

While tests and development work were still under way, full-scale production was gathering pace at Factory No. 22 in Kazan'. In 1947 production was extended to Factory No. 18 in Kuibyshev, and in 1948 to Factory No. 23 in Moscow. The three plants had produced 847 Tu-4s (of the 1,000 decreed by Stalin) when production ceased in 1952.

The following versions of the Tu-4 saw service with the Long-Range Aviation:

• Tu-4 – the basic bomber version built until 1952;

• Tu-4R long-range reconnaissance aircraft, converted from production examples of the Tu-4;

• Tu-4 REP (***rah***_dioelek_***tron***_noye podav_***len***_iye_ – electronic countermeasures) – production Tu-4 bombers fitted with ECM equipment;

• Tu-4 ELINT version retrofitted with electronic intelligence gathering equipment;

• Tu-4A (***ah***_tomnyy_) – ten examples modified to carry atomic bombs;

• Tu-4K (Tu-4KS) – a series of 50 Tu-4s adapted to carry KS-1 air-to-surface missiles;

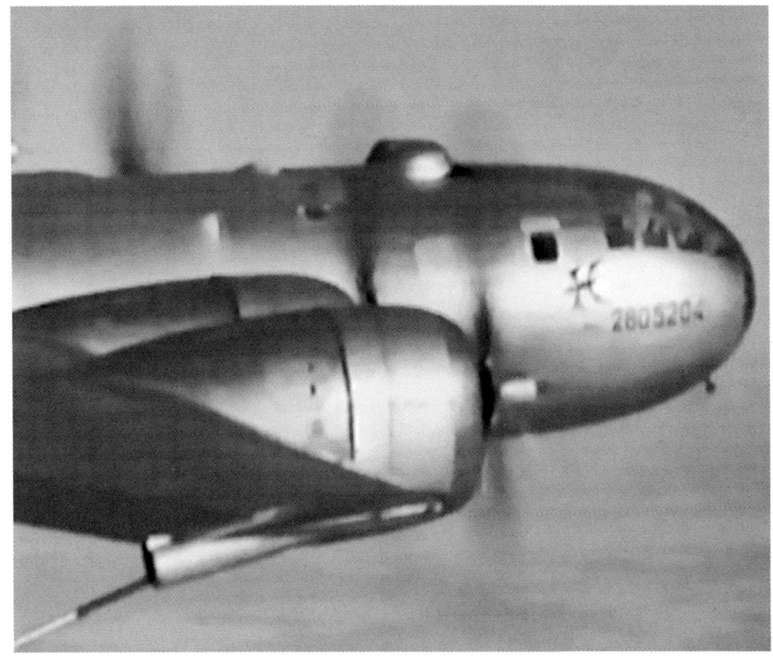

One of the Tu-4s converted into wing-to-wing refuelling tankers.

• Tu-4 (internal designation 'order 20'.) – a radiation reconnaissance aircraft specially equipped to monitor nuclear weapons tests;

• Tu-4 'Tanker' – several examples converted into in-flight refuelling tankers, using the wing-to-wing method for refuelling sister aircraft.

Specifications of the Tu-4	
Length overall	30.179 m (99 ft 0 in)
Height on ground	8.460 m (27 ft 9 in)
Wing span	43.047 m (141 ft 2¾ in)
Wing area	161.7 m² (1,740 sq ft)
All-up weight:	
normal	47,850 kg (105,490 lb)
maximum	55,600-63,600 kg (122,575-140,210 lb)
Top speed (with normal AUW):	
at sea level	435 km/h (270 mph)
at 10,250 m (33,630 ft)	558 km/h (346 mph)
Service ceiling	11,200 m (36,745 ft)
Range at 3,000 m (9,840 ft) until fuel exhaustion:	
with a 55,600-kg AUW and 1,500 kg (3,306 lb) of bombs	4,850 km (3,012 miles)
with a 63,600-kg AUW and 3,000 kg (6,613 lb) of bombs	6,200 km (3,850 miles)
with a 63,600-kg AUW and 9,000 kg (19,840 lb) of bombs	4,100 km (2,546 miles)
Defensive armament	10 x NR-23 cannons
Crew	11

Tu-16 *Badger* long-range bomber

In the early 1950s the creation of a jet bomber able to attack targets over a radius of 3,000 km (1,863 miles) with a speed twice that of the Tu-4 while carrying a comparable bomb load became a priority programme for the USSR. It had to be capable of striking at NATO bases in Europe and Asia, at the political, economic and military centres of America's allies, at NATO naval concentrations (in particular, carrier task forces) and shipping convoys from the USA to Europe and Asia without which any prolonged campaign by the Western allies against the USSR would be all but impossible.

Back in 1947-48 a Tupolev OKB team led by Boris M. Kondorskiy carried out research on high-speed jet aircraft, including those with swept wings. Meanwhile, the Il'yushin OKB brought out the IL-46 long-range bomber – a swept-wing design with two 5,000-kg (11,020-lbst) Lyul'ka AL-5 turbojet engines. When the IL-46 underwent its trials in 1952, it attained a top speed of 928 km/h (576 mph) and a range of some 5,000 km (3,100 miles). But the fact that Il'yushin had received the official commission did not prevent Tupolev from working unofficially along the same lines with the objective of producing an aircraft with better performance which would win round the Air Force. The combined research by TsAGI and the Tupolev OKB solved many problems affecting the aerodynamic configuration of a large swept-wing aircraft, the configuration chosen eventually having a wing aspect ratio of 7-9 and a sweepback at quarter-chord of 35°. In 1949 the OKB started work on a project known internally as 'aircraft 88' which received the official designation Tu-16. The preliminary research on the basic configuration and the calculation of the estimated characteristics was done by a number of recent grad-

An in-flight refuelling sequence involving a pair of Tu-4s; the tanker is in the background.

A Kazan'-built Tu-16A *Badger-A* nuclear-capable bomber (c/n 7203812) with white-painted undersides.

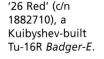

uates from the Moscow Aviation Institute, including the Chief Designer's son Aleksey A. Tupolev, together with Gheorgiy A. Cheryomukhin, A. A. Yudin, Igor' B. Babin and Vladimir A. Sterlin. The task was to create an aircraft with the following attributes:

- a bomb load of 6,000-12,000 kg (13,230-26,460 lb);
- a top speed at 10,000 m (32,810 ft) of 950-1,000 km/h (590-621 mph);
- a service ceiling of 12,000-13,000 m (39,370-42,650 ft);
- a range with a normal bomb load of 7,500 km (4,658 miles).

Within the confines of work on the preliminary design projects, the team considered a number of configurations powered by two to four AL-5 or AL-3 turbojets (the latter model was rated at 4,500 kgp/9,920 lbst). These included a project proposed by Aleksey A. Tupolev in which the engine nacelles were adjacent to the fuselage, which became the basis for further studies. After initial assessment, Andrey N. Tupolev approached the government with a proposition concerning the '88' for which he guaranteed a better performance than the IL-46. As the detail design progressed, Tupolev kept the work under constant scrutiny. Every morning he would call on Sergey M. Yeger's project team to find out how things were going, make any corrections and visit the mock-up shop where the full-size mock-up of the '88' was taking shape.

On 10th June 1950 the Council of Ministers issued directive No. 2474-974 for the Tupolev OKB to design and build the '88' with two AL-5 engines with the option of installing Mikulin AM-03 turbojets later. This was followed on 15th June by a specific operational requirement formulated by the Air Force. The project was completed on 20th April 1951 and reviewed by the Air Force, which confirmed its requirement for the version with the 8,750-kgp (19,290-lbst) AM-03 engines (production designation AM-3) – at that time the world's most powerful engine – in July 1951.

The Tu-16 was very different from the OKB's earlier designs. The central part of the airframe containing the wing/fuselage junction was area-ruled, a concept that became widespread

'26 Red' (c/n 1882710), a Kuibyshev-built Tu-16R *Badger-E*.

only somewhat later. The engines were located behind the wing torsion box, as close to the fuselage as possible, while the air intakes were positioned ahead of the wings so that the main inlet ducts passed through the specially designed wing spars (part of the air was routed below the wing torsion box). The problem of airflow disturbance at the wing/fuselage junction was solved by means of an 'active fillet' which used the engine exhaust to draw away the air flowing round the wings and fuselage, thus regulating the flow in that area. The wing sweep at quarter-chord was 35°, which created the optimum conditions for the control surfaces and their operating mechanisms. The tail surfaces were swept back more sharply than the wings (42° at quarter-chord), delaying the onset of shock stall and allowing an acceptable degree of stability and control to be maintained at comparatively high Mach numbers

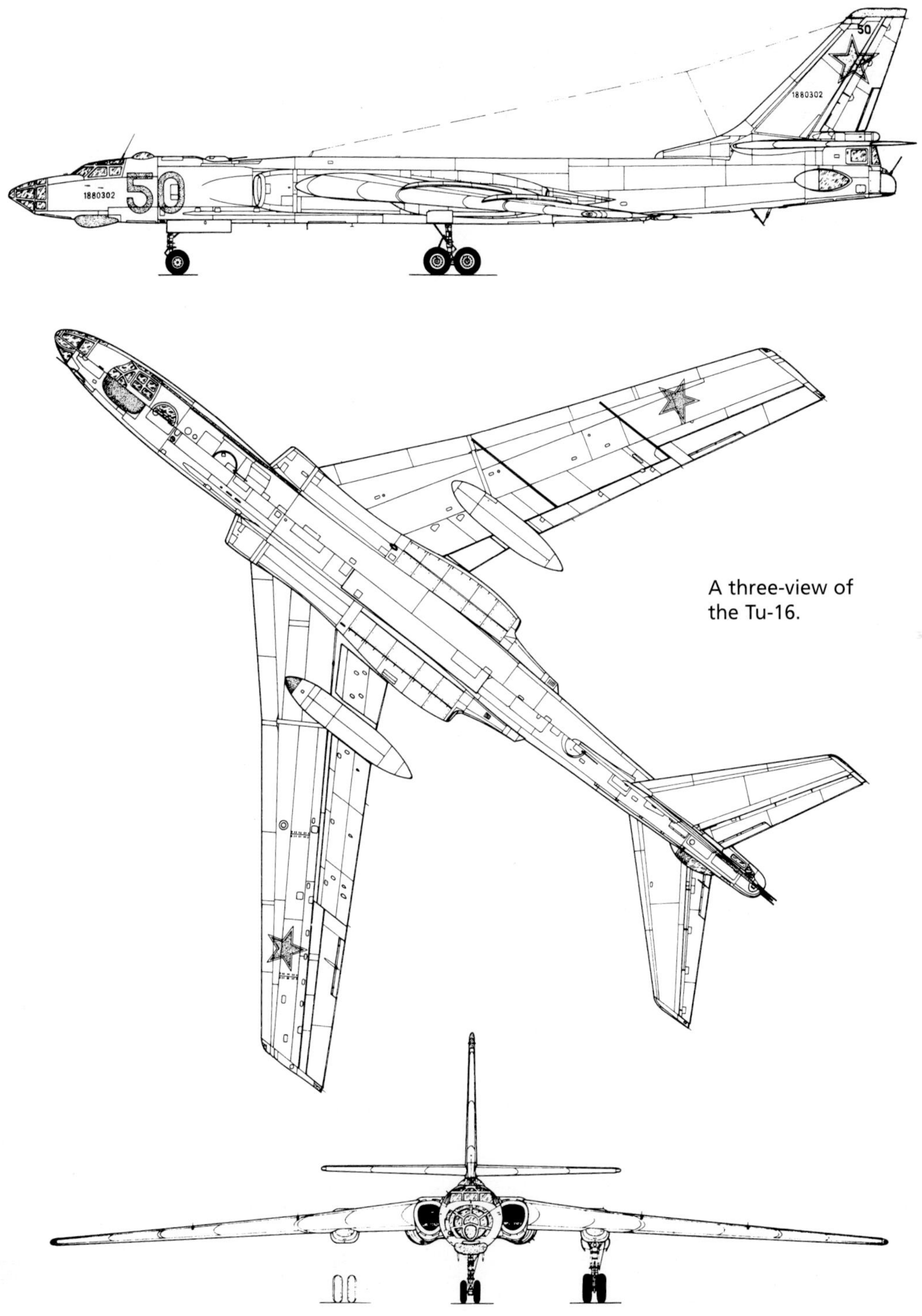

A three-view of the Tu-16.

A Tu-16A-KSR-2 *Badger-G* missile carrier (c/n 5201604) with bombs on adapters hooked up to the missile pylons.

(up to Mach 1.05). All these measures to enhance the lift/drag ratio, combined with the powerful engines, enabled the '88' to reach a top speed of Mach 0.92.

The high aspect-ratio (about 7) wings had a rigid two-spar design, the spar webs together with the upper and lower skin panels forming a strong box structure. This distinguished the Tu-16 from the Boeing B-47 Stratojet which had a flexible wing structure to dampen upsurges of air. The wings of the Tu-16 proved less prone to structural fatigue. Examples of the Tu-16 built in the 1950s remained active until the 1990s, whereas the wings of the B-47 began to crack after seven to ten years of service and the aircraft had to be retired in the 1960s.

The large bomb bay was located behind the rear spar so that the bomb load was carried close to the aircraft's centre of gravity. The fuselage's rigidity around the bomb bay were also enhanced by strong transverse beams.

The '88' also differed from preceding bombers in that the crew was accommodated in two pressurised cabins with ejection seats. The rear cabin housed both rear gunners, which allowed them to work more closely together in combat. The defensive armament consisted of Afanas'yev/Makarov AM-23 cannons in powered barbettes with optical sighting stations using either remote control or the PRS-1 gun ranging radar.

The main undercarriage units had four-wheel bogies that rotated aft through 180° on retraction to lie in special housings extending beyond the wing trailing edge. The nose leg was provided with twin wheels on a common axle to dampen shimmy effects on taxying – for the first time on a Soviet aircraft. Twin brake parachutes were also provided.

The working drawings for the first prototype ('88/1') were issued between February 1951 and January 1952, almost in parallel with the construction of the aircraft. In April 1951 preparation of the tooling began, and the prototype was been completed by the end of the year.

On 25th January 1952 the '88/1' was transported to Zhukovskiy for manufacturer's tests and the final fitting of equipment was

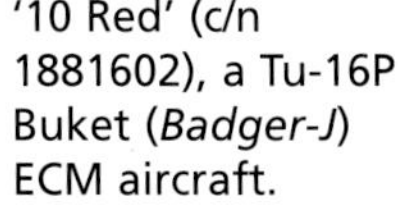

'10 Red' (c/n 1881602), a Tu-16P Buket (*Badger-J*) ECM aircraft.

Front view of a Tu-16E Azaliya (*Badger-H*) ECM aircraft.

completed three days before the aircraft was cleared for testing on 25th February. The maiden flight took place on 27th April 1952; the test crew was captained by Nikolay S. Rybko. Manufacturer's tests of the first prototype lasted until 29th October, the bomber attaining a top speed of 1,020 km/h (633 mph) – which exceeded the speed stipulated in the government directive – and a service range of 6,050 km (3,759 miles). On the other hand, the aircraft was 5,300 kg (11,680 lb) overweight. Bearing in mind that a full set of equipment and armament had not yet been installed, this was alarming.

The state acceptance trials began on 15th November 1952 and lasted until 30th March 1953. In spite of the good performance recorded at this stage, the '88/1' failed the trials, mainly because the special equipment functioned unsatisfactorily and the armament system was incomplete. It was decided to continue the trials with the second prototype ('88/2'), which was nearing completion.

The empty weight needed to be drastically reduced, and this was achieved on the second prototype. This work proceeded as a three-pronged effort: to lighten the non-stressed elements of the structure, to reduce the weight of load-bearing structures without detriment to their strength and to restrict the aircraft's speed at altitudes up to 6,250 m (20,500 ft) at which the Tu-16 would not normally operate. Thanks to these measures the empty weight was cut back from 41,050 to 36,490 kg (from 90,500 to 80,445 lb) – still above the target figure, but better than before.

Project work on the lighter version was finished in November 1952. Unfortunately, by then Factory No. 22 was gearing up for series production, using the old working drawings based on the '88/1', so that a changeover to the new lighter machine could have disrupted the deadlines for the first production examples to be rolled out in July 1953. Tupolev took the courageous and crucial decision to put the lightened version of the Tu-16 in production. Every effort was made to minimise the delay, and all the corrected drawings were supplied to Kazan' by the end of 1952. As a result the

Another Tu-16E Azaliya ('69 Red', c/n 8204214) with an SPS-151 jammer in a UKhO ogival tail fairing.

The second production Myasishchev M-4 *Bison-A* bomber.

rollout of the first production Tu-16 was postponed to October 1953.

The '88/2' was completed in early 1953, making the first flight on 6th April with a crew under Nikolay S. Rybko. With an almost complete systems and equipment fit the aircraft recorded a top speed of 1,002 km/h (622 mph) and a range of 6,015 km (3,737 miles). State trials began on 26th September, lasting until April 1954; this time the aircraft was recommended for service. Directive No. 1934-443 issued by the Council of Ministers on 18th May 1954 confirmed that recommendation.

As planned, production of the Tu-16 began in 1953. Subsequently various versions were built by three factories: No.22 in Kazan', No.1 in Kuibyshev and No. 64 in Voronezh. By 1963, a total of 1,509 examples had been built by the three factories (800 in Kazan', 543 in Kuibyshev and 166 in Voronezh). In addition, all three factories took part in modification and updating programmes, refitting production versions for a range of roles. Apart from the 11 versions built new at the three factories, there were about 40 others produced as mid-life updates. In the course of production the 8,750-kgp AM-3 engines were replaced by 9,520-kgp (20,990-lbst) RD-3Ms; the avionics suite was renewed; aircraft systems and parts of the airframe were changed; the armament was updated and the wing-to-wing IFR system introduced.

The following versions of the Tu-16 were operated by the Long-Range Aviation:

- Tu-16 (aircraft '88', *izdeliye* N) long-range-bomber. 293 examples built and supplied to the DA and the Naval Aviation (AVMF). Of these, 90 were refitted with IFR receptacles and 114 converted to tankers;
- Tu-16A (*izdeliye* NA) nuclear-capable bomber built at Factory No.22. 453 examples built and distributed about equally between the DA and the AVMF. Later, 155 Tu-16As were converted to carry KSR ASMs;

Initial production M-4s; the nearest aircraft is retrofitted with an IFR probe.

• Tu-16Z (Tu-16Yu, *izdeliye* NZ) wing-to-wing refuelling tanker. 114 Tu-16s were converted for the Air Force and the Navy; 20 later converted further to Tu-16NNs

• Tu-16N/Tu-16NN tanker (*izdeliye* NN). 23 Tu-16s and 20 Tu-16Zs were converted into hose-and-drogue refuelling tankers;

• Tu-16KS (Tu-16K, *izdeliye* NKS) missile strike version with two KS-1 ASMs, series built at Factory No. 22. 107 examples produced and supplied to AVMF. 40 examples transferred to Indonesia and Egypt, the remainder subsequently refitted as Tu-16KSR-2s;

• Tu-16KSR-2 (Tu-16K-16, *izdeliye* NKSR-2, izdeliye NK-3) missile strike version with two KSR-2 ASMs refitted from the Tu-16A and Tu-16KS as the basis of the K-16 weapons system;

• Tu-16K-11-16 (*izdeliye* NK-11-16, *izdeliye* NK-2) missile strike version with KSR-2 or KSR-11 ASMs forming the core of the K-11-16 weapons system. Refitted from the Tu-16A;

• Tu-16K-26 (*izdeliye* NK-26, *izdeliye* NK-4) ASM version with KSR-2, KSR-11 and KSR-5 ASMs forming the core of the K-26 weapons system; refitted from the Tu-16A and Tu-16K-11-16;

• Tu-16K-26P (*izdeliye* NK-26P) ASM version with KSR-2, KSR-11, KSR-5 and KSR-5P ASMs. Basis of the K-26P weapons system and converted from the Tu-16K-26;

• Tu-16KRM (*izdeliye* NKRM) carrier for air-launched KRM target drones converted from ASMs;

• Tu-16R (aircraft '92', *izdeliye* NR) photo-reconnaissance and ELINT version. 70 examples built at Factory No.1

• Tu-16P (Tu-16SPS, *izdeliye* NP) ECM version; 144 examples built at Factory No. 1. Subsequently other production examples of the Tu-16 were converted for ECM;

• Tu-16 'Yolka' (*izdeliye* NE); 42 examples of this version equipped with passive and active ECM were built at Factories 1 and 64.

M-4 *Bison-A* long-range bomber

Being a supporter of the long-range swept-wing jet bomber concept, Vladimir M. Myasishchev began preliminary design studies of the M-4 as early as 1948. The first proposals concerning the SDB were submitted by Myasishchev in February 1951. On 24th March 1951 the Council of Ministers issued directive No. 949-469 ordering the creation of the GSOKB-23 design bureau and appointing Myasishchev as its head. The OKB was to specialise in long-range heavy bombers. The directive further tasked GSOKB-23 with developing a strategic bomber (provisionally designated SDB) powered by either four Lyul'ka AL-5 turbojets or four Mikulin AM-3 turbojets. The aircraft was to be capable of covering a 12,000-km (7,450-mile) distance with a speed of 850-900 km/h (530-590 mph) and carrying a maximum ordnance load of 24 tons (52,910 lb). The first prototype was to enter flight test in December 1952. The general operational requirement (GOR) for the new bomber was endorsed by the Soviet Air Force Commander-in-Chief on 23rd June 1951.

Specifications of the production Tu-16A (RD-3M-500 engines)	
Length	35.2 m (115 ft 5 53/64 in);
Wing span	32.989 m (108 ft 22 5/32 in);
Height	9.85 m (32 ft 3 51/64 in);
Wing area	164.65 m² (1,772.28 sq ft);
Normal TOW	75,800 kg (167,110 lb);
Bomb load	3,000-9,000 kg (6,613-19,840 lb);
Max speed	
at 10,000 m (32,810 ft)	960 km/h (596 mph);
Service ceiling	12,800 m (41,990 ft);
Range	5,800 km (3,604 miles);
Defensive armament	7 x AM-23 cannons;
Crew	6

Leonid L. Selyakov was placed in charge of the SDB project. Quite a few configurations were considered for the new bomber. These differed in the wing and tail unit design, the number and placement of engines, but what they had in common was the large size, high wing aspect ratio and bicycle landing gear with outrigger struts retracting into the wingtip fairings. The ultimate configuration had swept wings, a conventional swept tail unit and four Mikulin AM-3 turbojets buried in the wing roots. The wings had 35° sweepback at quarter-chord.

The bomb bay was large enough to accommodate two 9,000-kg (19,840-lb) bombs one above the other. The defensive armament comprised three twin-cannon barbettes (dorsal, ventral and rear).

In November 1951 the OKB started manufacturing two prototypes and a static test article. The last of the manufacturing drawings were delivered by 1st April 1952, by which time the work was well advanced. Some Myasishchev OKB documents referred to the bomber as the 2M or VM-25. The Air Force, however, allocated the service designation M-4 under which the bomber would be best known.

A 3M *Bison-B* bomber at one of the Long-Range Aviation bases.

New production technologies were introduced as the M-4 programme gathered pace. For instance, to cut structural weight by reducing the number of skin panel joints the engineers decided to use duralumin sheets 2 m (6 ft 6¾ in) wide instead of the stock 1.5 m (4 ft 11 in) items offered by the Soviet metal industry; hence rolling mills had to be reconstructed and new thermal treatment kilns built.

The first prototype was rolled out in December 1952. After ground checks the aircraft was dismantled and transported by barge down the Moskva River to Zhukovskiy. There, at LII's airfield, the bomber was reassembled. The maiden flight took place on 20th January 1953, barely one year and ten months after the establishment of OKB-23. The aircraft was captained by Fyodor F. Opadchiy.

Full-scale production of the M-4 commenced at factory No. 23 in Moscow in 1954. Thus the Soviet Union became the world's first nation to field a new-generation strategic bomber (the M-4 became operational when the B-52 and the Tu-95 were still undergoing trials). The first few production aircraft participated in the state acceptance trials programme alongside the prototypes and were used for conversion training of service pilots which took place at the Myasishchev OKB's flight test facility in Zhukovskiy.

In 1955 plant No. 23 started manufacturing M-4s powered by RD-3M or RD-3M-500A turbojets; the existing *Bison* fleet was progressively re-engined by 1957. The RD-3M was more fuel-efficient and more powerful, with a normal take-off rating of 9,500 kgp (20,940 lbst) and a 10,500-kgp (23,150-lbst) contingency rating. The new powerplant increased range with a 5-ton (11,020-lb) bomb load to 10,500 km (6,520 miles).

Originally known simply as the *Bison* in NATO parlance, the initial 'glass-nosed' bomber became the *Bison-A* when new versions were identified by the West.

The Soviet Air Force was dissatisfied with the M-4's range which was only 9,800 km (6,090 miles) instead of the required 11,000-12,000 km (6,830-7,450 miles) – without bombs! Moreover, the wingtip-to-wingtip IFR system used by the Tupolev OKB was unsuitable for the M-4 because of the elastic wings. Hence Semyon M. Alekseyev's OKB-918 developed a probe-and-drogue IFR system for the M-4. The tanker's bomb bay accommodated fuel tanks and a hose drum unit (HDU) with a fuel transfer hose about 50 m (164 ft) long terminating in a stabilising drogue. This assembly was called KAZ (***kom****pleksnyy agre****gaht*** *za****prahv****ki* – integrated refuelling unit); the aircraft could be easily reconverted to bomber configuration by removing the HDU. The system was operated by the tail gunner.

The receiver aircraft featured a pneumatically operated telescopic probe atop the nose. The delivery rate was about 2,000 litres (440 Imp. gal.) per minute.

Tests of the probe-and-drogue IFR system on the *Bison* began in 1955. The second production M-4 was converted into the prototype of the M-4-2 tanker, while the first production aircraft was retrofitted with an IFR probe. In the course of the manufacturer's flight tests the receiver aircraft made 36 flights totalling 77 hours 7 minutes, while the tanker logged 63 hours 21 minutes in 32 test flights.

The state acceptance trials began on 27th September 1956 but were halted soon afterwards due to numerous problems which had to be rectified. There were several cases when the fuel transfer hose snapped; at worst the remnant of the hose whipped around the tanker's horizontal tail, which could result in damage to the elevators and loss of control.

Later, a different probe-and-drogue IFR system was developed in-house by OKB-23. The manufacturer's flight tests of this system were completed in February 1957. On one test mission the bomber received 35 tons (77,160 lb) of fuel en route to the target and another 24 tons

(52,910 lb) on the way home; as a result, the range was an impressive 14,500 km (9,006 miles)! Stage B of the trials ended in June 1958.

Starting in the late 1950s, the M-4 bomber fleet was progressively converted for the tanker role. The M-4-2 tankers worked with 3M, Tu-95 and Tu-22 bombers. All armament was deleted. The maximum transferable fuel load was 40 tons (88,180 lb).

3M long-range bomber (3MN/3MS *Bison-B* and 3MD *Bison-C*)

By the mid-1950s it was obvious that the Soviet Air Force would have to field both the M-4 and the Tu-95 rather than just one of them as originally planned. The two bombers complemented each other; while the *Bison* offered higher speed and a higher warload, the *Bear* could achieve longer range.

True enough, the fuel efficiency of the AM-3A and RD-3M turbojets left a lot to be desired. Hence OKB-23 decided to secure the Dobrynin VD-7 turbofan for the M-4. The *Bison* re-engining programme was formally launched in July 1954 when the Council of Ministers let loose with a directive ordering development of the M-6 bomber powered by VD-7 turbofans.

The different dimensions of the VD-7 brought about a redesign of the bomber's monobloc central structural assembly (the centre fuselage built integrally with the wing centre section). The rest of the airframe also underwent a major revision. New outer wings giving greater span and a larger wing area were designed. Wing aerodynamics were improved by eliminating the trailing edge kink which created vortices and hence drag; the wing camber was changed and the boundary layer fences were moved inboard. The fixed-incidence dihedral tailplanes gave way to new variable-incidence stabilisers featuring longer span and zero dihedral.

The fuselage nose ahead of the flight deck was extended by 900 mm (2 ft 11⅜ in) and recontoured. The navigator/bomb-aimer now sat aft of the radar instead of above and ahead of it. A welcome side effect of the new nose shape was that the IFR procedure became easier, as the airflow around the nose was less turbulent and the tanker's drogue was more stable. The redesign increased the lift/drag ratio from the M-4's 17.47 (an impressive figure as it is) to an unbelievable 18.5.

Analysis of operational experience with the M-4 made it possible to reduce the new bomber's structural weight by no less than 6,500 kg (14,330 lb). Updates were made to the systems and equipment. For instance, the flight control system incorporated yaw dampers; an ECM suite was added.

The maximum ordnance load remained unchanged at 24 tons (52,910 lb). The crew was reduced to seven; the flight engineer/gunner was replaced by an ECM officer and the radio operator was eliminated, his functions going to the dorsal gunner. The reduction of the crew and the relocation of the navigator's station allowed the forward pressure cabin to be made smaller.

The changes were so extensive that the bomber was for all intents a new aircraft. Hence the Air Force allocated a new service designation, 3M. Some OKB-23 documents, however, referred to the bomber as the M-6.

The prototype was converted from a standard M-4. Since flight-cleared VD-7 turbofans were still unavailable, the prototype had to be fitted with AM-3A turbojets as a stopgap measure. The aircraft made its first flight on 27th March 1956; the manufacturer's flight test programme continued until January 1957.

In 1956 factory No. 23 gradually started switching to 3M production. The first production aircraft was unique in that it had a mixed powerplant with two RD-3Ms to port and two VD-7s to starboard. The VD-7s were adjusted to limit their rating so as to avoid any asymmetrical thrust, thus providing a normal throttle position and coherent flight instrument readings. The third production example tested in September 1956 was the first 3M to feature the intended powerplant.

State acceptance trials of the 3M had to be postponed because of persistent problems with the VD-7 turbofans, which were prone to surging. It took almost a year to rectify this problem, and the final stage of the trials could not begin

An M-4-2 tanker refuels the M-4A ('85 Red') fitted experimentally with an IFR probe.

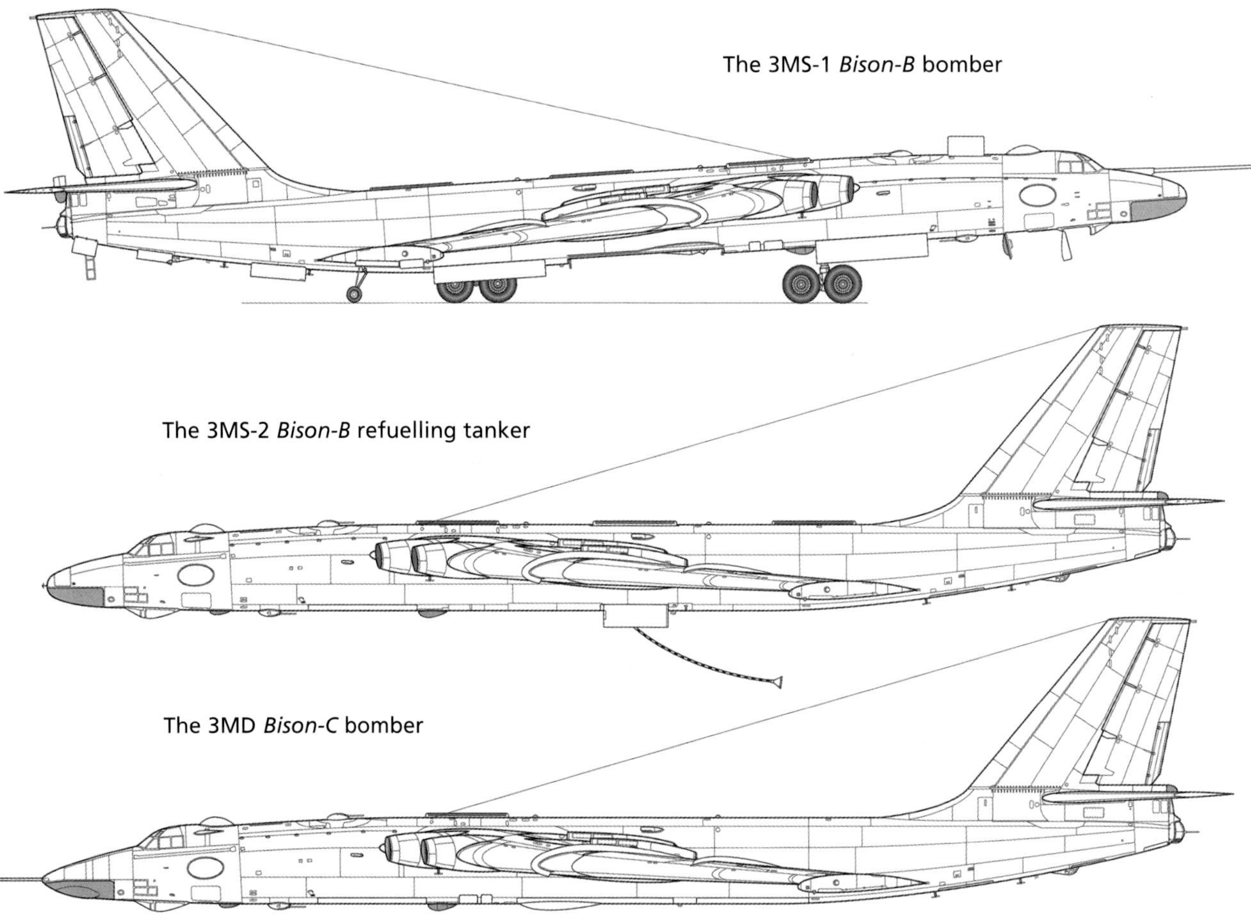
The 3MS-1 *Bison-B* bomber

The 3MS-2 *Bison-B* refuelling tanker

The 3MD *Bison-C* bomber

until 16th January 1958. The trials involved three aircraft; the first of these was used for performance and handling tests, the second machine served to put the equipment and armament through their paces and the third bomber was used for IFR system verification.

The 3M not only entered production but was actually included into the Air Force inventory *before* the state acceptance trials had even started, so acute was the need for the new bomber. Test pilots pointed out that the 3M was quite a handful during take-off and landing. A special panel was formed to look into the matter – and came to the conclusion that an averagely-skilled crew could not cope with the bomber. The Air Force acknowledged this; however, since the 3M was not produced in large quantities, finding an adequate number of highly professional pilots was no great problem.

Yet, new problems surfaced soon – and nearly wrecked the 3M's career before it had even started. Two brand-new bombers crashed fatally during pre-delivery test flights, stalling immediately after becoming airborne. What had happened was this. The nose gear unit had a special hydraulic damper which rotated the bogie when the nose gear was offloaded as wing lift increased on take-off, increasing the angle of attack and facilitating lift-off. However, unable to overcome their ingrained habits, some pilots would haul back on the control column to initiate rotation, just as they would on a tricycle-gear aircraft. This was the fatal error; the bogie would tilt faster than it should, catapulting the nose upward, and the considerable inertia of the heavy forward fuselage would then pitch the aircraft up into a super-stalled position.

The production-standard 3M was inferior in range to the prototypes – with an identical 5-ton (11,020-lb) bomb load the aircraft had an unrefuelled range of only 9,440 km (5,860 miles). In February 1957 a test crew successfully flew the 3M's first long-range mission which involved a refuelling from an M-4-2 tanker. On 19th July 1957 the 3M flew for the first time with drop tanks suspended under the wing roots. The bomber covered a distance of 12,050 km (7,484 miles) without 'hitting the tanker', staying airborne for 15 hours 15 minutes.

The introduction of IFR capability required the bombers to be equipped with short-range radio navigation systems. When the production 3M was discovered by the West, it received the reporting name *Bison-B*.

Not enough VD-7 engines could be manufactured for mass production of the 3M bomber because it took a while to overcome the engine's teething troubles. The problem was resolved when the Myasishchev OKB, the plant and the Air Force agreed to install RD-3M-500A, RD-3M or even AM-3A turbojets on early-production 3Ms. Such aircraft were designated 3MS (for ***sta****ryye* ***dvig****ateli* – old engines).

A version of the VD-7 turbofan derated to 9,500 kgp (20,940 lbst) to improve reliability was developed as the VD-7B. While having the same take-off thrust as the RD-3M-500A, it boasted a 20-30% lower fuel consumption. On 18th December 1958 the Council of Ministers issued a directive authorising plant No. 23 to manufacture 3M bombers powered by VD-7B engines. This version was designated 3MN (for ***nov****yye* ***dvig****ateli* – new engines). Since the VD-7 installation required structural changes to the *Bison*'s wings, the 'old' and 'new' engines were non-interchangeable; hence the 3MS served on alongside the 3MN.

The 3MS-1 and 3MN-1 bombers could be easily reconfigured for the tanker role by installing a KAZ HDU and the associated auxiliary tanks in the bomb bay. By analogy with the M-4-2 the resulting tankers were designated 3MS-2 and 3MN-2. At first they could be reconverted just as easily by removing the HDU; later the conversion was made permanent in the 1970s and 1980s.

The Tu-16K-10, Tu-95K-20 and other missile strike aircraft were seriously flawed in certain respects. Hence a Council of Ministers directive dated 7th August 1958 tasked OKB-23 with looking into the possibility of integrating stand-off air-to-surface missiles on the 3M with while still retaining normal bomber capability. Accordingly the OKB evolved the 3M-K-14 strategic weapons system comprising the 3MD bomber armed with two K-10S missiles. With one fuel top-up the 3MD would be able to attack targets up to 6,850-7,000 km (4,250-4,350 miles) away from base; the missiles would be fired 250 km (155 miles) from the target.

Until mid-1959 all work on the 3MD proceeded at the OKB's own risk. The OKB managed quite a lot during this period, performing wind tunnel tests and scaled-strength model tests with simulated external stores and so on.

Myasishchev M-4 and 3M family specifications

Type	M-4	M-4	3MN-1	3MS-1	3MD
Powerplant	4 x Mikulin AM-3A	4 x Zoobets RD-3M-500A	4 x Dobrynin VD-7B	4 x Zoobets RD-3M-500A	4 x Dobrynin VD-7B
Length, less IFR probe	47.665 m (156 ft 4½ in)	47.665 m (156 ft 4½ in)	48.76 m (159 ft 11⅝ in)	48.76 m (159 ft 11⅝ in)	49.20 m (161 ft 5 in)
Wing span	50.526 m (165 ft 9¼ in)	50.526 m (165 ft 9¼ in)	53.14 m (174 ft 4⅛ in)	53.14 m (174 ft 4⅛ in)	53.14 m (174 ft 4⅛ in)
Wing area, m² (sq ft)	326.35 (3,509)	326.35 (3,509)	351.78 (3,782)	351.78 (3,782)	370 (3,980)
Take-off weight, kg (lb):					
normal	138,500 (305,335)	140,000 (308,640)	140,000 (308,640)	140,000 (308,640)	145,600 (320,990)
maximum	181,500 (400,130)	184,500 (406,750)	193,000 (425,485)	193,000 (425,485)	193,000 (425,485)
Top speed at optimum cruise altitude, km/h (mph)	947 (588)	947 (588)	925 (575)	925 (575)	970 (602)
Service ceiling, m (ft)	11,000 (36,090)	11,000 (36,090)	12,250 (40,190)	12,250 (40,190)	12,000 (39,370)
Range on internal fuel with normal payload, km (miles)	8,100 (5,030)	8,000+ (4,970+)	11,800 (7,330)	10,500 (6,520)	10,950 (6,800)
Maximum payload, kg (lb)	24,000 (52,910)	24,000 (52,910)	18,000 (39,680)	18,000 (39,680)	18,000 (39,680)

A very early production Tu-95 *Bear-A* bomber.

On 22nd August 1959 the Communist Party Central Committee and the Council of Ministers let loose with joint directive No. 998-435 concerning the development of the M6K-14 strategic air-launched missile system including two K-14S cruise missiles (based on the K-10S) and a modified production 3M (M-6) bomber.

The design changes were kept to a minimum so as to ensure that a prototype could be completed before the year was out. Most notably, the nose was reshaped to improve the navigator's field of view. Other new features included a modified wing airfoil and a 40% smaller rudder easing rudder forces in emergency manual control mode. The systems and equipment were revised, too.

The first prototype 3MD was completed in November 1959, making its maiden flight on 25th November. A special joint flight test programme got under way on 1st February 1960. The second prototype joined the testing in 1960. Towards the end of the year, however, work on the K-14S missile system started winding down. Ten production examples of the 3MD were built but never carried missiles, being strictly bombers. The new front end of the 3MD was obvious enough to warrant a new NATO reporting name, *Bison-C*.

Tu-95 *Bear* Long-Range Intercontinental Strategic Bomber

As the Korean War demonstrated the inadequacy of piston-engined bombers, the Tupolev OKB abandoned further work on the Tu-85 (a Tu-4 derivative). It was essential to create a bomber matching the performance of the Boeing B-52. The new Soviet bomber had to enter service no later than 1954, the year in which the Kremlin anticipated the outbreak of nuclear war with the USA. It was to possess a top speed of 900-1,000 km/h (559-621 mph) and a range of no less than 13,000 km (8,077 miles) with a 5,000-kg (11,020-lb) bomb load.

Development of the intercontinental bomber designated 'aircraft 95' (Tu-95) or *izdeliye* V began in the spring of 1950. The machine was to be dimensionally similar to the Tu-85, with swept wings and tail surfaces; the wing sweep at quarter-chord was 35°. After exploring various powerplant options the design team settled for four turboprops, each rated at 12,000-15,000 ehp for take-off, as Tupolev believed turbojets would not provide the required range. With a take-off weight around 200 tons (440,920 lb), this would guarantee a 13,000-km service range and a speed of 800 km/h (496 mph).

The only viable Soviet turboprop at that time was the 6,250-ehp Kuznetsov TV-2F. Therefore it was decided to use coupled 2TV-2F engines on the prototype, with the intention of using the promising Kuznetsov TV-12 turboprops having the required output. The engines drove AV-60 eight-bladed contra-rotating propellers and were mounted in nacelles adhering to the wing underside; the inboard nacelles blended into the main landing gear housings.

On 11th July 1951 the Council of Ministers issued Directive No.2396-1137 calling for the design and construction of two versions of the '95' bomber: the first prototype (with four 2TV-2F turboprops) was to be ready for testing in September 1952 and the second (with four TV-12 turboprops) in September 1953. Factory No. 18 in Kuibyshev was earmarked for series production.

On 15th July 1951 the PD projects section under Sergey M. Yeger began draft design work, and in August the Air Force issued its own technical requirements. The bomber was to have a service range of 15,000 km (9,320 miles), a maximum range of 17,000-18,000 km (10,563-11,180 miles), a top speed of 920-950 km/h (571-590 mph), a service ceiling of 13,000-14,000 m (42,650-45,930 ft) and a take-off run of 1,500-1,800 m (4,920-5,900 ft).

Nikolay I. Bazenkov was in overall charge of the project. The PD project was completed in the autumn of 1951. The '95' benefited from the latest flight and navigation equipment that the Soviet industry was able to provide. New features included the use of aluminium wiring in the electrical system and electric de-icing on the wings and tail. On the other hand, the '95' had manual flight controls (unusually for such

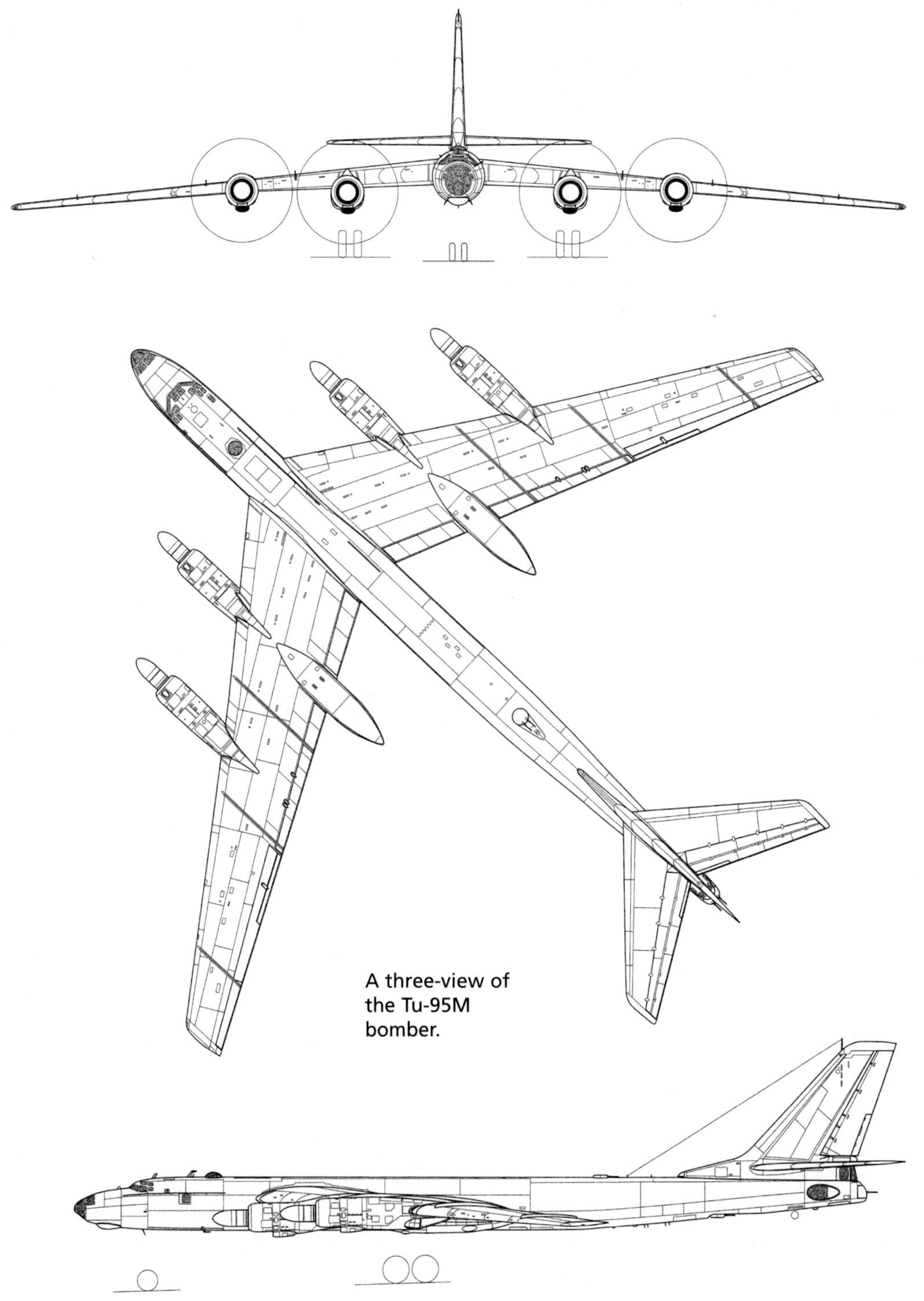

A three-view of the Tu-95M bomber.

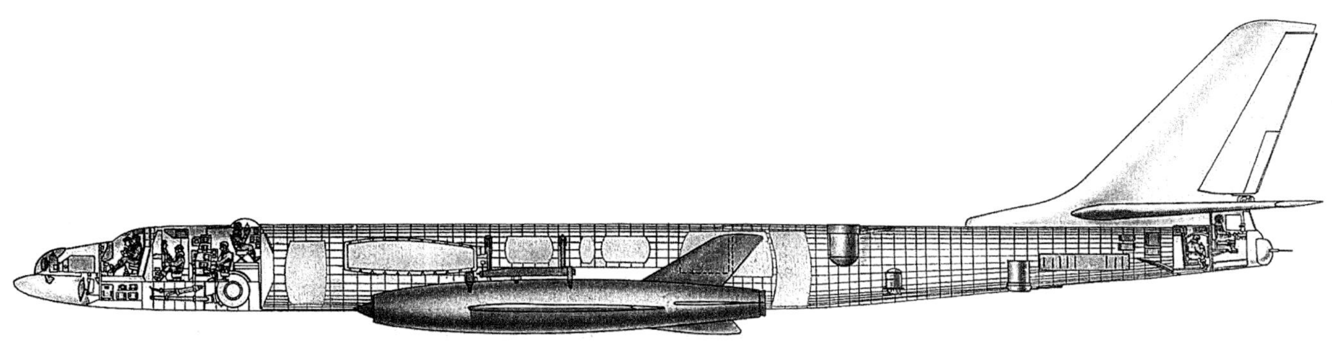

A drawing from the project documents showing the Tu-95K's internal layout.

a heavy and fast machine) because Tupolev continued to regard hydraulic actuators with suspicion. Ejection seats were also omitted to save weight – in an emergency the crew was to bail out conventionally. In the OKB's opinion this was perfectly acceptable given the speeds at which the Tu-95 was to fly.

Construction of the first prototype ('95/1') with 2TV-2F engines began in October 1951 and lasted a full year. On 20th September 1952 the bomber made its first flight, captained by Aleksandr D. Perelyot. Tragically, the '95/1' crashed on 11th May 1953 after a catastrophic engine fire, killing four of the crew. The crash, which was traced to the failure of the engine's reduction gearbox, could have had serious consequences; MAP was already considering terminating further work on the Tupolev machine. It was only thanks to the determination and patriotism of Tupolev and his colleagues that the Tu-95 programme was saved and work continued on the second prototype, the '95/2' with four TV-12 engines.

Design work on the '95/2' started in January 1952. Yet, due to the unavailability of the TV-12 engines, the aircraft was not flown until 16th February 1955. Manufacturer's tests lasted almost a year.

Meanwhile, Tu-95 production got under way at Factory No. 18 with the first two production examples rolled out in August 1955. Both of these together with the '95/2' were submitted for State trials which began in May 1956 with the first stage lasting until August. In the course of these the '95/2' achieved a range of 15,040 km (9,345 miles). As a result of the trials it was decided to install updated NK-12M engines and increase the fuel capacity. This updated aircraft designated Tu-95M was to serve as the pattern for production. Its flight testing ended in the autumn of 1957.

The Tu-95 family, including the Tu-142 anti-submarine warfare derivative for the Navy, remained in production until the early 1990s. During its long life the *Bear* was repeatedly updated, spawning a huge number of versions; the ones operated by the Long-Range Aviation are listed below:

• Tu-95 (*izdeliye* V) – the initial production model with NK-12 engines. In comparison with the prototype the production version had a take-off weight of 172 tons (379,195 lb) and

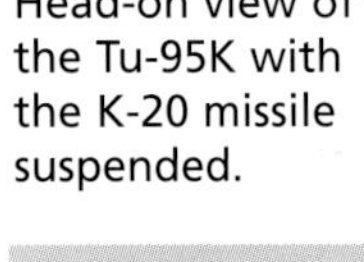

Head-on view of the Tu-95K with the K-20 missile suspended.

a range of 12,100 km (7,515 miles) with a 5,000-kg (11,020-lb) bomb load. A total of 31 were built between 1955 and 1958. Later the Tu-95 was updated with NK-12M (NK-12MV) engines and new equipment;

- Tu-95A – a version equipped to carry nuclear and thermonuclear weapons;
- Tu-95M (*izdeliye* VM) – updated version of the Tu-95 with 15,000-ehp NK-12M engines, greater fuel capacity, a take-off weight increased to 182 tons (401,240 lb) and a service range extended to 13,200 km (8,198 miles). 31 examples were built;
- Tu-95MA (first use of designation) – nuclear-capable version of the Tu-95M;
- Tu-95U (*izdeliye* VU) – Tu-95 and Tu-95M aircraft modified as conversion trainers;
- Tu-95MR (*izdeliye* VR) – four examples built as long-range strategic reconnaissance aircraft;

A Tu-95K-22 *Bear-G* with two Kh-22M missiles suspended under the wing roots.

The final version – the Tu-95MS-6 *Bear-H* missile carrier.

A rare view of the Tu-95MS-16 with ten Kh-55 cruise missiles under the wings.

- Tu-95V (order 242) – a modification of a production Tu-95 to carry the 100-megaton 'Ivan' hydrogen bomb;
- Tu-95 (order 244) – a production Tu-95M with increased fuel capacity;
- Tu-95K (*izdeliye* VK) – missile strike version with Kh-20 ASM forming the core of the Tu-95K-20 strategic ASM system. 48 examples produced;
- Tu-95KD (*izdeliye* VKD) – production Tu-95K with probe-and-drogue IFR system. 23 examples built;
- Tu-95KM (*izdeliye* VKM) – updated Tu-95K and Tu-95KD with new electronic and navigational equipment and armed with the updated Kh-20M ASM;
- Tu-95K-22 (*izdeliye* VK-22) – modification of production Tu-95KM to carry the Kh-22M cruise missile and the basis for the K-95-22 ASM complex;
- Tu-95KU (*izdeliye* VKU) – conversion trainer version of Tu-95K;
- Tu-95KM and Tu-95K-22 equipped with air sampling pods for monitoring nuclear tests;
- Tu-95MS-6/Tu-95MS-16 (*izdeliye* VP-021) – missile strike aircraft based on the Tu-142M and armed with 6 or 16 Kh-55 cruise missiles.

Specifications of the production Tu-95 (NK-12 engines) and Tu-95MS (NK-12MP engines)

	Tu-95	Tu-95MS
Length overall	46.17 m (151 ft 5 23/32 in)	49.13 m (161 ft 2¼ in)
Wing span	50.04 m (164 ft 2 5/64 in)	50.04 m (164 ft 2 5/64 in)
Wing area, m² (sq ft)	283.7 (3,053.7)	289.9 (3,120.4)
Max TOW, kg (lb)	172,000 (379,200)	185,000 (407,860)
Max speed, km/h (mph)	882 (548)	830 (515)
Service ceiling, m (ft)	11,900 (39,040)	10,500 (34,450)
Range, km (miles)	12,100 (7,520)	10,500 (6,520)
Bomb load, kg (lb)	12,000 (26,455)	none
Missile armament	none	6 x Kh-55MS;
Defensive armament	6 x AM-23	2 x GSh-23
Crew	12	7

Tu-22 *Blinder* supersonic medium bomber family

The OKB's draft work on transonic long-range bombers in the early 1950s led to the creation of the supersonic Tu-22. At the beginning of 1954 Andrey N. Tupolev approached MAP with a proposal for a supersonic long-range bomber which would replace the subsonic Tu-16 in due course.

On 30th July 1954 the Council of Ministers passed Directive No.1605-726 ordering the Tupolev OKB to design and build the 'aircraft 105' bomber based on the Tu-16 with two 18,510-kgp (40,810-lbst) Dobrynin VD-5F afterburning turbojets. The aircraft was required to have:

- a maximum supersonic speed of 1,400-1,500 km/h (870-931 mph);
- a service range of 5,800 km (3,604 miles) at subsonic speed, 4,000-5,000 km (2,485-3,105 miles) with a subsonic/supersonic mission profile, and 2,250-2,700 km/h (1,398-1,677 mph) at supersonic speed;
- a service ceiling while overflying the target at supersonic speed of 14,000-15,000 m (45,930-49,210 ft);
- a bomb load of 3,000-9,000 kg (6,610-19,840 lb).

The crew was to comprise three or four. The two prototypes were to be completed in 1956.

By November 1954 several different aerodynamic layouts had been prepared; these were based on the successful configuration of the Tu-16 but with the changes necessary for supersonic flight. On TsAGI's recommendation the engines were placed over the rear fuselage, flanking the base of the fin. In the summer of 1955 the VD-5F engines were replaced by 16,000-kgp (35,270-lbst) VD-7M afterburning turbofans. Initial design work was carried out in Sergey M. Yeger's PD project section, with Dmitriy S. Markov as programme chief.

An early production Tu-22R reconnaissance aircraft.

Actual design work began on 15th August 1955, with prototype construction started in November 1955 and concluded in December 1957. In the early summer of 1958, after final assembly and fitting, the final adjustment work, ground tests and first taxying trials were made.

Again, the '105' was very different from all the preceding designs produced by the Tupolev OKB. The long fuselage with its pointed nose, the swept wings placed far back on the fuselage and the unusual placement of the engines showed this was a machine designed to fly at very high speeds. The aerodynamically clean wings without wing fences had 55° leading-edge sweep. The main undercarriage bogies retracted inward into the fuselage, not aft. The crew of three was accommodated in the forward pressurised cabin; the defensive armament was limited to a tail cannon controlled by means of a television sight and a gun-laying radar. The tall fin meant that the crew had to eject downwards, which limited the minimum safe ejection altitude. The conditions of supersonic flight necessitated a variable-incidence tailplane and required the use of irreversible hydraulic actuators; manual controls were retained as a back-up.

On 21st June the 'aircraft 105' made its first flight, piloted by Yuriy T. Alasheyev. After only a dozen test flights the bomber was written off in a belly landing. It was decided to carry out further work on the second prototype, 'aircraft 105A' – the future Tu-22. Council of Ministers directive No. 426-201 on the Tu-22 was passed on 17th April 1958.

Design work on the '105A' started in August 1957. Unlike the '105', the second prototype had an area-ruled fuselage and the usual Tupolev main gear design, the bogies retracting aft into characteristic housings. Assembly of the '105A' began in January 1958 and was completed by the following summer. The bomber made its first flight on 7th September. Sadly, this aircraft was lost during its seventh test flight on 21st December. Only the gunner/radio-operator was able to eject. After this the structure of the aircraft was revised, and tests continued even on the first production examples.

While the '105A' was undergoing tests, Factory No. 22 in Kazan' was gearing up to produce it as the Tu-22 (alias *izdeliye* Yu, later renamed *izdeliye* A). The initial batch consisted of Tu-22A bombers. In 1960 the Tu-22 was revised as a matter of urgency: the struc-

'61 Red', a Tu-22KD missile carrier with dragon nose art.

ture was strengthened and slab stabilisers were used instead of conventional ones with inset elevators. The engine nacelles were also raised slightly to reduce the risk of engine surge.

Production of new aircraft was maintained even while the tests were being conducted. In July 1961 nine Tu-22s flew over Moscow-Tushino aerodrome during the annual Aviation Day display, whereupon the NATO reporting name *Blinder* was assigned. The Tu-22 proved to be quite temperamental, and actually the aircraft was not cured of its teething troubles until the 1970s. Series production went on until December 1969 with Factory No. 22 building a total of 311 examples. In December 1968 the Tu-22R, Tu-22K, Tu-22P and Tu-22U were officially included into the Air Force inventory. In the course of production the VD-7M engines were replaced by the more

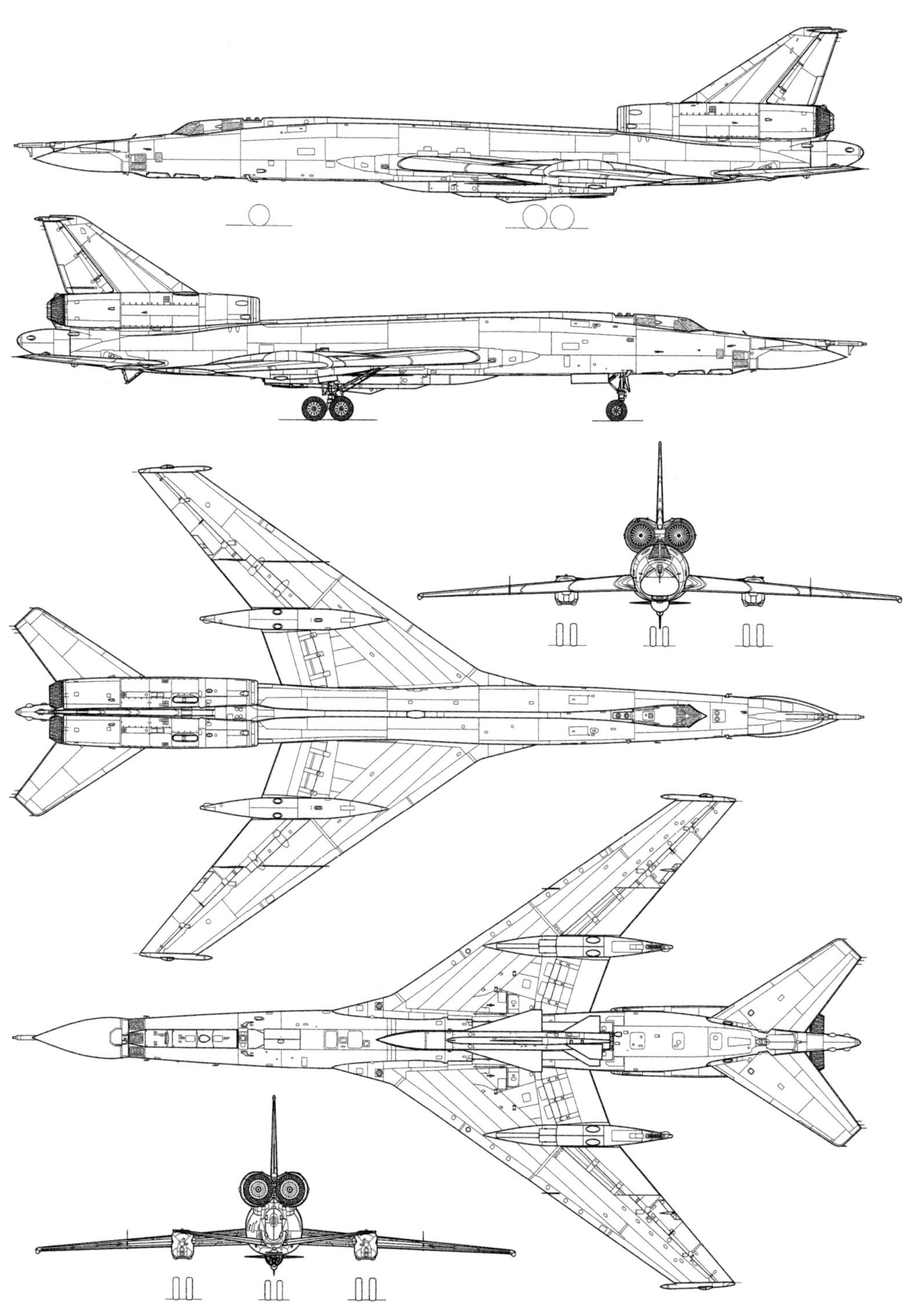

Six views of a Tu-22KD with a UKhO rear ECM fairing and a Kh-22 missile attached.

A Tu-22KD retaining the standard tail gun barbette and gun laying radar.

reliable RD-7M2s providing 500 kgp (1,100 lbst) more maximum thrust, a probe and drogue IFR system was fitted, and both the avionics and armament were constantly modernised. The following versions saw service with the Long-Range Aviation:

- Tu-22A bomber. 15 examples built;
- Tu-22R photo reconnaissance/ELINT version. 127 examples built;
- Tu-22K missile carrier armed with the Kh-22 ASM (part of the K-22 weapons system), 76 built;
- Tu-22P ECM version. 47 built;
- Tu-22U trainer version. 46 built;
- Tu-22RD, Tu-22KD, Tu-22PD – IFR-equipped production machines (176 examples built);
- Tu-22RK and Tu-22RDK – production reconnaissance machines with updated ELINT equipment;
- Tu-22RM – modernised reconnaissance version;
- Tu-22RDM – reconnaissance version with new mission equipment;
- Tu-22KP and Tu-22KPD missile carriers (part of the K-22P weapons system) armed with the passive radar homing Kh-22P ASM.

Specifications of the production Tu-22R (RD-7M2 engines)	
Length	41.04 m (134 ft 1⅝ in)
Wing span	23.646 m (77 ft 6 15/16 in)
Height	9.7 m (31 ft 9 57/64 in)
Wing area	162.25 m² (1,746.4 sq ft)
Max TOW	92,000 kg (202,830 lb)
Max speed with a 69,000-kg (152,130-lb)	
TOW at 11,000 m (36,090 ft)	1,600 km/h (991 mph)
Service range with a 92,000-kg TOW:	
at subsonic speed	5,000 km (3,105 miles)
at 1,300 km/h (810 mph)	1,800 km (1,118 miles)
Service ceiling	12,500 m (41,010 ft)
Defensive armament	1 x R-23 cannon
Crew	3

Tu-22M *Backfire* bomber

The considerable effort expended by the Tupolev OKB on the '106' and '125' high-altitude supersonic strike aircraft projects did not yield the required results, as the value of this concept was very much in doubt by the mid-1960s. A completely different approach was needed. First of all, the idea of a purely supersonic aircraft had to be abandoned.

This Tu-22KD has been retrofitted with a UKhO ECM fairing.

Front view of a Tu-22M2 *Backfire-B* with the IFR probe removed.

What the DA needed was a multi-mode aircraft optimised for supersonic flight at high altitude, long-range flight at subsonic speeds and low-altitude transonic flight. It would also need to have better field performance than its predecessors. The best way of meeting these requirements was to use variable-geometry (VG) wings.

Moderately swept wings improved aerodynamic efficiency at subsonic speed and gave longer range; the best field performance was obtained with minimum sweepback, while sharply swept wings were optimised for high supersonic speeds, and at maximum sweepback the aircraft was able to accelerate more quickly through the transonic zone. But this versatility had a price – the wing sweep change mechanism and structure incurred a weight penalty of 3.5-4%, depending on the type of aircraft and the state of the technology applied. The wing design required the manufacture of light but strong bearing assemblies, light but powerful drives to pivot the outer wings, effective lubricants for the bearings, an automatic wing sweep control system and so forth. The problem of ensuring stability and handling as wing sweep changed was solved (with the co-operation of TsAGI) by introducing a leading edge extension and by placing the pivots correctly to keep the wings' centre of pressure almost unchanged.

A side view of the same aircraft with multiple ejector racks under the air intake trunks.

Work on the 'aircraft 145' project began in 1965. The first stage was done by the OKB at its own initiative; since the work was carried out on a 'semi-legal' basis it was advertised a 'radical updating of the Tu-22K'. If this was more or less true at first, little remained of the original Tu-22 eventually; hence the '145' received the official designation Tu-22M (*izdeliye* 'YuM'/*izdeliye* 'AM'/*izdeliye* '45').

The configuration of the Tu-22M was not immediately arrived at; there were several interim projects which drew upon the development studies for the Tu-22 family. the first

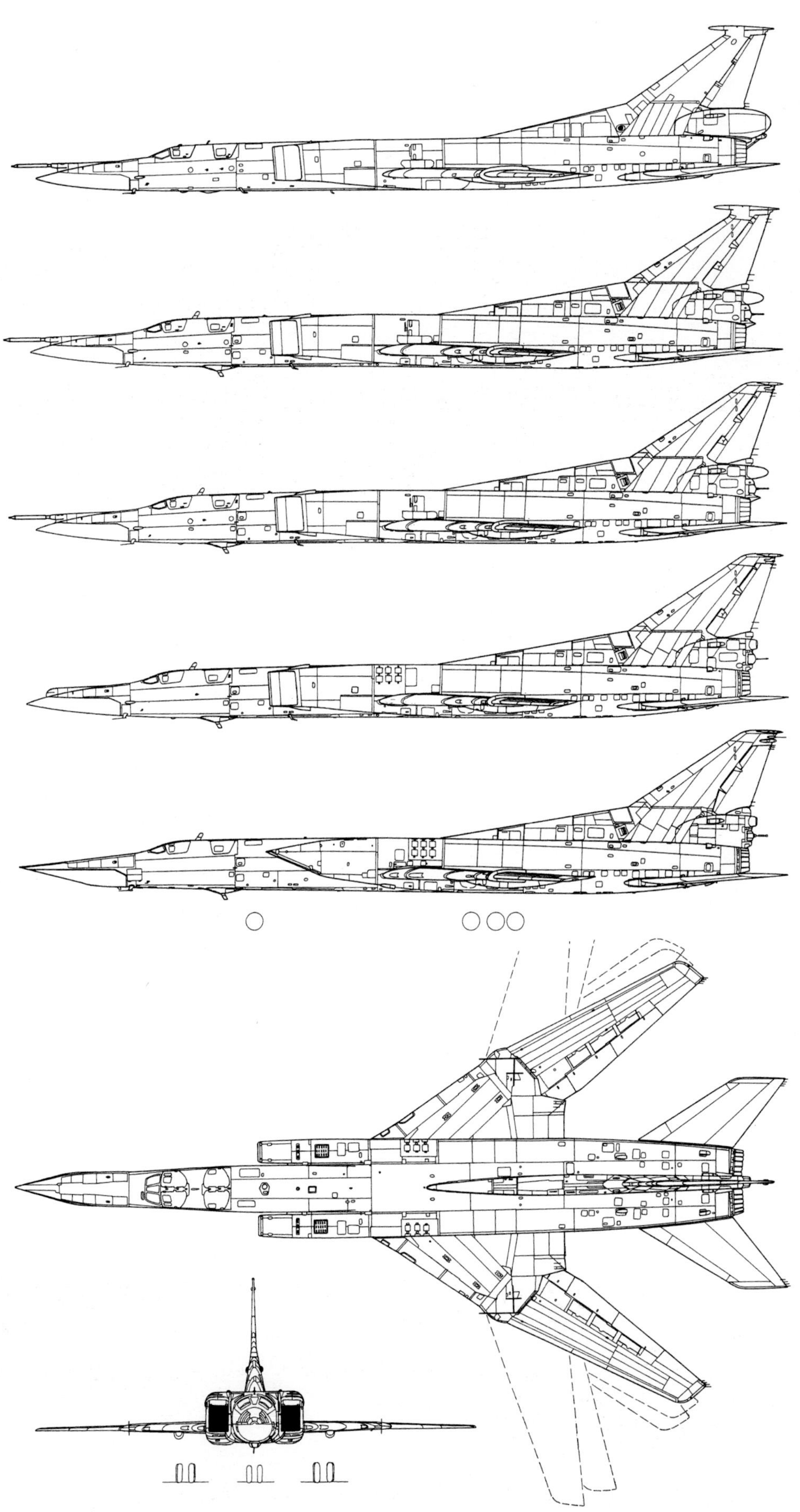

Top to bottom: Tu-22M0 prototype; Tu-22M1 pre-production aircraft; early production Tu-22M2; late production Tu-22M2 with no IFR prove; and three views of the Tu-22M3.

A Tu-22M3 *Backfire-C* with 36 FAB-250 bombs on four MBD3-U9 MERs.

version of the '145' based on the '106B' project (the autumn of 1965) retained the latter's fuselage layout, engine placement and armament. The VG wings were high-set, with 65° leading-edge sweep on the fixed wing gloves and 20°, 65° or 72° sweep on the outer panels; these settings were used for take-off/landing and maximum range at subsonic speed, for long-range supersonic flight and for low-level transonic flight respectively). The two Kuznetsov NK-6 afterburning turbofans were to be installed above the rear fuselage in a common housing with air intakes having vertical airflow control ramps. The main landing gear units retracted inwards.

The field performance of the '145' enabled it to operate from unpaved runways (unlike the '106B'). With a take-off weight of 105 tonnes, the '145' had an estimated top speed of 1,100 km/h (683.5 mph) at 50-100 m (164-330 ft) and 2,500-2,700 km/h (1,552-1,677 mph) at 14,500 m (47,570 ft). Supersonic cruising speed was to be 2,200 km/h (1,367 mph); estimated range was about 10,000 km (6,213 miles) at subsonic speed or 4,000 km (2,485 miles) at supersonic speed.

Later, at the advice of TsAGI, the aerodynamic layout of the '145' was changed considerably. Now the engines were buried in the rear fuselage, breathing through lateral air intakes with long inlet ducts. The OKB argued against this, as this entailed a more complex intake system and an additional weight penalty. Yet, TsAGI proved that it was unrealistic to expect engines mounted over the area of the wing trailing edge and fuselage to function properly at high supersonic speeds. This new version developed in 1967 introduced the Tu-22M designation.

The wings were now moved to a mid/low-set position. The air intakes were two-dimensional, with vertical airflow control ramps and boundary layer splitters. The new layout necessitated a significant rearrangement of the aircraft's systems, equipment and fuel tanks had to be moved. In the process, the aircraft's crew was increased to four by adding a co-pilot and the cockpit layout was radically

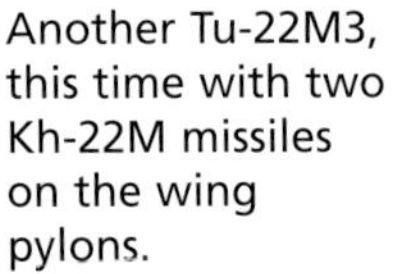

Another Tu-22M3, this time with two Kh-22M missiles on the wing pylons.

This *Backfire-C* carries a full complement of three Kh-22Ms.

revised; the two pilots were now seated side by side, with the navigator and the weapons systems operator (WSO) side by side aft of them; all crew members ejected upwards now. The wings were also altered, with the sweepback of the wing glove reduced to 56° and the outer wing section settings now varying smoothly between 20° and 60°, either automatically or by manual control. There were no ailerons; roll control was by means of spoilers and differentially movable stabilators, and leading-edge slats were fitted to improve field performance.

On 28th November 1967 the Council of Ministers passed directive No.1098-378, finally giving the Tu-22M official status. The OKB was now to produce the VG-wing Tu-22KM with NK-44 (NK-144-2) engines as a carrier for the Kh-22 missile. The directive specified a maximum speed of 2,300-2,500 km/h (1,429-1,552 mph) and a range of 7,000 km (4,350 miles) at subsonic speed with a single missile. State trials were scheduled to begin in the second quarter of 1969. As early as September 1967, the Air Force drew up its own requirements for the K-22M missile system, placing special emphasis on the ability to fly at low level.

Aware of the technical difficulties involved in this, the Air Force proposed that the system should be developed in two stages. Stage 1 featured NK-144-22 afterburning turbofans with a maximum thrust of 20,000 kgp (44,090 lbst); in the second stage NK-144-2 engines uprated to 22,500 kgp (49,600 lbst) would be used, with an attendant increase in performance. Stage 2 also involved a transition to updated equipment and automatic onboard control systems. The updating also included the Kh-22 missile as the Kh-22M.

The mock-up review took place in October-November 1967. Drawing on its results, it was decided to build an initial batch of Tu-22Ms with the first stage engines, equipment and armament as the Tu-22M0 (*izdeliye* '45-00'). All Tu-22M machines, including the first example, were built at the Kazan' Aircraft Factory (No. 22) in order to speed up the production

Another view of the same aircraft. Here the centreline missile is lowered into pre-launch position.

One more Tu-22M3 with two missiles and wings at maximum sweep.

process. In the traditional manner, Tupolev placed chief designer Dmitriy S. Markov in charge of the Tu-22M programme.

The first prototype Tu-22M0 was rolled out at Kazan' in early August 1969. After three weeks of ground checks, a crew headed by V. P. Borisov performed the first flight. Test and development work proceeded while further examples were under construction in Kazan'. Ten Tu-22M0s were built before the end of 1972, five being used for air and ground crew training.

The results of the flight tests showed that the aircraft needed further updating. Powered by the experimental NK-144-22 engines, the Tu-22M0 achieved a subsonic range of 4,140 km (2,573 miles) and a top speed of 1,530 km/h (950 mph) during tests with a single Kh-22M missile. This performance satisfied neither the Air Force nor the OKB, and in December 1969 it was decided to develop the Tu-22M1 version (*izdeliye* '45-01'). This was done in the course of 1970. The weakest parts of the structure were strengthened and the airframe was revised to reduce its weight by 3 tonnes (6,610 lb). Aerodynamic refinements were also made, mainly to the wings; the wing span was increased by 1.5 m (4 ft 11 in).

By the summer of 1971 the first Tu-22M1 with NK-144-22 engines had been completed, making the first flight on 28th July with Boris I. Veremey at the controls. Even before the

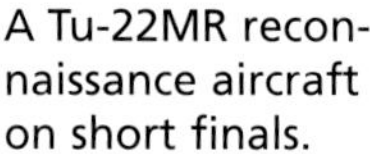

A Tu-22MR reconnaissance aircraft on short finals.

tests were completed, the decision to begin full-scale production in 1971 had been taken. Nine examples of the Tu-22M1 were built by the end of 1972, being used for test and development work (which lasted until the end of 1975) and crew training.

But the Tu-22M1 did not enter service as its basic performance failed to meet requirements. With one missile and a take-off weight of 122 tonnes (268,960 lb), its range was only 5,000 km (3,106 miles) subsonic and 1,560 km (969 miles) at supersonic speed. The maximum speed recorded in the tests was 1,660 km/h (1,031 mph).

Work on further improving the Tu-22M's performance continued with a new version, the Tu-22M2 (*izdeliye* '45-02'), which was powered by improved NK-22 afterburning turbofans delivering 22,000 kgp (48,500 lbst). The aircraft's empty weight was to be reduced by up to 1,500 kg (3,306 lb) and its aerodynamics improved. It was the first major production version built as a long-range missile-carrier and bomber with up-to-date equipment suitable for a wide range of operational applications as the K-22M weapons system.

As a missile carrier the Tu-22M2 could carry up to three Kh-22M missiles with various kinds of guidance systems. In bomber configuration it could carry conventional or nuclear bombs and mines to a total of 24 tonnes (52,910 lb).

The first Tu-22M2 was rolled out in the spring of 1973, making its maiden flight on 7th May. Joint trails and development were carried out until 1975. The K-22M weapons system built around the Tu-22M2 was accepted for service in August 1976.

The Tu-22M2 remained in production until 1983, by which time 211 examples had been built. Generally its service introduction in April 1974 brought fewer problems as compared to the Tu-22. The refinement and reliability of its structure was appreciated, and the reaction of both air and ground crews was positive. The aircrews liked the roomier cockpit, the addition of a co-pilot alleviating crew fatigue on long flights and the more modern crew escape system with upward ejection that was no longer subject to the minimum safe altitude restriction of the Tu-22.

The appearance of the Tu-22M was a cause of major concern for NATO. Information about the type reached the West in the early 1970s. Western experts credited it with the capability for intercontinental strikes against the USA; as a result the Tu-22M became a stumbling block in strategic arms limitation talks in the 1970s. After long and difficult negotiations it was decided to remove the IFR system from all Tu-22Ms so that they no longer qualified as 'intercontinental'.

The production Tu-22M2 had a range of 5,100 km (3,170 miles) and a maximum speed of 1,800 km/h (1,118 mph), but more was demanded. One particular problem was the engines. The NK-22 could not deliver its advertised thrust of 22,000 kgp and its fuel consumption had to be lowered. Aware of this, in the early 1970s the Kuznetsov OKB produced the new NK-25 afterburning turbofan which had a 20% higher maximum take-off thrust of 25,000 kgp (55,115 lbst) and lower fuel consumption at subsonic speed. The NK-25 engines underwent testing on the Tu-22M2-E testbed in 1974 and on the Tu-142LL testbed in 1975-76.

In December 1974 it was decided to further modify the Tu-22M2 by fitting NK-25 engines and making additional refinements to the airframe. As a result, on 26th June 1974, the Council of Ministers passed the appropriate directive No. 534-187. The new received the official designation Tu-22M3 (*izdeliye* '45-03').

As well as installing the new NK-25 engines, the OKB proposed the following radical design changes:

• Redesigned raked air intakes with horizontal airflow control ramps were incorporated;

• the maximum wing sweep angle was increased to 65°;

• the fuselage nose was reprofiled and fitted with a removable IFR probe;

• an aerodynamically cleaner single-cannon tail barbette replaced the earlier twin-cannon version etc.

A set of weight-saving measures was proposed to reduce the empty weight by 2,300-2,700 kg (5,070-5,950 lb). Changes were also made to the electrical supply system, the navigation suite and the gear ECM. At last the aircraft met the 1967 requirements.

The first prototype Tu-22M3 made its maiden flight on 20th June 1977 and series production commenced in 1978. Until 1983 the Tu-22M3 was built in parallel with the Tu-22M2, supplanting it completely from 1984 onwards, Altogether the Kazan' Aircraft Production Association (KAPO) built 268 Tu-22M3s.

Tests showed that the Tu-22M3's performance was significantly better than the Tu-22M2's: maximum speed had risen to 2,000-2,300 km/h (1,242-1,429 mph) and the combat radius increased by 14-45%, depending on flight speeds. The total operational

Specifications of the production Tu-22M2/Tu-22M3

	Tu-22M2	Tu-22M3
Length with IFR probe	41.46 m (136 ft 0 13/64 in)	42.46 m (139 ft 3 21/32 in)
Height	11.05 m (36 ft 3 in)	11.08 m (36 ft 4 7/32 in)
Wing span: at 20°	34.28 m (112 ft 5 39/64 in)	34.28 m (112 ft 5 39/64 in)
at 65°	25.0 m (82 ft 0¼ in)	23.3 m (76 ft 5 21/64 in)
Wing area, m² (sq ft): at 20°	183.58 (1,976)	183.58 (1,976)
at 65°	175.8 (1,892.3)	175.8 (1,892.3)
TOW, kg (lb)	122,000 (268,960)	124,000 (273,370)
Top speed, km/h (mph)	1,800 (1,118)	2,300 (1,429)
Combat radius, km (miles)	2,200 (1,367)	2,200 (1,367)
Service ceiling, m (ft)	12,600 (41,340)	13,300 (43,635)
Max bomb load, kg (lb)	24,000 (52,910)	24,000 (52,910)

effectiveness of the Tu-22M3 was 2.2 times better than the Tu-22M2's. Joint state trials ended in 1981 and the Tu-22M3 was recommended for service. Between 1981 and 1984 an additional test programme was held to expand the type's operational application; this took time, so the Tu-22M3 was accepted for service only in March 1989.

The Tu-22M0/Tu-22M1, Tu-22M2 and Tu-22M3 were codenamed *Backfire-A/B/C* respectively.

Additionally, the Tupolev OKB produced several versions which differed in their armament and equipment. As early as the 1970s work began on arming the Tu-22M2 with the Kh-15 short-range aero-ballistic missiles and in the 1980s its success produced a version of the Tu-22M3 with Kh-15 missiles on fuselage and wing multiple ejector racks. The Tu-22M3R long-range photo reconnaissance/ELINT aircraft entered test in December 1985. Its modern equipment combined with its performance was a major improvement on the Tu-22R. In 1989 it was placed in production as the Tu-22MR.

Tu-160 *Blackjack* intercontinental bomber/missile-carrier

On 28th November 1967 the Council of Ministers issued a directive tasking the Sukhoi and Myasishchev OKBs with developing a new multi-role strategic aircraft. This was to have a range of 11,000-13,000 km (6,035-8,077 miles) at a cruising speed of 3,200-3,500 km/h (1,988-2,134 mph) at 18,000 m (59,055 ft); at subsonic speed the required range was 16,000-18,000 km (9,941-11,184 miles) at high altitude and 11,000-13,000 km at low level. The machine was to carry a range of ASMs, as well as free-fall and guided bombs of various types. The total ordnance load was to be 45 tonnes 99,200 lb).

By the early 1970s both OKBs had prepared projects meeting the terms of the government directive and the GOR issued by the Air Force. Both projects were for four-engined aircraft with VG wings, but with completely different configurations. Sukhoi's T-4MS had a tailless, blended wing/body (BWB) configuration with the fuselage and wing centre section forming an integral whole, and with the pivoting wing sections attached to the wing centre section. The Myasishchev OKB came up with two proposals – the M-18 and the M-20; the former had a conventional layout but also used a BWB design, being strongly reminiscent of the Rockwell B-1 in overall layout. The M-18 was chosen as the more promising for future development. In 1969 VVS formulated its requirements for an advanced multi-role strategic aircraft and invited competing designs.

Until 1970 the Tupolev OKB had been involved only as an impartial observer and was heavily committed to other tasks, having no wish to take on new commissions, even though strategic aircraft had traditionally been its specialisation. In 1970, however, Tupolev entered the competition and set to work on a project to meet the terms of the 1967 requirements, having first assessed the current state of affairs and future prospects for a new strategic aircraft and compared his own ideas with those of his rivals. Project work took place under the guidance of Aleksey A. Tupolev. Subsequently the project was taken over by chief designer Vyacheslav I. Bliznyuk.

The new project was designated '160' (Tu-160), *izdeliye* 'K' or *izdeliye* '70'. The OKB had a free hand in deciding on a possible aerodynamic layout and the relevant design approaches for the future aircraft, opting to design a multi-role aircraft quite different from the T-4MS, M-18 and M-20. The overall performance set down in the government directive of 1967 posed an extremely difficult problem for the OKB. It should be mentioned that the OKB's Department K responsible for the effort was simultaneously working on a second-generation supersonic transport (the Tu-244) and as might be expected, some of this was drawn upon in deciding on the configuration for the Tu-160. The OKB opted for an updated form of the 'tailless' layout which had been successfully applied to the Tu-144 *Charger* and Tu-244 SSTs. The tailless layout would guarantee an increase in speed; in a bid to minimise the technical risk

An early-production Tu-160 in landing configuration.

for the new project, the OKB decided nonetheless – unlike its rivals – to restrict the cruising speed to Mach 2.3.

VG wings conferred a number of advantages but incurred a weight penalty and posed design problems. Yet the major attribute of a heavy multi-role aircraft was its considerable range utilising different flight modes, including supersonic speed at high altitude or subsonic speed at low level to penetrate enemy air defences. Most of the flight before and after encountering enemy air defences could be carried out at optimum altitude and at subsonic speed. Good field performance was also a requirement. A compromise between the aircraft's supersonic and subsonic speeds could only be achieved by using VG wings. Comparative research showed that the aerodynamic efficiency of variable-sweep wings was 1.2 to 1.5 times greater as compared to fixed swept wings. With the same type of engines, a VG-wing aircraft flying at medium altitude and subsonic speed had a range 30-35% greater (10% at low level) than an aircraft with conventional wings. The range at supersonic speed was 15% greater at low level with VG wings. A major issue for large supersonic strategic aircraft lay in determining the limiting speed. During research, a comparative range assessment for a VG-wing aircraft was made based on supersonic cruising speeds of Mach 2.2 and Mach 3.0. A lowering of the speed to Mach 2.2 greatly extended the range due to the reduced fuel consumption

An early-production *Blackjack* (note the five auxiliary inlet door) taxies at Kubinka AB during a demonstration to military top brass.

A Tu-160 is handled by a BelAZ-7420 tug at Priluki.

and the greater aerodynamic efficiency. Not only this, but an airframe designed for Mach 3.0 had to be made of titanium alloys, leading to a 15-20% higher cost, as well as greater technological and operating problems. In the course of further development these arguments were convincingly put to the Air Force.

The Sukhoi, Myasishchev and Tupolev projects were submitted for an MAP competition in 1972. An examination of the projects and an analysis of the American B-1 programme tipped the scales in favour of the M-18, which was backed by TsAGI and MAP's scientific-technical committee. The Myasishchev OKB, however, had no immediately available production base and a relatively small staff to tackle such a complex project, so MAP decided that the commission should be given to the better-resourced Tupolev OKB and the M-18 project should be transferred thereto for further development. Imagine how it feels to win and then have all the credit go to a competitor...

Using the M-18 as a basis, the Tupolev OKB settled down to design the Tu-160 with VG wings. In 1972 the Tupolev OKB, TsAGI, and other defence industry enterprises and research institutes – some 800 enterprises in all – embarked on a comprehensive programme to decide on the best layout and size of the future aircraft, its engines, structural materials, the devising of the necessary technologies and so on.

Initially, the NK-25 afterburning turbofan used on the Tu-22M3 was chosen to power the Tu-160. It was powerful enough but its fuel efficiency had to be improved, otherwise the aircraft would fail to meet the range requirement even with perfect aerodynamics. At that time the Kuznetsov OKB was just beginning development of the new NK-32 three-shaft afterburning turbofan rated at 13,000 kgp (28,660 lbst) dry and 25,000 kgp (55,115 lbst) reheat, which had an acceptably low specific fuel consumption. The NK-32 had a great deal in common with the NK-25, which guaranteed its practicality. In cooperation with TsAGI fourteen models with different engine arrangements were used in wind-tunnel tests. Finally the choice fell on the original version with paired engines in underwing nacelles with two-dimensional variable air intakes having vertical airflow control ramps.

The final version had a BWB layout, with the pivoting outer wing panels having a sweepback of 20° to 65°, and a cruciform tail assembly with slab stabilisers and a fin with an all-movable upper section. To optimise the aerodynamic efficiency of the area between the fixed wing glove and the pivoting outer sections, the inboard ends of the trailing-edge flaps were cunningly designed to fold upwards and form wing fences at maximum sweep. The lift/drag ratio proved to be 18.5-19 in subsonic cruise and over 6.0 at supersonic speed.

The structural design problems associated with the overall layout of the aircraft required the development of new technology. For example, the principal structural loads from the outer wings were carried by an all-welded titanium beam of complex shape. Unique technology was evolved for manufacturing this large airframe part as a by means of electron-beam welding in an autoclave, and this technology can be rightly considered national know-how. The chosen layout of the tail assembly enabled the powerful electro-hydraulic drives for the control surfaces to be accommodated in a limited space.

38% of the aircraft's structure was to be made of titanium alloys, 58% from aluminium alloys, 15% from high-quality steel alloys and 3% from composite materials. For the first time on a Soviet aircraft a fly-by-wire control system was used. The OKB co-operated with relevant research institutes and organisations in its search for the most effective missile armament for the new aircraft. In addition to low-level supersonic missiles, the Tu-160 was also to carry subsonic low-altitude terrain-following cruise missiles. MKB Raduga brought out the Kh-55 cruise missile and its Kh-55SM extended-range version carrying either a conventional or a nuclear warhead. The heads of MAP and the Air Force decided not to proceed with the Kh-55SM but changed their minds in 1976 when it became clear that the USA was

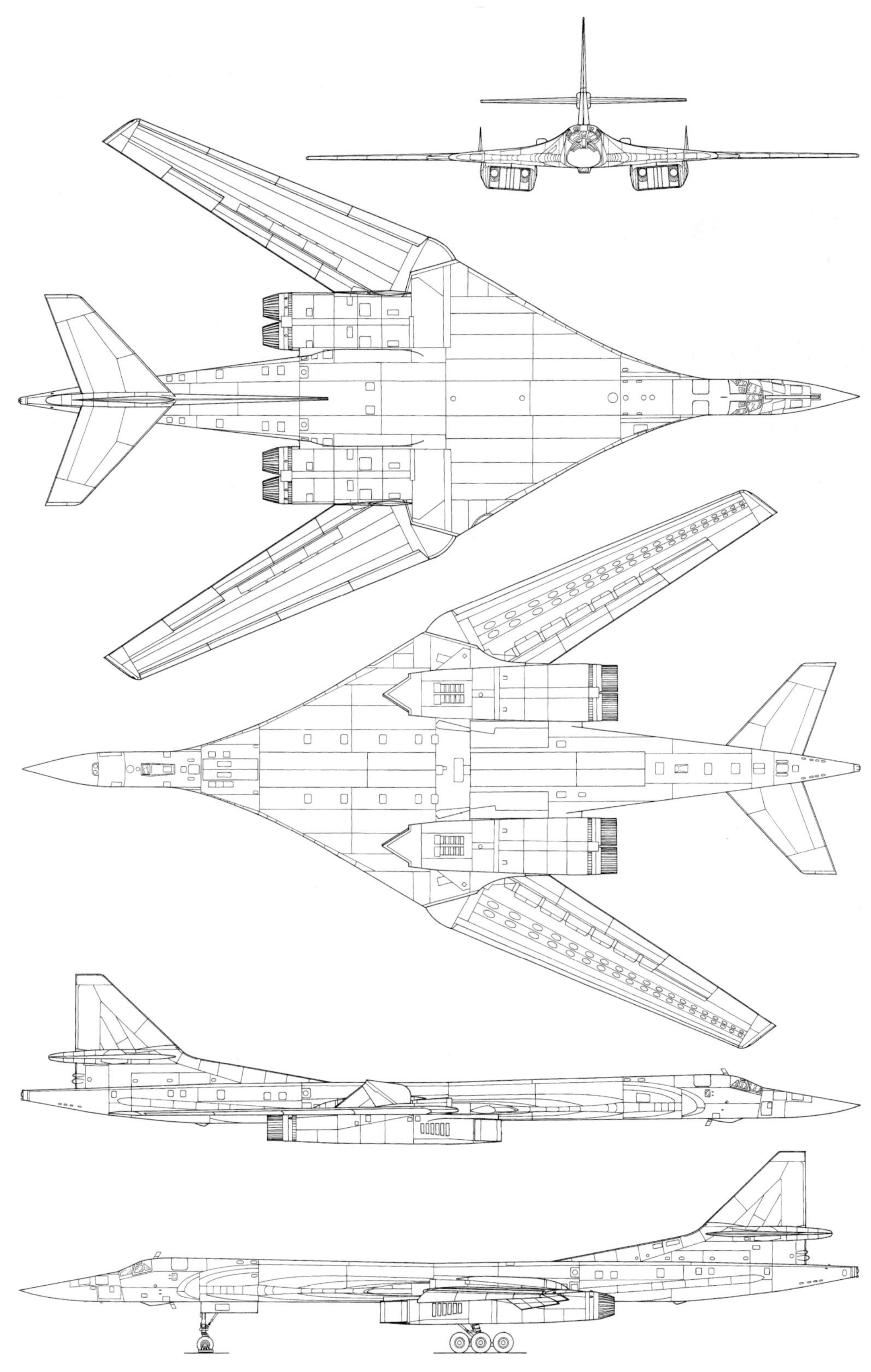

Five views of a Tu-160 with the wings fully swept (except the lower side view).

developing a similar weapon – the Boeing AGM-86B (ALCM-B).

The issue of the Tu-160's armament system was determined by the multi-role nature of the aircraft, and was based on the vague notion of a future geopolitical and defence situation (which became a harsh reality for Russia in the 1990s). It was planned to arm the aircraft with ultra long-range, long-range and medium-range missiles, short-range guided and unguided missiles and AAMs for defence. Preference was given to internally carried weapons able to hit targets, including poorly-defined ones, without the aircraft needing to enter the enemy air defence zone. The Air Force initially insisted that the Tu-160 should have a tail gun (the multi-barrel GSh-6-30), but the OKB managed to argue against this in favour of adding to the aircraft's ECM to save weight and space. The complex and multi-functional nature of the weapons' control system required the wide application of modern computer technology. The armament control system could go over to multiplex data exchange channels in a federal-centralised complex structure using modern digital electronic equipment. The onboard complex had a separate missile control system for the new generation of missiles which relied on the preparation and transmission of a large volume of data from the parent aircraft.

After the basic systems and layout and structural matters had been worked out and agreed with VVS and the other agencies involved, the go-ahead was given for the Tu-160 programme. Two Council of Ministers directives passed on 26th June 1974 and 19th December 1975 commissioned the creation of the Tu-160 strategic multi-role aircraft as a bomber and missile-carrier powered by NK-32 engines. The following requirements were set:

- a service range of 14,000-16,000 km (8,700-9,941 miles) with a 9,000-kg (19,840-lb) weapons load at a subsonic cruising speed;
- a range at subsonic and supersonic speeds including 2,000 km (1,242 miles) at low level (50-200 m) or 12,000-13,000 km (7,456-8,077 miles) at supersonic speed;
- a maximum speed of 2,300-2,500 km/h (1,429-1,552 mph) at altitude;
- a maximum speed at low altitude of 1,000 km/h (621 mph);
- a service ceiling of 18,000-20,000 m (59,055-65,620 ft);
- a normal weapons load of 9,000 kg and a maximum weapons load of 40,000 kg (88,180 lb);
- a missile complement of two Kh-45Ms or 24 Kh-15s or 10-12 Kh-55s;
- a bomb load of conventional or nuclear free-fall or laser/TV guided bombs.

The advanced development project and half-size mock-up were prepared in 1976-77 and approved in 1977. According to the ADP the Tu-160 was slightly larger than its American counterpart, the B-1A. The combination of weapons carried was modified to exclude the Kh-45 missile, leaving the Kh-55 on two launchers or Kh-15 on four launchers and bombs. Subsequently this was narrowed down to twelve Kh-55 missiles on two launchers.

Construction of the first three aircraft began at the Tupolev OKB's facility in Moscow in 1977 in close co-operation with KAPO where preparations for series production were under way. By the summer of 1980 the first prototype ('70-01') was partly completed and transported to Zhukovskiy. There, after all the usual system checks, on 18th December 1982 the Tu-160 made the first flight, captained by Boris I. Veremey. The second prototype flew on 6th October 1984, and manufacturer's tests continued using the two machines. In February 1985 the aircraft flew at supersonic speed for the first time. On 10th October 1984 the first Kazan'-built production machine made its maiden flight, followed by the second flight on 16th March 1985 and the third on 25th December 1986. Preparations were made for the Tu-160 to enter service. The first two production machines were delivered to the 184th GvTBAP at Priluki on 17th April 1987.

Plans called for the production of some 100 aircraft, but reduced defence spending in the second half of the 1980s, the dissolution of the USSR and the ensuing severe economic and political crisis which afflicted the new Russia brought about a curtailment of the Tu-160's production programme and wide-scale deployment. By the early the 1990s KAPO had built 34 Tu-160s, including two static/fatigue test airframes.

Specifications of the production Tu-160	
Length overall	54.095 m (177 ft 5 23/32 in)
Wing span (at 20°/35°/65° sweep)	57.7/50.7/35.6 m (189 ft 3 21/32 in/166 ft 4 in / 116 ft 9 37/64 in)
Height on ground	13.0 m (42 ft 7 13/16 in)
Total wing area, m² (sq ft)	293.15 (3,152.15)
Movable outer area, m² (sq ft)	189.83 (2,041.18)
Maximum take-off weight, kg (lb)	275,000 (606,260)
Fuel load, kg (lb)	148,000 (326,280)
Weapons load, kg (lb):	
normal	9,000 kg;
maximum	45,000 kg;
Max speed, km/h (mph)	2,200 (1,366)
Service ceiling, m (ft)	15,600 (51,180)
Range in supersonic cruise, km (miles)	2,000 (1,240)
Service range, km (miles)	13,200 (8,202)
Crew	4

An IL-78M *Midas-B* in standard Soviet/ Russian AF colours for the type.

IL-78 *Midas* refuelling tanker

In the early 1980s a requirement arose for a three-point tanker to replace the Tu-16N, M-4-2, 3MS-2 and 3MN-2 single-point tankers. The Il'yushin IL-76MD *Candid-B* four-turbofan transport represented an ideal basis for such a tanker; on 10th March 1982 the Council of Ministers issued a directive ordering the development of the IL-78 tanker. The design effort was led by project chief Radiy P. Papkovskiy and completed in 1983.

The aircraft was equipped with three UPAZ-1A podded HDUs developed by the Zvezda design bureau (formerly OKB-918). Two of these were conventionally mounted on pylons under the wings; the third pod was suspended from a short horizontal pylon on the port side of the rear fuselage. Normal delivery rate was 1,000 litres/min (220 Imp gal/min) but this can be increased to 2,200 litres/min (484 Imp gal/min) in case of need. 'Traffic lights' are installed at the rear end of the pod to indicate fuel transfer status to the pilot of the receiver aircraft.

Most of the fuel was carried in the standard wing tanks. Additionally, two cylindrical metal tanks, each holding 18,230 litres (4,010.6 Imp gal) or 14 tons (30,860 lb) of fuel, were installed in the freight hold; these could be easily removed if required, allowing the aircraft to be used for transport duties. Maximum transferable fuel with or without fuselage tanks was 85,720 or 57,720 kg (188,980 or 127,250 lb) respectively, equalling 111,620 or 75,160 litres (24,556 or 16,535 Imp gal) respectively. Take-off weight was 190 tons (418,870 lb) on paved runways and 157.5 tons (347,220 lb) on semi-prepared runways.

Unlike the IL-76MD, the tanker is unarmed; the former gunner's station is occupied by the refuelling systems operator. To ensure rendezvous with the receiver aircraft the IL-78 is equipped with an additional short-range radio navigation system providing mutual detection and approach at up to 300 km (186 miles).

With a 1,000-km (621-mile) combat radius the IL-78 can transfer up to 65 tons (143,300 lb)/84,639 litres (18,620 Imp gal) of fuel. Maximum combat radius with 32-36 tons (70,545-79,365 lb) of transferable fuel (equalling 41,668-46,877 litres/9,167-10,313 Imp gal) is 2,500 km (1,550 miles).

The IL-78 prototype (CCCP-76556) made its first flight in Tashkent on 26th June 1983

Unlike the basic IL-78s, which were mostly quasi-civil, few IL-78Ms wore civilian Aeroflot colours.

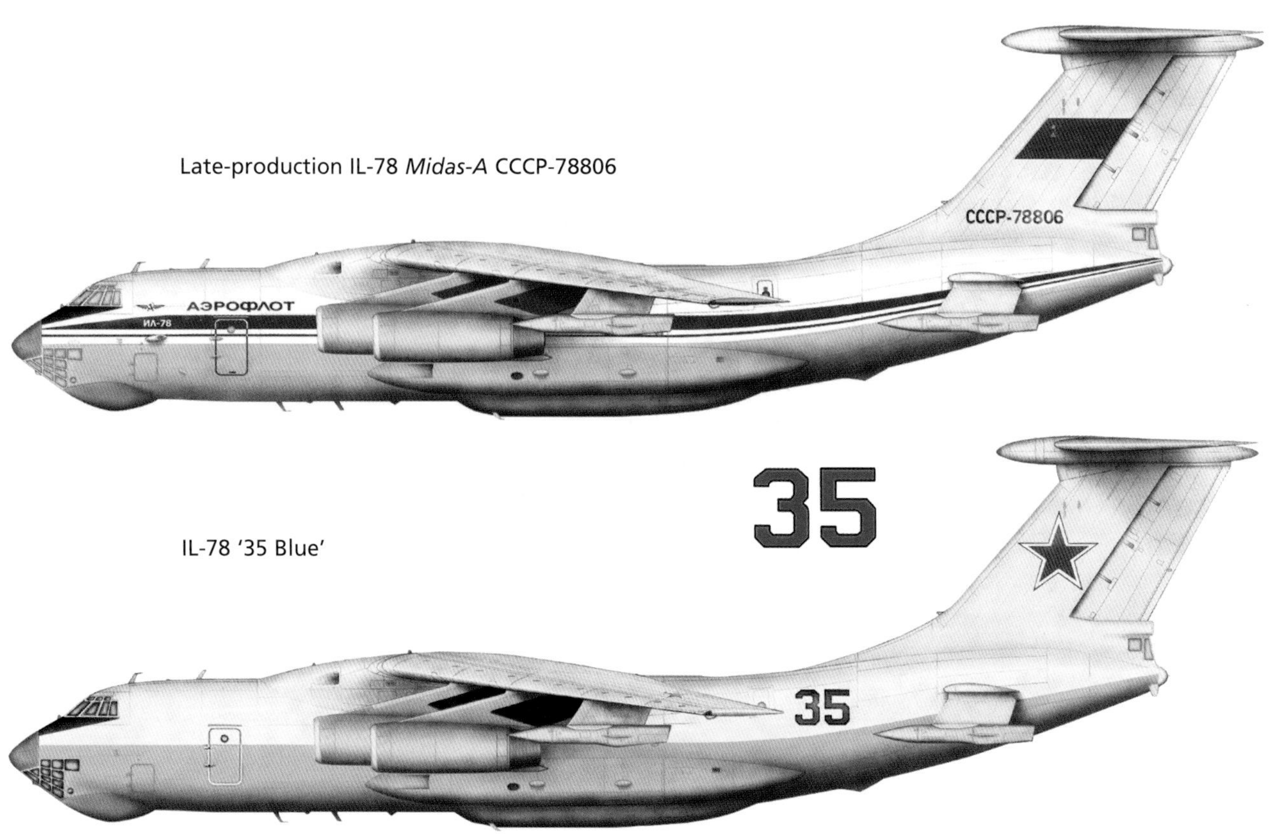

Late-production IL-78 *Midas-A* CCCP-78806

IL-78 '35 Blue'

with OKB test pilot Vyacheslav S. Belousov at the controls. Manufacturer's flight tests took place in September-December 1983, followed by state acceptance trials which began in March 1984 and were completed on 30th June. Deliveries of production IL-78s to the Air Force began in 1984, but it was not until 1st June 1987 that the tanker was officially included into the Soviet Air Force inventory.

On 20th December 1984, soon after the IL-78 completed its flight tests, the Council of Ministers issued a directive ordering the development of an upgraded tanker designated IL-78M. This is a dedicated (non-convertible) tanker version with a third fuselage fuel tank increasing total fuel to 138 tons (304,230 lb) or 179,965 litres (39,533 Imp gal); transferable fuel is thus increased to 105,720 kg (233,070 lb) or 137,662 litres (30,285 Imp gal). MTOW on paved runways is increased to 210 tons (462,960 lb); this required the wing torsion box to be reinforced. Besides, the IL-78M is equipped with improved UPAZ-1M pods having a higher delivery rate (2,340 litres/min or 514.8 gal/min). The deletion of the cargo doors and all cargo handling equipment cut structural weight by roughly 5,000 kg (11,020 lb) at the expense of versatility. The IL-78M prototype, CCCP-76701, entered flight test on 7th March 1987, again captained by Belousov. Unlike the basic IL-78, production IL-78Ms usually have overt military markings. 49 examples of both versions had been built by 1991.

Tu-124Sh *Cookpot* navigator trainer

The success of the Tu-104 *Camel* – the first Soviet jet airliner – prompted the development of smaller jets to be used on short-haul domestic and international services. The Tupolev OKB began development of such an aircraft class in 1958; designated Tu-124, the new machine was to be an 80% scale copy of the Tu-104, with the same 35° wing sweep, the trademark Tupolev main gear design and the engines buried in the wing roots. Its take-off weight was only half of the Tu-104's, with a passenger capacity reduced to 50-60. As the aircraft was to be smaller, less powerful engines could be used – the 5,400-kgp (11,900-lbst) Solov'yov D-20P turbofans.

The prototype of the baseline 44-seat passenger variant made its first flight on 29th March 1960. Production at Factory No. 135 in Khar'kov began that same year. After passing State trials between July 1961 and September 1962, the aircraft was recommended for airline service. Codenamed *Cookpot* by NATO, the Tu-124 was mostly delivered to the Soviet airline Aeroflot; the carrier performed its first revenue flight with the type on 2nd October 1962. The improved 56-seat Tu-124V was the main version.

However, the aircraft also had a navigator trainer version developed for the Soviet Air Force – the Tu-124Sh (***shtoor**manskiy*) featuring a different radar and racks for practice bombs. Two varieties of this were built in series and supplied to military pilot and navigator schools. The Tu-124Sh-1 was used for training the navigators of long-range bombers and transport, while the Tu-124Sh-2 was used for training navigators on tactical bombers. 55 Tu-124Sh trainers were produced between 1962 and 1968.

Specifications of the production Tu-124Sh	
Length	31.578 m (103 ft 7 15/64 in)
Wing span	25.55 m (83 ft 9 29/32 in)
Height	8.082 m (26 ft 6 3/8 in)
Wing area	119.37 m^2 (1,284.84 sq ft)
TOW	38,000 kg (83,780 lb)
Payload	6,000 kg (13,230 lb)
Max speed at 8,000 m	970 km/h (602.7 mph)
Cruising speed at 8,000-11,000 m	750-850 km/h (465-528 mph)
Service ceiling	11,500 m (37,730 ft)
Trainees	12
Crew	5

Tu-134Sh-1/Tu-134Sh-2 *Crusty-A* navigator trainer

Tu-134UBL *Crusty-B* pilot trainer

Experience gained with the Tu-124 enabled the OKB to take the next step, developing a short-haul airliner incorporating the latest trend with aerodynamically clean wings and engines mounted on the rear fuselage. It owed its existence to the French Sud-Est SE.210 Caravelle short-haul airliner, which impressed the Soviet leader Nikita S. Khrushchov and led him to request the development of a similar aircraft.

The other starting point was the Tu-124 proper. In order to minimise development time and costs, Tupolev opted for maximum commonality with the existing model, and therefore the new short-haul aircraft was initially known in-house as the '124A' (Tu-124A). The fuselage (with its distinctive glazed nose and chin radome) and the outer wings were largely unchanged. The powerplant consisted of the same D-20P turbofans mounted each side of the rear fuselage. The new engine location dictated the need for a T-tail; the Caravelle's cruciform tail surface arrangement was rejected because the sound waves impinging on the relatively

A brand-new Tu-124Sh awaits delivery at the Khar'kov aircraft factory.

The Tu-124Sh was identifiable by the larger-than-usual chin radome, faired bomb racks and two star trackers offset to port.

A Tu-134UBL in Soviet-era markings with a red lightning bolt cheatline and a red star on the fin.

low-set stabilisers could cause fatigue problems.

The chosen layout offered a number of advantages. Removing the engines from the wings allowed relative flap area and wing efficiency to be increased. The rear fuselage and tail unit were less affected by vibration and tailplane buffet caused by jet efflux. Likewise, the high-set stabilisers were less affected by wing upwash, which improved longitudinal stability in cruise flight. In addition, this improved engine operating conditions thanks to the short inlet ducts, reduced foreign object damage risk and facilitated engine maintenance and change. Passenger comfort was greatly enhanced by the low noise and vibration. Finally, there was no danger of fragments entering the cabin in the event of an uncontained engine failure. Yet the rear-engine, T-tail arrangement had some serious shortcomings, too. The wings were positioned further aft as compared to the normal layout, increasing fuselage area ahead of the CG; this meant vertical tail area had to be increased to ensure adequate directional stability, with an attendant increase in structural weight and thus an increase in operating costs. The fuselage and fin had to be reinforced, again increasing empty weight and reducing the payload. CG travel was increased, and the high position of the thrust line produced a pitch-down force that increased rotation speed on take-off and elevator control forces.

A Tu-134UBL takes off, showing its distinctive 'Pinocchio nose'.

On 1st August 1960 the Council of Ministers passed Directive No. 826-341 for the design of the Tu-124A airliner. By April 1961 the advanced development project had been drawn up. In the course of development the Tu-124A's payload was raised from 5,000 to 7,000 kg (from 11,020 to 15,430 lb), the number of passengers form 40 to 65-70 and the maximum service range extended from 2,000 to 3,000 km (from 1,242 to 1,863 miles).

The first prototype powered by 5,800-kgp (12,790-lbst) D-20P-125 engines and seating 52-56 passengers was assembled in the first half of 1963. The original designation was short-lived, however; Tupolev soon decided that the changes were serious enough to warrant a new designation. Pursuant to an order dated 20th February 1963 the Tu-124A was renamed Tu-134. On 29th July that year the airliner made its first flight.

The test results obtained with the second prototype built at Factory No.135 and again powered by D-20P-125 engines showed the need for more powerful engines, and it was decided to install the new Solov'yov D-30 turbofans rated at 6,800 kgp (14,990 lbst) on the production version.

Initial production of the Tu-134 *Crusty* in Khar'kov began in 1965; the first aircraft to have the intended D-30 engines and 44-ton 97,000-lb) TOW from the start was the third pre-production example, which flew on 21st July 1966. Upon completion of the manufacturer's tests and State trials the Tu-134 was officially accepted for passenger services by Aeroflot on 26th August 1967.

The initial production version was followed by the improved Tu-134A featuring a 2.1-m (6 ft $10\frac{43}{64}$ in) fuselage stretch, thrust reversers and an auxiliary power unit, which first flew on 22nd April 1969 and became the most widespread version by far. The Tu-134B version brought out in 1979 featured a new weather radar in a 'solid' nose (introduced on the export version of the A in 1973), featured improvements to the flight deck, cabin, and control system but was built on a small scale.

Dedicated military versions for the Soviet Air Force were developed as well. The first of these was the Tu-134Sh navigator trainer based on the 'glass-nosed' Tu-134A; it was designed in 1969-70 jointly with the Khar'kov aircraft factory as a successor to the Tu-124Sh.

Like its precursor, the aircraft had two subvariants differing in specialisation and hence equipment. The first of these, designated Tu-134Sh-1, was intended for training naviga-

Tu-134Sh-2 '38 Blue' in a non-standard blue/white livery 978th OVTAP, Klin-5 AB, Moscow Region

Tu-134Sh-1 '76 Blue' in standard red/white colours with BD-360 MERs

Tu-134UBL '27 Red' in early standard colours, Tambov VVAUL

tors for the Long-Range Aviation – specifically, navigators flying the Tu-22 and, to a certain extent, the Tu-22M2/Tu-22M3. The chin radome was much larger and deeper, housing an R-1 Rubin-1Sh panoramic navigation/bomb-aiming radar; the radar was linked with an OPB-15 optical bomb sight. Two star trackers were provided for celestial navigation training. Two removable BD-360 multiple ejector racks (MERs) were fitted under the inner wing sections, carrying four 120-kg (265-lb) PB-120 practice bombs each. In bombed-up condition the extra drag reduced the trainer's top speed from 860 to 800 km/h (534 to 496 mph). An AFA-BAF-40R vertical camera was housed in the rear fuselage to record the bombing results.

The cabin featured 12 trainee workstations associated with specific groups of equipment. Two shifts of trainees took turns using them during a typical sortie.

The first prototype Tu-134Sh-1 was manufactured on 29th January 1971. The second prototype followed on 17th March; this was possibly the Tu-134Sh-2 prototype. Tu-134Sh-1 trainers were mostly delivered to the

A Tu-134Sh-2 navigator trainer fitted with MBD3-U6-68A MERs.

Chelyabinsk Military Navigator College (VVAUSh – ***Vys**sheye voy**en**noye aviatsi**on**noye oo**chil**ischche **shtoor**manov*) in the Urals region of central Russia. A few saw service with the DA's 43rd TsBP i PLS at Dyagilevo AB near Ryazan'.

The other navigator trainer version called Tu-134Sh-2 was originally developed for training navigators of the Tactical Aviation, specifically Yakovlev Yak-28I *Brewer-C* and later Sukhoi Su-24 *Fencer* tactical bomber crews. The Tu-134Sh-2 was fitted with an Initsiativa-1Sh radar in an identical large radome and a different type of MERs (MBD3-U6-68Sh bomb racks). There were also structural changes to the fuselage. The Tu-134Sh-2 was mostly delivered to the Voroshilovgrad VVAUSh in the Ukraine.

Both sub-variants passed their state acceptance trials successfully and were cleared for service entry on 21st January 1972. Full-scale production began that same year and a total of 90 navigator trainers had been reportedly built when production ended in 1980; the proportion of Tu-134Sh-1s and Tu-134Sh-2s within this total is not known. Contrary to Western reports, the Tu-134Sh trainers were new-build aircraft, not converted Tu-134As and Tu-134s *sans suffixe*.

The second major military version was the Tu-134UBL (*oo**cheb**no-boye**voy** dlya **lyot**chikov* = combat trainer for pilots). Derived from the Tu-134B, this was a crew trainer for the Tu-22M2/Tu-22M3 and Tu-160. Its *raison d'être* is that, unlike the Tu-22 *Blinder*, these bombers did not have specialised trainer versions, and using them for conversion training would be a waste of their service life. The Tu-134 was selected for this role because it was similar to the bombers in thrust/weight ratio and low-speed handling. Development proceeded in parallel with the commercial 'donor' and was triggered by joint MAP/Air Force decision No. 3659 of 6th-7th August 1979.

The Tu-134UBL had a long pointed nose borrowed from the Tu-22M3; the lower half of this 'beak' was a huge dielectric radome. However, instead of the *Backfire*'s PNA navigation/target illumination radar the nose housed an ROZ-1 weather radar, since the aircraft was intended for flight training only. Originally the nose was to incorporate a telescopic IFR probe but this was never installed because the *Backfire* was stripped of IFR capability under the terms of the SALT II treaty.

The number of cabin windows was greatly reduced. The instrument panels in the flight deck emulated those of the Tu-22M. Three rows of seats were installed in the cabin, allowing 12 trainees to take turns flying the aircraft from the right-hand seat. The cabin also featured a rack for breathing apparatus and racks for the crew's and the trainees' parachutes; the rear baggage door was pneumatically actuated to permit bailing out in an emergency.

The first prototype Tu-134UBL was manufactured in January 1981. This and several more aircraft participated in manufacturer's flight tests coinciding with Stage A of the state acceptance trials which were held in May-June 1981. Stage B of the trials began in October 1981 and was completed in June 1982. The longer nose and hence increased area forward of the CG affected handling at high angles of attack to such an extent that spin recovery tests had to be held.

90 (some sources say 77) examples had been completed when production ended in late 1983. Again, contrary to allegations by some Western authors, all Tu-134UBL trainers were purpose-built aircraft, not conversions. Deliveries commenced in April 1981 – before the trials had ended, which was fairly common practice in the Soviet Air Force; a training regiment at Engels-2 AB was reportedly the first unit to receive the type. The Tambov Military Pilot College (VVAUL – ***Vys**sheye voy**en**noye aviatsi**on**noye oo**chil**ischche **lyot**chikov*) started re-equipping with the Tu-134UBL in August 1981; the Orsk VVAUL near Orenburg followed suit. Several *Crusty-Bs* were operated by Squadron 3 of the 184th GvTBAP at Priluki and by the 43rd TsBP i PLS at Dyagilevo AB.

Opposite page:

A US Marines McDonnell Douglas F/A-18A Hornet escorts a Tu-16SPS ECM aircraft away from the carrier USS *Coral Sea*.

A Tu-16P Buket ECM aircraft updated with additional strake-like aerials at the wingtips.

Tu-134 trainer version specifications

	Tu-134Sh	Tu-134UBL
Length overall	37.1 m (121 ft 8⅝ in)	41.918 m (137 ft 6½ in)
Wing span	29.01 m (95 ft 2⅛ in)	29.01 m (95 ft 2⅛ in)
Height on ground	9.02 m (29 ft 7⅛ in)	9.144 m (30 ft 0 in)
Wing area, m^2 (sq ft)	127.3 (1,168.81)	127.3 (1,168.81)
Operating empty weight, kg (lb)	n/a	28,840 (63,580)
MTOW, kg (lb)	46,500 (102,510)	44,250 (97,550)
Max. payload, kg (lb)	3,100 (6,830)	8,200 (18,080)
Cruising speed, km/h (mph):		
at 8,600 m (28,215 ft)	800/860 (500/534) *	884 (549)
at 10,000 m (32,810 ft)	n/a	904 (561)
Range, km (miles):		
with maximum fuel	3,900 (2,420)	3,400 (2,110)
with maximum payload	3,400 (2,110)	n/a
Service ceiling, m (ft)	11,000 (36,090)	11,800 (38,710)

* With/without practice bombs

11 In Times of Change The Demise of the Soviet Union

In 1980 yet another reorganisation befell the Long-Range Aviation. In accordance with the Soviet Minister of Defence's order No. 005 dated 5th January 1980 and a General Headquarters directive dated 13th March 1980, the Soviet Air Force's organisation was to change by the end of the summer; the separate Commands of the Air Force's various branches were abolished and the regiments, divisions and air armies were subordinated directly to the commanders of the Military Districts. Thus, the DA Command, a structure with a 35-year history that had exercised theatre-strategic control of the nation's strategic nuclear air strike component since the latter's birth, was eliminated. Instead, three Strategic Air Armies of the Supreme High Command (VA VGK (SN) – *voz**doosh**naya* ***ar**miya Ver**khov**novo **glav**noko**mahn**dovaniya strate-**gich**eskovo nazna**chen**iya*) were formed. These were the 37th VA VGK (SN) headquartered in Moscow, the 46th VA VGK (SN) headquartered in Smolensk and the 30th VA VGK (SN) headquartered in Irkutsk.

The headquarters of the 37th Strategic Air Army exercised control over four heavy bomber divisions operating Tu-95M/Tu-95MA *Bear-A* strategic bombers, Tu-95KM *Bear-C* missile carriers and Myasishchev 3MS-1/3MN-1

A Tu-16K-26 with a Rubin-1M radar carries a KSR-5 missile.

Bison-B strategic bombers. These were the 73rd TBAD based at Ookraïnka AB in the Far East, the 79th TBAD based near Semipalatinsk in Kazakhstan, the 106th TBAD based at Uzin AB in the Ukraine and the 201st TBAD based at Engels-2 AB in the Saratov Region of southern Russia. Between them the four divisions comprised nine heavy bomber regiments, four of which flew 3Ms (two each at Ookraïnka AB and at Engels-2 AB) and the remainder were equipped with Tu-95s (two regiments at Uzi AB, two at Semipalatinsk and one at Mozdok). By then a large proportion of the 3MS-1 and 3MN-1 bombers had been converted into 3MS-2 and 3MN-2 refuelling tankers to support the operations of the remaining *Bisons* and *Bear-Cs*.

The 30th Strategic Air Army included two heavy bomber divisions at Belaya AB and Vozdvizhenka AB, each with two regiments of Tu-16K missile carriers, plus an independent long-range reconnaissance air regiment at Spassk-Dal'niy equipped with Tu-16R *Badger-E/F* ELINT aircraft.

The 46th Strategic Air Army was a much larger formation, comprising four heavy bomber divisions (at Poltava, Ozyornoye AB, Bobruisk and Tartu) with four regiments each and two independent long-range reconnaissance air regiments equipped with Tu-22R *Blinder-Cs* (at Zyabrovka and Nezhin). Of the 46th VA's twelve bomber regiments, only two units based at Poltava and Sol'tsy AB were equipped with modern Tu-22M2 *Backfire-B* 'swing-wing' bombers; three more regiments (at Machoolishchi AB, Baranovichi and Ozyornoye AB) flew supersonic but obsolescent Tu-22K/Tu-22KD/Tu-22KPD *Blinder-B* missile strike aircraft and the remainder still operated various versions of the obsolete subsonic Tu-16.

Thus, in a situation when the confrontation between the two superpowers was growing ever fiercer and the Cold War was intensifying (all the more so because of the Soviet involvement in Afghanistan), the former Long-Range Aviation was badly in need of re-equipping with modern aircraft.

It took the top military authorities eight years to recognise the fallacy of this restructuring whose negative consequences by far outweighed the gains. Hence in accordance

A Tu-95K-22 missile carrier flying at high altitude.

A late-production IL-78 *sans suffixe* with all three drogues deployed.

with the Minister of Defence's order No. 0008 dated 25th February 1988 the headquarters of the 37th VA VGK (SN) was transformed into the reinstated Department of the Commander of the Long-Range Aviation, and the 30th and 46th VA VGK were subordinated to it. Additionally, the DA came to include the Arctic Operations Group (OGA – *Opera**tiv**naya* ***groop**pa v* ***Ark**tike*) which had no aircraft of its own but operated a number of tactical airfields beyond the Arctic Circle which could be used as staging points by DA aircraft flying combat sorties across the North Pole. Another formation placed under the direct control of

An IL-78 in Aeroflot livery prepares to take off.

A Tu-95MS tops up its fuel tanks from IL-78 CCCP-76632.

Heavy bombers like the Tu-95MS always use the IL-78's centre drogue.

the DA Commander was the 43rd TsBP i PLS at Dyagilevo AB in Ryazan', which comprised three instructional heavy bomber regiments based at Dyagilevo AB, Shaikovka AB (Kaluga Region) and Belaya Tserkov' (in the Ukraine). By the early 1990s these three regiments operated 27 Tu-16s, 19 Tu-22Ms and 11 Tu-95s (the *Bears* were stripped of armament and converted to trainers). The 37th VA VGK (SN) retained its status and subordination, remaining outside the DA Command.

By then the Long-Range Aviation's order of battle included ten heavy bomber divisions which, in turn, comprised 25 heavy bomber regiments. The 37th VA VGK (SN) headquartered in Moscow exercised direct control over another four heavy bomber divisions (the 73rd, 79th, 106th and 201st TBADs) operating intercontinental bombers. The Air Force's Combat Training Department came to include a section dealing specifically with the training of long-range and strategic bomber crews.

White on white: A production Tu-160 sits on a snow-covered hardstand.

Left and below: A Tu-160 with the wings at minimum sweep is refuelled by IL-78 CCCP-76675.

Below left: Unusually, this Tu-160 appears to have been refuelled with the wings fully swept back.

184th GvTBAP Tu-160s on the flight line at Priluki.

With a BelAZ-7420 tug attached, a Tu-160 sits in front of a lattice-like jet blast deflector.

The history of Soviet-American relations included a critical period of brinkmanship when nuclear deterrence was achieved not only by maintaining ground-launched intercontinental ballistic missiles (ICBMs) on constant alert and patrolling the seas by nuclear-powered missile submarines but also by having large numbers of strategic bombers with nuclear weapons on board patrol designated areas on a regular basis. This policy was pursued by both nations' governments. In the USSR, the Long-Range Aviation was assigned specific tasks in response to the SAC's bomber patrols along the Soviet Union's northern borders. Thus, the DA's aircraft also began systematically patrolling four designated areas of international waters in the Arctic. These missions continued for two years and two months (from January 1985 to April 1987); the strategic bombers made 170 sorties supported by 102 sorties of refuelling tankers, with a total time of 1,979 flight hours.

The Tu-160 looks rather ominous as it makes a high-speed dash with the wings fully swept.

The Soviet Air Force's Long-Range Aviation order of battle in the late 1980s

As mentioned earlier, the Long-Range Aviation command, which was reinstated in early 1988, controlled the 30th and 46th Air Armies of the Supreme High Command. The 37th (Strategic) Air Army of the Supreme High Command, which was equipped exclusively with strategic missile carriers, remained a direct reporting unit.

Wheels caught in mid-retraction, a Tu-160 shows its powerful high-lift devices.

A Tu-95MS visiting Kubinka AB.

A Tu-95MS on final approach. The blue tips of the propeller spinners are probably unit markings.

One more *Bear-H* prepares to make contact with an IL-78.

The flight line at Engels-2 AB with at least 12 IL-78/IL-78M tankers visible.

Thus, in the final year of the Soviet Union's existence the 37th (Strategic) Air Army of the Supreme High Command comprised four heavy bomber divisions. One of these, with two regiments of Tu-95KMs and Tu-95K-22s, was stationed in the Russian Far East; another, with two regiments of Tu-95MSs, was in Kazakhstan. The remaining two were deployed in the European part of the country – one division with a regiment of Tu-95MSs and a regiment of IL-78 tankers was based at Uzin in the Ukraine, while the fourth division

37th VA VGK (SN) Order of Battle			
Unit	**Base**	**Republic**	**Types operated**
364th OSAE	Vorkuta	Russian Federation	Transport aircraft and four Mil' Mi-8PS helicopters
106th TBAD (Uzin AB, Kiev Region)			
1006th TBAP 409th APSZ	Uzin AB Uzin AB	The Ukraine The Ukraine	21 Tu-95MS-16s IL-78s (number unknown)
79th TBAD (Dolon' AB, Semipalatinsk)			**13 Tu-95MS-16s, 27 Tu-95MS-6s**
1223rd TBAP 1226th TBAP	Dolon' AB Dolon' AB	Kazakhstan Kazakhstan	Tu-95MS-16, Tu-95MS-6 Tu-95MS-16s, Tu-95MS-6s
73rd *Ternopol'skaya* TBAD (Ookraïnka AB, Amur Region) *			**45 Tu-95K-22s, 15 Tu-95KMs**
40th Sevastopol'sko-Berlinskiy Red Banner GvTBAP 79th GvTBAP (Red Star Order)	Ookraïnka AB Ookraïnka AB	Russian Federation Russian Federation	Tu-95K-22, Tu-95KM Tu-95K-22, Tu-95KM
201st TBAD (Engels-2 AB, Saratov Region)			
184th Poltavsko-Berlinskiy Red Banner GvTBAP (Lenin Order) 1230th APSZ 182nd Sevastopol'sko-Berlinskiy Red Banner GvTBAP	Priluki Engels-2 AB Mozdok	The Ukraine Russian Federation Russian Federation	13 Tu-160s, Tu-134UBLs † 3MS-2s, 3MN-2s (number unknown) 22 Tu-95MS-16s

Notes: APSZ = *aviapolk* samo*l*yotov-za*pra*vshchikov – Aerial Refuelling Regiment

The honorary appellations Sevas*topol*'sko-Ber*lin*skiy and Pol*tav*sko-Ber*lin*skiy were given for these units' part in liberating the cities of Sevastopol' and Poltava (the Ukraine) and taking Berlin during the Great Patriotic War.

* The 73rd TBAD aircraft also operated from tactical airbases at Anadyr', Magadan and Tiksi maintained by the OGA.

† By the end of 1991 the 184th GvTBAP had increased its complement of Tu-160 missile carriers to 19 aircraft Squadrons 1 and 2; Sqn 3 operated Tu-134UBL aircrew trainers.

Long-Range Aviation Order of Battle			
Unit	**Base**	**Republic**	**Types operated**
43rd TsBP i PLS (DA), Dyagilevo AB, Ryazan'			
49th TBAP 52nd Brestskiy Red Banner GvTBAP 251st Red Banner GvTBAP	Dyagilevo AB Shaikovka AB, Smolensk Region Belaya Tserkov'	Russian Federation Russian Federation The Ukraine	11 Tu-95Us, Tu-95MRs and Tu-95KUs 19 Tu-22M3s (since 1981) 27 Tu-16Ks
46th VA VGK, Smolensk-Severnyy AB *			
11th Brestskiy GvODRAP 290th GvODRAP 103rd Krasnosel'skiy Red Banner GvOVTAP (DA) 64th Independent Communications Regiment	Nezhin Zyabrovka AB Smolensk-Severnyy AB Smolensk	The Ukraine Belorussia Russian Federation Russian Federation	26 Tu-22Rs/Tu-22RDMs and Tu-22UDs 29 Tu-22Rs/Tu-22RDMs, 13 Tu-16Rs An-12s, An-24s, An-26s
13th *Sevastopol'sko-Berlinskaya* GvTBAD (Poltava) †			
185th Kirovogradsko-Budapeshtskiy Red Banner GvTBAP	Poltava	The Ukraine	18 Tu-22M3s (since 1981), 6 Tu-16Ps
15th TBAD (Ozyornoye AB, Zhitomir Region)			
341st TBAP 121st Sevastopol'skiy Red Banner GvTBAP 203rd Orlovskiy Red Banner GvTBAP ‡	Ozyornoye AB Machoolishchi AB, Minsk Region Baranovichi	The Ukraine Belorussia Belorussia	32 Tu-22KDs and Tu-22KPs 34 Tu-22KDs and Tu-22KPs 32 Tu-22KDs and Tu-22KPs
22nd *Donbasskaya* Red Banner GvTBAD (Bobruisk, Mogilyov Region) §			
200th Brestskiy Red Banner GvTBAP 260th TBAP	Bobruisk Stryy	Belorussia The Ukraine	20 Tu-22M3s (since 1986), 18 Tu-16Ks 18 Tu-22M3s (since 1986)
326th *Tarnopol'skaya* TBAD (Kutuzov Order 3rd Grade) (Tartu)			
132nd Berlinskiy TBAP (Kutuzov and Aleksandr Nevskiy Orders) 402nd TBAP 840th Red Banner TBAP	Tartu Balbasovo AB, Orsha Sol'tsy-2 AB	Estonia Belorussia Russian Federation	18 Tu-22M3s (since 1984), 18 Tu-16Ks 17 Tu-22M3s (since 1983), 7 Tu-16Ks 19 Tu-22M3s (since 1980)
30th VA VGK, Irkutsk ¶			
219th ODRAP	Spassk-Dal'niy	Russian Federation	Tu-16Rs **
31st TBAD (Belaya AB, Irkutsk Region)			
1225th TBAP 1229th TBAP	Belaya AB Belaya AB	Russian Federation Russian Federation	Tu-22M2s Tu-22M2s
55th TBAD (Vozdvizhenka AB, Khabarovsk Area)			
444th Red Banner TBAP 303rd TBAP	Vozdvizhenka AB Zavitinsk, Chita Region	Russian Federation Russian Federation	Tu-16Ks Tu-16Ks

Notes: GvODRAP = Gvardeyskiy otdel'nyy dahl'niy razvedyvatel'nyy aviapolk – Guards Independent Long-Range Reconnaissance Air Regiment; GvOVTAP = Gvardeyskiy otdel'nyy voyenno-trahnsportnyy aviapolk – Guards Independent Military Airlift Regiment.

The honorary appellations Brestskiy, Krasnosel'skiy, Kirovogradsko-Budapeshtskiy and Orlovskiy were given for these units' part in liberating the city of Brest (Belorussia), the town of Krasnoye Selo (Russia), the cities of Kirovograd (the Ukraine), Budapest (Hungary) and Oryol (Russia) during the Great Patriotic War. The honorary appellation Donbasskaya was given for liberating the Donetsk coal mining area (Donbass) in the Ukraine.

* In the spring and summer of 1980 the command structure of the 6th OTBAK (otdel'nyy tyazhelobombardirovochnyy aviakorpus – Independent Heavy Bomber Corps) stationed at Smolensk served as the basis for the 46th (Strategic) Air Army of the Supreme High Command.

† In the 1980s the 13th GvTBAD comprised a different set of regiments – the 52nd GvTBAP at Shaikovka AB, the 184th GvTBAP at Priluki and the 185th GvTBAP at Poltava. In 1987 the 184th GvTBAP re-equipped with Tu-160s and was transferred to the 201st TBAD (see 37th VA VGK (SN)); two years later the 52nd GvTBAP was transferred to the 43rd Combat Training & Aircrew Conversion Centre. In post-Soviet times the 13th GvTBAD, which had just one regiment left by 1991, was augmented by transferring back the 184th GvTBAP (whose Tu-160s had been placed in storage and replaced by Tu-22M3s) and adding the 260th TBAP which was formerly part of the 22nd GvTBAD headquartered in neighbouring Belorussia. The division disbanded in May 2000.

‡ Now the 203rd GvOAPSZ (Gvardeyskiy otdel'nyy aviapolk samolyotov-zapravshchikov – Independent Guards Aerial Refuelling Regiment) at Dyagilevo AFB flying IL-78Ms

§ After the reorganisations of the late 1950s/early 1960s the 22nd GvTBAD included the 121st GvTBAP at Machoolishchi AB, the 200th GvTBAP at Bobruisk and the 203rd GvTBAP at Baranovichi. In the late 1980s the 121st and 203rd Regiments came under the command of the 15th GvTBAD (see above); in return, the 260th TBAP was transferred from the latter division.

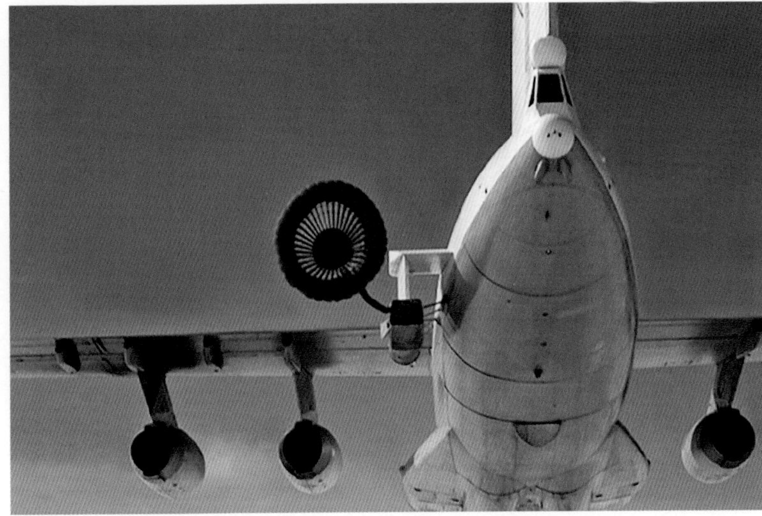

Clockwise from top:

The starboard UPAZ-1A podded hose drum unit of an IL-78M. The nose air intake is for the turbine driving the fuel pump; the rear one is for the hose drum drive turbine.

An IL-78M pays out the hose from the centre HDU. Note the red signal light and the design of the L-shaped pylon.

A Tu-95MS approaches the drogue of a quasi-civil IL-78M. The striped on the hose show the refuelling system operator how much of the hose has been paid out.

Contact has been made; the green signal light shows the bomber crew that fuel transfer is in progress.

The additional fuel tanks in the freight hold of an IL-78M. Note the triple fire extinguisher bottled beside each tank.

(notes continued from page 262)

¶ In the spring and summer of 1980 the command structure of the 8th OTBAK stationed at Blagoveshchensk served as the basis for the 30th VA VGK (SN). Apart from the 31st and 55th Heavy Bomber Divisions which had been part of the Long-Range Aviation, for a while the 30th Air Army included several Tactical Aviation units, such as the 21st TBAD which was deployed in the Trans-Baikal area in late 1979 and which, despite its name, operated Sukhoi Su-24 tactical bombers. The Tactical Aviation units were withdrawn from the 30th VA's structure in the middle of the decade. When the DA was reborn in April 1988, the 30th VA was included. Also, for a while the 30th Air Army included the 73rd TBAD based in the Amur Region.

** This was the last unit to operate the Tu-16, which was officially withdrawn from the Russian Air Force inventory in 1994.

The flight deck of an IL-78 tanker; the navigator sits at the lower level.

The badge of the 203rd GvOAPSZ established in 1941 as a bomber unit.

headquartered at Engels (Russia) comprised a regiment of Tu-160s at Priluki (the Ukraine), a regiment of Tu-95MSs at Mozdok (Chechen-Ingush ASSR, Russia) and a regiment of 3MS-2/3MN-2 tankers at Engels. The total number of strategic aircraft in the 37th VA as per early 1991 stood at 157 – 13 Tu-160s, 83 Tu-95MSs and 61 Tu-95KMs/Tu-95K-22s, and the Soviet aircraft industry was still turning out new *Blackjacks* and *Bear-Hs*.

The 30th Air Army of the Supreme High Command deployed east of the Urals Ridge

A pair of Tu-22M3s carrying two Kh-22M missiles each in low-speed configuration.

Above and below: 3MS-2s and Tu-95s being broken up at Engels.

A 3MS-2 at Engels during the final period of the type's service with the Russian Air Force.

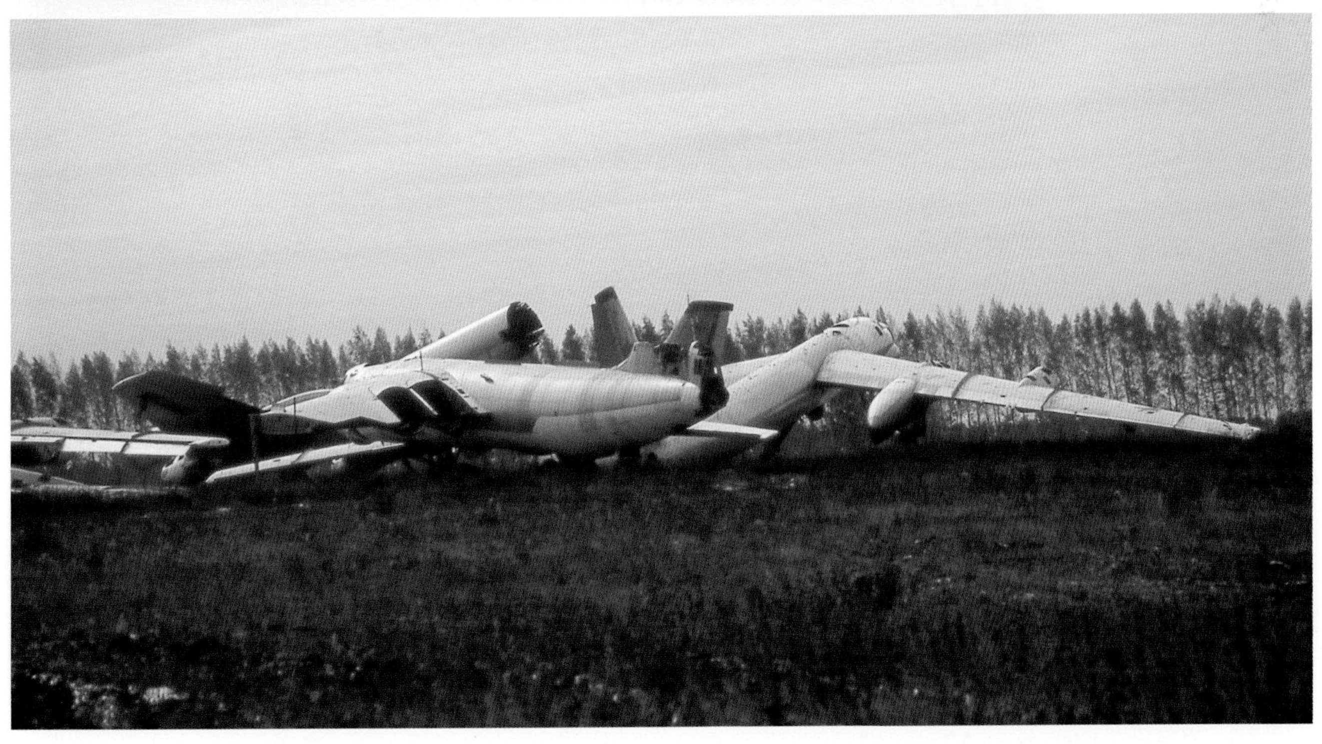

still consisted of two bomber divisions and an independent long-range reconnaissance air regiment. The two bomber divisions were based at Belaya AB near Irkutsk (with two regiments of Tu-22M2s) and Vozdvizhenka AB in the south of the Primor'ye Area (with two regiments of Tu-16Ks); the recce regiment operated Tu-16Rs from Spassk-Dal'niy. The 46th Air Army of the Supreme High Command was less lucky, falling victim to the Conventional Forces in Europe (CFE) treaty signed in 1990. Before its disbandment in accordance with the treaty it had a fleet of 347 combat aircraft operated by four heavy bomber divisions (in Poltava, Ozyornoye, Bobruisk and Tartu) and two independent long-range reconnaissance air regiments (in Nezhin and Zyabrovka). The bomber divisions operated modern Tu-22M3 bombers/missile carriers equipping six regiments (at Poltava, Bobruisk, Stryy, Tartu, Orsha and Sol'tsy). Most of these regiments, however, still operated the outdated Tu-16K in large numbers alongside the *Backfire*; three units (in Machoolishchi, Baranovichi and Ozyornoye) were still equipped with obsolete Tu-22s.

A pennant of the Long-Range Aviation's 43rd TsBP i PLS established in 1940.

The late 1980s witnessed a thaw in the Cold War – political and military tensions slackened as the East and the West became more open to talks. This change was brought about by the policy of *perestroika* (restructuring) and *glasnost'* (openness) initiated by the new Soviet leader Mikhail S. Gorbachov (later the sole President of the Soviet Union). One of the manifestations of this détente was that the Soviet Minister of Defence Marshal Dmitriy T. Yazov invited his American counterpart Secretary of Defense Frank C. Carlucci to visit the Soviet Union. On 2nd August 1988 Carlucci and his retinue were given an opportunity to examine the latest hardware of the Soviet Air Force, including the Tu-160 strategic missile carrier, at Kubinka AB near Moscow. For sheer effect a pair of Tu-160s flew over the runway at an altitude of 2,000 m (6,560 ft), followed by an ultra-low-level solo pass at just 50 m (164 ft); this was done at Yazov's personal orders, which ran contrary to current instructions.

By the end of 1988 the 'Iron Curtain' dividing the two political systems had begun to disintegrate. On 7th December that year, speaking at the United Nations General Assembly, Mikhail S. Gorbachov announced that the Soviet Union would undertake unilateral arms reductions and cut defence spending – a move that is still viewed as controversial in modern Russia. This created a 'domino effect' in the form of 'velvet revolutions' throughout the Eastern Bloc in which many of the communist leaders were deposed, and sweeping political changes in both the Soviet Union and its former allies. Some of the Soviet Union's constituent republics, too, clamoured for independence – first and foremost the Baltic republics. Here it should be noted that the DA units having the highest level of combat readiness were stationed in the western republics of the USSR (Estonia, Belorussia and the Ukraine). Growing separatism in these republics created a real danger that the units in question might suddenly find themselves abroad – and in unfriendly nations at that. These were troubled times for the Long-Range Aviation and for the country at large.

In early 1991 the member nations of the Warsaw Pact declared this organisation disbanded. Then, in August 1991 a handful of hard-line communist statesmen and military leaders who resented the political course taken by Gorbachov attempted a military coup. However, the Russian people refused to support the so-called National Emergency Committee and the putsch petered out, its authors receiving prison sentences. Yet, one of their goals was in fact attained; Gorbachov stepped down and was succeeded by Boris N. Yel'tsin who was later elected 'new' Russia's first President.

In November 1990 Col.-Gen. Igor' M. Kalugin was appointed the new Commander of the DA.

Finally, on 8th December 1991 representatives of the Russian Soviet Federative Socialist Republic (RSFSR), the Belorussian SSR and the Ukrainian SSR made a deal in Minsk, dissolving the Soviet Union and agreeing to form a loose confederation called the Commonwealth of Independent States (CIS). The founding members of the CIS were soon joined by all of the former Soviet republics except Latvia, Lithuania and Estonia.

After the demise of the Soviet Union a good deal of the former Soviet Air Force's strategic assets found themselves outside Russia. In the case of the 37th VA VGK (SN), two of the four regiments operating Tu-95MS missile carriers were 'left behind' in Kazakhstan (in Semipalatinsk); the Ukraine laid claim to one more Tu-95MS unit and the greater part of the DA's IL-78 tanker fleet (at Uzin AB) and the Tu-160s based in Priluki. Most of the Kazakh *Bears* were eventually recovered in keeping with a government-level agreement, Russia trading them for a number

A Tu-160 commences its take-off run, leaving a characteristic orange trail of engine efflux.

of Sukhoi Su-27 and Mikoyan MiG-29 fighters and Su-25 attack aircraft, which were more useful to the nascent Kazakhstan Air Force than the big bombers. The Ukraine, however, was not about to let go of the 19 Tu-160s (the entire operational *Blackjack* fleet!) and the 24 Tu-95MSs it had appropriated. The Long-Range Aviation was even worse off, losing two regiments of Tu-22M3s and two regiments of Tu-22s based in the Ukraine (the *Backfire-Cs* were based at Poltava and Stryy, the Tu-22KD/ Tu-22KP missile carriers at Ozyornoye AB and the Tu-22RD/Tu-22RDM reconnaissance aircraft at Nezhin). This amounted to 46 *Backfires* and 37 *Blinders* lost in one fell swoop. As if that weren't enough, five regiments of the former 46th VA VGK were stationed in Belorussia (two regiments of Tu-22M3s at Orsha and Bobruisk, two regiments of Tu-22KDs/Tu-22KPs in Machoolishchi and Baranovichi and a regiment of Tu-22RDs/ Tu-22RDMs at Zyabrovka). The sole DA unit stationed in Estonia and operating Tu-22M3s and Tu-16Ks redeployed from Tartu to Russia. From then on, the decimated strategic component of the Russian Air Force was concentrated at two bases – Engels-2 AB near Saratov and Ookraïnka AB in the Far East.

In Soviet days the Tu-160s were white overall, with none of today's colourful markings.

Index

AIRCRAFT TYPES

Soviet/Russian

Antonov
- An-2 78
- An-12 204, 264
- An-24 264
- An-26 264

Ilyushin
- IL-4 7, 8, 9, 128
- IL-14 78, 81
- IL-18 35
- IL-28 20, 62
- IL-38 35
- IL-46 219, 220
- IL-76 177
- IL-78 44, 51, 118, 249, 250, 257, 258, 259, 262, 263, 266, 268

Ilyushin/Beriyev A-50 172

Lavochkin
- La-9 78
- La-11 17, 24, 78

Lisunov Li-2 76, 78

Mikoyan/Gurevich
- MiG-15 30, 93, 123
- MiG-17 35, 46
- MiG-21 140
- MiG-29 269
- MiG-31 173

Mil Mi-4 76

Myasischev
- 3M 31, 32, 33, 34, 36, 37, 38, 39, 41, 43, 44, 47, 48, 51, 64, 65, 66, 68, 69, 70, 72, 73, 74, 82, 84, 86, 112, 131, 133, 152, 157, 173, 185, 187, 188, 189, 190, 194, 196, 197, 199, 200, 226, 227, 228, 229, 230, 255, 256, 263, 266, 267
- M-4 31, 32, 33, 34, 35, 36, 37, 39, 40, 41, 47, 48, 72, 78, 79, 82, 93, 112, 115, 185, 188, 196, 224, 225, 226, 227, 228, 229, 249
- M-18 244, 246
- M-20 244

Petlyakov Pe-8 8, 9, 14

Sukhoi
- Su-24 145, 206, 254, 265
- Su-25 206, 209, 269
- Su-27 173, 183, 269
- T-4MS 244

Tupolev
- Tu-2 7
- Tu-4 7, 8, 9, 10, 11, 12, 13, 14, 15, 16, 17, 18, 19, 20, 21, 22, 23, 24, 25, 26, 27, 30, 31, 51, 52, 53, 61, 76, 77, 78, 79, 80, 81, 93, 94, 95, 215, 216, 217, 218, 219, 230
- Tu-16 30, 31, 33, 34, 40, 41, 42, 43, 44, 45, 51, 52, 53, 54, 55, 56, 57, 58, 59, 61, 62, 63, 64, 65, 66, 67, 69, 70, 71, 73, 80, 81, 82, 83, 84, 85, 86, 88, 90, 91, 96, 97, 98, 99, 100, 101, 102, 103, 104, 105, 106, 108, 107, 109, 110, 111, 123, 124, 125, 132, 133, 134, 135, 140, 141, 144, 145, 157, 159, 160, 161, 163, 167, 168, 173, 182, 184, 185, 186, 187, 192, 193, 194, 195, 196, 197, 199, 201, 202, 204, 205, 206, 207, 213, 219, 220, 221, 222, 223, 224, 225, 229, 234, 249, 255, 256, 258, 264, 265, 268
- Tu-22 69, 97, 103, 119, 133, 134, 135, 136, 137, 138, 139, 140, 141, 142, 143, 144, 145, 146, 147, 148, 149, 150, 151, 153, 154, 155, 157, 165, 168, 173, 174, 191, 199, 203, 204, 211, 214, 227, 234, 235, 236, 237, 238, 243, 253, 254, 256, 264, 268, 269
- Tu-22M 52, 56, 69, 70, 71, 73, 132, 152, 153, 154, 155, 156, 157, 158, 159, 160, 161, 162, 163, 164, 165, 166, 167, 168, 169, 171, 172, 173, 174, 177, 182, 184, 206, 208, 209, 210, 212, 213, 214, 205, 237, 238, 239, 240, 241, 242, 243, 244, 246, 253, 254, 256, 258, 264, 266, 268, 269
- Tu-85 230
- Tu-95 6, 31, 33, 34, 44, 46, 47, 48, 49, 50, 51, 55, 60, 61, 62, 63, 73, 74, 79, 84, 86, 87, 88, 90, 91, 92, 103, 104, 105, 106, 107, 108, 109, 110, 111, 112, 113, 114, 115, 116, 117, 118, 119, 120, 121, 122, 123, 126, 127, 128, 129, 130, 131, 132, 185, 186, 196, 200, 226, 227, 229, 230, 231, 232, 233, 234, 255, 255, 256, 258, 262, 263, 265, 266, 267, 268
- Tu-104 250
- Tu-114 33
- Tu-124 250, 251, 252
- Tu-126 33
- Tu-134 167, 176, 184, 251, 252, 253, 254, 263
- Tu-142 33, 120, 121, 232, 234, 243
- Tu-144 244
- Tu-160 51, 123, 132, 170, 171, 172, 173, 174, 175, 176, 177, 178, 180, 181, 182, 183, 184, 244, 245, 246, 247, 248, 254, 259, 260, 261, 263, 264, 266, 268, 269
- Tu-244 244

Yakovlev
- Yak-25R 27
- Yak-28 254

Yermolayev Yer-2 8, 9

Non-Soviet/Russian

BAC Lightning 47, 105

Boeing
- B-17 Flying Fortress 8, 14
- B-29 Superfortress 7, 9, 10, 11, 30, 76, 215, 216, 217
- B-47 Stratojet 30, 222
- B-52 Stratofortress 37, 49, 226, 230

Consolidated
- B-24 8, 14
- PBY Catalina 76

Convair F-102A 109

Douglas C-47 76

Focke-Wulf Fw 200 Condor 76

Grumman
- A-6 Intruder 45
- EA-6 187
- F-14 Tomcat 52, 104, 117, 153

Lockheed
- F-16 154, 209, 210, 214
- P-3 Orion 129
- U-2A 49

McDonnell F-4 Phantom 47, 49, 61, 105, 132, 187

McDonnell/Douglas F-18 and F/A-18 Hornet 61, 67, 128, 255

North American B-25 Mitchell 8, 14

Rockwell B-1 244, 246

Sud-Est SE.210 Caravelle 251

Vought F-8 Crusader 187

BOMBS

FAB-100 103

FAB-250 103, 205, 214, 240

FAB-500 213

FAB-1500 24, 208, 209, 210, 214

FAB-3000 208, 210, 214
FAB-9000 37, 83, 213
IAB-500 26
IAB-3000 26
izdeliye 202 87, 88, 89, 91
M-46 213
M-54 213
RDS-1 18, 84
RDS-3 20, 23, 25, 26, 27, 30
RDS-4 21, 26, 30, 87
RDS-5 27, 30
RDS-6 83, 88, 90
RDS-37 83, 85, 86
SK-1 Skal'p 83
Vanya 87, 89

FACTORIES
No.1 Kuibyshev 33, 64, 224
No.18 Kuibyshev 11, 33, 114, 218, 230, 232
No.22 Kazan' 11, 33, 51, 95, 133, 157, 215, 217, 218, 223, 225, 235, 236, 241
No.23 Moscow 11, 32, 44, 48, 95, 218, 226, 227, 229
No.64 Voronezh 33, 224
No.135 Khar'kov 250
No.207 Doobna 94

LOCATIONS/BASES etc
USSR/CIS
Akhtoobinsk 59, 63
Amderma 65
Anadyr' 192, 194
Bagherovo 51
Balbasovo 26, 27, 30, 51, 63, 264
Baranovichi 51, 58, 69, 80, 134, 136, 141, 145, 148, 173, 211, 256, 264, 268, 269
Belaya 58, 61, 69, 71, 73, 87, 160, 161, 165, 171, 205, 206, 213, 256, 258, 264, 268
Belaya Tserkov' 71, 73, 87, 161, 205, 213, 258, 264
Blagoveshchensk 12, 124, 189, 195, 265
Bobruisk 58, 61, 71, 172, 173, 205, 256, 264, 268, 269
Bryansk 13
Cape Kanin Nos 88
Chagan 59, 73
Chekoorovka 65, 82
Chekoorovskaya 79
Chelyabinsk 59, 183, 254
Dolon' 33, 263
Domodedovo 72, 140
Dyagilevo 44, 60, 61, 62, 106, 107, 122, 141, 142, 157, 159, 254, 258, 264
Engels-2 31, 35, 36, 39, 44, 51, 58, 145, 167, 176, 199, 200, 254, 256, 263, 269
Feodosia 94
Gomel' 13, 14, 58
Graham Bell Island 79
Irkutsk 58, 124, 160, 195, 255, 264, 268
Ivanovo 14
Kalinin 30, 58
Kaluga 58, 172, 258
Kamensk-Ural'skiy 59
Karshi 206, 207, 213
Kazan'-Borisoglebskoye 10, 11
Kerch 51
Khabarovsk 7, 62, 264
Khanabad 207
Klin-5 253
Kubinka 184, 245, 262, 268
Kustanai 59
Leningrad 58, 134
Litovka 194
Machoolishchi 58, 69, 135, 136, 141, 145, 163, 173, 256, 264, 268, 269
Maryy-1 207
Maryy-2 206, 207, 208, 209, 210, 212, 213, 214
Migalovo 58
Minsk 58, 135, 145, 173, 264, 268
Mozdok 58, 113, 123, 126, 131, 214, 256, 263, 266
Murmansk 88, 128, 183
Nagoorskoye 82
Nezhin 58, 69, 135, 136, 141, 145, 150, 214, 256, 264, 268, 269
Noginsk 18
Noril'sk 79, 82
Novaya Zemlya 84, 88, 91, 183
Novgorod 58, 160
Oktyabr'skoe 58
Olen'ya 79, 82, 88, 92, 196
Omsk 40
Ookraïnka 31, 131, 194, 196, 256, 263, 269
Orsha 26, 51, 172, 212, 264, 268, 269
Ostrov 123, 124
Ozyornoye 58, 69, 139, 141, 145, 149, 150, 173, 211, 256, 264, 268, 269
Par'kova Zemlya Island 88
Polesskoye 151
Poltava 15, 58, 61, 63, 69, 149, 159, 164, 173, 208, 212, 213, 214, 256, 263, 264, 268, 269
Porkkala-Udd 187
Port Arthur 187
Priluki 57, 58, 69, 167, 171, 172, 173, 174, 176, 177, 183, 184, 246, 248, 254, 260, 263, 264, 266, 268
Pskov 123
Rogachovo 88
Ryazan' 44, 61, 122, 165, 264
Semipalatinsk 27, 30, 33, 59, 73, 83, 84, 86, 123, 131, 256, 263, 268
Severomorsk 65, 128, 130
Shadrinsk 59
Shaikovka 58, 69, 155, 172, 258, 264
Skomorokhi 58
Smolensk 7, 124, 189, 255, 264
Sol'tsy 58, 69, 160, 213, 256, 264, 268
Soomy 153
Spassk-Dal'niy 58, 71, 256, 264, 268
Sredniy Island 79, 82
Stryy 58, 71, 172, 173, 264, 268, 269
Taganrog 121
Tambov 59, 167, 253, 254
Tartu 57, 172, 256, 264, 268, 269
Tiksi 78, 79, 80, 81, 82, 183, 263
Totskoye 19, 27, 30
Tushino 13, 22, 46, 73, 133, 134, 184, 236
Tver' 58
Ussuriysk 58
Uzin 33, 73, 90, 113, 123, 130, 131, 256, 263, 268
Vayenga 88
Vesyolaya 59
Vinnitsa 7, 124, 189
Vladimirovka 59
Vorkuta 79, 82, 263
Voroshilovgrad 167, 254
Vozdvizhenka 58, 69, 141, 256, 264, 268
Wrangel Island 65
Zavitinsk 58, 264
Zhana-Semey 24
Zhitomir 58, 139, 145, 173, 264
Zhukovskiy 19, 37, 40, 59, 87, 121, 184, 222, 226, 248
Zyabrovka 58, 69, 135, 136, 141, 145, 154, 203, 204, 256, 264, 268, 269

Other Countries
Cairo-West, Egypt 204
Gerat, Afghanistan 214
Hiroshima, Japan 7, 9
Jakarta, Indonesia 201
Kabul, Afghanistan 205
Kandahar, Afghanistan 205, 208, 210
Maratam, Indonesia 201
Nagasaki, Japan 7, 9
Sumatra, Indonesia 201

MISSILES
K-10S 229, 230
K-14S 230
Kh-15 161, 244, 248
Kh-20 87, 103, 104, 112, 113, 116, 117, 126, 127, 234
Kh-22 103, 119, 120, 127, 136, 137, 140, 142, 151, 154, 159, 165, 168, 236, 237, 241
Kh-45 248
Kh-55 120, 121, 123, 131, 182, 234, 246, 248
KS-1 93, 94, 95, 96, 102, 103, 123, 202, 218, 225
KSR-2 97, 98, 99, 100, 101, 102, 103, 104, 105, 106, 124, 125, 126, 222, 225
KSR-5 69, 98, 101, 103, 104, 105, 106, 111, 124, 125, 126, 187, 225
KSR-11 98, 99, 100, 101, 102, 103, 104, 105, 107, 111, 124, 125, 126, 225

NATO REPORTING NAMES

Backfire 52, 69, 153, 157, 159, 160, 162, 164, 165, 167, 168, 169, 171, 172, 173, 174, 205, 207, 208, 212, 214, 237, 238, 240, 241, 244, 254, 256, 268, 269
Badger 30, 31, 33, 34, 40, 44, 51, 52, 54, 55, 56, 57, 58, 59, 84, 96, 98, 100, 101, 103, 104, 105, 155, 184, 193, 195, 201, 204, 205, 219, 220, 222, 223, 256
Beagle 62
Bison 31, 32, 33, 34, 35, 36, 37, 38, 39, 41, 43, 44, 47, 48, 49, 66, 86, 112, 188, 190, 200, 224, 225, 226, 227, 228, 229, 230, 256
Blackjack 51, 173, 174, 176, 177, 178, 180, 182, 183, 184, 244, 245, 266, 269
Blinder 69, 119, 133, 134, 135, 136, 139, 140, 141, 144, 145, 147, 149, 150, 153, 155, 157, 167, 168, 214, 234, 236, 254, 256, 269
Brewer 254
Bull 13, 23, 24, 215
Cab 78
Camel 250
Candid 177, 249
Charger 244
Cleat 33
Colt 78
Cookpot 250
Crate 78
Crusty 167, 251, 252, 254
Cub 204
Fagot 30, 93
Fencer 145, 206, 254
Fishbed 140
Flanker 173
Foxhound 173
Fresco 35
Frogfoot 209
Guideline 49
Kangaroo 112
Kelt 97
Kennel 93
Kingfish 103, 105
Kitchen 103, 119, 136
Mainstay 172
Midas 44, 51, 249, 250
Moss 33

NUMBERED DESIGN BUREAUS

KB-11 18, 19, 23, 24
KB-90 51
KB-201 48
OKB-1 94, 112
OKB-23 31, 45, 226, 227, 229
OKB-52 48, 51
OKB-155 93
OKB-156 9, 23, 94
OKB-918 226, 249

SHIPS/SUBMARINES

Altai 130
K-19 128
USS Abraham Lincoln 128
USS Coral Sea 49, 255
USS Essex 67
USS Midway 187
USS Nimitz 128

UNITS

Soviet Air Armies

1st 7, 8
2nd 7, 12
3rd 7, 12
5th 12
18th 7
30th 205, 255, 256, 257, 261, 264, 265, 266
37th 131, 175, 183, 207, 255, 257, 258, 261, 263, 264, 266, 268
40th 205
43rd 12, 14, 22, 27, 124
46th 128, 205, 255, 256, 257, 261, 264, 268, 269
50th 12, 13, 124, 189
65th 12

Soviet Regiments, Corps, Sqns etc

Indexed as unit numbers only; designations very from time to time between TBAP, UAP, APSZ etc, but the numbers remain constant as roles change.

1st 7, 182
2nd 124, 140, 189
3rd 7, 184
6th 84, 124, 126, 189, 264
8th 124, 189, 195, 265
11th 7, 264
12th 123, 124
13th 14, 15, 16, 17, 30, 34, 51, 52, 84, 86, 194, 197, 264
18th 8
22nd 8, 264
31st 160, 161, 264, 265
34th 84
37th 8, 131
40th 31, 128, 205, 263
43rd 51, 60, 61, 106, 120, 122, 133, 142, 157, 159, 161, 172, 190, 254, 258, 264, 268
45th 8, 13, 14, 26, 51, 80, 125, 204
49th 264
52nd 8, 26, 34, 80, 124, 125, 155, 158, 264
56th 201, 202
57th 8
73rd 32, 84, 256, 258, 263, 265
79th 31, 84, 86, 131, 194, 256, 258, 263
103rd 264
106th 84, 86, 90, 113, 128, 256, 258, 263
108th 8
111th 8, 124
116th 123, 124
121st 8, 81, 135, 136, 145, 165, 173, 264
132nd 124, 125, 126, 205, 264
157th 8
160th 30
165th 30
170th 8
171st 8
182nd 126, 131, 263
184th 57, 124, 168, 170, 173, 174, 175, 176, 177, 180, 182, 183, 184, 199, 248, 254, 260, 263, 264
185th 14, 15, 16, 51, 52, 69, 86, 124, 149, 159, 164, 172, 173, 207, 208, 209, 213, 214, 264
199th 135, 145, 150, 153, 154, 214
200th 8, 61, 71, 88, 124, 125, 126, 173, 205, 264
201st 31, 82, 84, 86, 256, 258, 263, 264
202nd 14, 51
203rd 8, 26, 34, 51, 133, 134, 140, 145, 148, 165, 173, 211, 214, 264, 266
208th 8
210th 8
219th 264
226th 14, 16, 17, 30, 51, 52, 61, 84, 142
240th 8
244th 202, 203
251st 71, 161, 205, 206, 213, 264
260th 71, 173, 264
290th 135, 145, 154, 264
291st 27
303rd 264
326th 84, 168, 211, 214, 264
330th 8
341st 139, 140, 145, 149, 173, 211, 214, 264
362nd 8, 26
364th 263
402nd 27, 34, 51, 63, 124, 125, 126, 212, 214, 264
409th 33, 128, 131, 263
444th 264
685th 123, 124
840th 11, 19, 22, 84, 124, 125, 126, 160, 165, 166, 172, 213, 214, 264
890th 8, 13, 14
978th 253
1006th 33, 128, 131, 263
1023rd 33
1096th 31, 51, 86
1223rd 131, 263
1225th 160, 161, 205, 264
1226th 33, 131, 263
1229th 160, 161, 264
1230th 31, 51, 73, 199, 263
Unit 78724 26, 27
LII 13, 19, 59, 157, 215, 226
NII VVS 18, 35, 59, 63
TsAGI 19, 25, 48, 219, 234, 238, 240, 246

US Navy Units

VF-1 52
VF-21 49
VF-51 117
VA-95 45
VF-111 104
VFA-133 61